InterPhases

For a complete list of titles published and in preparation for the series, see pp. 395–396.

InterPhases

Phase-Theoretic Investigations of
Linguistic Interfaces

Edited by
KLEANTHES K. GROHMANN

UNIVERSITY PRESS

OXFORD
UNIVERSITY PRESS

Great Clarendon Street, Oxford ox2 6DP

Oxford University Press is a department of the University of Oxford.
It furthers the University's objective of excellence in research, scholarship,
and education by publishing worldwide in

Oxford New York

Auckland Cape Town Dar es Salaam Hong Kong Karachi
Kuala Lumpur Madrid Melbourne Mexico City Nairobi
New Delhi Shanghai Taipei Toronto

With offices in

Argentina Austria Brazil Chile Czech Republic France Greece
Guatemala Hungary Italy Japan Poland Portugal Singapore
South Korea Switzerland Thailand Turkey Ukraine Vietnam

Oxford is a registered trade mark of Oxford University Press
in the UK and in certain other countries

Published in the United States
by Oxford University Press Inc., New York

British Library Cataloguing in Publication Data
Data available

Library of Congress Cataloging in Publication Data
Data available

Typeset by SPI Publisher Services, Pondicherry, India
Printed in Great Britain
on acid-free paper by
CPI Antony Rowe, Chippenham, Wiltshire

ISBN 978–0–19–954112–6 (Hbk)
ISBN 978–0–19–954113–3 (Pbk)

1 3 5 7 9 10 8 6 4 2

Contents

Part III. Ordering Issues

General Preface

The theoretical focus of this series is on the interfaces between subcomponents of the human grammatical system and the closely related area of the interfaces between the different subdisciplines of linguistics. The notion of 'interface' has become central in grammatical theory (for instance, in Chomsky's recent Minimalist Program) and in linguistic practice: work on the interfaces between syntax and semantics, syntax and morphology, phonology and phonetics etc. has led to a deeper understanding of particular linguistic phenomena and of the architecture of the linguistic component of the mind/brain.

The series covers interfaces between core components of grammar, including syntax/morphology, syntax/semantics, syntax/phonology, syntax/pragmatics, morphology/phonology, phonology/phonetics, phonetics/speech processing, semantics/pragmatics, intonation/discourse structure as well as issues in the way that the systems of grammar involving these interface areas are acquired and deployed in use (including language acquisition, language dysfunction, and language processing). It demonstrates, we hope, that proper understandings of particular linguistic phenomena, languages, language groups, or inter-language variations all require reference to interfaces.

The series is open to work by linguists of all theoretical persuasions and schools of thought. A main requirement is that authors should write so as to be understood by colleagues in related subfields of linguistics and by scholars in cognate disciplines.

In current minimalist theory, the notion of 'phase' has come to the fore as an architectural claim about the way that the syntactic system interacts with the interfaces to sounds and meaning. The idea is that the syntax is organized so as to deliver 'chunks' of information to the interfaces, rather than an entire tree structure. Kleanthes Grohmann brings together scholars from all over the world to explore the empirical and theoretical ramifications of this architectural claim.

David Adger
Hagit Borer

Preface

InterPhases was a successful occasion in all respects. The conference, subtitled 'A Conference on Interfaces in Current Syntactic Theory', took place at the beautiful Castelliotissa Hall in the Old Town of Nicosia, Cyprus from 18 to 20 May 2006. I could only have managed to organize the conference with substantial support from the Department of English Studies and the University of Cyprus whose financial contributions made the event possible in the first place. I would especially like to thank our administrative assistant, Thekla Constantinou, and the numerous student helpers for organizational and administrative help.

The *InterPhases* conference was immediately preceded by the *Edges in Syntax* conference held at Cyprus College in Nicosia 15–17 May 2006, organized by my colleague Phoevos Panagiotidis. We dubbed the entire six-day event the *Cyprus Syntaxfest*. The Syntaxfest attracted a lot of linguists from all over the world, partly due, I suspect, to the fact that the keynote address was delivered by Prof. Noam Chomsky who also was awarded an honorary doctorate from the University of Cyprus and delivered the 2006 Leventis Lecture. Noam Chomsky gave three talks in three days, participated in many other activities, and was simply a pleasure to have around. My deepest gratitude goes to Noam and his wife Carol for making the long trip, for so actively engaging with everyone, and simply for being who they are.

I would also like to thank my three invited speakers, Richard Kayne, Gereon Müller, and Howard Lasnik who, I can say with great pleasure, also contributes to this volume. The conference could not have been such an intellectual success had it not been for the active participation of all the linguists, colleagues and students, who attended in large numbers. Thank you, presenters and audience, for stimulating presentations, posters, and discussions. And a lot of social fun for everyone.

This volume took a lot of time and effort, but the result certainly makes it all worthwhile. Here I am very much indebted to David Adger and John Davey for their support, interest, and advice all along the way. Thanks are also due to the reviewers of all chapters collected here and everyone else involved in the assembly and production processes, especially Elena Shelkovaya-Vasiliou for compiling the index.

Finally, my deepest gratitude is due to Joy, who as my then wife did a fantastic job catering for our guests, organizing the Syntaxfest party, and contributing very much to the overall success of the *InterPhases* conference.

Notes on Contributors

Asaf Bachrach is a doctoral student at the Department of Linguistics and Philosophy at MIT. His work focuses on morphosyntax and neurolinguistics. His theoretical work centers on the representation and consequences of identity in a cyclic model of grammar. His brain research, using non-invasive imaging techniques as well as the study of impaired populations, investigates the neural correlates of syntactic complexity and online parsing and lexical access.

e-mail: asaf@mit.edu

Petr Biskup is an Assistant Researcher at the Institute of Slavistics of the University of Leipzig. He received his MA in Religious Studies from the Hussite Theological Faculty at the Charles University in Prague in 1997. In 2002 he completed his MA in Czech Studies at the Faculty of Philosophy and Arts of the Charles University in Prague. Since 2002 he has been involved in the Ph.D. program in Linguistics at the University of Leipzig with the dissertation entitled "The Phase Model and Adverbials".

e-mail: biskup@rz.uni-leipzig.de

Kleanthes K. Grohmann is Assistant Professor of Theoretical Linguistics at the University of Cyprus, where he has worked since 2003. Since his Ph.D. dissertation "Prolific Peripheries: A Radical View from the Left" (University of Maryland, 2000), he has published the monograph *Prolific Domains: On the Anti-Locality of Movement Dependencies* (John Benjamins, 2003) and the textbook *Understanding Minimalism*, with Norbert Hornstein and Jairo Nunes (CUP, 2005). Among other collections, some of which are in print, he has co-edited *Multiple Wh-Fronting* with Cedric Boeckx (John Benjamins, 2003) and guest-edited two special double-issues of *Linguistic Analysis* on dynamic interfaces (2007). He has published his research widely, in the form of numerous peer-reviewed journal articles, book chapters, and more. Jointly with Cedric Boeckx, he is also cofounding editor-in-chief of the new and free, peer-reviewed online journal *Biolinguistics* and together with Pierre Pica serves as the series editor of the new John Benjamins book series *Language Faculty and Beyoud*.

e-mail: kleanthi@ucy.ac.cy

Wolfram Hinzen obtained MAs in philosophy at Freiburg i. Br. and London Universities, did a Ph.D. at the University of Bern, a habilitation at the

University of Regensburg, and spent two postdoctoral years at Columbia University and New York University. After academic positions in Regensburg and Amsterdam, he became a full Professor of Philosophy at Durham University in 2006. His books include *Mind Design and Minimal Syntax* (2006) and *An Essay on Names and Truth* (2007).

e-mail: wolfram.hinzen@dur.ac.uk

Jiro Inaba studied linguistics at the University of Tokyo, the University of Tübingen, and at the University of Frankfurt am Main, where he got his Ph.D. in 2006. Since 2007 he has been Associate Professor at Hiroshima University.

e-mail: jinaba@hiroshima-u.ac.jp

Roni Katzir is a doctoral student at the Department of Linguistics and Philosophy at MIT. His work focuses on morphosyntax, semantics, and computation.

e-mail: trifilij@mit.edu

Howard Lasnik is Distinguished University Professor of Linguistics at the University of Maryland. He has played a prominent role in syntactic theorizing in the Chomskyan framework from the Extended Standard Theory, through Government-Binding Theory, to Minimalism. His main research areas are syntactic theory and the syntax-semantics interface. Alongside more foundational issues of language learnability and the general properties of linguistic theories, among the specific topics he has worked on are scope, anaphora, ellipsis, verbal morphology, Case, and locality constraints on movement. In the last few years, he has been exploring the phenomenon of "repair by ellipsis", where violations of constraints on syntactic movement are apparently remedied by deleting a portion of the structure containing the violation. His publications include eight books, the most recent being *Minimalist Investigations in Linguistic Theory* (Routledge, 2003) and, with Juan Uriagereka, *A Course in Minimalist Syntax: Foundations and Prospects* (Blackwell, 2005), and nearly a hundred articles. He is known as much for his teaching and advising as for his research, having supervised forty-eight completed Ph.D. dissertations, on morphology, on language acquisition, and, especially, on syntactic theory.

e-mail: lasnik@umd.edu

Franc Lanko Marušič got his Ph.D. from Stony Brook University in 2005, when he joined the University of Nova Gorica as an Assistant Professor. He teaches Slovenian syntax, general linguistics, and a language consultancy seminar. His main areas of interest are Slovenian syntax, comparative Slavic syntax, and syntactic theory. He has published papers in various journals (including *Linguistic Inquiry* and *Natural Language and Linguistic Theory*), given several talks at various (not only Slavic) conferences, and published several papers in refereed conference proceedings (*FASL, ConSOLE,* etc.). He also co-edited the volume *Studies in Formal Slavic Linguistics* with selected papers from a conference organized in Nova Gorica.

e-mail: franc.marusic@p-ng.si

Takashi Munakata received his Ph.D. from Yokohama National University in 2005 and currently teaches there as a part-time lecturer. His major publications include contributions to collected volumes, such as "Japanese topic-constructions in the minimalist view of the syntax-semantics interface" (*Minimalist Essays,* John Benjamins, 2006) and "Throwing in & Kicking out" (*Proceedings of WAFL 2,* MITWPL, 2007). His research focuses on the overall architecture of the language faculty and the syntax-semantics interface. He is currently working on the complementizer system and the derivation of *wh*-questions in Japanese and other languages in terms of the mechanism of Intermediate Agree.

e-mail: interface_condition@leaf.ocn.ne.jp

Masanori Nakamura is a Professor at Senshu University, Tokyo. He received his Ph.D. in linguistics from McGill University in 1996. His research interests are in comparative syntax, locality principles, and grammatical functions. His research results have appeared in such journals as *Linguistic Inquiry, The Linguistic Review,* and *Lingua* as well as in refereed conference proceedings volumes including *Is the Best Good Enough? Optimality and Competition in Syntax* (MIT Press and MITWPL, 1998), *The Minimalist Parameter* (John Benjamins, 2001), and *Dimensions of Movement: From Features to Remnants* (John Benjamins, 2002).

e-mail: masanori@isc.senshu-u.ac.jp

Anthi Revithiadou, currently Assistant Professor of Comparative Linguistics at the University of the Aegean, received her Ph.D. from Leiden University/HIL in 1999. Her dissertation *Headmost Accent Wins* dealt with a group of lexical accent systems and developed a theory of accentuation that relied on the inter-action of morphosyntactic principles with stress. Her research also extends to other areas of the morphosyntax-phonology interface. She is pursuing her work in the theoretical context of Optimality Theory, with emphasis on the structure of phonological representations and the issue of parallel grammars, and has published in journals (*Lingua, Journal of Greek Linguistics*) and edited volumes.

e-mail: revithiadou@rhodes.aegean.gr

Yosuke Sato is a Fulbright graduate student in the Department of Linguistics at the University of Arizona, Tucson. His research focuses on the

interface of syntax with phonology and morphology with special reference to Austronesian languages (Indonesian and Javanese) and Japanese.
His recent publications include the contribution "The distribution of the
active voice morphology in Bahasa Indonesia and *v*P Phases" to a *Festschrift*
for Masaru Nakamura, "P-Stranding Generalization and Bahasa Indonesia: A myth?" (*Snippets*, 2007) and "Semantic regularity in the alternation
in idioms" (*English Linguistics*, 2003). He is currently working on his dissertation entitled "Minimalist interfaces: Selected issues in Indonesian and
Javanese".

e-mail: yosukes@email.arizona.edu

Kayono Shiobara obtained her Ph.D. from the University of British
Columbia in 2004 for the dissertation "Linearization: A Derivational
Approach to the Syntax-Prosody Interface". Since 2005, she has worked
at Bunkyo Gakuin University in Tokyo. Recent publications include the
contribution "An interface approach to the linearization of verbal dependents
in English and Japanese" to a *Festschrift* for Kinsuke Hasegawa (2005) and
a review article of Hawkins (2004) in the journal *English Linguistics* 24
(2007).

e-mail: kayono@fs.u-bunkyo.ac.jp

Vassilios Spyropoulos received his Ph.D. from the University of Reading in
1999. He is a Lecturer at the Department of Mediterranean Studies of the
University of the Aegean and has worked on the synchronic and diachronic
(morpho)syntax of Greek, especially on issues regarding agreement and Case,
the derivation of subject, the morphosyntax of cliticization, the functional categories involved in the clause structure, and control. Another line of research
concerns issues about the morphology and morphosyntax of the Greek nominal system in its dialectal variation. He has published several papers in journals
(*Yearbook of Morphology, Linguistics, Journal of Greek Linguistics*) and edited
volumes.

e-mail: spiropoulos@rhodes.aegean.gr

Hedde Zeijlstra is Assistant Professor of Dutch Linguistics at the University
of Amsterdam. He has worked intensively on negation and on functional
categories in general, in the domains of syntax and semantics. He is the author
of *Sentential Negation and Negative Concord* (LOT Publications, 2004) and
has written various other papers, such as "On the Syntactic Flexibility of
Formal Features" (John Benjamins, 2008) and "Negation in Natural Language:
On the Form and Meaning of Negative Elements" (*Language and Linguistics
Compass*, 2008). His current research concerns the notion of uninterpretability

and the syntax, semantics, and typology of so-called doubling phenomena, i.e. multiple morphosyntactic manifestations of single semantic properties. He received his Ph.D. from the University of Amsterdam, where he also worked for the *Syntactic Atlas of Dutch Dialects* (Amsterdam University Press, 2005), and has occupied a post-doctoral research position at the University of Tübingen.

e-mail: zeijlstra@uva.nl

Abbreviations

[F]	(formal) feature
[iF]	interpretable feature
[uF]	uninterpretable feature
ACC	accusative
Adj	adjective
A-P	articulatory-perceptual (system)
BPS	Bare Phrase Structure (Theory)
C	complementizer
CED	Condition on Extraction Domains
C_{HL}	computational system of human language
C-I	conceptual-intentional (system)
C-S	conceptual-system
COMP	complementizer
CP	complementizer phrase
D	determiner
DAT	dative case
DP	determiner phrase
ECM	exceptional case marking
ECP	Empty Category Principle
EMG	Ellipsis Movement Generalization
EPP	Extended Projection Principle
EXPL	expletive pronominal form
FFFH	Flexible Formal Feature Hypothesis
FI	full interpretation
FL	faculty of language / language faculty
FocP	focus phrase
GB	Government-and-Binding (Theory)
HDS	hierarchical dimensional semantic interpretative structure

IC	interface condition
IP	inflection phrase
I-S	intentional-system
LA	lexical array
LCA	Linear Correspondence Axiom
LEX	lexicon
LF	Logical Form
LI	lexical item
L-to-R	left-to-right
MC	Mapping Condition
MP	Minimalist Program
MSO	multiple Spell-Out
MSOH	Multiple Spell-Out Hypothesis
N	noun *or* numeration
NC	negative concord
NEG	negation
NOC	New Outcome Condition
NOM	nominative
NP	noun phrase
NS	narrow syntax
O	object
Op	operator
OS	object shift
OT	Optimality Theory
P&P	Principles-and-Parameters (Theory)
PF	Phonetic Form
PhonC	Phonological Component
PIC	Phase Impenetrability Condition
PO	prosodic object
PP	prepositional phrase
PRES	present tense
pro	phonetically empty pronoun

PS	phrase structure
QNP	quantified noun phrase
QR	quantifier raising
RC	relative clause
REFL	reflexive pronominal form
RNR	right-node raising
S	subject
SC	Syntactic Component
SemC	Semantic Component
SG	singular
SM	sensorimotor (system)
SMT	Strong(est) Minimalist Thesis
SO	syntactic object
Spec	specifier
SPVH	Strongest Parametric Variation Hypothesis
TopP	topic phrase
TP	tense phrase
UG	Universal Grammar
V	verb
*v*P	light verb phrase
VP	verb phrase
XP	maximal projection

*I dedicate this volume to the memory
of my father Helmuth Grohmann
(17 November 1939–18 May 1991)*

1

Phases and Interfaces*

KLEANTHES K. GROHMANN

1.1 Introducing the Volume

The present volume is a collection of carefully chosen contributions with particular attention paid to thematic coherence as well as broad coverage of topics. The overall goal is to present a unique mix of takes on interface properties within the phase-theoretic approach to the grammar. This collection addresses the fundamental issues in the phase-based approach to the mental computation of language that have arisen from recent developments in the Minimalist Program (Chomsky 1993 *et seq.*). Leading linguists and promising young scholars from all over the world focus on two themes that are at the centre of current theorizing in syntax—the interaction of the syntactic computation with the interpretive interfaces (commonly dubbed the conceptual-intentional system and the sensorimotor system) and current formulations of Phase Theory (capitalized to identify a particular strand of current minimalist theorizing).

Phases are a recent way of modeling the *computational system of human language* (C_{HL} or simply the computation) in relation to the interfaces between the syntactic derivation and the *levels of representation*, known as Logical Form (LF, not to be confused with the logical form used in philosophy) and Phonetic Form (PF, sometimes also called Phonological Form). The original formulation of the notion "phase" goes back to Chomsky (2000), circulated in manuscript form since early 1998. It has undergone serious revisions in both Chomsky's own subsequent writings (which appeared as Chomsky 2001,

* This selective collection derives from oral presentations at the *InterPhases* conference, held 18–20 May 2006 in Nicosia as part of the (unofficially titled) *Cyprus Syntaxfest* (see the Preface for more information). Thanks to all the contributing authors for their patience and cooperation, and for accompanying me on the not always easy route to final publication.

Parts of this chapter build on the two introductions written for two *Linguistic Analysis* special double issues, which I guest-edited (vol. 33, issues 1–2 [2003]: *Dynamic Interfaces, Part I* and vol. 33, issues 3–4 [2003]: *Dynamic Interfaces, Part II*; cf. Grohmann 2007a, 2007c).

2004*a*, 2007*a*, 2008[1]) and many other scholars' contributions (too numerous to mention all[2]). The central idea is that particular substructures of the syntactic computation play an important role in the computational process, also with respect to interpretation at the interfaces.

But in terms of the relation between C_{HL} and the interpretive interfaces, a number of issues remain to be settled. What exactly, for example, does the operation Spell-Out do? How often, and when, does it apply, and to what kind of structures? Where do morphology and phonology kick in? Are the two levels of representation, LF and PF, sufficient, too many, or not enough? How can the interaction between syntax and prosody be formally represented? The contributors to the present volume discuss these and other central questions including the degree to which phases are the right way to think about the dynamic system of language. They consider how far the answers are likely to come from conceptual and theoretical considerations or from experimental and empirical research, which key components might be missing, and how the system can be improved.

Before addressing the main facets of a minimalist approach to linguistic theory as relating to interface issues relevant to the present volume, let us be clear on how the term "interface" is used here. It can be argued, as done somewhat subjectively in Grohmann (2007*a*, 2007*c*), that there are two types of interfaces—*linguistic interfaces* and *modular interfaces*.[3] The latter term was chosen to capture interfaces understood as interactions between separate modules or components of the grammar. For example, there is no shortage of research on the syntax-semantics interface or the syntax-phonology interface, as pretty much all of the subsequent chapters pursue. If LF is the level of representation that sends instructional signals to the systems of thought, which interpret the meaning of a linguistic expression and capture the "meaning side" of language, research in syntax-semantics interactions could thus be considered interface-related. The same goes for syntax-phonology interactions, given that phonology is concerned with the "sound side" of language, the sensorimotor systems, and by extension the level of representation known as PF. The same applies to any number of other combinations, also relating

---

[1] Subsequently often referred to as "Chomsky (2000 *et seq.*)"—the more technical papers on Phase Theory (but note also the important Chomsky 2005).

[2] Excellent recent dissertations on Phase Theory include Richards (2004), Hiraiwa (2005), and Gallego (2007), to name but a few. For shorter textbook presentations, see e.g. chs. 10 of Adger (2003), Radford (2004), and Hornstein *et al.* (2005) or Lasnik & Uriagereka with Boeckx (2005: sect. 7.4) and Boeckx (2008*a*: sect. 3.2).

[3] See also Chomsky (2008), although with different terminology. In a sense, then, the distinction drawn here relates to the LF/PF vs C-I/SM distinction within Phase Theory starting with Chomsky (2000).

to morphology (including the lexicon), pragmatics (and/or discourse, information structure, etc.), and so on. Such a view of interfaces would concentrate on common properties and divergences between two or more (possibly autonomous) components of grammar. The recent collection of state-of-the-art research compiled in Ramchand & Reiss (2007) provides plenty of further discussion, also investigating interactions between phonetics and phonology, between morphology and syntax, and so on.

However, the study of interfaces need not be concerned with trying to find out something deep about the conceptual-architectural properties of the sound and meaning interface systems, the systems that "translate" linguistic properties into signals to the brain to produce or process language. This is done by the modular interfaces,[4] identified in minimalism as LF and PF.[5] The interface levels LF and PF are systems of representation, in the formal sense of Chomsky (1955); see e.g. Chomsky (1975: 99, 103), and especially Uriagereka (1998, 2008a), for valuable discussion. Under this view, the structure assembled in the syntactic component is handed over to the semantic component and to the phonological component, which in turn produce as their output the interface levels LF and PF—steps that are being investigated theoretically and empirically in this volume as well. Standard minimalist assumptions hold that the external systems of thought and the sensorimotor systems read off these levels of representation at the interface.[6]

The following three sections introduce some of the specific questions which can be taken as central to the topic and at the same time mirror the organization of this collection. The twelve contributions have been arranged into three sets of four, fitting the three part titles. Admittedly, this is not, and cannot be, a perfect one-to-one fit, thus some overlap between a particular contribution and the part it has been assigned to may be observed, but by and large the approximation is fittingly close and, it is hoped, transparent. One group largely discusses conceptual issues, sketching the theoretical framework of minimalism and Phase Theory (but often, of course, providing empirical discussion as well); one recurring aspect here is the LF part of interface

---

[4] This corrects the unfortunate typographical error in Grohmann (2007a: 6).

[5] The nature of these signals, and how the brain deals with them, arguably goes beyond the formal study of theoretical linguistics, and also beyond the present volume. The increase in linguistically motivated investigations in areas of neuro- and psycholinguistic research over the past decade, in which linguists participate alongside neurologists, biologists, and other scientists, can, however, be taken as a good sign for interest and progress in this area. This issue is closely related to what Poeppel & Embick (2005) have called the "Granularity Problem" (for further discussion, see also Hornstein forthcoming).

[6] "External" is understood as being outside the faculty of language, whereas the "internal" mechanics are part of our language system. The contributions collected in this volume are for the most part concerned with issues relevant to the faculty of language.

interpretation, the nature of the conceptual-intentional system (Section 1.2). A second bunch explores articulatory issues, focusing on the point(s) of Spell-Out applications and the mapping from syntax to phonology; in this way, the chapters address the PF side of interface interpretation, the nature of the sensorimotor system (Section 1.3). The third part addresses ordering issues at large, in particular linearization and cases of deletion; it deals with other interpretive issues at the interface(s), such as word order and ellipsis phenomena (Section 1.4). The remainder of this introductory chapter thus puts the ensuing discussion, and thereby the articles collected here, into the wider perspective of Chomsky's work on Phase Theory as well as critique, suggestions, and revisions provided elsewhere. The final section of this chapter provides a brief outlook for future investigations, also beyond the concerns addressed here (Section 1.5).

1.2 Conceptual Issues: The Theoretical Framework

Part I contains discussions of largely conceptual issues, thereby sketching the theoretical framework of minimalism in general and Phase Theory specifically. A recurring aspect in all four chapters is the LF part of interface interpretation, that is, the nature of the conceptual-intentional system and how it is fed by the syntactic computation. The Minimalist Program, often simply abbreviated as MP, is the currently prevailing approach to grammar and goes back at least to Chomsky (1993), which circulated in manuscript form and by word of mouth much earlier. The theoretical developments and advances over the past decade and a half fall into two major strands, minimalism as formulated in Chomsky (1995) on the one hand, especially chapter 4 (an expanded version of Chomsky 1994), and in Chomsky (2000) and subsequent work on the other. The former can be classified as embracing at its core *Checking Theory*, the latter as developing *Phase Theory*.

Here the classification is used in this sense, where Checking Theory considers the entire derivation and assumes that movement is feature-driven, triggered by the computational need to check formal features in a specifier-head configuration, or Spec-Head for short. Checking may be source-driven, triggered by the moving element's properties (*Move*, in the sense of Chomsky 1993) or target-driven, where a higher functional element attracts a lower phrase to satisfy feature licensing (*Attract*, in the sense of Chomsky 1995: ch. 4).

Phase Theory, on the other hand, eliminates the structural configuration Spec-Head, which has been a staple property of generative grammar for a very long time, much longer than what can be called "minimalist approaches to the grammar" in the technical sense. It, and thus Checking Theory as a whole, is replaced by the operation *Agree* which holds between a higher functional head, the *probe* P, and a lower linguistic expression, the *goal* G.[7] The formal relation that must hold for Agree between P and G to take place is c-command: P may enter into an Agree relation with G if P c-commands G. Other relevant aspects involve *feature interpretability* and some notion of locality at large, expressed through the property "active": In order for an element to act as a probe, it must bear an uninterpretable feature that is not yet valued, and in order for an element to be a possible goal it must be active in some sense to be determined. "Uninterpretable" means that the feature needs to get valued and deleted, since it cannot be interpreted at the interfaces; to become a suitable goal, the element must in addition bear an interpretable feature that matches the uninterpretable feature of the probing element. Thus P with an uninterpretable feature $[uF]$, in the terminology of Pesetsky & Torrego (2001), must c-command an active G with a matching interpretable feature $[F]$.[8]

The references mentioned in *n.* 2 lay out the basics sketched here in more detail, and for the most part the contributions collected here do not deal with the specifics of the Agree framework to feature licensing, and neither do they directly explore the notion "active"—but indirectly they do. Being active requires the element to be accessible in a particular technical sense, simply put within the same phase.[9] And this leads us to Phase Theory.

The cornerstone of Phase Theory is the hypothesis that the syntactic derivation proceeds phase by phase—by building up a smaller chunk of syntactic structure, evaluating it at several time steps, and then continuing to successively construct the next relevant chunk(s) until the *numeration* or *lexical array* is depleted. In order to demonstrate the rationale behind Phase Theory and address some of the issues that arise, the *architecture of the grammar* needs to be considered in some semi-historical perspective.

For starters, the type of architectural design of the grammar minimalism challenged from the outset is the Government-and-Binding Theory (GB, Chomsky 1981) organization of four levels of representation and their interplay, where each is subject to a number of specific filters and constraints:

---

[7] This is a simplified characterization, of course, but it should suffice for present purposes since none of the following chapters deals in any deep sense with Agree and movement issues that bear on the status or replacement of Checking Theory in Phase Theory. It is probably more accurate to say, as Petr Biskup (p.c.) points out, that the Spec-Head configuration is replaced by the operation *Agree* coupled with the (generalized) EPP (Chomsky 2000, 2001) and that Agree replaces F(eature)-movement.

[8] See Adger (2003) for the earliest textbook presentation of this notation and a coherent (if, at times, non-standard) feature-licensing system, ideal as an overview for novice minimalists.

[9] In an earlier formulation, the goal could also be active when in a lower phase (e.g. Chomsky 2001: 14), but this raises the issue of strong vs weak phases, which will be ignored here.

D-structure (Projection Principle) feeds S-structure (Move α) which in turn branches off and leads to the semantic interpretation (LF) and phonetic output (PF). Particular conditions (such as Subjacency or the Extended Projection Principle) apply and individual modules (such as Theta Theory, Case Filter, PRO Theorem, and so on) have to be satisfied at the respective level of representation (see also van Riemsdijk & Williams 1986; for a recent review of subsequent developments, see e.g. Hornstein *et al.* 2005). In contrast, the classic minimalist architecture eliminates the levels of D- and S-structure, as in (1): The Lexicon (LEX) feeds the syntactic derivation directly, which thus allows interspersing of *Merge* and *Move* rather freely (certainly not as constrained as in older models), in accordance with the licensing mechanism of formal properties, as briefly mentioned above (such as Checking Theory vs Agree), and other conditions on interpretation.

(1)   LEX (*qua* numeration or lexical array)

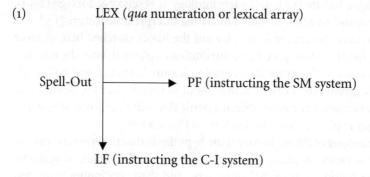

Spell-Out ├──────────▶ PF (instructing the SM system)

LF (instructing the C-I system)

Noteworthy here is the operation *Spell-Out*, which will be addressed in Section 1.3. Other than that, standard minimalist reasoning holds that only such entities should exist in the grammar that either follow from *(virtual) conceptual necessity* or fall into the category *bare output conditions* (Chomsky 1995: 169–71, 219–25), now called *interface conditions* in Phase Theory (Chomsky 2004a: 2). LEX, the collection of lexical items and functional elements in the human mind/brain, is arguably conceptually necessary, whereas LF and PF are clearly interface conditions.[10] As just mentioned, these are linguistic levels of representation which the relevant language-external systems read off. These levels, which Chomsky (1995) calls the *conceptual-intentional (C-I) system* and the articulatory-perceptual system, these days more commonly known as the *sensorimotor (SM) system* (Chomsky 2000 *et seq.*), respectively, are clearly

---

[10] Returning to one of the questions from Section 1.1, note that Uriagereka (1999a) makes the interesting case for a revival of DS. He argues that many aspects of DS are essentially still packaged in minimalism as hidden assumptions and carefully teases apart the relevant issues: What is a "level of representation" (as opposed to a "component")? How can we integrate their role in a minimalist approach? The reasoning laid out in more detail in Uriagereka (2008a) will probably play an important role in the near future, but not in this volume.

"(virtually) conceptually necessary" if there is anything to the characterization, roughly going back to Aristotle, that language is the pairing of sound and meaning. If language at some level boils down to such a pair—often expressed as the pair $<\pi, \lambda>$, where π is the phonetic output and λ the semantic one or the pair $<$Phon, Sem$>$ (see below)—then sound and meaning need to be represented somehow, to yield the two objects that make up language.

Or so goes the mainstream view. Two contributions to the present volume deal specifically with the C-I interface system(s). **Wolfram Hinzen** casts some doubt on the characterization of (virtual) conceptual necessity to include the C-I system. When Hinzen asks whether the successor function plus the lexicon equals human language, he not only plays with the title of a workshop recently held in Berlin (cf. Sauerland & Gärtner 2007). Hinzen really asks to what extent the equation in the title is a useful idealization of evolutionary facts. He wants to know what interfaces "motivate" exactly (thereby getting even closer to the title of that particular workshop). And he has some answers, too. He motivates the equation by assuming a radical simplification of the computational system of the language faculty (FL^{11}). This explanatory vision operates with a minimal conception of recursive structure-building, modeled on the recursive structure of the natural numbers. The results of the discussion of conceptual and empirical difficulties for the latter may be taken as a reformulation, but not necessarily an abandonment, of the so-called *Strong Minimalist Thesis* (Chomsky 2000 *et seq.*; Lasnik 2002), to be addressed presently, viewed as a guideline of empirical research in the evolution of language.

In contrast, **Takashi Munakata**, working from within the hypothesis that the C-I system is conceptually necessary, argues for a division of the C-I system, into a *Conceptual-System* and an *Intentional-System* as opposed to one unified system, and suggests that both systems interface with the language faculty. He also proposes that the different interface conditions imposed by these systems regulate a number of otherwise unmotivated syntactic properties and mechanisms, such as the A/A'-distinction, the difference between lexical and functional elements, thematic properties, or the dual nature of semantics. Munakata's investigations into the nature of the input within a phase-theoretic approach thus lead to a different perspective from Chomsky's on the output (*vis-à-vis* multiple applications of Transfer; cf. Section 1.3).

To continue with the brief sketch of basic minimalist assumptions and terminology in Phase Theory, C_{HL} thus essentially maps items from the Lexicon

---

[11] The language faculty is also referred to as the (human) faculty of language, then often abbreviated as FL. Both terms are used in this volume. For a wider discussion of FL issues, including evolutionary speculations and the larger biolinguistic perspective, see Hauser *et al.* (2002) and Chomsky (2005, 2007*b*).

to the LF representation of an expression (Exp)—call this *narrow syntax* (NS). The mapping proceeds from either a unique numeration (as in the earlier minimalist approach of Chomsky 1995) or from several lexical (sub)arrays (as in the current phase-based model of Chomsky 2000 *et seq.*). Spell-Out, or a subapplication of *Transfer* (see Section 1.3), is the operation that applies to the derivation computed within NS, once all uninterpretable features have been licensed (but see the presentation on Spell-Out below). It sends the derivation, or the relevant subpart (the "chunk" called phase), to PF for phonological manipulation in order to obtain a legible, i.e. pronounceable, representation. By assumption, the derivation continues, but without effect on the PF output, in order to obtain a unique LF representation corresponding to the meaning of the linguistic expression computed. The final outcome is a paired expression, namely Exp = <Phon, Sem> (or $<\pi, \lambda>$ in earlier notation).[12] In more recent work, Spell-Out has received a lot of attention, which will be presented briefly in the next section.

Whatever the details, a linguistic theory must above all be able to take care of, and explain, those (unique) properties of human language that make language such a special object to study. Four such properties are (i) the existence of uninterpretable formal features, (ii) dislocation effects, (iii) the cross-linguistic flexibility of morphosyntactic categories, and (iv) the existence of cross-linguistic variation—a wild mix that so far seems to have resisted a clean explanation and has sometimes been characterized as "imperfections" of language. One aspect of the conceptual underpinnings of the Strong(est) Minimalist Thesis (SMT) is the idea that language is, despite appearances, a "perfect" solution to the task of relating sound and meaning.[13] In other words, this perspective takes language to be an optimal solution to conditions that are imposed to FL by the mental modules, the C-I and the SM systems.

However, as **Hedde Zeijlstra** argues, the idea that language is "perfect" in this sense seems to be at odds with several "imperfections" found in grammar, such as those just mentioned. Zeijlstra argues that these four properties are not linguistic imperfections, but are actually predicted by the Perfectness Hypothesis—specifically, that the different conditions imposed by FL are not always compatible to each other, and that therefore FL can offer multiple,

---

[12] To be more precise, here's the latest formulation in the original (Chomsky 2004a: 107):

Assume further that [language] L has three components: *narrow syntax* (NS) maps [the lexical array] LA to a derivation D-NS; the *phonological component* Φ maps D-NS to PHON; the *semantic component* Σ maps D-NS to SEM. Σ is assumed to be uniform for all L; NS is as well, if parameters can be restricted to LEX (as I will assume). Φ, in contrast, is highly variable among Ls. Optimally, mappings will satisfy the *inclusiveness condition*, introducing no new elements but only rearranging those of the domain.

[13] The SMT has undergone some changes in its formulation since Chomsky (1995) but can be summarized as follows: "[L]anguage is an optimal solution to interface conditions that the Faculty of Language (FL) must satisfy" (Chomsky 2005: 3).

equally optimal solutions to these conflicting interface conditions. His contribution thus deals with consequences of conflicting interface conditions: being a perfect solution to one interface condition may imply that another interface condition cannot be maximally solved, and vice versa. Hence perfect solutions to interface conditions, which are in conflict with other interface conditions, can only exist by virtue of less perfect solutions to these other interface conditions. The central claim of this chapter is that the existence of the aforementioned properties are all epiphenomena of the perfectness hypothesis.

A final aspect of interface interpretation relevant for the following chapters concerns binding, captured in earlier theoretical approaches, predominantly in GB, by the Binding Theory which is made up of three binding principles or conditions (Chomsky 1981, 1986*b*): Condition A governing the interpretation of anaphors, Condition B licensing pronouns, and Condition C relating R(eferential)-expressions. Binding is perhaps the interface phenomenon *par excellence*—certainly from a linguistic interface perspective, in the sense understood here. Binding concerns cannot be accommodated without the interplay of at least both syntax (*qua* derivation, yielding the relevant structural configurations) and semantics (*qua* interpretation of individual linguistic expressions, possibly in context). Hornstein *et al.* (2005: ch. 8) provide a larger background of binding issues in a minimalist approach. As for treatments of binding in Phase Theory specifically, not so much work has been done yet. Perhaps Phase Theory has not (yet) much to contribute to standard (minimalist) treatments of binding phenomena in language. One notable exception is work by Uriagereka & Gallego (2006) who propose (multiple) Agree as relating binder (probe) and bindee (goal), where the classic binding domain is recast in terms of the phase (originally suggested in Lasnik & Uriagereka with Boeckx 2005). They thus replace the relation Binding with the operation Agree, develop the notion of multiple Agree to capture Condition A, and derive Condition B from associating subject and object with different probes (Uriagereka & Gallego 2006: 7).

They remain silent, however, on Condition C. **Petr Biskup** pays attention to R-expressions in his contribution and Condition C effects within a phase-based approach to C_{HL}. Concentrating on the role of adjuncts, he revisits the well-known asymmetry between reconstruction and Condition C and the timing question of adding adjuncts to the derivation. Biskup first makes the strong case that there is a need to differentiate between clausal and non-clausal adjuncts with respect to Condition C effects, which only the former can obviate. Condition C effects themselves consequently do not constitute a uniform phenomenon; they can be induced by three different factors (stemming from phrase structure, tripartite quantificational structure, and information structure). He argues further that the Condition C data cannot be accounted for by acyclic merger of adjuncts or by the special status of (late) adjunct merger, and concludes that all adjuncts are merged cyclically. On the verge of leaving the conceptual part this chapter has been assigned to, Biskup presents a thorough discussion of actual language data and discusses a wealth of relevant data from Czech.

1.3 Articulatory Issues: Points of Spell-Out

Part II explores articulatory issues within Phase Theory with two major focal points—the mapping from syntax to phonology (with a recurring theme of prosodic issues) and further details concerning the operation Spell-Out (such as when and where it applies). In this way, all chapters address the PF side of interface interpretation, the nature of the SM system, from both a linguistic and a modular interface perspective in the sense outlined above.[14] Chomsky (1993, 1995) originally introduced Spell-Out as that kind of operation in NS that replaced the S-structure level of representation. It was assumed to take the final product of the syntactic derivation and send meaning-relevant information to LF and sound-relevant information to PF for interpretation.

The following briefly summarizes the status of Spell-Out in Chomsky's (2000 *et seq.*) more *dynamic model* of Phase Theory (see also the references cited in *n.* 2). It should be prefaced with the observation that many of the properties hold for all recent proposals, to some degree, after the original introduction of multiple Spell-Out by Uriagereka (1999*b*)—which itself picks up on ideas expressed first in Bresnan (1971, 1972). This includes Uriagereka's own explorations of multiple Spell-Out (1998, 2002*c*, 2008*a*, 2008*b*), Chomsky's phase-based model (2000, 2001, 2004*a*, 2005, 2007*a*, 2008), the Spell-Out-as-you-merge approach by Epstein *et al.* (1998) and Epstein & Seely (2002*a*, 2006), the related single-output model of Groat & O'Neil (1996) and others, and Grohmann's (2000, 2003) dynamic spelling out of Prolific Domains, for example, which are briefly summarized in an overview at the end of this section for completeness.

There are at least two major issues concerning the articulatory interface theme in minimalism or, more specifically, some version of multiple Spell-Out and the organization of the grammar—the two issues that connect the chapters in this part (and some others). On the one hand, it needs to be seen empirically whether the notion of multiple Spell-Out has a practical application, and what details of such an application would look like. On the

---

[14] In this sense, they also contribute to conceptual advances of the framework, of course, but since emphasis is put clearly on Spell-Out effects and phenomena, the four chapters have been included here.

other hand, the terms and conditions relating to multiple Spell-Out have to be made concrete. One exciting aspect of linguistic minimalism (in the sense of Boeckx 2006) is, then, that the study of the linguistic interfaces opens new doors in the large hallway of the architecture of the grammar.

As depicted in (1) above, the so-called Y-model of the grammar, (narrow) syntax feeds the interpretive interface levels LF and PF directly, without assuming additional levels of representation. The operation Spell-Out was originally introduced in Chomsky (2003) to apply at one point and hand the derivation over to the interface levels. With the rise of the Multiple Spell-Out Hypothesis (Uriagereka 1999*b*), however, the conception of this transfer became more "dynamic" in a way (see also Uriagereka 1998, 2002*c*, 2008*a*, 2008*b* as well as the approaches mentioned at the end of this section), while Uriagereka suggested applying Spell-Out to "command paths" with the (simplified) effect of "freezing" left branches of assembled tree structures. Chomsky (2000) picked the idea up and developed a notion of cyclic Spell-Out (other approaches are briefly presented at the end of this section): Spell-Out applies in a cyclic manner over specific subparts of the derivation. These cyclic subparts he called phases, identified on the clausal level as *v*P and CP on the basis of a number of properties (as discussed here by Marušič who provides plenty of references; see also Boeckx & Grohmann 2007 and literature cited for a critical overview). Phases then are the relevant derivational subparts at which Spell-Out applies cyclically.

Since the focus of the chapters contained in this part falls on spelling out to PF, this aspect will be given more emphasis here.[15] More recently, Chomsky (2004*a*) employs the "superoperation" Transfer (Lasnik & Uriagereka with Boeckx 2005: 240), which sends the relevant information (interpretable features) to the interpretive interfaces (LF and PF). Spell-Out, under this view, is the suboperation "Transfer to PF" (as opposed to the alternative, "Transfer to LF"[16]). For the remainder of this chapter, unless otherwise noted, "Spell-Out" is used interchangeably with "Transfer to PF" understood in this sense. And it is this sense that leads to the articulatory issues discussed here.

To start with, **Lanko Marušič** balances his discussion between conceptual and articulatory issues. Following standard assumptions, as laid out in the previous section and continued below, when a phase is completed, the structure is

---

[15] Note that Nissenbaum (2000)—taking his cue from the single-output models of Brody (1995), Bobaljik (1995), Pesetsky (1998), and Groat & O'Neil (1996)—assumes Spell-Out to apply solely for PF purposes. This single-cycle grammar replicates the effects yielded by the Y-model (cf. (1)) without losing the dynamic character of the phase-based model.

[16] On a par with *Spell-Out* as Transfer to PF, Lasnik & Uriagereka with Boeckx (2005: 240) suggest the term *Interpret* for Transfer at LF.

sent simultaneously to the two interfaces where it gets interpreted. But certain syntactic constituents do not have phasal properties at both interfaces. This suggests that Transfer sometimes occurs to a single interface, that is, to PF but not simultaneously to LF, or vice versa (note the conceptual resemblance to Zeijlstra's suggestion: "Being a perfect solution to one interface condition may imply that another interface condition cannot be maximally solved, and vice versa"). This tool of *non-simultaneous Spell-Out* could place this chapter in the conceptual part of the volume. However, Marušič also provides a host of relevant data from Slovenian, zooming in on both PF- and LF-relevant aspects. Here he finds strong evidence in favor of (non-simultaneous) Spell-Out at both the clausal and the nominal level, i.e. within DP.[17] He further argues that non-simultaneous Spell-Out derives reconstruction effects and covert movement, the two cases where place of interpretation differs from the place of pronunciation.

But in "standard" Phase Theory as proposed by Chomsky (2001 *et seq.*), Spell-Out (Transfer to PF) applies at the phase level on a par with Transfer to LF (see also *n.* 15). The phase is thus argued to be an indispensable property of any well-designed language system that conforms to the SMT. In essence, phases are the only relevant units for the mapping from NS to the external systems, the C-I system fed by LF and the SM system fed by PF. This process supposedly allows for optimal computational efficiency, eliminating redundant internal levels and compositional cycles in favor of the generation of a single cycle with periodic transfer to the interfaces. The units sent to Spell-Out are syntactically defined as the locus of uninterpretable features, which need to be eliminated (and whose cyclic valuation ensures Full Interpretation at the interfaces).

As noted above, the assumption that Spell-Out is not an operation fundamentally different from other operations in the grammar in that it applies exactly once in a given derivation leads to more dynamic conceptions (for book-length treatments, see Uriagereka 2002c, 2008b). Rather, it may apply several times, giving rise to a "multiple Spell-Out" model—and what makes these "several times" of application appropriate is somehow encoded in the dynamics of the syntactic computation. This can be illustrated as below (taken from Boeckx 2008a: 45), where LF and PF are assembled cyclically in some fashion (via "mini-interface components" *lf* and *pf*)—leaving out details at this point in the introduction as to how exactly the dynamics of the system is computed. The latter is, of course, identified as the phase, more specifically,

---

[17] On the phasal status of DP, see Svenonius (2004) as well as Hiraiwa (2005), a possibility acknowledged in Chomsky (2008). Note that Abels (2003b) also makes the case for the phase-relevance of PP (by means of a modern twist on van Riemsdijk 1978), but these issues are not discussed in the present volume.

tied to the point at which a phase head is merged into the derivation and ranges over its domain—its complement up to and excluding the next lower phase head and structures c-commanded by it, but including its edge (see below for more).

(2)
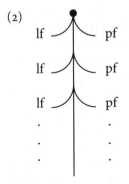

$$lf \qquad pf$$
$$lf \qquad pf$$
$$lf \qquad pf$$

Under such an approach, Spell-Out applies several times in the course of the derivation—and the question is to find out which units are the relevant subparts of the derivation at which Spell-Out applies. Chomsky's (2000 *et seq.*) answer is that phases are instrumental; potential alternatives will be briefly presented at the end of this section.

As roughly portrayed in (2), cyclic Spell-Out allows for the dynamic linearization of syntactic structures, where each phase forms a separate linearization domain. If linearization algorithms operate on syntactic information (a reasonable assumption, but see Section 1.4)—such as c-command relations, as under Kayne's (1994) Linear Correspondence Axiom—dynamic linearization is not just a possibility but in fact a necessity in a phase-based system. This is because such information is lost in the course of cyclic computation, which, in accordance with the SMT, leads to minimization of computational complexity, at least by hypothesis, via a reduction in memory load. This property of a phase-based computation yields the strict cyclicity effects captured under the Phase Impenetrability Condition (PIC). The PIC originally proposed in Chomsky (2000) has received some modification, specifically in Chomsky (2001), on the basis of work by Nissenbaum (2000). The latest installment of the PIC is as follows:

(3)   At the phase ZP containing phase HP, the domain of H is not accessible to operations, but only the edge of HP. (Chomsky 2004a: 108)

For Chomsky, then, the PIC is an inevitable consequence of any "meaningful" system of cyclic computation. In his words, "Φ [the phonological component] is greatly simplified if it can 'forget about' what has been transferred to it at earlier phases; otherwise, the advantages of cyclic computation are lost"

(Chomsky 2004*a*: 107). Most research inspired by Chomsky in this area tends to be done by syntacticians, and thus focus on (syntacticians' conceptions of) the mapping from syntax to PF. But of course, a phonologist's perspective might be equally revealing, if not more (or at least, differently).[18]

A relevant contribution to this aspect is the chapter by **Kayono Shiobara**, who provides a phonological perspective on syntactically derived phases. She thus focuses on the sound side of the two interfaces and considers potential advantages of a phonologically based approach to phases. Shiobara shows that a phonological approach to phases calls for left-to-right, as opposed to the standardly assumed bottom-up, structure-building in C_{HL} and argues that this assumption has independent motivations. First and foremost, left-to-right is the way terminal elements are produced or processed online in performance. In addition, left-to-right structure-building in the computational component is empirically supported by syntactic and phonological facts, and possibly by scope phenomena related to the syntax-LF mapping, for which Shiobara provides evidence. She argues specifically that locality effects captured by the PIC may be reinterpreted in a left-to-right derivation, where it is always the "right" edge of a phase that is accessible to the next computational cycle, without any additional problems.

Current dynamic approaches to the syntactic derivation capitalize on the notion of syntactic cycles, be it in the sense of phases, derivational cascades, or other alternatives. Such models also raise a number of interesting issues regarding the way in which phonology processes the syntactic output. **Anthi Revithiadou & Vassilios Spyropoulos** provide a case study from prosodification of clitic-doubled DP-objects in Greek to implement a dynamic approach to the syntax-phonology interface. They essentially propose that the derivational status of syntactic material is reflected on the way PF organizes the output of syntax into phonological phrases. On the basis of empirical evidence, Revithiadou & Spyropoulos propose that elements which exhibit derivational islandhood form independent phonological phrases and, significantly, are

---

[18] The subsequent three chapters cite plenty of relevant sources, such as work by Gorka Elordieta, Shinichiro Ishihara, Hubert Truckenbrodt, and, of course, Lisa Selkirk, the pioneer on these issues for the past few decades, who has also worked on Phase Theory in recent years (Selkirk 2006*b*, Kratzer & Selkirk 2007), among many others, naturally including the individual authors' own research. A very recent and highly stimulating piece of research is Chung's (2007) dissertation on the "ecology" of PF. Other relevant research is carried out by Tobias Scheer and colleagues (e.g. Newell & Scheer 2007), who also provide a "little interface library" (http://www.unice.fr/dsl/tobweb/interfacelib.htm). However, the phonology aspect of these chapters will not be discussed in this syntax-orientated introduction (but see the respective chapters of Revithiadou & Spyropoulos, Sato, and Shiobara).

Another perspective comes from morphology, especially the framework of Distributed Morphology (Halle & Marantz 1993); see Embick & Noyer (2001) and Embick (2007) for interesting proposals concerning the "road to PF" (Grohmann 2007*b*).

impervious to PF restructuring mechanisms. They further explore the limits of this isomorphism by investigating the derivational and prosodic status of preverbal Greek subjects and conclude that their syntactic non-islandhood is matched by an analogous behavior at PF since they are subject to restructuring. This particular type of isomorphism provides empirical justification for drawing a distinction between two different implementations of Spell-Out, as originally proposed in Uriagereka (1999*b*).

A comparison, or integration, of the Multiple Spell-Out Hypothesis and Phase Theory is also the concern of **Yosuke Sato**, who provides arguments for multiple Spell-Out through an application to prosodic domains. In this third and final "phonological perspective" on dynamic interfaces and Phase Theory, he proposes a syntax-prosody mapping hypothesis within the recent derivational theory of syntax. This hypothesis yields predictions about possible structural domains for phonological rule application that are indeed borne out by a variety of phonological alternations across languages. The empirical data Sato discusses are rich and varied: Taiwanese tone sandhi, French liaison, Gilyak lenition, Kinyambo high tone deletion, and Welsh consonant mutation are all explored in this chapter.

Expanding on the above presentation and thus going slightly beyond the scope of the present volume, the following list provides a short overview—with no claim to exhaustiveness—of some recent proposals, in chronological order, that are relevant to what has been called here the "dynamic model" (from Grohmann 2007*a*: 11–12):

(i) *Multiple Spell-Out*
Uriagereka (1999*b*), originally circulated in 1996, who proposes multiple Spell-Out every time a 'command path' is formed, which essentially breaks down to left branches (apart from Uriagereka 2002*c*, 2008*a*, 2008*b*, see also his follow-up work with Jairo Nunes and other work inspired by it);

(ii) *Spell-Out-as-you-merge*
Epstein *et al.* (1998), based in part on the previous work of the co-authors, who argue essentially that every application of Merge spells out (see also recent fruitful collaboration of Samuel Epstein and Daniel Seely as well as other scholars' contributions to this line of research);

(iii) *Phase Theory*
Chomsky (2000), originally circulated in 1998, who introduces phases as Spell-Out domains and who refined the notion of phase in Chomsky (2001, 2004*a*, 2008) and other work (see also a lot of recent research within the phase-based approach by a host of different scholars);

(iv) *Prolific Domains*
Grohmann (2003), based on his 2000 dissertation, who suggests Prolific Domains to spell out dynamically (and here too there is much follow-up and related research by Grohmann and co-authors as well as other linguists; see Grohmann, forthcoming).

1.4 Ordering Issues: Linearization and Deletion

Part III addresses ordering at large, in particular how C_{HL} linearizes syntactic constituents and deals with deletion issues; it also deals with other interpretive effects at the LF and PF interfaces, such as word order and ellipsis phenomena. Since linearization must take place in the phonological component (as argued for under minimalist considerations by Chomsky 1995, Uriagereka 1998, Nunes 1999, and many others), dynamic/cyclic linearization goes hand in hand with SMT-conforming dynamic/cyclic Spell-Out. In short, linearization in Phase Theory should take place on a phase-by-phase basis if the phonological component gets constructed piecemeal via phases. The following sketches some issues relevant to linearization and then briefly presents the remaining chapters; deletion and ellipsis will not be discussed here.[19]

In the course of the derivation, "all NS does is to create new objects out of pre-existing morpho-lexical units" (Piattelli-Palmarini & Uriagereka 2004: 355). These new objects are sets which the syntactic operation Merge combines. Merging two items, α and β, thus creates the set $\{\alpha, \beta\}$, in which α and β remain distinct; in natural language, this operation can be reiterated (recursively). This way, the phrase marker is built bottom-up in a recursive manner through the successive application of the operation Merge (but see Shiobara's chapter). The interface with the SM system imposes that the hierarchical structure resulting from merging objects iteratively be linearized. As Uriagereka (1998, 1999*b*) notes, the objects assembled by Merge are (at least) two-dimensional, whereas speech is one-dimensional. Therefore, all the objects NS (or rather D-NS, as per *n.* 12) sends to PF, and ultimately the SM system, must be submitted to some ordering relation—linearization.

However, linearizing the objects in a given phrase marker would, as a consequence, destroy all hierarchical relations, which in turn would result in feeding the C-I system with uninterpretable material. Thus, as Piattelli-Palmarini &

---

[19] A major concern for deletion relates, of course, to deletion of copies, or whatever multiple occurrences of syntactic constituents be referred to. This is not the right place to open that can of worms, which bears on many issues beyond chain formation (see e.g. Nunes 1995, 2004 and Hornstein 1998, 2001 for extensive discussion).

Uriagereka continue, one of two assumptions must apply. First, one could argue that linear order unambiguously reflects hierarchical structure (as in Kayne 1994, briefly addressed right below). Second—alternatively or in addition—one could capitalize on some marker that the SM system can detect (such as an agreement or Case marker, as Uriagereka 1999*b* suggests) which is attached to one item in the string; according to Uriagereka, this marker corresponds to a marker attached to another item in the string in ways that the C-I system can process, which would suffice to feed the C-I system with specific constructs that can be interpreted there.

One of the most explicit translations from syntactic structure to phonological/phonetic output (i.e. PF) in recent years is however based on some version of Kayne's Linear Correspondence Axiom (LCA). The major insight here (call it the Dominance Hypothesis, with Lechner 2006) is that syntactic relations refer to dominance (via c-command), but not to precedence. Uriagereka (1998, 1999*b*) suggests that the syntactic representation can be likened to a Calder mobile, whose root X is fixed, but whose branches swing freely in a two-dimensional plane—the result of a recursive application of Merge where the output of one application can be the input of the next. But at least at the point at which the product of the completed derivation is submitted to the PF component, an ordering of the two terms has to be specified. That is, the two-dimensional tree has to be mapped onto a one-dimensional phonetic representation. More precisely, it is the two-dimensional circle that results from letting α and β rotate freely which needs to be mapped to a one-dimensional string. Given that this information cannot come from any other source than from LEX and the properties of the syntactic derivation (which are possibly restricted by some kind of IC or "interface readability"), and given that LEX is inherently unordered (which also goes for any implementation of a presyntactic numeration or array that enters NS), it follows that the tree somehow must also contain information about order.

For the sake of completeness, and to allow a better processing of the following discussion, (4) reproduces the original formulation of the LCA and (5)-(6), from Uriagereka (2008*b*: ch. 1), illustrate it further (even though it may not bear directly on Phase Theory, at least not in current research[20]):

(4) *Linear Correspondence Axiom* (*LCA*; Kayne 1994: 6)
     d(A) is a linear ordering of T.

---

[20] What may not be so prominent in current phase-based research is Kayne's specific formulation within his Antisymmetry Theory, and Uriagereka provides an interesting alternative formulation. What is prominent, though, is of course the idea that linearization must be captured somehow, and that this is done at PF. Uriagereka's rendering of Kayne's LCA turns out to be a theorem, rather than an axiom. This is surely a step in the right direction, but whether it suffices remains to be seen.

(5)   *Linear Correspondence Axiom* (partial statement; Uriagereka 2008*b*: ch. 1)
      When x asymmetrically c-commands y, x precedes y.

(6)   *Linearization Induction* (Uriagereka 2008*b*: ch. 1)
      If a non-terminal X dominates a terminal y, and X is linearized with
      regards to terminal z, then y is linearized with regards to z.

Aside from transitivity, the LCA is specified through two conditions. First, for
each pair of terminals, it must be possible to find two nodes that dominate
these terminals and which asymmetrically c-command each other. This condition, the "Totality Clause" of the axiom, requires that all pairs of terminals
satisfy this condition. Second, by the "Antisymmetry Clause," there should
be no two non-terminals above the terminals that reverse the asymmetrical
c-command order. The main objective of the LCA is to derive basic properties
of X′-Theory related to generalizations of ordering (specifiers precede heads,
complements follow, adjunction is to the left—whether this is to be implemented through Kayne's Universal Base Hypothesis or derived some other way
with slight alterations; cf. *n*. 20). A second goal is to find a mapping structure
to order. The fact that some terminal α precedes some terminal β in a given
structure does not necessarily mean that the two terminals are pronounced in
that order.

      An alternative to the Dominance Hypothesis would be what Lechner calls
the Precedence Hypothesis: hierarchical order (*vis-à-vis* syntactic structure)
encodes linear order. This view is espoused in recent work that does not
assume the LCA (see Williams 2003, Fox & Pesetsky 2005, and Müller 2007,
for example). On analogy with the Dominance Hypothesis, it could be
defined in such a way that syntactic principles refer to precedence, not to
dominance (c-command). Richards (2007) critically examines this hypothesis and argues against it (at least in the formulation of Fox & Pesetsky
2005).

      What is interesting to note at this point is that an adoption of either
hypothesis has important repercussions for the theory of syntax. Beyond
particular assumptions on phrase structure (an LCA-conforming X′-Theory
vs Bare Phrase Structure Theory, for example) and feature checking (see also
the discussion of "natural relations" in Grohmann 2003), something has to
be said about how unordered items from LEX are arranged in NS in such a
way that all relevant hierarchical relations come out (quantifier scope, binding
possibilities, and other LF-interpretable properties) and the desired linearized
object emerges (the pronounced PF-output).

      On the task of linearizing derivational units to comply with observed word
order, grammarians have been taxed for a long time by postverbal sentential

complements in German since in all other relevant respects, German seems to be OV. **Jiro Inaba** revisits this puzzle from a phase-theoretical perspective. Based on the concept of postsyntactic linearization and cyclic Spell-Out from the bottom, Inaba proposes (i) that the element spelled out earlier is realized in the phonological component later and (ii) that CPs, as opposed to DPs, constitute an independent Spell-Out domain. This chapter thus contributes to the mechanics of linearization in Phase Theory.

Other complications for linearization are raised by all kinds of deletion phenomena in the grammar. This goes beyond the need to delete "copies" of displaced, or syntactically moved ("internally merged"), material (see *n.* 19). Two such cases are discussed in the present part of the collection, namely, ellipsis in general and a possible subcase, right-node raising.

Turning their attention to the latter special case of deletion, **Asaf Bachrach & Roni Katzir** provide new data showing that right-node raising can feed *wh*-movement and that this movement is exempt from certain locality constraints. They use these observations to argue that right-node raising should be analyzed in terms of multiple-dominance, a concept they put in the right context and provide relevant references for in their chapter. Bachrach & Katzir further discuss the implications of this conclusion for the architecture of grammar, thereby, of course, contributing to the conceptual theme of this volume as well. These include a discussion of the effects of *delayed Spell-Out* at the phonological interface.

Based on Holmberg's (2001) analysis of ellipsis combined with a particular characterization of phase, **Masanori Nakamura** explains a cross-linguistic generalization, which he dubs the *Ellipsis Movement Generalization (EMG)*: If a language allows ellipsis of a particular category in a certain structure, that category cannot undergo movement except when it is phonologically null. Following a discussion of facts from English, Irish, and Japanese, Nakamura puts the EMG in relation to the notion phase. He suggests a modification of the operation Transfer (to PF): "Transfer applies to the complement domain of head H as soon as all of the uninterpretable features of H are eliminated" (cf. Svenonius 2004; Gallego 2006*b*). In other words, in adopting the hypothesis Nakamura holds—very much with Chomsky (1986*a*)—that any projection can in principle be a phase (see also Boeckx & Grohmann 2007). He then modifies it slightly by restricting the relevant domain Transfer to which applies to the Φ-interpretable complement domain of H.

The final contribution to this volume combines investigations relevant to all three parts, and thus relates to much of what has been said above. On a conceptual note, **Howard Lasnik** addresses the organization of the grammar, arguing for *one-cycle syntax*, which has proven very productive with its concomitant cyclic Spell-Out, but it also raises certain problems. Concerning articulation issues, Lasnik examines what is really meant by "Spell-Out"—at least on the PF side—which he puts in a wider discussion of some of these problems thrown up by one-cycle syntax. It is here that his contribution does fit the ordering part in that Lasnik considers ellipsis phenomena, island constraints, and overt-covert movement asymmetries, and combines the theoretical and empirical concerns just mentioned.

1.5 Outlook and Beyond

The final section of this chapter provides a brief outlook for future investigations and related concerns beyond those addressed here. The following chapters contribute, as outlined above, to the three aspects of *InterPhases*—the relation between the interpretive interfaces and phase-based approaches to minimalist investigations of the grammar. They all explore, to varying individual extent, conceptual, articulatory, and ordering issues within Phase Theory. As regards interface explorations, they also all investigate linguistic and modular interfaces, as the two major types of interface-relevant research have been dubbed here—again to varying individual extent.

And also to varying extent, they all embrace Phase Theory, as laid out in Chomsky (2000 *et seq.*) and other work. While adopting existing notions and hypotheses of Phase Theory, even in detail (and at times even going beyond them), the present collection does not, however, question fundamental assumptions of Phase Theory (as per Chomsky 2000 *et seq.*). Neither do the following chapters deal with certain notions of Phase Theory that might require rethinking or working out of details (as done in Boeckx & Grohmann 2007, for example). And they do not, to end these introductory remarks on a positive note, even address certain aspects of Phase Theory, whether contentious or not (some of which have been raised above)—but the following are aspects of Phase Theory that should be mentioned, if only in passing, even in a sketch as brief as this. So this section completes the rough overview of Phase Theory and interpretive interfaces within linguistic minimalism as relevant to the present volume but also slightly above and beyond, with some pointers to critical or more reflective literature.

Without doubt, the phase-based model of Chomsky (2000 *et seq.*) is an influential approach; however, it is not without its problems, and a number of issues remain to be resolved. For example, to repeat some of the questions posed in Grohmann (2007*a*): What exactly is the relation between phases and Spell-Out—do phases undergo Spell-Out, or just the domain of a phase head, or is the mapping not one-to-one after all? Or to call the relevant interface operation Transfer, does Transfer take place simultaneously to LF and PF? (Of course, Marušič's contribution bears on this question as well.) Likewise, if phases are domains opaque for further computation once spelled out or transferred to the interfaces, does the Phase Impenetrability Condition apply to all narrow-syntactic operations? What is the relation between Agree and Move (or Merge, if Move boils down to the distinction between Internal and External Merge)? The first question is addressed throughout the following chapters, at least within Phase Theory, at times also incorporating the specific details of Uriagereka's (1999*a*) Multiple Spell-Out Hypothesis, which are not always in line with phase-theoretic assumptions. Alternative approaches were briefly presented towards the end of Section 1.3.

Another very important issue for Phase Theory to be solved satisfactorily, which is here being addressed to some extent by Marušič, concerns the "diagnostics" used to identify phases at the interfaces. Richards (2004, 2007), for example, explores an alternative to purported phonetic independence and isolability at PF and/or propositionality at LF, "standard" tools that have proven quite difficult to ascertain (see e.g. Bošković 2002*c*, Matushansky 2004, and Boeckx & Grohmann 2007 for recent criticism).

Likewise, much more can be said on the issue of intervention, be it expressed through the PIC or some other means, such as integration of optimization procedures in a minimalist computation at large. Research by Gereon Müller may lead the way on this route (among others, Müller 2007 and fruitful collaboration with Fabian Heck), which often incorporates insights from Optimality Theory (Prince & Smolensky 2004 as well as much work of the last decade in phonology, but also increasingly in syntax).

More can, and probably should, be said about feature interpretability. This goes for minimalism in general and is not specific to Phase Theory, but it certainly goes hand in hand with (further) interface-related research. How is the existence of uninterpretable features justified in the grammar? The standard answer Chomsky (1995, 2000) gives relates interpretability of formal properties of the grammar to (im)perfectness issues. In a series of papers, Pesetsky & Torrego (2001, 2006, 2007) offer an alternative conception. See also Roberts & Roussou (2002), Vangsnes (2002), Sigurðsson (2004, forthcoming), Zeijlstra (2008, forthcoming). Svenonius (2007), in particular, offers an interface perspective on features.

Other aspects of the phase-driven grammar that require better answers include the operation Agree (when and how it applies, single vs multiple applications, the definition of "active" goal, and many other issues) and the perennial difficulty of not only describing, but also explaining, islands (Ross 1967)—syntactic or otherwise—and extraction phenomena (both of which are intimately related to the previously mentioned issues), to mention but a few.

This volume is by no means an exhaustive collection on the topic. This said, however, it will surely not remain the last volume dedicated to the study of *InterPhases*—whether minimalist theorizing will continue and develop in Phase Theory or move on, interface studies will remain an integral part of any future investigations in linguistic theory. Likewise, any continuation and development of Phase Theory will by definition put a strong emphasis on the role of the interpretive interfaces. Phases and interfaces are intricately linked with one another.

Part I
Conceptual Issues

2

The Successor Function + LEX = Human Language?

WOLFRAM HINZEN

2.1 Introduction

What in syntax do so-called "interface conditions," in current minimalist conceptions of the language faculty, explain? Virtually everything, to the extent that the *Strong Minimalist Thesis* (SMT) holds, which stipulates that language is an optimal response to interface conditions externally imposed on the language faculty prior to its insertion into a language-ready but prelinguistic brain. The idea is that prior to and independent of the evolution of language, systems of "thought" or semantics were in place that the emerging language system had to "interface" with. Clearly, then, the language system will have to satisfy certain minimal conditions on usability imposed by these non-linguistic systems ("bare output conditions"): conditions the language system has to satisfy to be usable at all.

It is hard to see—and I will here concur—that such usability conditions could fail to be met. Yet, I will argue that this particular conceptual necessity is a very different demand from another and much stronger one, to the effect that there are richly structured non-linguistic systems of thought on the other side of the interface (so-called "Conceptual-Intentional" or "C-I"-systems), whose structures mirror and explain the syntactic forms that we find on the inner, linguistic side of this interface.

To illustrate how minimalist explanation by appeal to conditions imposed by the interface (the semantic one, to which I largely confine my discussion here) work, consider the question why adjunction should exist as an operation in the grammar. Chomsky (2004*a*) suggests that at least *prima facie* there is no principled ground for such an operation to exist in addition to the operation standardly called Merge, which combines lexical items into binary sets. The suggestion is that Merge is conceptually necessary, hence does not need to be especially justified, and hence that adjunction, if it exists additionally, needs to be so justified. Why is Merge conceptually necessary? Because any combinatorial system exhibiting discrete infinity needs an operation putting some primitive items together into larger, complex units containing the former as parts. Merge as currently defined is meant to achieve exactly that and nothing more. If Merge is defined so as to capture what is minimally needed—it simply includes the items in question into unordered binary sets, giving rise to a relation of containment—Merge can be viewed as coming for free and as having found a "principled explanation." How then is adjunction to find such an explanation, too? Answer: The C-I-systems "require an operation of predicate composition," as Chomsky (2004a) puts it, and adjunction ("pair-Merge") provides just that.

At the heart of this explanation is the positing of a certain functional need, whose existence rationalizes a given computational operation. Inevitably, for such an explanation to work there needs to be evidence for the functional need in question which is independent of the operation to be motivated itself. But as Chomsky himself has often emphasized, such evidence is not in general to be expected, given the evolutionary and conceptual entanglement of language (on the inner side of the putative interface) and "thought" (on its outer side). We don't have much independent grasp—if indeed grasp at all—of the semantic systems or systems of "thought" on the non-linguistic side of the semantic interface. Therefore, any attempt to explain language from interface conditions imposed on it will have to figure out the nature of those conditions by looking at how narrow syntax satisfies these very conditions.

A circularity problem thus looms, though one that is not necessarily either vicious or unfamiliar from other areas in biology (e.g. the adaptationist program in biology) or cognition (e.g. the study of neural nets). On the other hand, there is a danger of mistakenly assuming that as we pile up explanations of features of language in terms of "interface conditions," we have actually provided independent evidence for what these interface systems are like—instead of merely getting results that are artefacts of our research methodology. The problem of merely providing "just-so" stories arises in the biolinguistic program as much as it does in evolutionary thinking at large.

The problem worsens if we add to this a rather simple-minded conceptual point. Any textbook introduction to linguistic minimalism repeats that the very existence of a "C-I"-interface is a "virtual conceptual necessity." But it isn't: It goes beyond conceptual necessity. By a merciless minimalist logic it would have to go for this reason alone. All that's conceptually necessary is that language is used. This weaker statement does not entail, firstly, that there is an interface where linguistic representations arrive tuned to (independently given) requirements of some "outside systems of thought": Language and thought could be more entangled and could obviously have co-evolved in such a way that no conceptual distinction between the two can be drawn (and none of the two "answers" any conditions imposed by the other). Secondly, there is no entailment that the language system will be anything more than *usable* by the outside systems. That is, it may as well be no more than partially used, hence not meet conditions on expressive potential optimally or in full. Thirdly, and relatedly, it doesn't follow that the language system will actually be *explained* by the outside systems or the conditions imposed by them. To conclude from the system's *being* used that we can *explain* it by reference to systems that use it, is a non sequitur.

Ludwig Wittgenstein, when proposing a "use-theory of meaning," stayed clear of this last error. His thesis that "meaning is use" does not suggest that we can explain the meaning of an expression from its use. Indeed, obviously this very use is what does itself need to be explained (in part by conditions that may be internally imposed). Transferred to the context of the MP, a use theory of meaning would not assume that language answers to independently given thoughts or semantic contents that we somehow "grasp" in our C-I systems and that the linguistic system is somehow designed to "express." Instead, the workings of the computational system and how its productions are being executed by systems of use could be all there is. That these productions are used implies that other cognitive systems using linguistic structures must be rich enough in themselves to be able to use these structures somehow, but not that they "rationalize" them or impose conditions on which structures need to be delivered by the syntax in order to meet certain independent semantic conditions. The importance of this distinction will be clarified through examples later on.

If human syntax is to essentially boil down to Merge, as on the standard minimalist view, it is natural to attempt to blame as much as possible on "bare output conditions." Accordingly we may expect that the current tendency to *deflate* phrase structure and linguistic structure-building will correlate with an *inflated* conception of what conditions of language the extra-linguistic "semantic systems" impose. And indeed it seems to me that the more minimal the syntax has become in recent years and the more flatter and thinner our trees, the more maximal the conditions imposed by the semantic interface have become. Current empirical evidence in comparative cognition, I will argue, does not support this asymmetry and in fact suggests pursuing the opposite strategy: inflating our notion of syntactic categorial hierarchy and deflating the role of the interfaces, particularly the semantic one.

(1), below, is a long list of linguistic properties that have been said to be motivated from interface conditions—this is virtually all of the theory of syntax except Merge and principles of efficient computation (giving rise to locality effects):

(1) a. adjunction

  b. the A/A' distinction

  c. displacement

  d. the binary nature of Merge

  e. the EPP-principle

  f. the relation Agree

  g. phases

  h. hierarchy

I will here conclude that what can be motivated from interface conditions may as well reduce to (1a), alone, and that, moreover, an "I"(ntentional) interface, in the sense of something that could motivate LF-like structures, likely does not exist. Empirical differences between conceptual (C) and intentional (I) structures or information, and the dependence of the latter on the former (which does not hold the other way around), suggest that at least the intentional ones are narrowly linguistic and likely originate *with* the very syntactic structures that are often said to merely "express" them.

In the following section I will turn to the "deflated" conception of Merge or combinatoriality that has been thought to yield human language, after being added to (i) a lexicon, (ii) interface conditions, and (iii) language-independent economy principles, in the way that the title of this chapter suggests. Section 2.3 turns to some available evidence from comparative cognition regarding thought in non-linguistic animals. Section 2.4 turns to adjuncts specifically and argues that the very reason why adjunction perhaps can be motivated from semantic interface conditions also reveals why probably little else in syntax can. I also sketch a hypothesis for where the actual locus of hierarchy in the linguistic system lies, and why, in particular, it cannot be based algebraically on the kind of structures that the successor function in arithmetic yields. Section 2.5 concludes.

2.2 Deflating Phrase Structure

2.2.1 *Arithmetic and Merge*

Chomsky (2008: 139) argues as follows:

(2) *Merge*
     "Suppose that a language has the simplest possible lexicon: Just one LI,
     call it 'one'. Application of Merge to the LI yields {one}, call it 'two'.
     Application of Merge to {one} yields {{one}}, call it 'three'. Etc. In effect,
     Merge applied in this manner yields the successor function. It is straight-
     forward to define addition in terms of Merge (X,Y), and in familiar
     ways, the rest of arithmetic. The emergence of the arithmetical capacity
     has been puzzling (...) and it has often been speculated that it may be
     abstracted from FL [the faculty of language] by reducing the latter to its
     bare minimum. Reduction to a single-membered lexicon is a simple way
     to yield this consequence."

Arithmetic, that is, is the "minimal language," and iterating the operation "set-
of" generates the natural numbers:

(3) *Enumerating a series I*
     $\emptyset$ = 1
     Merge (1) = {$\emptyset$} = 2
     Merge (2) = {{$\emptyset$}} = 3
     Merge (3) = {{{$\emptyset$}}} = 4
     etc.

The broader idea is: If we generalize the generative principle of the series (3),
i.e. Merge, and add the full set of lexical features characterizing FL, language-
specific properties will emerge. On the other hand, the successor function
is standardly defined as the transitive closure of the "immediate successor"
function defined in (4):

(4) *Immediate successor*
     $\text{Succ}(X) =_{\text{def}} X \cup \{X\}$

Note that applying this definition yields not the sequence generated by Merge
in (2), but the full ordinal sequence in (5), in which every number is the set of
its predecessors:

(5) *Enumerating a series II*
     $\emptyset$ = 1
     Merge(1) = {$\emptyset$} = {1} = 2
     Merge(2) = {$\emptyset$, {$\emptyset$}} = {1, 2} = 3
     Merge(3) = {$\emptyset$, {$\emptyset$}, {$\emptyset$, {$\emptyset$}}} = {1, 2, 3} = 4
     etc.

Once Succ/Merge is defined, algebraic operations + (addition) and (.) (multiplication) are definable, and if these conform to relevant axioms, we obtain a mathematical space that is a *group*. I will here think of a space like that as providing the mind with a particular "ontology": Any structured mathematical space, having elements in certain structural relations (including entailments), contains objects of a particular kind and formal nature. In geometric terms, the particular space built by the generative principles above can be represented as a line; in algebraic terms, as a vector space, every element of which can be expressed as a linear combination of the vectors in its *base*. In this particular case, there is one single vector in the base, namely, 1, scalar multiplications of which suffice to span the entire space in question (they yield all of its elements). By consequence, the dimension of the space so constructed is one: Merge as conceived in (2) yields a *one-dimensional vector space*. If Merge in language and Merge in arithmetic are species of the same operation, as per Chomsky's quote above, linguistic objects will be of the same mono-dimensionality as the natural numbers. That this is so is an empirical claim about the productions of the human faculty of language, right or wrong. In principle, syntactic objects could vary across more than one dimension.

Note that the space of the numbers as such (which of course includes more than the naturals) is *not* one-dimensional in this sense. That is, if the successor function was the only generative principle the human mind could employ, our mind would be mathematically impoverished in a way it is factually not. To characterize all the other numbers that exist, from the whole numbers to the rational, real, complex, and hypercomplex numbers, the dimensionality of the vector space involved has to be steadily increased. Since a higher-dimensional system cannot evolve from a lower-dimensional one in a linear fashion, the mathematics/language capacity must involve non-linear operations alongside a linear Merge-operation. These operations are needed to as it were catapult us from one dimension to the next containing different kinds of objects, as our mathematical insight grows and we discover that one number system can be recursively employed as a basis for constructing another one. It is interesting to ask whether this process might find a reflection in human language: Whether, in short, non-linear operations are generative for certain aspects of linguistic objects as well, generating more and other hierarchies than those that linear and one-dimensional Merge as applied in the language system can. If arithmetic evolved from language, this is perhaps what we would expect.

There is an interesting consequence of the potential fact that human language may, in a relevant sense, be "multi-dimensional," relevant to the problem with which we began. The consequence, if indeed we wish to motivate language from interface conditions, is that either the extra-linguistic systems are multi-dimensional too, in which case we have simply shifted the explanatory problem, or they are not, in which case we must essentially give up the whole project of principled explanation, to whatever extent it is tied to the idea of motivating syntax from interface conditions. On the latter option, it must have been narrow syntax itself, in evolution, which helped to boost the dimensionality of the human mind and the thoughts or objects it can recursively generate: "thought" wasn't multi-dimensional before these specific computational operations of language (or arithmetic) evolved. Put differently, the language system was creative for the kinds of thoughts we can think (Uriagereka 2008a; Hinzen & Uriagereka 2006).

2.2.2 *Phrase Structure in Minimalist Syntax*

Let us turn now to the conception of phrase structure (PS) that results (or perhaps rather fails to result), when we think of Merge as little more than a way of generating hierarchies in the way of Merge, as in (3). If Merge is set-formation, there is no reason to restrict it to singleton sets. Thus, let Merge form n-ary sets, and let the restriction of $n=2$ follow from "interface conditions" (as is standardly assumed). The result of this is a *label-free bare phrase structure* in something like the sense of Collins (2002), with lexical items replaced by numbers, as before:

(6)   Merge $(1, 2) = \{1, 2\}$
      Merge $(3, \{1, 2\}) = \{3, \{1, 2\}\}$
      Merge $(4, \{3, \{1, 2\}\}) = \{4, \{3, \{1, 2\}\}\}$
      etc.

As Collins points out, labels go beyond "virtual conceptual necessity"; hence they cannot be part of a system that is defined by this very notion. There are lexical items, there are (sets of) sets of them, and there are syntactic relations (Theta(X,Y), EPP(X,Y), Agree(X,Y), and Subcat(X,Y)), which hold between features or lexical items X and Y; and there is nothing else. Three explanatory factors for syntax therefore suffice:

(7)   (i)   the interaction of properties of lexical items

      (ii)   economy conditions

      (iii)   interface (bare output) conditions.

Syntax on this construal is no longer about part-whole relations among syntactic categories or phrases, but *lexical items* and relations between them. There is no such thing as projection, in particular. PS in this sense seems exactly as "flat" and one-dimensional as our number line above. It does exhibit hierarchy in a sense, but that is a deflated form of hierarchy, which, as Chomsky puts it, is "automatic for recursive operations, conventionally suppressed for those that merely enumerate a sequence of objects" (2008: 158). Does this view amount to a (i) "derivation," "reduction," or "naturalization" of PS on the basis of barren Minimalist machinery, or (ii) its elimination? The question hasn't been much discussed, but Chametzky (2003) has extensively argued for the latter conclusion: Minimalist syntax is a non- or post-phrase-structural phase in the theory of grammar. If this is true, it is unclear whether the dismissal of PS has actually been widely noticed among practicing linguists, who may be under the impression that what one does using minimalist technology is what one did all along, though now the descriptive machinery has been "minimized" and "derived." Let us go through some problems which arise when attempting to make phrase-structural syntax compatible with minimalism.

First, Chametzky argues that contrary to claims of e.g. Epstein *et al.* (1998), syntactic relations defined on traditional phrase-structure trees such as c-command actually don't fall out naturally from the minimalist structure-building operation, Merge. This is in line with arguments of Chomsky (2005) to the effect that all syntactic relations reduce to two, set-membership (a consequence of Merge) and probe-goal relations, leaving out c-command.

Second, Chametzky argues that minimalist theory has failed to give an argument for the fact that Merge should not be simply concatenation, where:

(8)   Concatenate (A,B) $=_{def}$ A$^\wedge$B, with A, B atoms

That is, there is no *prima facie* reason why a minimalist syntax, if indeed minimal, *should be* phrase-structural. Hornstein (2005), from where (8) is taken, argues that concatenation doesn't yield phrase-structural hierarchies, and is a weaker notion. If it is more minimalist, preference should go to it, other things being equal. But he also argues that other things are not equal, given that the hierarchical organization of linguistic expressions is a basic assumption of modern syntactic theory. Hence a more PS-like system has to be reconstructed, by adding something to a bare concatenative system: categorial *labels*. In short, labels are needed to upgrade a purely concatenative system to a phrase-structural one. Against this particular line of reasoning one can object on several fronts, however:

(i) Why there *should* be such a hierarchy is precisely the question we have to ask in this minimalist context, and we can neither take it as a traditional assumption nor in particular appeal to some mysterious external "demand for the system to be hierarchical," when giving an explanation of that fact.

(ii) Why could Concatenate defined as in (8) not yield hierarchy as Merge did, above, through a restriction to being binary?

(iii) Why is recursive set-formation not essentially *simpler* than concatenation, as it does not depend on principles of ordering?

(iv) If accepted as a foundation for the system, Merge *qua* recursive set-formation makes labels in Hornstein's sense *unnecessary* for hierarchy: A Collins-style system yields it as well, in the trivial and automatic sense described above.

(v) Adding labels to a concatenation-based system is also not *sufficient* for hierarchy in a phrase-structural sense. Suppose hierarchy is somehow imposed on the system as a "demand" it has to meet, and that it will meet it with a minimum of resources, ones it already uses for other purposes: lexical items. Labels are thus lexical items. But, if a projection amounts to no more than the copying of a lexical item that yields this projection, as in standard minimalist syntax, nothing strictly speaking projects. If labels are lexical items again, hierarchy within syntax does not get off the ground.

Adding labels to a concatenation-based system so as to obtain phrase structures is thus a problematic move. But neither is concatenation as such, as Chametzky argues, a plausible minimalist foundation of the system. Assuming merely recursive set-formation, therefore, without adding labels, in principle appears as the more minimalist and principled move, supporting Chomsky's conclusions that PS is unneeded from a minimalist point of view.

Chametzky offers a third argument for the same conclusion, to the effect that an essential *interface aspect* of earlier Government-and-Binding (GB) conceptions of PS (e.g. Speas 1990) is ignored or in fact denied in standard minimalist syntax: Here there is said to be *no* interface between lexical argument structure and the syntax. PS is said to be "derived" in Chomsky (1995: 378), but the interface aspect of earlier PS does not seem to be a part of this derivation. I have argued elsewhere (Hinzen 2007), consistent with Chametzky's claims, that this interface aspect of PS is crucial and should be preserved within minimalist grammar, although this leads to a different and more differentiated ("layered") view of the semantic interface and semantic interpretation as such (see Uriagereka 2008a on this "distributed interface" hypothesis).

A fourth reason that Chametzky offers is that GB-theory freely generalizes PS and projection from lexical categories to functional ones. But, as Grimshaw

(1990) has argued rather convincingly, (i) the relation of a functional head to its complement is not one of selection; and (ii) it is not one of "extended projection" (Grimshaw's alternative, based on a rejection of selectionalist approaches) either. Maybe then there are no functional projections. But then, are there lexical ones, given that the prime argument for the existence of functional projections seems to be that there is *one* (X-bar-theoretic) paradigm that generalizes from lexical to functional projections? So again a projection-free and non-phrase-structural grammar appears on the horizon.

Arguably, this last problem is aggravated in minimalism. Chomsky (1995) wants to license functional projections if and only if they have features that are semantically interpretable. However, he sees these semantic effects as rooted in the semantic interface, whereas it seems actually to be a characteristic feature of earlier thinking on interpretability in syntax that the semantic effect of the functional portion of the clause is defined *syntax-internally*. Thus, e.g., Abney (1987) talks about the "second-order semantic contribution" of functional heads: They regulate the given descriptive content of the sentence, while not adding any such content to it; that is, they apply to certain "first-order" structures already constructed within narrow syntax, and their semantic contribution is in this sense *not* one that can be said to be due to the (crucially non-syntactic) interfaces.

Independently of this specific proposal by Abney, it is obvious that functional categories have interpretive properties of a rather abstract kind—things like specificity, definiteness, finiteness, force, modality, or negation—the grasp of which does plausibly depend on representational resources of language (or a system isomorphic to it in its formal aspects), as opposed to merely being a function of non-linguistic conceptualization abilities. In line with this, it seems that in various language pathologies (such as Specific Language Impairment) functional, closed-class vocabulary is often more severely disturbed than substantive, descriptive, or open-class vocabulary. The latter systems, which are more semantics-based, may still be in place—which may well be as if a person deprived of the functional-categorial system of language can still use whatever is left of its non-linguistic C-I systems to find her way around in the world and achieve some communicative success. This situation then shows both what non-linguistic systems of "thought" can achieve, and what they cannot—hence which semanticity finds its origin in language itself and syntax-internal mechanisms, as opposed to originating independently of them.

A fifth and final reason Chametzky gives for the fact that minimalist syntax is not phrase-structural is that notions like "head" and "adjunct" that are central to syntactic theory have resisted definitions in terms of configurational, phrase-structural notions: Both of these aspects of language express kinds of dependencies, not kinds of configurations. The failure of their reconstruction in phrase-structural terms may point to the fact that they *cannot* be captured in these terms, and are really part of *another*, non-phrase-structural conception of grammar.

Overall, then, it seems a reasonable case can be made that the minimalist program confronts us with a new system that may not resemble much the ideas of PS and hierarchy of early generative models. It is as if we do not really understand any more (lack principled understanding) of the old phrase-structural notions, and thus feel inclined to conclude that all that is left and needed is the kind of linguistic hierarchy that is an "automatic consequence of the recursive enumeration of a sequence." Perhaps, indeed, there is nothing more to be explained. There is no PS, no projections, and no configurations internal to the syntax around which it is organized. All of these old notions may be unprincipled, in the minimalist sense, and the dull routine of Merge is all there is. Our most dignified human possession would then be way less remarkable and special than thousands of years of philosophy assumed (see Boeckx 2008*b* for a line of argument in this spirit).

When in this radical sort of minimalist mood we may well be unsympathetic to Chametzky's (2003) playing with the idea of reinstituting phrase structure and using it as an argument *against* minimalist syntax, or Hornstein's above reinstitution of labels. Also Fukui (2005), rather tellingly, asks, in an interesting note directly inspired by the passage quoted in (2):

(9)   "Is the nature of the fundamental operation in human language really 'combination' alone?"

Like Chametzky and Hornstein, Fukui opts for a more substantive conception, on which the compositional process does not depart "from the bottom-up" (as in Chomsky 1995, where two syntactic objects, A and B, form, when merged, the labeled set {A,{A,B}}), but is rather "top-down," from the "label" itself. The label A is now said to "self-embed" in the set {A, B}, where B, the complement, is taken from a "Base Set" (BS), which is one of the two arguments of the Merge(=Self-embedding)-operation. We can think of BS as a Lexicon with n elements ($n \in \mathbb{N}$):

(10) $BS = \{a_1, \ldots, a_n\}$

Merge *qua* self-embed is then defined as follows:

(11)   Merge $(a_i, BS) =_{def} \{a_i, BS\} = \{a_i, \{a_1, \ldots, a_n\}\}$

Now consider again the "minimal" language, with $n=1$. Merge then yields, if $BS=\{\emptyset\}$, following the definition in (11), the object in (12):

(12)   Merge(∅, {∅}) = {∅, {∅}}

In turn, if we have $n=2$, with, say, $BS_1 = \{kill, Bill\}$, then we get either (13a) or (13b), depending on which lexical item self-embeds:

(13)   a.   Merge (*kill*, {*kill*, *Bill*}) = {*kill*, {*kill*, *Bill*}}

       b.   Merge (*Bill*, {*kill*, *Bill*}) = {*Bill*, {*kill*, *Bill*}}

A claimed advantage of the proposal is that labeling is now a trivial consequence of what Merge happens to apply to: If it applies to A, A self-embeds. Otherwise, B does. No potentially stipulative "labeling algorithm" (determining which label a given unordered set of two lexical items bears) is needed. But note that this system takes labels and the hierarchy they imply simply for granted, whereas Chomsky's bare phrase structure project at least aims to either derive or eliminate them. Even taking labels and projections for granted, the purpose of going beyond the austerity of recursive set formation and the minimal sense of hierarchy it entails does not become clear. If anything becomes a part of a whole here, it's the head that Merge applies to, which becomes a part of the base set. The latter embeds the former, rather than the base set becoming a part of a higher-order structure. We don't here capture, for all I can tell, the fact that a head's projection is a function of a complement it applies to.[1]

Here again, then, as in Hornstein or Chametzky, we see an attempt to go beyond the deflated conception of Merge implicit in (2) and to regain a richer form of hierarchy employing labels in a more substantive way. But the mystery of what hierarchy really means remains. This problem even affects Chomsky's deflated or austere conception of hierarchy, at the point where we make the move from the empty set to a set containing the empty set as its only member. This picture presupposes, on pain of violating Russell's axiom of foundation, that the empty set is an object, not a set. Sets must be objects of a different and higher type than the objects that figure in them as their members. Burying the problem of syntactic hierarchy in the problem of getting to singleton sets is perhaps to bury much of the mystery involved (Juan Uriagereka, p.c.).

All that said, that (5) is a minimal conception of structure-building in a discretely infinite system *is* a powerful argument in favor of it. Again, we *have* obtained some notion of hierarchy, after all, namely that of a recursive embedding within a linearly progressing sequence. This alone buys us discrete infinity—yet is this enough? If the linear routine of Merge is all there is, then virtually everything we need to explain in language will have to have been

---

[1] A technical problem is that if we identify the empty set with the number "1," then self-embedding it in the case of $n=1$ yields a formal object that is usually identified with "3" (see (12) and (5)).

there already, on the "other side" of the interface. Having impoverished the computational system of language, we will not know how it all got there, and we will have to blame this complexity on the outside systems. Whatever complexity we see beyond the minimal core of discrete infinity will free-float of what computational resources narrow syntax provides our minds with; for we have dumped it on the other side, where syntax does not reach. Put differently, "semantics" will be largely unaccompanied by a restrictive theory of syntax that makes specific predictions for which kinds of semantic contents can be thought by a creature, and with which types of syntactic structures it can do so. In Section 4, I will make a specific proposal in the spirit of such a restrictive theory: Merge *qua* successor yields the semantic correlate of adjunction, and of adjunction alone, which is indeed hierarchical in a no more interesting sense than is implicit in enumerating a sequence.

2.3 The Other Side

The prime characteristic of a one-dimensional sequence in the sense of Section 2.2.1 is that it never yields anything new. As I will put it here, it is not "ontologically productive": It only ever produces objects of the same type or category. A syntax of that sort is exactly what we hope for if our attempt is to motivate syntax from interface conditions. For if that is the project, the best syntax is no syntax, and the second-best syntax is a syntax that merely linearly combines what the lexicon provides it with, adding nothing to that (except brackets and certain laws governing such bracketing). Syntactically combining lexical items *shouldn't* ever yield anything new, since, if it did, the extra-linguistic semantic systems likely couldn't read it. "Inclusiveness" is the very principle that bars the ontological or categorial innovativeness of syntax in this sense.

In short, if the evolutionary novelty that yielded language is merely to "link" already given extra-linguistic systems, then the lack of a substantive contribution of syntax to semantic interpretation or thought, and its merely "satisfying expressive conditions imposed on it," is precisely what we expect and hope. By contraposition, if there is hierarchy in a more genuine sense and violations of Inclusiveness, both governed by narrowly linguistic combinatorial principles, we must conclude that language is *not* (merely) a linking system and cannot be rationalized in the way minimalism has largely suggested. With the linguistic combinatorics *new* forms of thoughts will arise.

Since it seems virtually certain that there isn't thought and semanticity in its *full* propositional glory independently and prior to language (so that any thought whatsoever can also be thought without language), it seems equally certain that one will have to ground at least *some* of human thought in the existence of structural operations that the language faculty made available, and hence that the computational system will *have* to be ontologically productive to some positive extent. This raises the fundamental question of how syntax— if it is *bound* to be semantically productive to some non-zero extent—*can* be productive in this way. I return to this question briefly at the very end, even though one way in which it can be, should by now be clear: by instantiating a multi-dimensional syntax in the sense of Section 2.2.1.

Turning now to evidence of what is there on the "other side," let us start by noting that studies of animal cognition face an "other minds" problem of daunting proportions, and that it remains perfectly possible, as a large philosophical tradition starting from Descartes has suggested, that this problem is not an empirical but a logical one, hence cannot be resolved by empirical means. As Povinelli has pointed out with specific reference to the issue of mind-reading in non-human primates, for the problem of the inscrutability of reference no sound methodology as yet exists (Povinelli 2004; see also Cheney & Seyfarth 1997 for discussion). If that is the nature of the problem we face, there is not even the possibility that the SMT will be validated by research in comparative cognition.

Seyfarth *et al.* (2005) claim the existence of a capacity for "propositional" thought in baboons, as witnessed in their comprehension of grunt-scream sequences which the authors argue exhibit features of hierarchical classification and perhaps even recursion, though they categorically deny such evidence for production. Even the claim about comprehension is problematic. As of now, we don't really know whether "propositions" in the sense of Seyfarth *et al.*, on the one hand, and the linguistic propositions we study in linguistic theory, on the other, even form a natural kind, and which evidence would tell that they do. Propositionality is a technical term coming out of a Fregean– Russellian philosophical tradition, not an empirical notion. The notion can be given an empirical content by analyzing in detail the structures of the linguistic expressions identifying and encoding such propositional contents. The more we do that, however, the notion of a proposition, to the extent that it has an empirical content, will have a linguistic empirical content.

Propositionality in this linguistic sense exhibits both conceptual and intentional properties, each associated with different layers of the human clause (in essence, the thematic layer, and the functional one, respectively). The question whether non-human thought exhibits intentional properties as opposed to merely conceptual-thematic ones, or doesn't even exhibit the latter, is widely open. Do non-humans have intentional reference, categorical judgements and truth (as opposed to being governed by principles of probability, reliability, and adaptation)? Again, for the question to have an answer, the difference will have to be given an operational empirical sense.

In human language, the difference between mere conceptual combination and intentional uses of these combinations seems clear enough. Thus, combining the concepts of "blue" and "house" yields the conceptual structure *blue house*, in the potential absence of any ability to actually *refer* to blue houses or judge a particular house to be blue on an occasion. Grammatical principles structuring such intentional judgements or acts of reference ("that (is a) blue house"), on the one hand, and modificational adjective-noun combinations ("blue house"), on the other, are empirically distinct. Can this distinction be made on non-linguistic grounds, or by invoking non-linguistic structuring principles? Wouldn't the object of study itself change if we changed the structural properties of expressions that define the phenomenon in question, at least in formal and logical respects? If so, that then would be an argument that when we abstract from the formal-syntactic nature of particular kinds of thoughts, we may lose our grip on what we are talking about, thereby providing evidence that these thoughts probably lack a non-linguistic nature.

Note moreover that a linguistic proposition, studied as an empirical object, is a highly *specific* one, deriving from a rigid sequence of a number of clausal "zones" (Cinque 1999, 2004*a*; Ernst 2002) or "layers" (Hinzen 2006; Uriagereka 2008*a*) each encoding distinct kinds of information. The more we see such semantic or informational layers intrinsically correlating with specific structural conditions, the less we are inclined to see their identity and specificity originating on non-linguistic or non-syntactic grounds, or in supposed external systems of "thought." Some candidates for such close form–meaning correlations are listed in (14):

(14) *Form–meaning correlations (candidates)*

SEMANTICS	SYNTAX
predicate composition	adjuncts
predication	"bare" small clauses (see Moro 2004)
events	VP/*v*P
tensed events	TP
events placed in discourse	CP
kinds	nouns
reference	DP
event-participant	argument
adjective	property
etc.	

A system merely having the argument-of relation of thematic structure, in addition to merely compositional or adjunctive operations, already requires a context-free grammar, which the non-linguistic mind probably lacks. Since Fitch & Hauser (2004) studied Tamarin monkeys' apparent failure to grasp $A^n B^n$ grammars (n As followed by n Bs), this lack has often been claimed. As has been frequently pointed out, the significance of the result is unclear, as a counting routine added to the basic cognitive design of a finite state machine could handle the task the Tamarins were given. If so, the Tamarins may lack even this simpler computational capacity. Perhaps it is no great surprise to find starlings actually *mastering* the $A^n B^n$ grammar for small n (Gentner *et al.* 2006): They would do so on the basis of counting, without the machinery of a phrase-structure grammar. Yet, that ability still does not carry us very far towards the human intentional capacity.

Note that as structure-building in language proceeds, systematic (compositional) semantic effects of specific categorial types arise cyclically: As we build up a proposition, we go through particular stages, like building a VP first, then its shell, a vP, then a TP, then a CP, with new semantic effects (aspect, tense, finiteness, force) and concomitant entailment patterns arising at every step. Note that the ability to make a truth-judgement arises at the very *end* of this long structure-building process: Nothing short of an expression that has the form of a full CP (or contains reference, predication, finite tense, force, etc.) is truth-evaluable. If so, we simply do not expect such kinds of thoughts to be given independently of this form, on the "other" side of the interface (Hinzen 2007).

Whether ritualized alarm-calling for certain predators in the wild, perhaps the best bet for the existence of (at least functionally) referential vocalizations in non-human primates, is the precursor of human words, can also be doubted on reasonable grounds (e.g. Tallerman 2007). Terrace (2005), reviewing decades of communication with sign-language-trained apes, confirms a categorical absence of symbol use with intentional meaning or for the sake of sharing information in this domain. There is, he claims:

(15)   "No evidence that apes used any of the symbols they learned to *refer* to
        objects or events, or that those symbols had any function other than to
        request food or drink."   (Terrace 2005: 101)

The "multi-sign combinations" in ape symbol use are not "sentences," Terrace asserts, and there is no evidence for "proto-declarative" communication following a "proto-imperative" phase, as in all normally developing children.

On a more positive note, McGonigle *et al.* (2003), reporting results from the most far-reaching longitudinal and learning-based studies in meaningful size seriation tasks with monkeys ever, provide evidence for the robust emergence of hierarchical, concurrently disjoint, reciprocal, and even "recursive" classification in *cebus appella*. Perhaps plausibly, then, the non-human primate mind is not merely an *associative* but a systematic and compositional one, in the classical sense of Fodor & Pylyshyn (1988), as the authors argue. Perhaps, as discussed in McGonigle & Chalmers (2006), prior to the evolution of a linguistic communication system, "relational codes" were in place in the non-human primate mind: primitives of cognition lending an objectivity to the processing of input that can form the basis of a "language," once relevant means of externalizing these internal codes have evolved. These studies nonetheless don't lend support to what the SMT as currently formulated requires, namely rich non-linguistic structuring of systems of thought on the non-linguistic side of the semantic interface. Firstly, the primitives that enter the relevant primate computations (algebraic relations, hierarchical organization, etc.) do not seem logically *distinct* from those we find in the computational system of language in humans. Secondly, the monkey mind as depicted in these studies does not suggest the specificity of intentional reference, propositional kinds of thoughts, or of the categorial architecture of meaning in human thought. However impressive the "relational" competences that McGonigle & Chalmers have "brought on" in the non-linguistic minds of monkeys through extensive training and tutelage, it is still probably only a platform from where intentional and propositional structures of greater specificity might evolve.

Whatever is the right conclusion from this sketchy survey of the state of the art in animal propositional thought, (16), at least viewed as an empirical claim about the putative C-I systems, seems a highly dubious contention:

(16)   "C-I incorporates a dual semantics, with generalized argument structure as one component, the other being discourse-related and scopal properties."   (Chomsky 2005)

Taking this as a basis, Chomsky speculates that language can be rationalized as a system "seeking to satisfy the duality" in question, "in an optimal way": "EM [External Merge] serving one function and IM [Internal Merge] the other" (*ibid.*), with both finding a "principled explanation" in this fashion. This clearly *is* a functional explanation—an explanation of structural conditions internal to FL from external demands "imposed" on that system, a function it "needed to satisfy." The explanation only makes sense if the functional need in question is given prior to and independently of the evolution of FL, and evidence to that effect is not provided. In line with (16), Chomsky (2004a) also explains the operation of "Internal Merge" on the basis of the suggestion that "movement provides new interpretations which would *not otherwise be expressible*." So, Internal Merge operates, because, if it didn't, the expression of something that is as such independently given would not be possible. But the argument does not hold: There is no evolutionary impossibility in FLs not satisfying any "expressive needs" imposed on it (*if* these pre-existed FL). If it didn't, then we simply wouldn't express propositions, say, even if we could think them. Worse accidents have happened in evolution. That we couldn't have achieved certain things, if certain mechanisms hadn't existed, is no reason why these exist.[2]

The consequences from the above for the assumption of the existence of the "I(ntentional)" part of the "C-I"-interface are clear. Intentionality in humans goes with reference, judgements, propositionality, and truth. All of these *presuppose* "conceptual" information, which needs to enter a derivation *before* any judgement can be made on its basis, or any expression is put to a referential use, or any truth is asserted. I have now argued that the existence of structures like DPs, TPs, and CPs specifically encoding these intentional semantic properties cannot be explained by appealing to a need to express the semantic properties in question. There *is* no "functional need" for a communication system to express reference and truth, and no evidence for their existence independently of the clausal layers that code them. In short, and quite simply, I conclude that there isn't any current empirical evidence for an "I"-interface, in the sense of a system where syntactic objects with a particular kind of semantic interpretation are delivered to an extra-linguistic system of thought that is as such, or independently of the syntactic objects in question, capable of intentionality and reference, and hence capable of imposing conditions on syntactic objects having such thoughts as their contents. The more plausible alternative is that the semantic objects in question are creatures of the syntax itself: Syntax was and is innovative for them.

Whether the same skeptical conclusion holds for conceptual (as opposed to intentional) structures in non-humans I leave open here, but given that these also exhibit recursion and context-freeness, their non-availability in creatures

---

[2] An alternative conception is that both internal and external Merge were in place, and *because* they were, they were then co-opted to a novel function, that of expressing the two kinds of semantic properties in question. On that alternative, performing the function in question is a *consequence* of the presence of certain structural conditions that lend themselves to these uses, not what explains them. This would leave open whether the duality of semantics *pre-existed* FL and CS (for, not *explaining* the latter does not yet mean that the duality didn't exist independently of them). Even so, the project of motivating language and syntax from interface conditions externally imposed in it looks bogus, and neither does it make (16) more plausible. (16) remains implausible in the light of persistent failures to find intentional reference and truth in non-humans, and in the light of the fact that the two layers of semantic complexity in question are supported by combinatorial systems of different degrees of computational complexity and plausibly depend on these systems.

who lack formal-computational procedures equivalent to those involved in their linguistic encoding is at least likely (see further Hinzen 2007: ch. 3).

2.4 Adjuncts

I will now argue that the very reason for the *non-existence* of interface conditions imposed on *intentionally* interpreted structures in narrow syntax is, at the same time, a reason for the existence of adjunct structures there. The idea is that semantics as such, in the non-linguistic sense, cannot support what is in some essential sense *syntactic* (which, if I am right, intentional information is), but that adjuncts are the most plausible candidate for what is *not* essentially syntactic. As Chomsky has put it: If α adjoins to β, β behaves as if α was "not there, *apart from semantic interpretation*" (Chomsky 2004a: 117, my emphasis)

He also notes that adjunction of α to β does not change any properties of β—in particular it does not affect its category, projection status, or theta role—and that an adjunct construction is not the projection of any head. As one might put these observations, there isn't much syntax to adjuncts. Adjuncts are not selected, they don't take part in feature checking or control, have different island properties, etc. Overall, thus, adjuncts attach in different (weaker) ways to a given syntactic object than arguments do: They are relatively more independent.

In what follows I will be talking about adjuncts primarily in the sense of right-merged adverbials (which behave differently from adverbs merged to the left of the VP), or nominal modifiers. Adjuncts in this sense are linguistic objects that may crucially stack (they iterate, hence are subject to much lesser restrictions than the tightly constrained argument system), and in none of these iterations do they contribute a new categorial label to the syntactic object to which they attach. As Pietroski & Uriagereka (2002) argue, categories are useful only if they are few, so that the computational system, when recognizing one of them, will take a certain action irrespective of which open-class lexical element fills the position that has that specific categorial label. Thus, if adjunction is unbounded, either there are infinitely many labels, which does not seem to be the case, or adjunction never involves a change in category.[3]

Unsurprisingly, the syntactic properties of adjuncts have semantic consequences. As Chomsky (2004a: 117) points out, the kind of semantic

---

[3] That does not necessarily mean that "adjunction" is a unified phenomenon, and other kinds of adjunction do not exist that are much more limited and are different semantically as well, behaving more like specifiers of appropriate functional projections (see Scott 2002).

interpretation we are getting with adjuncts is "not the one of standard X-bar-theoretic constructions." This would be much in the spirit of the restrictive theory of the syntax and the syntax-semantics mapping envisaged above: If we get different structural conditions (of different computational complexity) within the computational system, we also get different semantic effects correlating with these conditions (and we don't get the effects otherwise). Let us specifically assume, with the Neo-Davidsonian (e.g. Pietroski 2002; Larson 2004), that right-merged adverbials have a very simple—though still compositional—conjunctive semantics: Their interpretation consists in conjoining predicates. Intuitively, *walk quickly* means that there is a walking and it is quick:[4]

(17)   *Interpretation of adjuncts*
      walk quickly: (∃e) e is a walking & e is quick
      blue house: (∃x) x is a house & x is blue

Arguments crucially lack this semantics: *John ran* does not mean: ∃e[e is a running & e is John], but:

(18)   ∃e[ran(e) & THEME (John, e)]

With the participant-of relation (thematic roles) something entirely different enters the computational system of human language, which the adjunct system—and probably the putative systems of thought on the other side of the interface—know nothing of.

The path is now free for my claim that adjuncts in the above sense, but not likely much else in human language, may well be motivatable from the interface. Put differently, adjuncts may well have existed in a protolanguage that had a simpler semantics than the semantics that plausibly depends on a more elaborate syntax that includes the argument-of relation, categories, A′-relations, etc. This fits well with the consideration that processing modificational structures like *(the) [blue, [square, [heavy [large [box]]]]]* could well be within the scope of simian cognition. It is as if we can subtract argument-structures from language and keep something back: a fully operational, productively combinatorial and compositional system based on predicates, whose essential function is to combine them.[5] One can't make any judgement in it, of course, in the above sense: Though one can combine

---

[4] The semantics is not *purely* conjunctive, in that some other operation will have to bind the two (or more) predicates to one single referent somehow.

[5] Again, restrictions on adjectival modifiers as found in the human modifier system (see e.g. Scott 2002) do not entail that adjunction as a merely conjunctive mode of attachment does not also exist in human language and could have provided a functional protolanguage deprived of arguments.

blue and *house*, one will never be able to think about *a blue house* or *This is a blue house*. But that might as well have been our predicament, had we not found some queer trick to somehow bootstrap an entirely new system with a more dependent mode of attachment, the argument system. The adjunct system gives us a window into a mind more impoverished in syntactic terms.

Let us now hold these adjunct facts together with what I argued in the beginning: that a successor-style Merge operation does not yield phrase-structural and categorial hierarchies in any serious sense either. We are then led to the suggestion that what it yields is adjuncts. It's in the case of adjuncts that no projection takes place; and neither does projection exist in minimalist syntactic trees as built by Merge in the sense above. It's adjuncts where β, if α is adjoined to it, is simply reproduced at the next level, as if nothing had happened to it; and nothing else happens in standard labeling proposals in minimalist "bare phrase structures." It's adjuncts that are purely symmetrical (in the way that conjunction as an algebraic operation is), because no projection takes place in them that creates asymmetries; and it's minimalist Merge that's said to be purely symmetrical as well. Finally, it's adjuncts that iterate indefinitely; and so does minimalist Merge. The inability of minimalist syntax to get hierarchy off the ground, as I discussed earlier when reviewing various proposals, attests to the fact that its syntax is essentially adjunctive or iterative. The lack of categorial projection, of ontological innovation, and the one-dimensionality of the system all converge to this conclusion.

Chomsky (2004a, 2005) argues to the contrary that Merge (viewed as generating the *argument*-system) is symmetric, while adjunction is crucially asymmetric. More generally, he construes adjunction as an evolutionary extra (a *prima facie* "imperfection") that should not exist in a system that has only Merge, hence which putatively violates the SMT. Thus it has to be provided with a special motivation and novel operation (see Section 2.1), and the semantics is then invoked to supply one. If I am right, it is exactly the other way around, with adjuncts coming virtually for free (by needing very little structural support), while arguments provide a first crucial evolutionary innovation that gave us the thought and conceptual structures that we more routinely think.

The reason Chomsky (2004a) gives against the symmetry of adjunction is that when α, the adjunct, is adjoined to β, β is a head, α not, and β behaves "as if α isn't there, apart from semantic interpretation." But semantic interpretation treats them precisely as symmetrical, or as on a par: Predicate composition is symmetric, as conjunction is, and the adjunct system *is* crucially semantic, by Chomsky's own suggestion. There is a difference between β and α for sure, but the adjunct system is too primitive to "see" it. If you can't see heads and projections, the syntactic object that at a later evolutionary stage will look to you as a head will look as just a further predicate. Using the earlier geometric metaphor, from the perspective of a one-dimensional system, the difference between a line and a plane cannot be seen. Adjuncts are the linguistic reflex of generative principles that span a one-dimensional space, with all objects in it being of the same ontological kind (or categorial nature).

But language is not like that. It generates objects in several dimensions recursively, with entailment relations systematically ensuing from the part-whole relations that are built. Both within N and V we see lexical items of different categorial complexity, with each type of higher complexity entailing the types of lower complexity. Thus there is no such thing as a concrete object expressed by a count noun without a mass, expressed by a mass noun (that is, conceptually, where there is *a lamb* there is also *lamb*, i.e. the relevant meat, by conceptual necessity); in a similar way, any verb of accomplishment presupposes the state that forms its *telos* or intrinsic end. There are similar entailments inside the categorial skeleton of the clause, where a finiteness projection presupposes a proposition, a proposition a verb, and so on.

As argued elsewhere (Hinzen & Uriagereka 2006), higher-dimensional syntactic objects generated where we leave adjuncts for arguments are moreover not just that: higher-dimensional. Rather, the dimensions must be *based* and *built* on one another so as to stand in asymmetric relations of dependence (entailment): The clausal categorial hierarchy is a rigid one, with a D necessarily presupposing an N, and v presupposing in its internal architecture an unaccusative V, T presupposing v, and so on. Assuming a highly restrictive theory of how narrow syntax can be interpreted (or generates new interpretations, if I am right), these presuppositions have an immediate semantic correlate in certain entailments that they license, as when the event of Caesar's having destructed Syracuse necessarily entails the state of its being destroyed. For syntax to have this semantic effect, the dimensional layers in which higher categories in the clausal skeleton live have to be *built* so as to contain the less complex structures. As plausible as it is, perhaps, that adjunction is an operation that is "semantically driven," it is implausible that a semantic (non-syntactic) "motivation" of this categorial hierarchy will go very far beyond the very first of these recursive steps, by means of which our conceptual world gradually opens up.

2.5 Conclusion

We began with the project of principled explanation and the SMT, and I have argued that we should replace the project of "motivating language from interface conditions" by an older Wittgensteinian, and effectively much more minimalist, "use theory of meaning." Perhaps the role of interfacing systems, if they have one, is not the positive one that Minimalism has by and large ascribed to it, but a primarily *negative* one: They *restrict* the powers of the generative engine that define our minds, since not all of its products may be usable. Also, we will very likely have to accept that language has been innovative for what thoughts we can think, and for what categories figure in our mind.

As for the equation in my title, syntax likely isn't one-dimensional seriation, though it is possible that evolutionarily the system has begun there. Reconstructing structure-building in successor terms leaves out the categorial hierarchies which mark out language against iterative and adjunctive, label-free and projection-free systems, and which do not engender necessary entailment relations among categories. Merge in the sense of endless recursive embedding may be real in language, but if so, it will not be, if I am right, its distinctive mark (*contra* Hauser *et al.* 2002). Its distinctive mark is the way it breaks out of a given dimension of mental reality by projecting new categories upon merging two given syntactic objects, or by enacting categorial "jumps" that give us a different kind of object to think about.

3

The Division of C-I and the Nature of the Input, Multiple Transfer, and Phases*

TAKASHI MUNAKATA

3.1 Introduction

In this chapter, I argue that the language faculty is connected not to a single Conceptual-Intentional System (C-I) on the meaning side, but to two different external cognitive systems, a Conceptual System (C-S) and an Intentional System (I-S). Furthermore, I argue that these two systems compel the syntactic computational mechanism to make use of different types of syntactic inputs (lexical elements for a C-S and functional elements within the CP domain for an I-S) and produce corresponding syntactic outputs (i.e. phases). A syntactic derivation consists of two types of "phases" (lexical phases and functional phases). Consequently, Transfer should apply to these different types of phases separately (hence, multiply). In other words, I argue that the existence of phases is derived from interface conditions (IC) and the properties of external cognitive systems on the meaning side, which implies that phase status should be determined by these properties.

It will also be shown that the characterization of SC based on C-S and I-S gives rise to a number of interesting consequences, such as what I call "parallel consistency and asymmetry" within the language faculty, and allows for a principled explanation for several syntactic notions, such as Multiple Transfer,

* A version of this paper was presented at the *InterPhases* conference (Nicosia, Cyprus, May 2006). I would like to thank the audience for helpful comments and suggestions. I am also very indebted to Kleanthes Grohmann for his efforts to organize the conference, edit this book and for providing great help at the several stages of this work. Furthermore, I am very grateful to Wolfram Hinzen, Daisuke Inagaki, Lanko Marušič, Takashi Toyoshima, Akira Watanabe, and especially to Yoshio Endo, Roger Martin, and Christopher Tancredi for comments, suggestions, and insightful discussions. Needless to say, all errors are of my own.

the dual nature of semantics (cf. Chomsky 2005), different nature of lexical and functional items, initial Merge based on θ-grid, and the A/A$'$ distinction, in terms of the Strong Minimalist Thesis (Chomsky 1994).

3.2 Syntactic Computation and the Language Faculty

Chomsky (2004*a*) assumes that the language faculty is connected to two external cognitive systems: the Conceptual-Intentional System and the Sensorimotor System (SM).[1] He further assumes the need for two interface components, the Semantic Component (SemC) and the Phonological Component (PhonC), in addition to the Syntactic Component (SC), the computational mechanism that maps a numeration to a syntactic derivation, deriving a syntactic object.[2] SC sends the syntactic object into the interface components by Transfer (Chomsky 2004*a*). It is argued that Transfer must apply multiply to erase a valued uninterpretable feature as soon as possible to satisfy Full Interpretation (FI) and reduce computational complexity (cf. Chomsky 2001, 2004*a*, Epstein & Seely 2002*a*, and Uriagereka 1999*a*). Chomsky (2000, 2001, 2004*a*) assumes that Multiple Transfer is applied at the phase level, where phases are defined as propositional—namely, v^*P and CP.

The numeration, which is defined as a set of lexical items, indicates what lexical choices are and how many times each lexical item is selected (cf. Chomsky 1995). Chomsky (2000, 2001) suggests that the numeration is divided into subsets (i.e. subnumerations), which correspond to phases. Normally, it is assumed syntactic arguments should be merged into a θ-position (cf. Chomsky 1995, 2000 and Hale & Keyser 1993*a*). Recently, Chomsky (2005) suggests that Merge into a base-position (i.e. External Merge) correlates with argument structure and establishes "base-structures" within the GB framework, whereas Move (Internal Merge) correlates with edge properties such as scope or discourse-related properties.

Importantly, given the Strong Minimalist Thesis, SC must create a syntactic derivation which obeys IC, such as FI, imposed by the interface components.[3] Otherwise, the syntactic derivation is illegitimate and crashes.

---

[1] I will occasionally continue to use C-I to refer to the external cognitive system on the meaning side, though I adopt the claim by Uriagereka (1999*a*) that C-I is actually divided into two systems.

[2] I mean "derived syntactic object" by the term "syntactic object" throughout the chapter.

[3] In this chapter, I assume that SC as well as the interface components SemC and PhonC should also satisfy IC. That is, it should indirectly satisfy requirements of the external systems. Since SemC and PhonC are interface components, IC are directly imposed on these components by C-I and SM. Then, one might argue that it should be possible that SC ships an inappropriate syntactic object to SemC and PhonC and these interface components might modify this shipped syntactic object to be able to be read off by C-I and SM, providing an appropriate readable linguistic object for these external systems.

Another such IC is the Inclusiveness Condition, which says that any structure formed by the syntactic computation is composed of elements already present in the lexical/functional items selected for the numeration; new objects cannot be added in the course of computation apart from rearrangements of lexical properties (cf. Chomsky 1995, 2005, 2008). A strong version of the Inclusiveness Condition requires that no features or lexical/functional items be introduced in the course of the syntactic computation (cf. Chomsky 2000, 2001).[4]

In the next subsection, I will discuss the numeration, the status of phases and Multiple Transfer in light of IC and argue that these notions, as they are conceived by Chomsky (1995, 2000, 2001, 2004*a*), are not motivated by IC and hence it is necessary to reevaluate them in light of the Strong Minimalist Thesis.

3.3 Interface Conditions and the Syntactic Component

As noted, given the Strong Minimalist Thesis that the language faculty is an optimal solution to IC, it is plausible that the components of the language faculty are also an optimal solution to relevant IC. In essence, IC are imposed on the language faculty by C-I and SM. Since SemC and PhonC are interface components, IC are directly imposed on these components. That is, these interface components should be organized hand in hand with C-I and SM.

Also, it seems that SC needs to generate a legitimate syntactic object, which can be appropriately interpreted and used by the interface components. This indicates that SC may also obey IC. For example, FI is an IC imposed on SC, requiring that only legitimate (i.e. interpretable) objects survive at the interfaces (Chomsky 1995).

Moreover, given that a syntactic object is a source of the linguistic output, which is used by external systems and thus needs to satisfy IC, it seems that this syntactic object also needs to satisfy IC: If it violates IC, it should be the case that a linguistic output, derived from a syntactic object, results in violating IC, too.

However, it does not seem that this is the case. Rather, as will be discussed, SC produces a legitimate syntactic object, which can be made use of by the interface components to provide an appropriate linguistic object to the external systems. For example, FI is an IC imposed by the interface components, not the external systems, in order that SemC and PhonC can ship legitimate linguistic objects satisfying IC to these systems.

[4] I will claim below that this part of the strong version of the Inclusiveness Condition is imposed by C-S and should be observed up to TP, which implies that it may be violated when SC generates functional projections within the CP domain.

Thus, given that the Strong Minimalist Thesis assumes that IC characterize the language faculty, it may be that SC is also characterized by IC. Given this, it is reasonable to assume that every syntactic notion of SC should be principally characterized by them within the minimalist framework. However, it will turn out that this assumption cannot always be upheld.

3.3.1 *Numeration*

The numeration is defined as a lexical choice from the lexicon (Chomsky 1995: 225–7). Given that lexical items are initially merged in θ-positions (cf. Chomsky 1995, 2001, 2005), this choice is presumably based on selectional requirements and θ-properties of syntactic heads, which are not motivated by IC but rather reflect argument structure.[5] Essentially, these requirements and properties only deal with lexical items and light verbs v/v^*, whereas functional items within the CP domain like Topic and Focus are irrelevant to them. This raises a question whether a numeration needs to contain these functional items. Actually, selectional requirements and θ-properties are necessarily satisfied, and, thus, lexical verbal heads and their arguments always appear in a sentence. The same thing is applied to light verbs: light verbs should appear always when selectional requirements require the external argument and Agent θ-role is selected in argument structure. On the other hand, functional items within the CP domain are optional. It is generally unnecessary for them to appear; the sentence may be uttered without a sentential topic and a focus element, for example. In addition, these functional items may freely appear in the structure, whatever selectional requirements and θ-properties are. Thus, it is unnatural for the numeration, which is considered to be based on lexical requirements and θ-properties of syntactic heads, to contain these functional items within the CP domain, since nothing, including IC, seems to require these functional items to always appear and to be contained in the numeration.

It might be argued that the numeration should initially involve functional items within the CP domain in order to reduce the computational burden of SC by limiting access to the lexicon to one-time formation of the numeration. However, this argument is hard to maintain, because there is no obvious basis on which to choose these items and, consequently, the choice plausibly

---

[5] Uriagereka (1999a) correctly points out that some justification is necessary to explain why a numeration as well as an initial Merge of lexical items is based on selectional requirements and θ-grids. He notes that this problem is solved if the numeration reflects conceptual matters (e.g. conceptual structure of lexical items), including an argument structure. Also, he claims that C and I should be separated from one another and that the numeration (in his terms, D-structure component) is an interface component accessed by C-S whereas SemC (in his terms, LF Component) is accessed by I-S. I will adopt and discuss this proposal later, showing that it brings several desirable consequences in view of the Strong Minimalist Thesis.

demands a great deal of computational burden (cf. search domain), unlike lexical items, the selection of which can be based on selectional properties and θ-grids.[6] In addition, given that selection of these functional items is not required and that there is no clear-cut way to derive this optionality from properties of syntactic elements in the numeration, it is difficult for SC to determine which functional items should be present in the numeration. This seems to require the ability to "look-ahead," further increasing the computational burden. Rather, it seems more economical to insert functional items within the CP domain into the derivation directly from the lexicon only when "needed," thus limiting the search by SC and avoiding excess computational burden. If so, functional items are not present in an initial numeration but are inserted derivationally.

Also, it might be argued that functional heads within the CP domain need to appear in the numeration initially because of the selectional requirement by the next relevant head. For instance, Cinque (1999), who proposes forty-seven functional categories, argues that all functional projections must be present, because each of these functional categories is semantically selected by the next higher functional head (cf. Ernst 2002). However, this claim seems to leave the apparent optionality of the meanings expressed by certain functional categories unexplained. First, such functional categories would exist merely to satisfy the selectional requirements syntactically. Furthermore, since they do not make any semantic contribution in SemC, their very existence at the interface would seem to violate FI.

Finally, one might say that C should be present in the numeration, because it plays the important role in determining the subnumeration and due to its status as a phase head. However, as I argued above, C, one of functional heads within the CP domain, seems irrelevant to selectional requirements of lexical heads and it is unmotivated for C to be included in the numeration.[7]

---

[6] A great deal of look-ahead is necessary to select syntactic items from the lexicon in building the numeration; or, if we maintain the organization of the language faculty assumed by Chomsky, selection of lexical items should be the random as Uriagereka (1999a) claims. However, this problem can be avoided if we assume that the numeration is an interface to C-S and C-S provides information about lexical choice for the language faculty, as discussed below, though it may be possible that the numeration plays no role in SC as Collins (1997) and Frampton & Gutmann (2002) claim.

[7] Chomsky (2007a, 2008) no longer mentions the numeration/lexical array. Roger Martin (p.c.) points out that the notion of numeration/subnumeration does not seem to play such an important role in the syntactic derivation. For example, the status of a phase head is derived from different factors in these papers. Also, the economy principles (cf. fewest steps) regulating the syntactic computation, and for which the numeration was needed in order to properly define, vanish. However, even if the numeration is no longer assumed, many of the problems raised in this chapter remain and must be dealt with.

3.3.2 *Phases*

Chomsky (2000, 2001, 2004a, 2005, 2008) suggests that phases correspond to CP/v*P, since these syntactic objects both have a coherent and independent status in SemC and PhonC and are considered to be propositional: v*P is equipped with a full-fledged argument structure and CP has a clausal status since it contains tense and force. However, this assumption is also questionable given IC. That is, it is unclear in view of IC why these quite distinct syntactic objects should be regarded as the same, i.e. propositional.

As discussed above, Chomsky (2000: 106, 2001: 12) claims that phases are CP/v*P. Also, he assumes that they correspond to subnumerations and, accordingly, a subnumeration must contain either C or v*. However, as I reasoned above, there is no clear reason why the numeration should contain C. Also, according to Chomsky (cf. Chomsky 2000), the phase status of v*P is attributed to its full-fledged argument structure, which is a conceptual matter (cf. Jackendoff 1969, 1996 and Chomsky 2005, 2008) and clearly motivated by the selectional requirements of lexical heads, whereas the phase status of CP arises from the presence of tense and force, which are not so obviously conceptual in nature and cannot be motivated by the selectional requirements of lexical heads. That is, the phase statuses of v*P and CP are attributed to different sources, although it is claimed that they are related to propositionality. Consequently, there is no strong reason to regard v*P and CP as phases uniformly.

In addition, one may say that because a subnumeration corresponds to a phase and a phase is a propositional CP/v*P due to the requirement of C-I, a subnumeration should involve one of the phase heads C or v* beforehand. However, this argument involves a look-ahead property and should be abandoned. Provided that a phase is the target of Multiple Transfer and the size of a phase is principally determined by the requirements of the interface components, phasehood is identified in the course of syntactic derivation after a syntactic object is created. Yet, since a subnumeration is made before a syntactic computation begins, SC would have to look ahead to know whether some syntactic head is a phasehead and that the subnumeration containing this syntactic head thus corresponds to a phase.

Chomsky (2001) claims that C-I requires propositional structures with a force indicator (CP) and full argument structure (v*P)—that is, a clause.[8] However, this is mysterious. First, it is unclear why vP and TP do not count as phases, even though they seem to be propositional: vP has full argument structure and TP seems to express indicative force in a root clause

---

[8] Thanks to Roger Martin (p.c.) for this point.

(cf. Uriagereka 1999*a*; Epstein & Seely 2002*a*; Legate 2003*b*). In addition, there is no reason why C-I requires a propositional clause: It may demand the whole sentence (i.e. Single Transfer) or separately pick up sentential-force information, discourse-oriented properties like topic and sentential modality such as evaluation and evidentiality, rather than picking up all information of the propositional clause once and for all.

Recently, Chomsky (2007*a*, 2008) regards a phase as the domain of syntactic locality by arguing that all syntactic operations such as Transfer, Agree, and Internal Merge (i.e. movement) apply at the phase level and the phase is the domain where uninterpretable features are valued. Also, he links the phase status to the possession of uninterpretable features, such as case features and edge features (cf. EPP), claiming that C and v^* are the locus of such features and, consequently, the triggers of all syntactic operations. Though this might be reasonable given that a phase is the syntactic unit which Multiple Transfer targets, there is no reason why this is the case in view of IC. If one sticks to the Strong Minimalist Thesis, this should be derived from IC and properties of the external cognitive systems or the interface components.[9]

3.3.3 *Multiple Transfer*

In the previous section, I have argued against the claim that CP/v^*P correspond to phases because IC do not motivate it. Accordingly, given that Multiple Transfer is deeply related to the nature of phases, it may be said that Multiple Transfer is not motivated by IC, either.

---

[9] Chomsky (2007) gives a further argument for the phase-head status of C and v^*, based on Richards (2007), which relies on feature inheritance and the treatment of valued uninterpretable feature. According to Chomsky (2000, 2001, 2004*a*, 2007, 2008), uninterpretable features need to be valued not to trigger derivational crash at the interfaces. Also, he notes that once valued, these features should be transferred as soon as possible because they are indistinguishable from interpretable counterparts when the next phase head is introduced (cf. Chomsky 2007, 2008). For this reason, Chomsky claims, adopting Richards's (2007) observation, that not TP but CP should be a phase. Suppose that T is a phase head, it cannot transmit its uninterpretable features to v^* because the latter is also an independently motivated phase head. In addition, even if these uninterpretable features on T are valued via Agree, they cannot be transferred soon because they wait until the next phase head is introduced to be transferred due to PIC, where they cannot be distinguished from interpretable features. Then, Transfer cannot know which features are uninterpretable and remove uninterpretable features, causing the derivation to crash. Therefore, it is impossible that T is a phase head.

However, this argument goes through only under a particular view of the Agree mechanism. If feature interpretability is determined in another way, distinguished easily by Transfer, this argument cannot be maintained. For example, Munakata (forthcoming) suggests that feature interpretability is determined depending on which head a (valued) feature is associated with. Under this view, Transfer only needs to know which head a certain feature is combined with in order to know whether it is interpretable or not.

Transfer is an operation which ships a derived syntactic object to the interface components SemC and PhonC. A phase is a syntactic unit Transfer applies to. Then, it may be that the size of the phase is determined by Multiple Transfer.[10] Since Multiple Transfer applies to a derived syntactic object so that the interface components can make use of it and create an appropriate linguistic output for the external cognitive system, it is natural, given the Strong Minimalist Thesis, that the transferred syntactic object should be derived from IC and properties of the interface components.

As already discussed, Chomsky states that the external cognitive systems, especially C-I, require propositional structures. However, as I have argued, there is no strong reason that C-I (and SM) require propositional structures. Also, given IC and computational efficiency, SC might need to transfer an appropriate syntactic object so that SemC (and PhonC) can efficiently compute it and give it a semantic interpretation, which is read off by C-I. Again, it is unclear whether propositionality is relevant in forming the appropriate syntactic object in terms of computational efficiency of SemC. Rather, it seems necessary to consider whether propositionality is really motivated by an interpretative mechanism and properties of SemC (and PhonC) and C-I (and SM).

In addition, according to Chomsky (2001, 2004a), application of Multiple Transfer reduces computational complexity and computational load. In particular, Chomsky argues that Transfer should be applied multiply to erase a valued uninterpretable feature as soon as this uninterpretable feature is valued via Agree: if not, it is impossible to distinguish between normal interpretable features and valued uninterpretable features. However, Epstein & Seely (2002a) point out that this analysis faces a problem: if minimality is a primary factor in the determination of the target of Transfer, the target should be a minimal syntactic unit (i.e. all syntactic units), not v*P/CP, irrespective of propositionality. Consequently, Multiple Transfer should always apply shortly after SC merges a syntactic element with an existent syntactic object. Of course, since this proposal does not take the properties of the interface components and the external cognitive systems into account, it might be refuted if such minimal syntactic units are not appropriate objects of interpretation in the interface components. Nonetheless, it indicates that it is questionable that v*P/CP is the target of Multiple Transfer given minimality, since other syntactic units like VP, AP, and TP appear more minimal.

---

[10] Of course, it is possible that the size of the phase determines the timing of Multiple Transfer.

3.4 Reconsidering C-I

In the previous section, I have claimed that the numeration should be based on θ-properties and selectional requirements of lexical heads and that this is apparently not justified by IC.

Nonetheless, Chomsky (2007a, 2008) hypothesizes that C-I incorporates a dual semantics, with generalized argument structure as one component and with discourse-related and scopal properties as the other component. In particular, he claims that initial (i.e. External) Merge yields generalized argument structure, adding that C-I will assign a theta-role to an argument NP according to its initial merge position, presumably based on the argument structure of lexical heads after SemC computes a transferred syntactic object. However, if so, it does not follow that the numeration should be motivated by θ-properties and selectional requirements of lexical heads and that initial Merge is restricted by θ-configurations (cf. Hale & Keyser 1993, Chomsky 1995, 2000, and Saito 2003b), because C-I is not directly connected to the numeration. Whatever External Merge (i.e. initial Merge) is, it should not be restricted by θ-configuration, because C-I has no way to directly control initial Merge of SC, which means that it does not necessarily follow that External Merge yields generalized argument structure.

Another problem with Chomsky's claim is that it requires look-ahead. SC cannot directly access C-I information regarding argument structure and, accordingly, should not know where NP arguments must be merged or move, necessitating look-ahead.[11] It might be argued that C-I imposes an IC on SC through SemC, regulating θ-grids and requiring SC to build a syntactic object based on these θ-grids.[12] However, this kind of condition is untenable and should be abandoned. Under Chomsky's approach, it might be stated that SC should merge an argument NP into a θ-position blindly when this merge appears suited to a θ-grid.[13] Yet, it seems that this kind of syntactic derivation would have to resort to an unprincipled and unsystematic computational mechanism which yields a syntactic derivation somewhat randomly,

---

[11] This special look-ahead property can be called "supra look-ahead" in that SC needs to look ahead not into the components of the language faculty but C-I outside it.

[12] For example, it could be said that selectional features of a lexical head reflect a θ-property of this lexical head. Then, it is necessary for SC to satisfy selectional features to merge this lexical head with a syntactic element (cf. Collins 2002).

Actually, Chomsky (2007a) seems to assume that this kind of information is stored in label of a phase head (v^* in case of transitive verbs and C in case of unaccusative and passive constructions), though it is quite unclear how to utilize it. See the discussion in the text.

[13] Possibly, this IC merely says that a first merged argument must be merged into VP-Comp and a second merged argument NP v^*P-Spec. However, this faces a problem because a first argument NP is an external NP with Agent in case of an unergative verb, while an argument NP which is first merged with VP is an internal NP with Theme in case of an unaccusative verb and a transitive verb.

incidentally producing appropriate syntactic outputs (see *n.* 12). Clearly, this is quite the opposite of what is assumed for the syntactic computational mechanism of SC, namely, that it is highly efficient and systematic, generating only well-formed syntactic derivations (cf. Chomsky 1995, 2001, 2004*a*, 2007*a* and Frampton & Gutmann 2002). If so, blind initial Merge should be abandoned.

Instead, Chomsky (2007*a*) states that the label of a (phase) head bears information about selection and Merge including initial (i.e. External) Merge, which seems to circumvent a looking-ahead problem.[14] However, in Chomsky's (2007*a*) model, the only domain where selection enters is possibly C-I, which indicates that this kind of information may be only derived from it. Thus, the selectional information formed by generalized argument structure must be transmitted to label from C-I, which should be impossible because C-I is not directly connected to SC and does not have any influence on its lexical selection. Then, SC must make use of a looking-ahead property, which should be abandoned.

Moreover, it is unclear why the numeration satisfies the selectional requirements of lexical heads like V even though lexical choice is made, and the numeration is created, before Merge applies. To implement this proposal, this information must be available when creating the numeration, which should be abandoned because of the look-ahead property. Rather, it is good to assume that the numeration reflects the event structure of lexical heads and lexical choices are made accordingly. Similarly, given that an initial Merge applies to syntactic elements in the beginning of a syntactic derivation, it is unclear how this kind of IC is stated without the look-ahead property (cf. Uriagereka 1999*a*).

Finally, Chomsky (2007*a*) states that the smallest domain where the V-Object relation (and possibly an external argument) may be checked with its θ-role at C-I is above vP in case of passive and unaccusative and v^*P in case of transitive, which means that the V-Object relation and a relevant argument structure are unsettled at the point of the derivation at which VP is created. He argues emphatically that "phases are as small as possible consistent (possibly) with assignment of argument structure, CP and v^*P," which makes it possible to signal anomalous derivation quickly without resorting to selectional features of lexical items (cf. label). However, there is no reason why the syntactic expression needs to wait at C-I not within the language faculty to be checked with its argument structure and thematic anomaly. Also, this seems unnatural and uneconomical in that it basically allows SC to generate syntactic

---

[14] Note that External Merge is based on generalized argument structure, which implies that information about generalized argument structure (cf. θ-grid) should also be involved in label.

expressions with semantic anomaly, because thematic anomaly is known only at C-I, where the linguistic computation finishes and everything goes out of the language faculty, disallowing SC to regenerate syntactic derivation by removing semantic anomaly and making it irrecoverable: that is, it is too late to know thematic anomaly. Rather, it is good that the language faculty identifies thematic anomaly of a syntactic expression at a much earlier stage by receiving the information about argument structure and thematic properties, enabling SC to avoid generating syntactic expressions with thematic anomaly.

Thus we need something to motivate an initial Merge of an argument NP into a θ-position without a look-ahead property. This initial Merge is based on the θ-properties of a lexical predicative head. As argued in the previous section, the numeration should also be based on the θ-properties of a lexical head, which is irrelevant to IC, because C-I cannot influence the formation of the numeration. Clearly, this is unfavorable in light of the Strong Minimalist Thesis, given that the numeration functions as an input and plays a very important role in the syntactic computation.

To solve these problems, I propose that C-I is actually divided into a Conceptual-System (C-S) and an Intentional System (I-S), following Uriagereka (1999a). In particular, I assume that C-S is connected to the numeration and imposes IC on SC through the numeration, whereas I-S is connected to SemC and imposes IC on SC through SemC. Hereafter, I refer to this model as the C/I model.

I assume that C-S deals with the event structures of predicates as well as selectional and θ-properties, whereas I-S deals with intentional matters such as discourse-oriented properties and sentential mood in addition to truth values and reference. Basically, I suggest that C-S provides the language faculty with the necessary information involving selectional requirements and θ-properties of event structure to build the numeration and generate lexical projections, whereas I-S computes the intentional-semantic interpretation of sentences by accessing SemC.[15]

---

[15] A reviewer points out that this proposal is similar to the design of the language faculty proposed by Jackendoff (1996). Though I partly sympathize with his proposal about conceptual properties, my approach is quite different from Jackendoff's in important points. For one thing, I argue that conceptual and intentional properties are quite different and cannot be dealt with by the single cognitive system, unlike Jackendoff, who says that the single cognitive system—what he calls "the conceptual structure"—includes both properties. In addition, I insist that C-S gives conceptual information to the language faculty via the numeration without resorting to any mediating rules before syntactic derivation starts, whereas he claims that syntactic structures are converted and mediated to conceptual units by applying correspondence rules between the language faculty and the conceptual structure after Transfer, where syntactic derivation ends.

If this is so, it is natural that the numeration is formed based on selectional requirements and θ-properties of lexical heads, if C-S requires that the numeration should reflect conceptual matters. To achieve this aim, I propose that C-S imposes the Conservation Condition in (1) on the language faculty:

(1) *Conservation Condition*
     SC must conserve the properties of C-S without any change throughout a syntactic derivation to reflect these properties properly in the syntactic derivation and mirror them in SemC.

This condition is natural because the properties of C-S (i.e. selectional requirements and θ-properties) are indispensable for linguistic expressions and I-S needs to access these properties to process the intentional-semantic interpretation appropriately.

Also, we can give a principled explanation to why an argument NP must be initially merged into a θ-position. The Conservation Condition requires SC to initially merge an argument of an event structure into a θ-position, because a θ-grid that this event structure has is also a property of C-S and SC should initially merge an argument according to the θ-grid to conserve this property. This is plausible because both SemC and I-S should easily read off the information about θ-roles from the transferred syntactic object based on the θ-grid.[16]

Similarly, this condition may restrict an application of Merge by SC to the instances where it satisfies the selectional requirements of lexical heads (selectional Merge in Saito 2003*b* and selectional features in Collins's 2002 terms), if it is assumed that Merge by SC is also restricted by the Conservation Condition via the numeration and is allowed only when its application results in reflecting the properties of C-S—in this case, the selectional requirements.

Due to the Conservation Condition, selectional requirements of an event structure need to be expressed by lexical categories and by v/v^* since they are involved in an event structure as a functional head projecting an external argument. In addition, assuming that an event structure necessarily selects a temporal argument which expresses a specific time and T embodies this temporal argument syntactically (cf. Stowell 1981), it is natural to conclude that tense has C-S properties. This indicates that C-S requires the syntactic computational mechanism to treat lexical categories and v/v^*/T as its syntactic input via the numeration, and consequently these categories obligatorily appear in a sentence. Here, I suggest that in order to assure an appropriate

---

[16] Perhaps C-S requires the numeration to involve rather enriched information about a θ-grid to achieve this aim.

mapping to SemC, the Conservation Condition requires that the syntactic object serving as the target of Transfer (i.e. syntactic output) contains only categories that are part of a C-S-related syntactic input. Assuming that a syntactic object that is the target of Transfer forms a phase, TP, created from syntactic elements in the numeration, should constitute a phase. I refer to this type of phase as a "lexical phase" (cf. Φ-domain in Grohmann 2003).[17] This is a conceptually favorable and reasonable assumption since TP can be thought of as a lexical maximal projection which corresponds to Core Functional Complex (Chomsky 1986b) or the Lexical Relational Structure (Hale & Keyser 1993) where all lexical properties like case and θ-properties are satisfied.

Interestingly, the Conservation Condition has another consequence; namely, the effect of the Projection Principle is also derived from this condition. Basically, this principle says that the properties of lexical items project onto the syntax of the sentence. In the present terms, this means that the properties of lexical items are projected onto the syntactic derivation. This is naturally derived from the Conservation Condition, because the properties of lexical items can be thought as the selectional requirements and θ-properties of lexical heads, which this condition requires SC to reflect (i.e. project) in a syntactic derivation. Moreover, it requires SC to project these properties onto the domain of SemC by necessitating that SC initially merges an argument of lexical heads based on θ-grid and conserves a syntactic object obeying this θ-grid without affecting any changes to it, transferring this syntactic object into SemC. Because this syntactic object is computed and given a semantic interpretation according to a conserved θ-grid, it follows that the lexical properties of lexical heads are projected and conserved throughout the language faculty and are properly read off by I-S.

On the other hand, I suggest that many I-S-related properties, which are optional and not involved in event structures of predicates, are expressed by functional categories within the CP domain (cf. Rizzi 1997). Because the numeration does not involve these functional items, it is necessary for the syntactic computational mechanism to apply some syntactic operation derivationally to insert these functional items. In Section 3.5, I will propose a syntactic operation *Throwing in* that inserts functional heads within the CP domain, functioning as the narrow syntactic "input" to I-S.

---

[17] It might be argued that TP should not be a phase since C is normally thought to select T (cf. Chomsky 2007a). As will be made explicit below, I do not assume that T is selected by C. Rather, C is added to syntactic derivation to continue syntactic derivation after SC forms TP, which I regard as a basic syntactic structure encoding the necessary information to yield a sentential interpretation (i.e. event structure).

This division of C-I into C-S and I-S is reasonable and theoretically favorable.[18] For one thing, it is very strange that the same cognitive system (i.e. C-I) deals with both conceptual and intentional matters, because the former, including θ-properties and selectional requirements, are intimately related to individual words in the lexicon (cf. Pustejovsky 1995), and exhibit quite distinct properties from the latter, which are thought to deal with extra-sentential properties and extra-linguistic issues (cf. Uriagereka 1999*a*).[19]

Also, it was noted that look-ahead is necessary under Chomsky's system in building the numeration based on selectional requirements and θ-properties of a predicative lexical head (see also *n.* 5), because the information about selectional requirements and θ-properties is thought to be part of C-I, to which the numeration is not connected. However, if C-I is divided into C-S and I-S, this look-ahead is unnecessary, since the numeration is the interface to C-S and, consequently, C-S provides the language faculty with the necessary information involving selectional requirements and θ-properties of the predicative head. SC already knows a θ-grid of a predicative lexical head and initial Merge positions of arguments which are necessary to generate syntactic derivation up to vP/v^*P (and other relevant projections). In addition, thematic anomaly can be detected as soon as an argument is merged in a wrong position due to the information C-S supplies.

Finally, this proposal may be evidenced linguistically: conceptual matters are ordinarily expressed by lexical words, whereas intentional matters are functional categories within the CP domain (Speas 2004 and many papers in Rizzi 2004, for example). For example, a predicative lexical head is the core of event structure (i.e. argument structure), which is clearly a conceptual matter. Also, its arguments are lexical nominal elements. On the other hand, discourse-oriented things, such as the selection of topic, and the evaluation of sentential meaning, which can be regarded as intentional matters, are

---

[18] Uriagereka (1999*a*) notes one important difference between SM and C-I. The concept of SM as a unified component is empirically based in the motor theory of speech perception, which assumes that the perception of sounds is partly based on aspects of production (cf. Ryalls 1996). On the other hand, Uriagereka claims that, provided that "meaning" is used vaguely in the sense that it consists of conceptual information (cf. the distinction of predicates from arguments, generalized argument structure, θ-hierarchy, and so forth) and intentional information (cf. reference, calculation of truth, context confinement, and so on), it is at best slightly unjustified that a single external cognitive system (and the interface of the language faculty) deals with both types of information. It is hard to verify whether or not intentional matters and conceptual matters form two sides of the same coin (see the discussion in Uriagereka 1999*a* for details and see Jackendoff 1996 about the different views of the conceptual domain of the external system).

[19] In addition, conceptual matters are often associated with perception and concepts and images of events, things, acts, and situations, whereas intentional issues are related to pragmatics and discourse.

expressed by functional elements such as a topic-marker and the evidential morphemes, which are normally positioned within the CP domain (cf. Cinque 1999).

3.5 *Throwing in* and *Kicking out*

In Subsection 3.3.1, I argued against the assumption that the numeration contains all lexical and functional items, claiming instead in the previous section that the numeration should be derived from C-S and formed based on θ-properties and selectional requirements of lexical heads. Along this line, I define the numeration as follows:

(2) The minimal set of lexical and functional elements which must be present to satisfy the event structure of a main predicate and to express a tense.

I assume that SC initially creates the "Lexical Relational Structure" (Hale & Keyser 1993*a*) or a "Complete Functional Complex" (Chomsky 1986*b*): that is, TP. This assumption is reasonable, provided that an event structure necessarily selects a temporal argument expressing a specific time and T syntactically embodies this temporal argument (cf. Stowell 1981). Also, an event which is expressed by an event structure needs to be anchored to a specific time to be expressed and T or the projection of T (as a temporal argument) functions as anchoring events to a specific time.

How about functional heads within the CP domain? SC can only generate TP from a numeration as defined above. To treat functional heads within the CP domain, I propose two syntactic operations *Throwing in* and *Kicking out*. When SC exhausts lexical and functional items in the numeration, *Throwing in* can insert certain functional heads directly from the lexicon thus enabling SC to continue the syntactic derivation by generating functional projections within the CP domain. Whereas *Kicking out* signals the end of syntactic computation of a derived syntactic object by removing it from the syntactic derivational workspace, ultimately enabling it to be transferred to SemC and PhonC. Given that SC must send a syntactic object to the interface components, *Kicking out* is indispensable and default.[20] It follows that *Throwing in*

---

[20] One may wonder how *Kicking out* differs from Transfer. Basically, *Kicking out* removes the syntactic object from the syntactic workspace but it remains in SC until Transfer applies, shipping it at SemC and PhonC. I assume that *Kicking out* "collapses" a syntactic object into "a compound" in Uriagereka's (1999*b*) sense, which implies that a *kicked-out* syntactic object may be reused by SC and merged with a newly created syntactic object in a new syntactic computational workspace. Also, I assume that Transfer only applies to *kicked-out* syntactic elements and only sends a *kicked-out* syntactic object to the interface components, which makes *Kicking out* a prerequisite for Transfer.

is not default but optional, and that its application thus needs to be justified by IC (cf. Chomsky 2004*a*, 2005). Note that SC must apply *Throwing in* to generate functional projections within the CP domain after lexical projections are created, since functional heads within the CP domain do not exist in the numeration. On the other hand, if SC does not resort to *Throwing in*, *Kicking out* must apply in order to make the syntactic object ready for Transfer to the interface components.

3.5.1 *Interface Condition and Syntactic Operations*

I claimed that *Throwing in* is optional and needs to be justified by IC above. In this subsection, I take the analysis of object shift (OS) in Chomsky (2001) as a starting point and claim that *Throwing in* applies freely if its application influences the interpretation of the outcome by SemC. Specifically, I will propose that *Throwing in* is an instance of a warping operation (Uriagereka 2002*b*), which always results in having an effect on the semantic interpretation.

Chomsky assumes, following Holmberg (1999*a*), that OS is an optional movement operation of an object into v*P-Spec, for which he proposes the following analysis (Chomsky 2001: 60–1):

(3) Optional operations can apply only if they have an effect on outcome: in the present case, v* may be assigned an EPP feature to permit successive-cyclic Ā-movement or Int (under OS).

   (i) v* is assigned an EPP feature only if that has an effect on outcome.

   (ii) The EPP position of v*P is assigned Int.

   (iii) At the phonological border of v*P, XP is assigned Int′.

Because OS only applies when the EPP position of v*P is assigned Int, the application of OS should create a new interpretation and have an effect on outcome.

In sum, Chomsky argues that all optional syntactic operations are constrained in that they can apply only if their application yields a direct effect on "interpretation" of the output at the interface, hence satisfying IC. I restate Chomsky's proposal as the New Outcome Condition in (4), limiting attention to SemC:

(4) *New Outcome Condition (NOC)*
    An optional syntactic operation applies freely only if its application influences the interpretation of this output by SemC.

I assume that *Throwing in* is possible only if its application satisfies NOC.

3.5.2 *Interpretation and Dimensionality*

I proposed above that *Throwing in* may be applied only when it satisfies the NOC. Then, it seems necessary that SC knows beforehand whether the application of *Throwing in* influences the interpretation of the output by SemC, hence satisfying NOC, which would necessitate look-ahead. In this subsection, I will argue that this is not the case and the semantic interpretative mechanism and an IC regulating Multiple Transfer from SC into SemC provide a welcome solution to this puzzle. Before entering the discussion, however, consider how "influence on the interpretation by SemC" should be defined. To answer this question, I first discuss the relationship between SC and SemC.

In Section 3.3, I noted that SC should obey IC imposed by SemC, even though they are independent components, which implies that SC has some dependency on SemC. Consequently, it may be the case that SC exhibits much parallelism to SemC. Also, it transfers a hierarchical syntactic structure into SemC by Multiple Transfer, observing all IC like FI. Plausibly, IC should require that transferred syntactic objects are readable by SemC; that is, the computational mechanism of SemC needs "readable" syntactic objects for its computation and a hierarchical syntactic structure satisfies this necessity. Therefore, it is quite probable that this mechanism uses a hierarchical structure equivalent to syntactic structure and therefore can interpret syntactic structure easily.

Based on this consideration, I propose, incorporating Uriagereka's (2002*b*) idea that the language faculty makes use of a hierarchical dimensional structure, that SemC utilizes a hierarchical dimensional semantic interpretative structure (HDS) to compute a transferred syntactic structure. HDS is essentially divided into two parts: a simple dimension (1D) and multiple-dimensions.[21] According to Uriagereka (2002*b*), 1D is made up of some elementary elements. Here, I presume that 1D corresponds to lexical projections where all lexical properties like case and θ-properties are satisfied and the Lexical Relational Structure and the Core Functional Complex are created— that is, TP.

Also, I assume that the semantic interpretation assigned in 1D must be simple due to the simplicity of this dimension; hence only an existential interpretation is available. Concretely, I suggest that the semantic unit in 1D, which

---

[21] Actually, I propose in Munakata (2006, 2007) that HDS is composed of four dimensions, following the idea of Uriagereka (2002*b*). Accordingly, I argue that functional projections within the CP domain should be divided into the three zones (cf. Enç 2004), necessitating the split-CP hypothesis (Rizzi 1997). I suggest that these dimensions are distinguished depending on which types of semantics they utilize and that the higher the dimension is, the richer interpretation is assigned to a linguistic object. See Munakata (2006) for details.

Uriagereka (2002*b*) regards as an elementary unit, expresses a propositional meaning given that a proposition is an essential unit for the calculation of meaning.[22] Normally, syntactic expressions that convey a propositional meaning are (full or embedded) sentences, which always contain predicates.[23] Following Davidson's (1967) claim that predicates of natural languages are predicates of events (see also Tenny & Pustejovsky 2000), I assume that sentential predicates predicate events.[24] Thus it follows that sentences expressing propositional meaning always involve a predication of events. If so, it is plausible to think that an atomic unit which expresses propositional meaning involves events as well as proposition, functioning as an essential unit in SemC.[25]

In addition, I assume that it is necessary for events to be anchored to a specific time to be assigned a truth-value (Parsons 1990; Ogihara 2006). This suggests that linguistic objects in 1D syntactically correspond to TP, given that T functions to anchor events to a specific time. This is natural given the traditional assumption that an event structure necessarily selects a temporal argument which expresses a specific time and T syntactically embodies this temporal argument (cf. Stowell 1981).[26] Following Ogihara (2006), I assume that this specific time anchor gives an existential interpretation to a whole sentence involving events and event participants. Thus, the interpretation which is given to syntactic objects (actually, syntactic elements within TP and TP itself) in 1D in HDS is an existential interpretation, which goes along with Uriagereka's (2002*b*) suggestion that 1D consists of simple materials given that an existential interpretation is semantically simple. For example, sentences, such as (5), simply express a past event, exhibiting an existential interpretation in the sense that there was an event of "Kyoko meeting Hideki" at a certain past time, and are analyzed as bare TPs, involving no functional elements within the CP domain:

[22] This is a reasonable assumption, because truth-values are usually computed at the level of a proposition.

[23] Small clauses are another candidate, though it is uncertain whether they express a proposition. Rather, it may be plausible to think that they simply express an event. Below, I claim that an event needs to be anchored at some specific time (I will assume that an infinitival *to*, whose tense is discussed in detail in Chomsky & Lasnik 1993 and Martin 1996, also expresses a specific time). Because small clauses lack a tense value (cf. Parsons 1990: 15) and their tense should be provided by a matrix or an embedded tense, I exclude it as a possible candidate here.

[24] Note that events cover states within a Davidsonian framework.

[25] Actually, events are not an appropriate term. Here, I mean an "event structure," which contains a conceptual representation of an event, an event argument, argument structure, and necessary arguments involved in this event. Throughout this chapter, I refer to an event structure as simply an event.

[26] Although this traditional assumption is not completely compatible with Ogihara's claim, I assume in this chapter that there is a syntactic element within TP that embodies a temporal argument and this temporal argument functions as a specific anchor. I will not discuss this further in this chapter.

(5)   Kyoko-ga   Hideki-ni   atta.
      Kyoko-NOM Hideki-DAT met
      'Kyoko met Hideki.'

It might be said that TP is the extended vP/v^*P-projection, where the event structure of predicates is expressed and an event argument and all arguments are base-generated.[27] Furthermore, given that vP and v^*P are the extended projection of VP and that TP is often thought of as the basic syntactic projection where all lexical properties are satisfied, as Chomsky (1986*b*) and Hale & Keyser (1993*a*) argue, the assumption made in this chapter that TP is a maximal lexical projection is supported.[28]

If so, it is natural that TP is syntactically the lexical maximal projection and semantically the simplest dimensional syntactic object in HDS. This is quite reasonable given the Conservation Condition (1), which states that C-S properties are projected onto TP and TP is the target of Transfer, forming a lexical phase. This lexical phase is transferred into 1D of HDS, where I-S easily recognizes this isolated unit and can read off C-S properties and the relevant interpretation (i.e. an existential interpretation) without difficulty. The lexical projection only contains simple syntactic elements such as lexical heads and relevant functional heads like T and v/v^* which might be called extended lexical functional heads. In this sense, T and v/v^* are different from functional heads within the CP domain like Topic or Force in that the former have grammatical functions connected to lexical heads such as case-marking and the assignment of an external θ-role, whereas the latter do not have such grammatical functions. Similarly, 1D objects also consist of simple elements like events and a specific time anchor and receive a simple existential interpretation.[29]

On the other hand, multiple dimensions are composed of complex 1D-elements (cf. lexical projections). Given that functional projections within the CP domain are projections where new functional heads are added to lexical ones, it is natural to think that multiple dimensions correspond to them. Thus, I suggest that the multiple dimensions deal with discourse-oriented properties, such as, topic and focus, evidential and modality and quantifier-related

---

[27] This is reasonable given that θ-properties of an event structure are satisfied within vP/v^*P.

[28] For example, Chomsky (1986*b*) suggests that TP corresponds to a Complete Functional Complex in which all grammatical roles like the subject and the object are satisfied. Additionally, Hale & Keyser (1993*a*) assume that TP is the syntactic projection where the Lexical Relational Structure is fully expressed.

[29] Lanko Marušič (p.c.) points out the possibility that aspect rather than tense is the key to represent proposition. Although I have to admit that aspect may play an important role in the determination of truth conditions, it seems that the reference time aspect represents is subject to tense in some sense, implying that tense is a supra element. I leave this question for future research.

interpretation (cf. wh-scope), which are usually treated by functional items heading functional projections within the CP domain. This is natural because these functional heads have essentially different linguistic functions (cf. the indication of topic and operator quantification) from lexical elements, which denote properties.

Here, I assume that functional heads within the CP domain and their associated phrases, which are usually located in Spec, are assigned sophisticated interpretations (cf. discourse-oriented interpretations and quantified interpretations) in the multiple dimensions in SemC after they are transferred from SC.

There are three reasons favoring the assumption that SemC separately deals with lexical projections and functional projections within the CP domain in different domains.

First, as I said, lexical projections reflect event structures and their selectional requirements and θ-properties, due to which I suggest that the core units of 1D are events. On the other hand, semantic elements involved in the multiple dimensions, such as topic and wh-scope, are totally irrelevant to event structure and its requirements, which means that they cannot be dealt with by event structure of 1D. Thus, the semantic elements (cf. topic and evidentiality) relevant to functional projections within the CP domain should not be involved in 1D where events play an important role.

Second, given that the semantic units corresponding to functional projections within the CP domain cannot be dealt with by events, they should be treated by another type of semantic units. Because 1D and the multiple dimensions are totally different in nature and a 1D semantic unit is an event structure, it is natural to assume that the multiple dimensions not 1D involve the semantic units that yield semantic interpretations reflected by functional projections within the CP domain.

Finally, the linguistic elements mapped to 1D are lexical elements: nouns, verbs, adjectives, and adpositional phrases. These elements denote properties of (concrete and abstract) objects including conceptual ones, which is natural given that lexical elements are oriented to C-S. Also, some of these elements are countable: nouns can have plural forms and the event times denoted by verbs can be quantified by an adverbial phrase. On the other hand, functional heads within the CP domain do not denote properties of objects. Rather, they encode the point of view of the speaker with respect to which elements are topicalized, thematicized, or focalized in the discourse, the evidentiality of the proposition denoted by the sentence, and so on. In addition, these elements are not countable in the sense that lexical items are. In short, these elements are fundamentally different from lexical items which are mapped to 1D. Thus,

1D should not be able to deal with these functional heads. Below, I argue that these functional heads denote I-S semantic properties which are reflected by multiple dimensions.

There is abundant evidence that functional projections within the CP domain correspond to the sorts of semantic properties that I argue are dealt with by multiple dimensions. Rizzi (1997) and Speas (2004) (as well as the papers in Rizzi 2004) demonstrate that functional heads within the CP-domain are strongly connected to discourse-oriented interpretations, evidentiality and modality. For example, in Italian (Rizzi 1997), topicalized and focused elements are clearly located in functional projections within the CP domain (topicalized elements are indicated in bold and focused ones are underlined):

(6) a. A **Gianni**, <u>questo</u>, domani gli   dovremmo dire.
         to Gianni this   tomorrow to-him should   tell.2SG
         'As for Gianni, this, you should tell it to him tomorrow.'

     b. **Un libro di poesie**, <u>a Gianni</u>, lo regalerete.
         a   book of poems to Gianni you will-give-it
         'As for a book of poems, Gianni, you will give it to him.'

In fact, it is well known that topicalized elements appear to be universally located in sentence-initial positions, which suggests that topic-markers are located in the functional projections within the CP domain. Also, some authors argue that topic elements need to be initially interpreted in a special fashion in semantics (see Portner and Yabushita 2002). In our terms, it can be said that they need to be mapped into multiple dimensions. We can observe similar phenomena in other types of topic constructions such as hanging-topic left dislocation (7a) and contrastive left dislocation (7b) in German and clitic left dislocation (7c) in Greek (see Grohmann 2003, where these examples are taken from, for discussion of such topic constructions):[30]

(7) a. **Diesen Mann** — ihn habe ich noch nie   gesehen.
         this.ACC man   him have I   yet never seen
         'This man, I have never seen him before.'

     b. **Diesen Mann**, den   kenne ich nicht.
         this   man   that-one.ACC know I   not
         'This man, I do not know him.'

---

[30] Akira Watanabe and Chris Tancredi (p.c.) point out that a potential problem for my proposal is raised by the fact that phrases can be focused even in situ. One possibility is that these elements are licensed in situ via agreement with a focus operator (cf. Bruening 2001) in the CP domain and indirectly assigned a focus interpretation.

c. **Afton** **ton** **andra,** dhen ton ksero.
   this.ACC the.ACC man.ACC not him know.1SG
   'This man, I do not know him.'

In Japanese, a topic element (NP-*wa*) must be positioned sentence-initially to be interpreted as a genuine topic. This can be seen clearly in the sentences in (8), where a generic interpretation is possible only when the topic element is located sentence-initially:[31]

(8) a. **Doobutu-wa** riku-ni sum-u.
        animals-TOP land-on live-PRES
        'As for animals, they live on land.'

     b. Riku-ni doobutu-wa sum-u.
        land-on animals-TOP live-PRES
        'Animals will live on land.'

Given these observations, it is not unreasonable to assume that topic elements are positioned in peripheral functional projections and that they are mapped into the multiple dimensions in HDS, where they receive a discourse-oriented interpretation.

Japanese has numerous particles expressing modality and evidentiality (cf. Endo 2006, 2007), which are also located in functional projections in the CP domain (that these sentence-final particles appear in the right, as opposed to left, periphery simply follows from the fact that Japanese is a head-final language):

(9) a. Kyoko-ga ku-ru-yo.
        Kyoko-NOM come-PRES-emphatic
        'I am sure that Kyoko will come.'

     b. Kyoko-ga ku-ru-kana.
        Kyoko-NOM come-PRES-uncertain
        'I'm wondering if Kyoko comes.'

Speas (2004) observes that evidential morphemes appear in sentence-final peripheral positions in Quechua:

(10) a. Wan˜u-nqa-paq-mi.
        it-will-die-evidential
        'It will die (I assert).'

---

[31] NP-*wa* in (8b) is interpreted as a contrastive topic. Here, I assume that a contrastive topic is also located in a functional projection within the CP domain, and mapped into the multiple dimensions, though it is positioned in a lower position than a genuine topic element. See Munakata (2006) for discussion.

b. Wan˜u-nqa-paq-shi.
    it-will-die-evidential
    'It will die (I was told).'

c. Wan˜u-nqa-paq-chi.
    it-will-die-evidential
    'It will die (perhaps).'

Given these sorts of examples, I assume that evidential morphemes are also universally located in functional projections within the CP domain. Also, because evidential elements can be said to take scope over propositions, it is natural to think that these evidential morphemes are mapped into multiple dimensions.

I schematize my proposals regarding HDS below:

(11) *Hierarchical Dimensional Structure (HDS)*

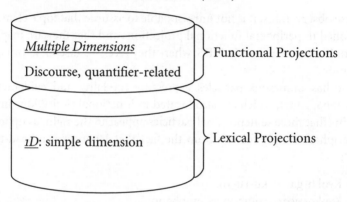

Suppose that relevant functional heads and accompanying NPs need to be interpreted in the appropriate dimension in HDS. If so, IC should require an appropriate mapping of these syntactic materials in transferring SC into SemC (cf. Diesing 1992; Chierchia 1995). I call this IC the Mapping Condition (MC):

(12) *Mapping Condition*
     Syntactic materials are mapped into the appropriate dimension, depending on their syntactic height.

Given my proposal that TP is the maximal lexical projection, MC requires it to be mapped into 1D by Multiple Transfer, whereas functional projections within the CP domain are necessarily mapped into multiple dimensions. This systematic correspondence between the syntactic structures created by SC and HDS implies that the latter, a property of SemC, characterizes the former and that MC is a necessary IC assuring an appropriate mapping.

Returning to the question raised at the beginning of this subsection, it is clear that semantic interpretation is directly related to HDS, which is the mechanism that gives a semantic interpretation to a transferred syntactic object. Also, since MC dictates the dimension where syntactic materials are mapped is determined by their height in SC, the influence on the semantic interpretation should be reflected in SC. Given that 1D corresponds to lexical projections and multiple dimensions correspond to functional projections within the CP domain, a syntactic operation that dislocates syntactic materials from lexical into functional projections should trivially result in influencing the semantic interpretation. Thus it follows that this kind of syntactic operation, for which I have argued that *Throwing in* is the sole candidate, always influences the semantic interpretation and, consequently, satisfies NOC.

3.5.3 Throwing in *and* Kicking out *Revisited*

In this section, I discuss *Throwing in* and *Kicking out* in more detail based on the architecture of HDS proposed in the previous section. I will argue that there are two types of phases—lexical phases and functional phases—and suggest that this categorization of phase can be derived from IC and HDS.

As discussed above, *Throwing in* a functional head, which I argued is the only possible syntactic warping operation, enables SC to generate a higher functional projection, and moves a relevant NP to this projection if its Spec must be filled for an EPP reason.[32] Given MC, this should result in mapping this functional head and accompanying NP into a higher dimension in HDS, where a new richer interpretation is made available. In sum, application of *Throwing in* results in projecting the thrown-in functional head and an accompanying NP into a higher dimension and influencing the interpretation by SemC, trivially satisfying NOC without requiring look-ahead; hence it is always justified when available.[33]

In this section, I would like to ask a further question: What drives *Throwing in*? As argued in Section 3.3, the numeration is based on the event structure of a lexical predicative head, a property of C-S and determined by selectional requirements and θ-properties of this event structure (cf. Chomsky 2000,

---

[32] I assume that an EPP feature is attached to a functional head when it is taken from the lexicon if its selectional properties require its Spec to be filled.

[33] In Munakata (2006, 2007), where it is proposed that the "multiple dimensions" consist of three different dimensions, I assume that information about the dimension in which functional heads are interpreted is specified in the lexicon. Given NOC, this implies that *Throwing in* is unavailable when there are only the functional heads which are interpreted in a lower dimension(s) than those which have been already inserted. Also, NOC may be stated in a similar way: *Throwing in* applies freely if it inserts a functional head which is interpreted in a higher dimension than the current one. I am grateful to Roger Martin (p.c.) for this suggestion.

2004*a*, 2004*b* and Collins 2002) and thus contains only lexical heads and lexically oriented functional heads such as *v*/*v** and T. SC can only generate TP from the numeration. Also, given that a sentence is supposed to express an event, syntactic elements which an event structure selects are obligatory in nature (cf. the Conservation Condition) and should be always reflected in the numeration.

On the other hand, I argued that functional heads within the CP domain are irrelevant to selectional properties and θ-properties of an event structure and optional in the sense that they need not always appear.[34] Thus they need to be introduced into the syntactic workspace directly from the lexicon derivationally. *Throwing in* is indispensable in order for functional heads to be introduced and obtain the interpretations available in the multiple dimensions (discourse-oriented properties). Moreover, the optionality of the application of *Throwing in* explains why these interpretations are optional (see the discussion in Section 3.6 below).

3.5.3.1 Kicking out *and HDS*   Above I proposed that SC must apply either *Kicking out* or *Throwing in* once the syntactic elements in the numeration (or subnumeration) have been exhausted. If *Kicking out* applies, the syntactic object is removed from the computational workspace, inducing Multiple Transfer. *Kicking out* must apply to the maximal lexical projection TP in cases where SC does not resort to *Throwing in*. Even in situations where *Throwing in* does apply, *Kicking out* must still apply at least to the resulting syntactic object when SC cannot continue any syntactic computation (e.g. when application of *Throwing in* is no longer able to satisfy NOC and is inapplicable), triggering Transfer of this syntactic object to SemC and PhonC.

As discussed in the previous subsections, MC requires that syntactic materials are mapped into an appropriate dimension. This means that MC also requires that SC should apply *Kicking out* so that syntactic materials can be transferred to the appropriate dimensions depending on their syntactic height. Thus Multiple Transfer is conceptually justified, given HDS and MC.[35] I speculate that in order to obey MC and transfer syntactic materials appropriately into HDS, SC must kick out a complement of a functional head as soon as it

---

[34] It might be argued that at least one of the functional heads within the CP domain is necessary because of the need for sentential force to be expressed. However, this is not the case. As discussed in the previous section, an event only needs to be fixed at a specific time in order that it is evaluated with respect to its truth-value, which might mean that TP is equivalent to a proposition. Also, a complementizer like *that*, which is also a functional C-head, apparently does not always need to be present, to determine sentential force.

[35] Single Transfer would not suffice, since it can only map syntactic materials into one of the two types of dimensions in HDS, which violates the MC.

throws in this functional head and its Spec is filled by an appropriate NP (if it has an EPP feature).

Also, I suggest that the need to apply Transfer to the output stemming from the syntactic derivation that exhausts the elements in the numeration and the output of application of *Throwing in* follows from the Conservation Condition, which states that it is necessary for C-S and I-S properties to be clearly differentiated from each other and reflected in different places in syntactic structures and in the mapping to SemC. Thus, *Kicking out* ought to apply after application of *Throwing in*, triggering Transfer.

Then, we can derive the timing of Multiple Transfer and the phase status from the interaction between *Throwing in* and *Kicking out*. Because *Kicking out* induces Multiple Transfer, Multiple Transfer also occurs soon after *Throwing in* is applied. Consequently, the timing of Multiple Transfer depends on application of *Throwing in* as well as the availability of this operation. Since *Throwing in* and *Kicking out* are conditioned by IC (i.e. the Conservation Condition, NOC, the MC) and HDS, the timing of Multiple Transfer and what categories count as phases are also derived.

3.5.3.2 *The Inclusiveness Condition and C-S*   In this subsection, I return to the Conservation Condition in (1), which regulates the mapping of the properties of C-S to I-S. In particular, I will show that the Conservation Condition is responsible for one part of the strong version of the Inclusiveness Condition.

The strong version of the Inclusiveness Condition states that no features or syntactic items can be introduced in the course of the syntactic computation by SC (cf. Chomsky 2000, 2001). This also prohibits SC from accessing the lexicon more than once in a given derivation, disallowing an operation like *Throwing in*.[36] Apparently, this condition strongly denies the existence of *Throwing in*, which means that the approach adopted in this chapter faces a potentially serious problem.

Of course, it is reasonable for the Inclusiveness Condition to prohibit the introduction of syntactic artefacts, such as traces which are not present in the lexicon and are hard to motivate within the minimalist framework (cf. Chomsky 1995, 2000, 2005, Hornstein 1998, 2001, and Nunes 2004). However, with respect to features and elements present in the lexicon, it is not

---

[36] I will refer to this part of the strong version of the Inclusiveness Condition as "one-time lexical access."

Throwing in does not violate the weak version of the Inclusiveness Condition, which does not restrict access to the lexicon but merely prohibits SC from introducing any syntactic artefacts such as traces, chains or indices (see Hornstein 1998 and Nunes 2004).

Other researchers have proposed that SC freely accesses the lexicon throughout the derivation (cf. Collins 1997, 2002 and Frampton & Gutmann 2003), which obviously violates one-time lexical access of Inclusiveness and is also incompatible with the "mixed" theory proposed here.

unnatural that the Inclusiveness Condition allows SC to introduce them into the syntactic derivational workspace in the course of its syntactic computation; that is, *Throwing in* should be possible.

In the minimalist program, the Inclusiveness Condition is normally taken for granted and presumed to be natural. However, generative linguists have not shed much light on this part of the Inclusiveness Condition in view of IC.

One possibility is that the Inclusiveness Condition is a sort of economy condition imposed on the computation, which restricts available materials to features and syntactic lexical and functional elements in the lexicon. Given this, one may say that economy necessitates this part of the Inclusiveness Condition, because adding new objects is in itself uneconomical. Nonetheless, economy does not seem to work in this way.

Although this sort of economy of design (computational efficiency) may reasonably prohibit SC from introducing new items into a syntactic derivation if it results in added computational complexity, more typically we observe economy of the locality type; that is, the computational mechanism of human language is characterized by economy conditions which require that computation proceeds step by step in some local domain, without look-ahead (cf. phases). For example, suppose that syntactic derivations proceed locally. After the numeration is made, SC may create a subnumeration from the numeration, and then builds its syntactic derivation based on syntactic elements in this subnumeration. Then, after it finishes building its subsyntactic derivation locally, it returns to the numeration and repeats the same procedure again and again until it completes building the entire syntactic structure. This kind of computational mechanism suggests that computational economy obeyed by the language faculty may prefer computational locality of syntactic derivation to computational efficiency of the sort discussed in the beginning of this paragraph and may allow SC to introduce a new syntactic element or feature if this introduction is favorable given computational locality. If so, economy does not necessitate one-time lexical access of the Inclusiveness Condition.

Also, non-one-time lexical access does not seem incompatible with the view of Ontological Minimalism (Martin & Uriagereka 2000) given that natural systems often employ mechanisms that create a new entity by adding some feature or object to an existing entity; for instance, a biological organ may create a new kind of protein by adding and combining amino acids with an existing protein. Moreover, the language faculty itself admits this in PhonC, where phonological operations add phonetic features or prosodic features quite freely.

Then, what is responsible for the one-time lexical access part of the Inclusiveness Condition, in so far as it holds? My answer is that it should be attributed to the Conservation Condition in (1), which is deeply connected to the properties of C-S involving the conceptual structure of lexical properties and an event structure.

Note that according to the proposal adopted in this chapter, the numeration is connected to C-S and the requirements of C-S, which form the basis to give a sentential meaning, are reflected in the input to SC, whereas the output is accessed by I-S at the interface with SemC. Consequently, I-S accesses the properties of C-S by looking into HDS. In addition, as discussed in Section 3.4, given that an event structure is fixed and its selectional requirements and θ-properties are determined in C-S, it is natural that C-S imposes the Conservation Condition on the language faculty, requiring it to reflect these properties in the numeration and preserve them throughout the syntactic computation. Consequently, it is natural to assume that SC has to preserve C-S properties throughout the syntactic derivation, conveying them to I-S. In other words, that SC should be prohibited from inserting new syntactic objects or features is plausibly motivated by the need to ensure that C-S properties are fully reflected in 1D of HDS.

As discussed in Section 3.4, the Conservation Condition imposes many restrictions on SC. For example, it requires SC to initially merge an argument of an event structure into a θ-position, due to the fact that a θ-grid is also a property of C-S, projecting C-S properties onto syntactic derivation up to TP and 1D of HDS in SemC without affecting any changes to it. Then, these C-S properties SC has conserved are properly read off by I-S.[37] It seems that the one-time lexical access part of the Inclusiveness Condition should follow from the Conservation Condition as well. This can be accomplished by slightly revising the Conservation Condition as in (13):

---

[37] It might be possible to assume that an EPP feature on T (as well as an additional EPP feature on v^*) is necessary to reflect the properties of C-S. As discussed above, T is necessarily involved in the numeration because an event structure necessarily selects a temporal argument which expresses a specific time and T embodies this temporal argument syntactically (cf. Stowell 1981); in this sense, it is natural to conclude that tense has C-S properties and T is selected by C-S to express an event structure appropriately. Turning to an EPP feature on T, this feature may be necessary to complete TP and map this syntactic object into 1D, if one speculates that the only syntactic object that SC may ship into 1D is TP by the MC. More specifically, satisfaction of this feature and subsequent A-movement into TP-Spec may be used as obvious signal indicating that TP has been completed, differentiating the completed syntactic object (i.e. TP) which reflects all properties of C-S from a syntactic object (cf. v^*P/vP/VP) purely based on an event structure and its selectional requirements and letting SC kick out this completed syntactic object and transfer it into 1D. In this sense, A-movement (specially, A-movement into TP-Spec) might be driven by the Conservation Condition. Uninterpretable Case-features on v^* and T are possibly selected for the same reason.

(13)   *Conservation Condition (revised)*
SC must conserve the properties of C-S without any change throughout a syntactic derivation to reflect these properties properly in the syntactic derivation and mirror them in 1D of HDS.

The one-time lexical access part of Inclusiveness, as derived from the Conservation Condition in (13), dictates that SC should use only syntactic elements in the numeration, the interface to C-S, to generate a lexical maximal projection TP. However, I argue that nothing prevents SC from throwing in functional heads within the CP domain after TP is generated. This is a natural consequence of the current proposal because functional heads within the CP domain are not involved in the numeration and irrelevant to C-S. Rather, these elements are relevant to intentional matters and seem to be one of the properties of I-S. The Conservation Condition as stated in (13) is only concerned with preserving C-S properties, as expressed in the numeration, and does not prohibit the addition of I-S properties "on top" of those. SC thus does not need to observe the one-time lexical access part of Inclusiveness when generating functional projections within the CP domain.

This is a welcome result since, as discussed above, the properties of I-S can be mirrored in the syntactic derivation only by adding some syntactic objects or features in the course of the derivation and *Throwing in* satisfies this demand by inserting functional heads within the CP domain.

In the next section, I will discuss the parallel consistency between SC and SemC and the asymmetry between numeration/TP/simple dimension and *Throwing in*/CP/multiple dimensions, as well as address the question why *Throwing in* exists.

3.6 Parallelism and Asymmetry

In the previous sections, I suggested that the numeration corresponds to the lexical maximal projection TP. TP corresponds to 1D in HDS, the linguistic objects of which receive an existential interpretation. Also, I claimed that a lexical choice in the numeration is based on the properties of C-S and thus the numeration is obligatory. For this reason, the numeration is the source of TP, where these lexical properties are satisfied. In turn, TP is the source of 1D, where I assume syntactic arguments of an event structure must be reflected. In turn, I suggested that C-S imposes the Conservation Condition on SC, requiring that SC conserve the properties of C-S throughout a syntactic derivation so that these properties are reflected in the syntactic derivation and in 1D of HDS.

Because the Conservation Condition and MC require that SC should map TP into 1D in HDS, SC should kick out TP and transfer it to 1D after it exhausts syntactic elements in the numeration and generates TP, regardless of whether *Throwing in* applies. This implies that TP is always the target of Transfer and always constitutes a lexical phase.[38] A lexical phase is formed only after the selectional properties of T, such as an EPP and Case, are satisfied, filling TP-Spec, and TP has been "completed" (see *n.* 37).

On the other hand, I maintain that functional heads within the CP domain may be introduced into the syntactic derivational workspace only by *Throwing in*, which means that only this syntactic operation is able to generate functional projections within the CP domain. Also, I assumed that syntactic materials within these functional projections are mapped into multiple dimensions in HDS due to the MC, which suggests that these functional projections correspond to the multiple dimensions in HDS. Since the interpretations available in multiple dimensions express the properties of I-S, it may be that these functional projections reflect the properties of I-S. Also, I argued that *Throwing in* is optional and thus needs to satisfy NOC to apply, which results in the optionality of the functional projections within the CP domain. Because these functional projections are optional, the corresponding interpretations in multiple dimensions are optional. This optionality is plausible given that the properties of I-S apparently do not always need to be expressed linguistically.

Because *Kicking out* (and Transfer) applies after the application of *Throwing in*, functional projections within the CP domain should be the target of Transfer, forming (layers of) phases. I refer to this type of phase, which is deeply connected to properties of I-S, as a "functional phase."

This formation of the two types of phases (lexical phases and functional phases) has an interesting consequence, given that phases are responsible for syntactic locality within the minimalist program. That is, syntactic locality should be shaped by the formation of a lexical phase and a functional phase.[39]

---

[38] It might be possible that there is a subphase within the lexical phase TP so that v^*P also constitutes a phase. I will not pursue this possibility in this chapter.

[39] The C/I model gives rise to implications concerning the PIC (cf. Chomsky 2001, 2004a), although the differences from other models are minimal in many respects. For example, since a lexical phase (TP) is transferred soon after *Throwing in* applies, syntactic items must move to edge positions of functional phases (functional projections within the CP domain) in order to "escape" from the lexical phase. I assume that this kind of movement is EPP-driven and is made possible when a functional head is thrown in with an EPP feature. I assume that TP is transferred immediately after any EPP feature on the functional head is satisfied. This implies that syntactic elements cannot escape from a lexical phase if they remain within TP, which means that edge positions of TP cannot be used as escape hatch. Also, edge positions of v^*P (and possibly, vP) cannot be used as escape hatch for the same reason (vP/v^*P adjunction, however, may be possible, and perhaps even necessary for minimality reasons; cf. Boeckx 2003). Consequently, vP/v^*P/TP-adjunction and CP-adjunction are differentiated, unlike other models (cf. Chomsky 2004a). In addition, this may suggest that successive-cyclic movement takes place not by

TABLE 3.1 Parallel consistency and asymmetry

	Input	Syntax	Semantics
Obligatory	Numeration	TP (lexical projections)	1D (event + tense)
Optional	Throwing in	CP (functional projections)	multiple dimensions

Phase status is clearly derived from the proposed division of C-I into C-S and I-S with different syntactic inputs (lexical categories plus $v/v^*/T$ in the numeration as opposed to functional heads within the CP domain, which are introduced by *Throwing in*). It is easy for SemC to interpret syntactic structures if objects coding C-S-related lexical information and objects I-S-related functional information are transferred separately; different types of interpretations can be assigned without confusion. In addition, different properties of lexical items and functional items within the CP domain are also derived from the C/I model since these syntactic items are different types of syntactic inputs corresponding to these two different systems. If Transfer works multiply in this way, different types of phases (the target of Transfer) are inevitable.

Also, a distinction between lexical items and lexical-functional items, on one hand, and functional heads within the CP domain, on the other, follows from properties of C-S and I-S. Namely, lexical items as well as lexical-functional items such as v/v^* and T are associated with the properties of C-S and selected by these properties and C-S, whereas functional heads within the CP domain are associated with I-S and express the properties of this system.

We can now see that there exist the asymmetries in Table 3.1 between obligatoriness and optimality across inputs, syntactic projections, and semantic interpretations in terms of HDS, which I refer to as "parallel consistency and asymmetry".

As was discussed above, the parallel consistency of syntax and semantics is rather natural because it is regulated by MC and perhaps arises from internal consistency within the language faculty, whose source is not certain. Also, the Conservation Condition gives a plausible explanation to why there exists consistency among the numeration, TP and 1D.

Given that an event structure and θ-properties and selectional requirements of lexical heads are properties of C-S and obligatory, I argued that, for this reason, C-S imposes the Conservation Condition on the language faculty,

way of Spec of v^*P (or vP or TP) but only by way of Spec of CP (more precisely, Specs of functional phases within the CP domain) as has been assumed in more traditional analyses, because only Spec of CP works as an "escape hatch" under the model advocated here.

necessitating that these properties of C-S should be always expressed in the numeration, functioning as input to SC. Also, the Conservation Condition requires that these properties of C-S be conserved throughout the syntactic computation and mirrored in 1D of HDS. This is the reason for the fact that the properties of C-S are expressed with consistency in the numeration, TP and 1D.

The optional side reflects the properties of I-S, which are also linguistically optional in that speakers do not always necessarily express an intention. For example, speakers do not always use a sentential topic or focused element, even though these can be expressed by topic-markers and focus-related positions, and so on, belonging to discourse-oriented properties. The optional syntactic operation *Throwing in* is also relevant to the properties of I-S, because its application results in creating the intentional interpretations available in the multiple dimensions of HDS. I-S deals with the optional side of the language faculty, necessitating the consistency among *Throwing in*, functional projections within the CP domain and multiple dimensions in HDS. Finally, I-S imposes NOC on SC, which regulates the *Throwing in* of functional heads, restricting their appearance to multiple dimensions in HDS.

Note that the correspondence between lexical/functional phases and simple/multiple dimensions in HDS naturally follows from the C/I model. Given the different interpretational characteristics of conceptual and intentional matters, it is not likely that SemC interprets lexical phases and functional phases in a similar fashion. Thus, in addition to assuming that the syntactic computational mechanism transfers these phases separately, it is natural that SemC incorporates a hierarchical structure, making use of different domains, namely HDS, for these phases to be computed. This parallel computation between SC and SemC seems not only empirically plausible but conceptually reasonable under the C/I model, given that conceptual and intentional matters are distinct and that C-S and I-S require the language faculty to reflect these properties in different ways by imposing different IC (e.g. the Conservation Condition and NOC).

We should also consider why *Throwing in* is necessary and intimately related to functional projections within the CP domain and multiple dimensions in HDS. In order for the external cognitive systems to reflect its relevant properties on SC, an input is necessary. Because C-S is connected to the numeration, which is an input to SC, it can reflect its properties. On the other hand, because I-S is connected to SemC, there is no input corresponding to the properties of I-S. Thus, the language faculty should resort to some other syntactic operation which may function as input to SC in order to reflect the properties of I-S. This syntactic operation is *Throwing in* functional heads within the CP domain.

TABLE 3.2 Parallel consistency and asymmetry (refined)

	Obligatory	Optional
IC	Conservation Condition	NOC
Input	Numeration	*Throwing in*
Syntactic element	lexical items & v/v^*/T	functional items
SC	TP	CP
	lexical maximal projection	functional projections
	lexical phase	functional phase
	A-movement	A$'$-movement
SemC	1D/ simple dimension	multiple dimensions

Then, I-S can reflect its properties only through *Throwing in* and the language faculty satisfies these properties of I-S by this syntactic operation; therefore, *Throwing in* is necessary. For this reason, it is optional because the properties of I-S are optionally expressed in language unlike the properties of C-S.

We can now consider a more refined sketch of the properties illustrating "parallel consistency and asymmetry," illustrated in Table 3.2.

The exhibited parallel consistency and asymmetry originates from IC and properties of the external systems. On the obligatory side, conceptual matters are indispensable for language. Consequently, C-S requires that conceptual properties are reflected in SC and 1D by imposing the Conservation Condition. On the optional side, intentional matters are optionally expressed in language, and only when this is the case does I-S necessitate that they are reflected in SC and the multiple dimensions in HDS.

Needless to say, I-S always processes the semantic interpretation of sentences by accessing SemC. For example, it contributes to filling in the linguistic meaning by fixing the reference of nominal elements, such as proper nouns and pronouns, because this system is responsible for the determination of reference and the interpretation of binding relationships.[40]

Chomsky (2008) claims that the language faculty expresses a "dual semantics," with conceptual matters, such as generalized event structure, on the one hand, and intentional matters, such as discourse-related and scopal properties, on the other hand. Chomsky argues that C-I incorporates such a dual semantics and that the language faculty seeks to satisfy the duality in an optimal way, External Merge (i.e. initial Merge) serving one function and Internal Merge (i.e. movement) the other. The C/I model derives this dual nature of semantics

---

[40] Lanko Marušič (p.c.) points out that another possibility is that sentences always make use of topic and focus, which may sometimes be expressed by null topic, focus, and modality elements, which means that SC always resorts to *Throwing in*.

because the language faculty is connected with C-S and I-S by way of different interfaces—namely, the numeration and SemC. Additionally, the A/A′ distinction can be easily stated within the C/I model: lexical phases consist of A-positions and involve A-movement whereas functional phases consist of A′-positions and involve A′-movement. This asymmetry is also reflected in SemC, because the properties of C-S and I-S need to be expressed in the different domains of SemC, as discussed above.

3.7 Conclusion

To summarize, the C/I model is favored in view of IC and the Strong Minimalist Thesis since, as I have shown, taking C-S and I-S to be independent systems, which interface with the language faculty by way of distinct interfaces, enables us to characterize the architecture of SC and SemC, including the "parallel consistency and asymmetry" illustrated in Table 3.2, in terms of IC and to provide principled conceptual explanations for several syntactic notions, such as the nature of phases and so on. In particular, recognition of the "parallel consistency and asymmetry" is important because it reveals the way in which C-S and I-S unitarily characterize the syntactic computational mechanism and SemC. C-S, by imposing the Conservation Condition, requires that syntactic elements expressing C-S properties always appear in the numeration and are merged into A-positions according to θ-grids. Such elements exhibit A-properties and are transferred into the C-S-related dimension in SemC (cf. 1D). According to I-S, on the other hand, syntactic elements expressing certain I-S-related properties are (optionally) inserted into functional projections within the CP domain by *Throwing in*. Such elements possess A′-properties and are transferred into multiple dimensions where complex (intentional) semantic interpretations are assigned. The "asymmetry" must be observed because C-S and I-S involve different properties and access different interfaces, requiring the language faculty to differentiate these properties in SC and SemC by imposing different types of IC. The C/I-model can give a principled explanation to the asymmetry and consistency depicted in Table 3.2, showing that the language faculty may indeed be an optimal solution to IC.

4

Dislocation Effects, Uninterpretable Features, Functional Heads, and Parametric Variation: Consequences of Conflicting Interface Conditions

HEDDE ZEIJLSTRA

4.1 Introduction

In current minimalist reasoning language is assumed to be a "perfect" solution to the task of relating sound[1] and meaning (Chomsky 2000, 2001, 2005, 2008; Lasnik 2002). This perspective takes language to be an optimal solution to conditions that are imposed on the faculty of language by its neighboring mental modules, the Sensorimotor system and the Conceptual-Intentional systems.

However, the idea that language is "perfect" in this sense seems to be at odds with several "imperfections" found in grammar, such as agreement phenomena or the dislocation property. Implemented in linguistic theory, at least four properties of language appear to be "imperfections" rather than "perfections": (i) the existence of uninterpretable formal features; (ii) dislocation; (iii) the cross-linguistic flexibility of morphosyntactic categories; and (iv) the existence of cross-linguistic variation.

In this chapter I argue that all four properties addressed above are not linguistic imperfections, but are actually predicted by the Perfectness Hypothesis. In a nutshell, I argue that the different conditions imposed on the faculty of language are not always compatible to each other, and that therefore the

---

[1] As is well known, sound is interpreted in a broad sense, including signs in sign languages, gestures, etc.

faculty of language can offer multiple, equally optimal solutions to these conflicting interface conditions. In this sense, fulfilling interface conditions is some kind of a trade-off. Being a perfect solution to one interface condition may imply that another interface condition cannot be maximally solved, and vice versa. Hence perfect solutions to interface conditions, which are in conflict with other interface conditions, can only exist by virtue of less perfect solutions to these other interface conditions. Consequently, some linguistic imperfections are consequences of conflicting interface conditions and thus epiphenomenal in nature.

The central claim of this chapter is that the existence of uninterpretable formal features, dislocation effects, the cross-linguistic flexibility of morphosyntactic categories and the existence of cross-linguistic variation are all epiphenomena of the Perfectness Hypothesis.

This chapter is organized as follows: In Section 4.2, I discuss Chomsky's Strongest Minimalist Thesis (Chomsky 2005) which takes the language to be an optimal solution to interface conditions that are imposed on the faculty of language and I discuss the nature of two such interface conditions (one sound-based, one meaning-based). In Section 4.3, I introduce the four linguistic "imperfections" and explain why they appear to be problematic for the Perfectness Hypothesis. In Section 4.4, I discuss the notion of optimality in grammatical architecture and demonstrate why dislocation effects and uninterpretable formal features result from conflicting interface conditions. In Section 4.5, I discuss the notion of functional heads and projections and I argue that the set of formal features is not universal but triggered during L1 acquisition as a consequence of the existence of uninterpretable features. In Section 4.6, I argue that the different marking strategies that are pregiven by a "perfect" grammatical architecture constitute the range of parametric variation that is attested in natural language. Section 4.7, finally, concludes.

4.2 The Perfectness Hypothesis

4.2.1 *The Strongest Minimalist Thesis*

Chomsky's Strongest Minimalist Thesis (SMT) states that "language is an optimal solution to interface conditions that the Faculty of Language (FL) must satisfy" (Chomsky 2005: 3). This thesis, tracing back to the philosophical view that language enables human beings to express their thoughts (a view endorsed in the biolinguistic program) is implemented in the current perspective on the architecture in the following way: The faculty of language (FL), a mental organ, is connected to both systems that deal with the expression of a sentence and the meaning it conveys, the Sensorimotor (SM) system and the Conceptual-Intentional (C-I) system respectively, as well as with an instance of memory, the lexicon. This is illustrated in (1) below:

(1)

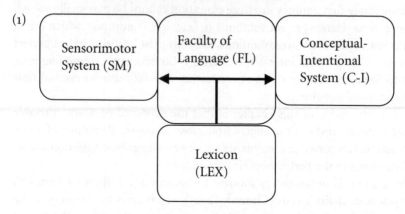

In the diagram in (1) the input for FL consists of a lexical numeration and the output (after separating at Spell-Out) passes on either to the SM interface or to the C-I interface. Consequently, since the output of FL is the input for the SM and C-I systems, the outputs of the derivation should be fully legible to each connected mental component. This amounts to saying that the two interpretational systems impose conditions on the structures that have to be met at the interface.[2]

It is important to distinguish two different types of conditions: hard and soft conditions. Hard conditions are conditions that must always be satisfied. The Principle of Compositionality, which states that the meaning of a sentence follows from the meaning of its parts and the way in which these parts are ordered, for instance, is a hard condition that the C-I system imposes on FL. If Compositionality cannot be applied, the derivation will crash at the level of Logical Form (LF), the interface between FL and C-I. Soft conditions, on the other hand, are conditions that express preference. Economy conditions are well-known examples, such as the last-resort constraint with respects to movement. This constraint does not rule out movement, but only states that movement must be as late as possible. In other words, it favors late movement over early movement, but does not exclude early movement *a priori*. Such a constraint does not rule out any kind of early movement *a priori*, but compares a number of possible derivations and assigns grammaticality to only one candidate.

[2] I do not take into account the possibility that the lexicon should be considered a mental module as well. Note that nothing in this study is incompatible with that idea either.

Hence, in principle, a grammatical architecture like (1) allows in total four kinds of conditions: Both neighboring mental modules may impose both hard and soft conditions. Whereas hard conditions must be completely satisfied, soft conditions must be optimally satisfied.

However, nothing entails that the different soft conditions cannot be in conflict to each other. On the contrary, it is much more likely that, if mental components function autonomously, soft conditions from different mental modules are not always compatible. It could in fact very well be the case that by satisfying a particular interface condition imposed by the SM system, some other interface condition, for instance applying at the C-I interface, cannot be maximally satisfied any more, and vice versa. This implies that if two soft conditions are in conflict with each other multiple, equally optimal, solutions may fulfill these conditions.

Hence, natural language cannot be seen as a single optimal solution to different interface conditions, but its various instantiations should be thought of as multiple, equally complex, solutions to different interface conditions. The central aim of this chapter is to reduce existing cross-linguistic, or more specifically parametric, variation as a result from SMT. This amounts to adopting the following hypothesis:

(2)   *The Strongest Parametric Variation Hypothesis* (SPVH)
      The Strongest Minimalist Thesis governs the entire range of parametric variation.

Under (2) parametric variation is no longer an imperfection that natural language seems to exhibit, but an epiphenomenon of the supposed perfection of natural language.

Thus, the SPVH leads to a view on individual grammars that takes the SMT not only to be a hypothesis on FL and the nature of natural language. The SMT now also applies to individual natural languages and possible grammars. The variety of natural languages, or to be more precise, the different characteristics they exhibit, follow from different conflicting soft conditions imposed at the interfaces FL shares with other mental components.

Before discussing the range of variation that the SPVH constitutes, let us first discuss two important interface conditions that are imposed on FL.

4.2.2 *Optimal Design in the Architecture of Grammar*

In this subsection I take a closer look at the kind of hard and soft conditions that apply at the two interfaces. I first argue that the hard C-I condition that interpretation follows from Functional Application and Predicate Modification results in a simplicity metric that favors structures that lack uninterpretable features over structures that have them. Then I argue that, from the SM perspective, light prosodic structure is preferred over rich prosodic structure.

4.2.2.1 *Optimal Design from the C-I Interface Perspective*   Let us try to enter the mind of a purely semantically (C-I) biased language engineer in order to investigate what kind of conditions the C-I systems impose on FL. From the semantic perspective the most important requirement on linguistic structure is that it allows for compositional interpretation (Frege 1892; Janssen 1983; Partee 1984; Hendriks 1993; Szabó 2000). This means that a particular inter-pretation of a non-terminal element α (as in (3)), $\|\alpha\|$ follows from $\|\beta\|$ and $\|\gamma\|$ through Functional Application (FA) or Predicate Modification (PM), as defined by Heim & Kratzer (1998) and illustrated for extensional semantics in (4) and (5) respectively.[3]

(3)

(4)   *FA*: If f is the set of daughters of branching node α, and $[[\beta]]$ is in $D_{<a,b>}$ and $[[\gamma]]$ is in D_a, then $[[\alpha]] = [[\beta]]([[\gamma]])$

(5)   *PM*: If $\{\beta, \gamma\}$ is the set of daughters of branching node α, and $[[\beta]]$ and $[[\gamma]]$ are both in $D_{<e,t>}$, then $[[\alpha]] = \lambda x.[\ [[\beta]](x)\ \&\ [[\gamma]](x)]$

Consequently, from the semantic/C-I perspective there is no reason to assume more structure to be present than the compositional interpretation of the top node requires. In other words, there is no reason to assume any abstract struc-ture projected by semantically vacuous elements. If a particular lexical item does not contribute to the meaning of the sentence there is no need to assume its presence at LF. This assumption leads to the following two conclusions: (i) the C-I systems prefer no semantically vacuous elements at the level of LF as they cannot be motivated by any C-I condition and (ii) nothing *a priori* rules out the presence of semantically vacuous material at LF. These two conditions allow us to formulate the following semantic simplicity metric:

(6)   *Semantic Simplicity Metric*
        A structural representation R for a substring of input text S is simpler than an alternative representation R′ iff R contains fewer uninterpretable features than R′.

---

[3] For illustratory purposes I have only included the extensional definitions.

Note that (6) is a weaker version of Full Interpretation (Chomsky 1995) as it does not forbid the occurrence of semantically vacuous material at LF.[4] If for an independent reason uninterpretable material can be motivated at LF, nothing would rule out the sentence. In the following section I demonstrate that SM-based soft interface conditions may in fact require the presence of semantically vacuous material at LF.

4.2.2.2 *Optimal Design from the SM Interface Perspective*   It is a well-known fact about natural language that syntactic structure is not always identical to the simplest structure that meets all compositionality requirements. This must be due to the fact that language, apart from semantic requirements, also needs to satisfy conditions, which are imposed by the SM system. Otherwise, following the SMT, syntactic structure should only reflect the simplest possible configuration that would allow for a compositional interpretation. Once again, we should try to enter the mind of a language engineer, but this time the mind of a purely phonologically (SM) biased one.

Work by McCarthy (1986) and Hopper & Traugott (1993) on phonological simplicity and grammaticalization claims that the SM system prefers phonologically weak items over strong ones: affixes over clitics, particles over lexical words, etc. (see (7)).

(7) a. *Word > Foot > Syllable > Mora*   (McCarthy 1986)

     b. *Content word > Particle > Clitic > Affix*   (Hopper & Traugott 1993)

Although generalizations like the ones in (7) have been formulated from the nineteenth century onwards, these preferences are puzzling from the perspective of the SM system. In the previous subsection on semantics I argued that elements lacking meaning, i.e. elements that are uninterpretable for the C-I system, are dispreferred. But there is no preference in favor of "small meanings" over "large meanings." Hence, the fact that small words like affixes are preferred over big words such as content words may seem intuitive, as has been argued for in studies on grammaticalization, but the SM system does not disfavor large words in any way.

However, the crucial distinctions in (7) are not about word length, but about what separates different words or word parts. Adopting a proposal by Neeleman & van der Koot (2006) that prosodic representations are string-based, in the line of Chomsky & Halle (1968) and McCawley (1968), prosodic

---

[4] The idea that Full Interpretation requires that the semantic content of structures at LF must be interpretable and that there is no ban against uninterpretable material at LF, as long as its syntactic licensing requirements have been met, could be expected to rule in vacuous quantification. However, the constraint on vacuous quantification has been argued not to be a necessary constraint on syntax in the first place. See Potts (2002c) for a series of arguments in favor of this view.

categories (utterances (U), intonational phrases (I), prosodic phrases (Φ) prosodic words (ω), feet (F), and syllables (σ)), are considered to be prosodic boundaries. This means that phonological elements are interrupted by phonologically uninterpretable, unpronounceable, material, as their example (8) shows.

(8)   U John's ω father Φ suggested ω a two-seater I but ωJohn's ω mother Φ preferred ω a fur ω coat U.

Thus the preferences in (7) can be replaced by the single preference in (9).

(9) $\sigma > F > \omega > \Phi > I > U$

Similar to the semantic case, nothing *a priori* bans prosodic boundaries, but they are not motivated by the SM system, for it is a system that merely interprets phonological material. The fact that prosodic boundaries are neither motivated nor forbidden by the SM system, induces a phonological simplicity metric (10).

(10)   *Phonological Simplicity Metric*
       A structural representation R for a substring of input text S is simpler than an alternative representation R′ iff R contains fewer prosodic boundaries than R′.

What (10) reflects is that prosodic phrase boundaries are dispreferred over prosodic word boundaries, which in their turn are dispreferred over foot boundaries, etc. Note that (10) can be regarded as an SM variant of the Principle of Full Interpretation. In other words, the expression of two particular elements carrying semantic content preferably constitutes a single word (e.g. a root affix combination (11) rather than two different prosodic words (12)).

(11)   [$_{PW}$ Root$_1$-AF$_2$]

(12)   [[PW$_1$] ... [PW$_2$]]^5

Of course, it is not the case that structures that are prosodically richer than what would be desired from an SM-based perspective are excluded from natural language, as there is no principled motivation to rule out rich prosodic structures. Again, the preference takes the shape of a soft condition that prefers to assign poor rather than rich prosodic structure to a particular string of phonological elements.

---

^{5} In this study I concentrate only on the difference between affixes and prosodic words.

4.3 Four Linguistic "Imperfections"

In the previous section I have presented two different simplicity metrices that are both soft conditions imposed on FL. However, these two principles only induce the SM-based preference for poor prosodic structure and the CI-based preference against uninterpretable material. However, natural language features many more characteristics, which do not seem to be the result of the simplicity principle behind the SPVH (and therefore behind the SMT). For instance uninterpretable features are dispreferred from the Semantic Simplicity Metric, but still widely attested in natural language. In this chapter I introduce, next to the notion of uninterpretable features, three other instances of linguistic imperfections that do not seem to result from the SMMT: dislocation effects, the cross-linguistic flexibility of functional heads, and the existence of parametric variation. After this section, I demonstrate that each of these four linguistic imperfections are actually the result of the SPVH and are thus correct predictions of the Perfectness Hypothesis.

4.3.1 *Dislocation Effects*

First, dislocation effects. The fact that a Lexical Item (LI) may occupy a different position in the structure (its position in the phonological representation of the sentence) to that in which it is interpreted semantically (the position of the semantic representation), seems to be one of the core properties of natural language. As is well known, many LIs contribute to dislocation effects, such as fronting of *wh*-elements, topicalization, scrambling, verb movement, Quantifier Raising (QR), etc. Against the background of the Perfectness Hypothesis this immediately leads to the question as to why the semantic position of a particular LI does not simply coincide with its phonological position. Note that this question is a different one to the question as to why dislocation is possible in the first place. Arguing that there is no principled ban on remerging elements has adequately solved this question (Starke 2001; Chomsky 2005, 2008), although this leaves unexplained how semantic compositionality requirements remain unviolated after remerging a linguistic object. However the fact that Remerge (or Internal Merge) is not blocked as a matter of principle does not answer the question why natural language exhibits dislocation. In other words, the existence of unrestricted Merge, accounts for the possibility of dislocation, since there is no principled ban on remerging. However, that does not mean that dislocation effects are immediately expected to occur. As is well known, remerging, and therefore dislocation effects, are heavily restricted. The question why dislocation, despite being freely available is so much restricted, must be due to the fact that although it is possible, it is not necessary, and since

it is not necessary it is ruled out. The notion of Merge suffices to explain the
possibility of dislocation, but not its necessity.

In Chomsky (2005) it has been argued that the duality of semantics (i.e. the
distinction between the expression of argument structure and discourse properties) calls two different modes of syntactic structures into being: Argument
structure is realized by External Merge, and discourse properties are expressed
by means of Internal Merge. This idea has, however, met a fair amount of
criticism in the literature (cf. Moro 2000, 2004; Hinzen 2006), who, apart from
presenting some arguments against a semantic motivation for Internal Merge
on evolutionary grounds, argue that there is no independent evidence for the
duality of semantics. Moreover it is not clear why discourse properties cannot
be expressed by means of External Merge. In fact many markers of discourse
properties are externally merged, such as West Germanic discourse particles
or Classical Arabic focus particles. Hence the question why natural language
exhibits dislocation effects is still in need of a principled explanation, as it does
not seem to be inevitable in order to perfectly connect sound to meaning.

4.3.2 *Uninterpretable Features*

Second, the notion of uninterpretable formal features requires a principled
explanation. Uninterpretable features are those features that cannot be interpreted, neither by the SM system, nor by the C-I systems. This immediately
opens the question as to why natural language would allow for redundant
material in the first place? At first sight language seems to be full of redundancy as suggested by concord phenomena (such as Negative Concord) or
overt agreement (subject-verb agreement). The line of reasoning developed
in Chomsky (1995) was to take one imperfection to license the other. Following the principle of Full Interpretation (Chomsky 1986a) that states that
the interfaces should be free of uninterpretable material, uninterpretable
features ($[uF]$s) must be deleted during the derivation, before reaching LF
or PF. Deletion takes place by establishing a feature-checking relationship
with a local element carrying an appropriate interpretable formal feature.
However, if the structural distance between a particular LI carrying some
uninterpretable feature and its possible feature checker (i.e. an LI that carries
a matching interpretable feature) is too big to allow for feature checking,
a syntactic operation such as Move may be triggered, thus motivating the
triggering of Internal Merge. Not moving this element would lead to a violation of Full Interpretation at LF. The necessity of an instance of dislocation
has thus been triggered by the presence of redundant material. Note that
this may very well explain the presence of dislocation effects, but that it

leaves the existence of redundant material itself an open question (Chomsky 2006).

4.3.3 *Functional Heads*

Third, natural language exhibits a flexible distribution of functional heads. Since the introduction of multiple clausal functional heads (most notably by Pollock 1989) it is observed that languages differ with respect to which functional heads are (overtly) realized. Why would a particular language exhibit some F⁰ if another language can do without it? Roughly speaking, two different approaches have been proposed to account for this flexible distribution of functional heads. The first approach, the so-called cartographic approach,[6] has taken the strong, radical claim that each language underlyingly has the same functional structure that reflects the many hierarchies that have been observed in natural language (Larson 1988; Rizzi 1997; Cinque 1999; Belletti 2004a; Ramchand 2008) and that grammatical variation is restricted to which positions are overtly realized. Proposals along these lines have been formulated by Cinque (1999), Kayne (2000), Starke (2004), and (to a lesser extent) Rizzi (1997).[7] If this approach is on the right track, (rich) functional structure can be taken to be part of UG and the language-specific realization can be reduced to parametric variation. Under such an approach, the abstractness of functional structure (i.e. why several functional are heads allowed to be covertly realized whereas others are realized overtly) remains unexplained and therefore lacks principled explanation. As there is no explanation why UG should innately be equipped with such a rich structure, several scholars (e.g. Svenonius 2002a; Ernst 2002; Nilsen 2003) have argued against such a universal UG-based functional sequence (terminology due to Starke 2001). These scholars have pointed out several problems with respect to the cartographic approach by arguing that the clausal hierarchy that the cartographic approach imposes turns out to be problematic, as many functional orders can in fact be reversed. Moreover, it has been argued that many hierarchical effects, as well as the observed transitivity failures can be explained by adopting a semantic motivation for the orderings observed within clausal structure. Under such an approach the universal functional sequence is rejected and functional heads themselves become subject to parametric variation. However, also under this

---

[6] Not every analysis that is cartographic makes this strong assumption. Several analyses actually allow for cross-linguistic differences with respect to clausal structure; cf. Iatridou (1990) and Giorgi & Pianesi (1997), among many others.

[7] Many papers written within this cartographic approach can be found in the collections by Cinque (2002), Rizzi (2004), and Belletti (2004b).

perspective, it remains unclear what determines the existence/availability of functional heads if they are not innately provided by UG.

4.3.4 *Parametric Variation*

Finally, if language performs a perfect task in relation to sound and meaning, why would different instantiations of it (i.e. different languages) opt for so many differences? Why would morphosyntax not be identical across different languages? The introduction of the Principles and Parameters program (Chomsky 1981) has provided an initial answer to this question by arguing that linguistic variation is not unlimited and the notion of parameter has been introduced.[8] Still, the fact that grammatical variation is limited by a fixed number of innately present parameters lacks a principled explanation. It is not clear why languages must vary syntactically. The need for such an explanation becomes more and more urgent since modern research, especially due to the success of microparametric studies, has revealed that the number of parameters is no longer easily countable. Even the most optimistic analyses take the number of parameters to be larger than 100–150 (cf. Newmeyer 2004). At the moment there is no clear notion what the exact number should be, but given the idea that each human I-grammar results from a different parameter setting, the number of parameters must be accordingly large. Since previous and future I-grammars must be taken into account as well, the number may grow excessively large. If the number of parameters is indeed as high as it is esteemed these days, their innate status is getting less and less likely, not only because such a large amount of innate acquisition instructions is hard, if not impossible, to explain in terms of language evolution and genetic encoding, but also since an explanation for such a distribution of innately present parameters is lacking. If linguistic variation is indeed constrained by parameters, what constitutes parameters themselves? Why do parameters exist in the first place?

A hypothesis put forward by Baker (2001, 2008) is to separate different types of parameters, thus distinguishing microparameters from macroparameters, and possibly intermediate types, such as mesoparameters. Whereas microparameters can be reduced to particular properties of functional heads (following the Borer-Chomsky conjecture (Borer 1984 and Chomsky 1995), macroparameters should distinguish different types of language families. However, this distinction between possible types of parameters does not solve the problems that have been addressed. First, even under a perspective that only macroparameters are innately present (not a conclusion that Baker is

---

[8] For a recent debate on the status of parameters in linguistic theory, see Newmeyer (2004, 2005, 2006), Roberts & Holmberg (2005), and Baker (2008).

necessarily committed to), the question as to why a perfect system like natural language would allow for parameters, remains unanswered. The major question is not how many parameters there are, or what form they can have, but why they are there in the first place. Second, even if many parameters are reduced to properties of functional heads, we still need to account for what properties enable functional heads to constitute the particular amount of cross-linguistic variation that has been attested.[9] Moreover, if parametric variation reduces to properties of functional heads, the previously addressed question again emerges: What determines the set of functional heads? Why would natural language allow a series of functional heads if, at least from a superficial point of view, not every language exhibits all possible functional heads?

4.3.5 *Line of Argumentation*

In this chapter, I address all four "imperfections" that require principled explanation, and I argue that the existence of dislocation effects, uninterpretable formal features, functional heads and parameters follows from the fact that language constitutes an optimal solution to the task of mapping meaning to form, but that it is not the perfect solution. In its very essence the proposal that I formulate amounts to saying that natural is an optimal solution to conditions imposed by the different interfaces. However, the fact that these interface conditions can be conflicting opens up the possibility that different grammars may equally optimally satisfy their interface conditions. This already creates a grammatical space that allows for cross-linguistic variation. I propose the radical hypothesis, that this room for grammatical variation, which follows from conflicting interface conditions, forms the entire parametric space.

I demonstrate that dislocation operations are required in order to spell out two markers of different semantic operations in one and the same position. If two semantic functions cannot be interpreted in one and the same position, since for instance their semantic types form a mismatch, Remerge creates a second syntactic position, so that each semantic function can be interpreted in a unique position. This argument is close to the argument following from the duality of semantics (since it derives movement from the fact that LIs may induce multiple semantic functions), but crucially differs from it since it takes SM-based soft conditions to be responsible for the fact that multiple semantic functions are spelled out in one syntactic position.

Remerge is, however, not the only available mode of repairing the fact that mismatching semantic functions are realized in one syntactic position.

---

[9] See Longobardi *et al.* (2008) for an analysis of these properties.

A second, equally economical alternative is to assume that if two semantic functions are marked on one LI, one of these two markers can be semantically vacuous and licenses the presence of a phonologically abstract element that is interpreted as the second semantic function. Note, however, that this mode of repair calls uninterpretability into being as such elements need to carry uninterpretable formal features in order to license the higher abstract semantic function. Hence the same mismatch between phonological and semantic economy conditions that causes movement is also the cause of the existence of redundant material in natural language.

Finally, I discuss the relation between functional heads and formal features, demonstrating that feature projection is only allowed for formal features, and that the set of functional heads in a particular language depends on which formal features are available in that language. This alludes to the cartography-flexibility debate: Is the set of formal features identical cross-linguistically or not? In this chapter I demonstrate that formal features must be acquired through positive evidence. In short, I demonstrate that features can only be taken to be formal if there is positive evidence that at least one instance of this formal feature is uninterpretable. This explains why the set of functional heads is flexible. Only if [F] is some formal feature in a particular language, may F project in this language. If a language lacks a particular formal feature [F], it must also lack a syntactic head F°. I discuss some phenomena (Negative Concord, Modal Concord) that support this prediction.

The most far-reaching consequence of this idea is that the notion of parameters, as well as the motivation for other syntactic operations, such as Move (Remerge) and the feature-checking system underlying Agree, are pregiven by the language system as a result of the fact that it is a perfect system. Thus, simply arguing that natural language is an optimal system connecting the thought and speech systems already accounts for the available linguistic tools (dislocation, uninterpretable formal features, the flexible distribution of functional projections and parameters) without having to allude to biologically innate knowledge or to argue against the consequences of poverty of the stimulus arguments. In this sense these characteristics can be seen as "Factor III" properties in the sense of Chomsky (2005).

4.4 Uninterpretability and Dislocation as a Result of the Mismatch between SM and C-I Interface Conditions

In this section I argue that in many cases the two simplicity metrices, (6) and (10), cannot always be satisfied simultaneously. To be more precise, in every case where two semantic operators are not of a matching type, it is impossible to have these semantic expressions spelled out in a prosodically poor construction, and at the same time have them take scope from that position. To illustrate this I demonstrate that grammatical tense cannot be interpreted from the same position where it is spelled out, namely on the finite verb. In a nutshell, this opens up different marking strategies for natural language to express tense: either by an adverbial operator, which occupies a different clausal position than the verb (as is the case for instance in Greenlandic), or by merging the finite verb in two different positions while spelling out only one copy (e.g. French), or by taking the tense markers on the verb to be semantically vacuous, i.e. pure scope markers realizing a higher covert operator (e.g. Dutch).

In order to see this, take the following sentence:

(13)   John loved Mary.

The sentence contains two arguments (*John* and *Mary*) as well as a finite verb marked for third person singular and past tense. Focusing on the latter, the question arises as to where past tense is actually interpreted in the sentence. As von Stechow (2002) has demonstrated, the first suggestion that may come to mind, namely that past tense is interpreted in situ (i.e. on the finite verb), cannot be correct for semantic reasons. This is illustrated in (14).

(14)   Wolfgang played tennis on every Sunday.   (von Stechow 2002)
        = 'For every Sunday in Past c there is a time t at which Wolfgang plays tennis.'
        ≠ 'There is past time on every Sunday at which Wolfgang plays tennis.'
        ≠ 'For every Sunday, there is time before it such that Wolfgang plays tennis at that time.'

As can be seen from the correct interpretation in (14), past tense cannot be interpreted in the same position where the verbal content ("play") is interpreted since the past tense outscopes the quantifying PP *on every Sunday*, whereas the predicate "play" is outscoped by this PP. In more technical terms, the logical types of "play" and the past tense operator (Op_{PAST}) do not match.[10]

The prosodic word *played* thus cannot induce the semantic contents of the predicate "play" and Op_{PAST} at the same time. In other words, what seems to be the case here is that the phonological preference to express Op_{PAST} by means of single affix (*-ed*) yields a semantic problem: How is past tense interpreted in sentences like (14)?

---

[10] Adopting von Stechow's representation for Op_{PAST}: $[[PASTc]] \ c = \lambda w.\lambda P_{it}.\exists t[t < t_c \ \& \ P(t)]$.

As it is obvious that *-ed* is the only marker of past tense in this sentence, two logical possibilities arise. The first possibility is that the finite verb does not move to a higher position, but that it somehow licenses the presence of a phonologically abstract operator that has the semantics of Op$_{PAST}$. The second possibility is that the finite verb (*loved/played*) has remerged (Chomsky 2005) in such a way that past tense is interpreted in the higher copy and the predicate in the lower copy (i.e. partial reconstruction after movement). The abstractions behind both options are illustrated in (15).

(15)　a.　　　　　　　　　　　　　　b.

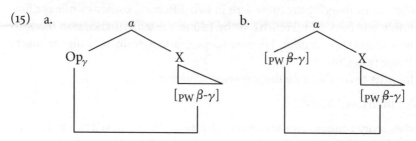

In the next subsections I argue that the first possibility is an instance of the syntactic operation known as Agree and the second possibility reflects Move. Moreover I argue that both strategies cannot be instantiated without the linguistic notion of uninterpretable features. When I refer to both strategies in (15), I use the term doubling, as in both strategies, γ is manifested more than once in the syntactic structure.

4.4.1 *Uninterpretable Features*

Let us first concentrate on the first strategy to express multiple markers of semantic functions on one and the same element. In the previous subsection I explained how the existence of additional structure hosting an abstract operator follows from the SM desideratum for phonological economy. However, nothing yet has been said about how this extra functional structure arises; it has only been explained why it must arise.

In the case of (15a) it is a property of the prosodic word $[\beta\text{-}\gamma]$ that γ has no semantic value itself, but that the presence of γ implies that it is c-commanded by an abstract operator Op$_\gamma$ that is responsible for the semantics that correspond to the affix γ. Hence the prosodic word $[\beta\text{-}\gamma]$ has an additional particular property such that it meets the following three criteria:

(16)　a.　　$[Op_\gamma [\ldots [\beta\text{-}\gamma] \ldots]]$

　　　b.　*$[\ldots [\beta\text{-}\gamma] \ldots]]$

　　　c.　*$[Op_\gamma [\ldots [\beta] \ldots]]$

The criteria in (16) state that $[\beta\text{-}\gamma]$ is grammatical if c-commanded by Op_γ, but that ungrammaticality is yielded either if Op_γ is merged in the clause without the occurrence of the affix γ, or if the affix γ occurs without being c-commanded by Op_γ. In other words, γ is a morphosyntactically visible element that is semantically empty, but simultaneously requires the presence of an operator that dominates it in order to survive at LF. Readers who are familiar with the minimalist program will immediately recognize γ as the phonological realization of a so-called uninterpretable formal feature $[uF]$ that must establish a syntactic relationship with an interpretable formal feature $[iF]$ in order to prevent crashing at LF (in the sense of Chomsky 1995).

It should be noted, however, that the perspective on uninterpretable features in this sense is not exactly similar to the perspective in Chomsky (1995). Uninterpretable features as described above are not illegible to the C-I system. They are thought to be semantically vacuous, which basically means that the C-I system is blind to them, contrary to the view in Chomsky (1995) where the presence of undeleted uninterpretable features at LF makes the derivation crash. Consequently, this means that uninterpretable formal features do not have to be deleted before or at the level of LF. They only need to be properly licensed in syntax. Note also that such a definition for uninterpretable features prevents look-ahead problems. As no uninterpretable feature needs to be deleted, its semantic status does not play any role during the syntactic derivation. The only information that uninterpretable features carry, and which is lexically encoded, is purely syntactic in nature.

Now let us see how exactly the three criteria in (16) are met, given the notion of uninterpretable features introduced above. Clearly the case of (16a) follows immediately, since the $[uF]$ feature that γ carries is properly licensed by Op_γ. Note that, contrary to more traditional analyses of feature checking the hierarchical structure here is the reverse: It is the element carrying $[iF]$ that c-commands $[uF]$. The reversal of this hierarchical structure has been proposed on different grounds by, amongst others, Pesetsky & Torrego (2001, 2006), Adger (2003), Wiklund (2005), and follows the essentials behind Rizzi's (1997) notion of criteria (where semantic operators occupy specifier positions that must share their features with their heads).

The second condition in (16) is also immediately met as, by definition, any $[uF]$ requires checking by an element carrying $[iF]$.

The third criterion, however, is not directly met. Given the nature of Merge, nothing in principle forbids merger of an abstract operator carrying $[iF]$ with a syntactic object that does not include $[uF]$. This is not a problem particular to this theory, but is a more general one concerning the nature of abstract operators, or even more generally, the nature of abstract material. In order to restrict the inclusion of abstract material to those cases in which it is required, i.e. cases like (16c), let us adopt the following condition:

(17)   Only postulate a covert element if a particular sentence is grammatical and none of its overt elements is responsible for the grammaticality of the sentence.

Note that (17) is a truism, if feature checking is the mechanism behind grammaticality. It only states that if no overt element can be responsible for the fact that some uninterpretable feature has been checked, it must be a covert element. Note that (17) is not a condition that allows inclusion of abstract material in order to save sentences from ungrammaticality. It only states that if a sentence is grammatical, it may be the case that abstract material is responsible for it.[11] Condition (17) is a soft condition in the sense that abstract material may occur in those cases where its presence is somehow unavoidable. It is exactly this economy condition that has also been applied to license *pro* (Rizzi 1986) and it permits inclusion of abstract material only in those cases where the derivation would not have been convergent otherwise. Adopting (17) derives the ban in (16c): The fact that there is no γ-affix carrying an uninterpretable feature [uF] renders the sentence without Op$_\gamma$ grammatical (all other things being equal) and thus (17) can never be applied.

The status of (17) depends on the perspective on grammar one adopts. In a representational system it operates as a filter on representations, which excludes configurations like (16c). In a derivational system, condition (17) cannot be properly implemented, as nothing can forbid the creation of (16c) and filters do not apply at the interfaces. However, (17) does not necessarily have to function as a syntactic filter. Following Ackema & Neeleman (2002), who take rightward movement to be banned on parsing grounds and do not take it to be ruled out in syntax proper (as opposed to Kayne 1994), (17) can be thought of as a parsing constraint as well. Hence, although grammatical background assumptions may alter the status of (17), they do not block its application.

Thus far we have reached the following situation: On the basis of the two simplicity metrices defined in Section 4.3, it follows that there are already two, equally optimal solutions to express two semantic functions β and γ that are not each other's semantic complement. Either β and γ are introduced in

---

[11] One may wonder why languages can realize an overt operator if a covert operator is also available. An example would be the realization of a pronominal subject in a pro-drop language. Note, however, that such an overt realization always comes about with a particular semantic effect, such as topicalization or emphasis. As such, overt realization not only denotes the semantic properties of the subject, but also additional semantic/pragmatic properties.

the clausal position from which they take scope, or they are expressed on one and the same prosodic word. In the first case the semantic simplicity metric is fully satisfied, but the phonological simplicity metric is not, as the two elements must both be prosodic words. In the second case β and γ are expressed on one word only, but as both semantic functions cannot be interpreted in the position where the prosodic word has been base-generated, one of the two markers actually carries an uninterpretable feature that marks the presence of an abstract operator. In this case the phonological simplicity metric is fully satisfied, but the semantic simplicity metric is not, as the structure now contains an uninterpretable feature $[u\text{F}]$, carried by γ and checked by Op_γ.

4.4.2 *Dislocation*

However, marking abstract operators is not the only way to optimally fulfill the phonological simplicity metric. Another way, represented in (15b), is to remerge a particular word that contains two semantically mismatching elements, to a higher position in the tree and have one of the two take scope from the higher position, and the other one from the lower position.

Following Truckenbrodt (2006) and Zeijlstra (2006), who argue that V-to-C movement in the Germanic languages is always semantically motivated (contra Chomsky 1995, 2000, who postulates that this movement in fact takes place at PF),[12] let us focus on verbal movement triggered by imperative morphology. Take an imperative verb, V_{imp}. V_{imp} contains two pieces of semantic information: its verbal (i.e. predicative) property and its imperative (i.e. speech-act property). Although both semantic functions (the predicate and speech-act operator) are encoded on the verb, they cannot be interpreted in the same position:

(18) Slaap niet!   Dutch
      sleep not
      'Don't sleep!'

Sentence (18) means "it is imperative that it is not the case that you sleep." The imperative operator (i.e. the operator that has the illocutionary force of an order) takes scope above the negation, whereas negation outscopes the predicate. The scopal relationships immediately follow if movement is assumed to be a marking strategy as sketched above. In order to see this, let us go through the derivation step by step.

---

[12] See also Lechner (2007) for a number of arguments in favor of the idea that head movement causes interpretable effects.

First the entire prosodic word V-IMP is copied (or remerged) in the higher position:

(19)   [V-IMP] → [[V-IMP] ... [V-IMP]]

Now the formal, phonological and semantic content of the prosodic word V-IMP has been copied. However, although the possibility of remerging is given by any system that allows unrestricted application of an operation like Merge, from the semantic and phonological perspective, it faces serious problems. Semantically speaking, the operation applied in (19), is a blatant violation of compositionality. The only way to avoid this violation is to delete all semantic features that have been copied, once. In principle, it does not matter on which copy which semantic feature is deleted, as long as compositionality is maintained. This means that deletion could target all semantic features in one copy or some in one copy and some in the other copy. In this case, given the semantics of both predicate and speech-act operators, the only division that would not yield any uninterpretable construction at LF is one in which the imperative feature is deleted below, and the verbal feature above, as shown in (20). Semantically speaking, (20) has escaped its compositionality violation.

(20) $[\text{V-IMP}_{[\text{V}][\text{IMP}]}]$ → $[\text{V-IMP}_{[\text{V}][\text{IMP}]}$ ... $\text{V-IMP}_{[\text{V}][\text{IMP}]}]$

From the phonological perspective, doubling all phonological features would introduce an uneconomical effect, as there is no reason to spell out lexical material twice, when spelling it out once suffices. In fact, the general idea behind movement is that it fulfills the phonological simplicity metric. However, just as deletion may target semantic features, it may also target phonological features. Following standard minimalist assumptions, the phonological features of the lower copy are deleted and will thus not be realized. It should be addressed however, that contrary to semantic deletion, phonological deletion does not have to take place, as no SM hard condition is violated if phonological material is spelled out twice. This also explains why in some languages in cases of e.g. *wh*-movement traces of movement are phonologically realized (McDaniel 1989; Cheng 2000).

Hence, remerging does not suffer from any phonological or semantic problems. However, (20) is still invalid from a syntactic point of view. If, as in (20), all verbal features are deleted in the higher copy, the moved element could no longer be analyzed as a (finite) verb. Yet, clearly the moved element's category remains unchanged. A moved verb remains a verb and behaves like a verb in every respect. But even more crucial: If the finite verb lacked any formal feature in the first place, no feature could ever have projected it. Although the higher copy no longer carries any semantically verbal properties, it must thus still have purely formal verbal properties. In other words, the higher copy must have such a feature that is syntactically recognizable as a verb, but semantically not. The most likely hypothesis now is that the highest copy must carry an uninterpretable verbal feature, whereas the lower copy carries an interpretable one. Then, (21) denotes correct representation after movement has taken place.

(21) $[[\text{V-IMP}_{[\text{IMP}][u\text{V}]i}] \dots [\text{V-IMP}_{[\text{IMP}][i\text{V}]i}]]$

All features, except the verbal features, are present at only one copy. The verbal feature must be a formal feature that remains present on both copies, albeit with a different value. Again, $[u\text{V}]$ exhibits the diagnostics of an uninterpretable feature: It does not contribute to the semantics of the sentence, and it must stand in a syntactic relationship with a particular element carrying $[i\text{V}]$.

The movement solution to optimally fulfill the requirements of the phonological simplicity metric mirrors exactly the agreement approach described in the previous section. There it was the affix that had to be realized by a formal feature; here it is the root itself. Note that this account of movement comes about with two major benefits. First, it accounts for the fact why uninterpretable formal features are involved in enabling movement. If there was not any formal verbal feature, movement could never have taken place. In a sense the formal feature in the case of movement functions as the vehicle. Note that the verb's higher $[u\text{V}]$ and lower $[i\text{V}]$ feature exactly represent the earlier probe-goal configuration underlying movement, but this configuration has now received an explanation in terms of linguistic simplicity. Second, it enables marking by means of uninterpretable features, the strategy discussed in the previous section. This can be explained as follows: Suppose movement did not involve uninterpretable features, then movement could in principle take place without violating the semantic simplicity metric. Hence movement would be a more economic strategy than the Agree strategy, thus ruling out the latter. The fact that movement cannot be realized without uninterpretable features, motivates the notion of semantically redundant features in natural language.

To conclude, what we have seen thus far, is that in each instance of dislocation (resulting from the operations Move and Agree) formal features have played crucial roles. It has been demonstrated that without formal features movement and Agree cannot take place. Dislocation, as shown above, is a result of a semantics-phonology mismatch, and formal features must exist in order to establish the required dislocation effects. This means that a second imperfection in grammar (dislocations), similar to uninterpretable formal features, follows from conflicting soft interface conditions.

4.5 Functional Structure

4.5.1 *Functional Projections*

The third imperfection to be discussed in this chapter concerns the functional structure. Several scholars have argued that (the amount of) functional structure is a property of UG. One such proposal has been Cinque's adverbial hierarchy; cf. Cinque (1999), who provides a template for the adverbial distribution, as illustrated in (22). Since Cinque's proposal is one of the most radical ones in terms of fixed templates, it is one of the most interesting ones to discuss here.

(22) [*frankly* Mood$_{speech\ act}$ [*fortunately* Mood$_{evaluative}$ [*allegedly* Mood$_{evidential}$ [*probably* Mod$_{epistemic}$ [*once* T(Past) [*then* T(Future) [*perhaps* Mood$_{irrealis}$ [*necessarily* Mod$_{necessity}$ [*Possibly* Mod$_{possibility}$ [*usually* Asp$_{habitual}$ [*again* Asp$_{repetitive(I)}$ [*often* Asp$_{frequentative(I)}$ [*intentionally* Mod$_{volitional}$ [*quickly* Asp$_{celerative(I)}$ [*already* T(Anterior) [*no longer* Asp$_{terminative}$ [*still* Asp$_{continuative}$ [*always* Asp$_{perfect(?)}$ [*just* Asp$_{retrospective}$ [*soon* Asp$_{proximative}$ [*briefly* Asp$_{durative}$ [*characteristically(?)* Asp$_{generic/progressive}$ [*almost* Asp$_{prospective}$ [*completely* Asp$_{SgCompletive(I)}$ [*tutto* Asp$_{PlCompletive}$ [*well* Voice [*fast/early* Asp$_{celerative(II)}$ [*again* Asp$_{repetative(II)}$ [*often* Asp$_{frequentative(II)}$ [*completely* Asp]]]]]]]]]]]]]]]]]]]]]]]]]]]]]]]]]

Cinque's analysis is based in two different claims: (i) he argues that selectional hierarchies are part of UG; (ii) he argues that each adverb occupies the specifier position of a functional projection that exhibits an X-Bar skeleton. In this chapter I will not discuss the syntactic nature of hierarchies. Rather, I want to address the claim that each class of adverbials universally requires a functional projection of its own.

Opposed to Cinque's view that the set of functional projections is uniform across languages is the view that the set of available functional projections is flexible (Ackema *et al.* 1993; Weerman & Neeleman 1997; Koeneman 2000; Zeijlstra 2008). In a flexible system, the existence of a particular functional projection in one language does not imply the existence of such a projection in another language. One can compare the two perspectives with respect to the English adverb *often*. Under Cinque's analysis, *often* should be located in the specifier position of Asp$_{frequentative(I)}$P; under a flexible approach it can be taken to be an adjunct to *v*P. The two options are illustrated below:

(23) a.

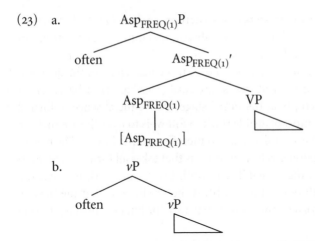

b.

The question to be asked now is how these two structures can be distinguished empirically. Cinque suggests that since adjacent adverbs in principle allow a verbal participle between them, this indicates that an empty head position should be available in between every two adverbs.

(24) Da allora, non hanno <rimesso> di solito <rimesso> mica
      since then NEG have.3PL <put> usually <put> NEG
      <rimesso> più <rimesso> sempre <rimesso> completamente
      <put> any longer <put> always <put> completely
      <rimesso> totto bene in ordine
      <put> everything in order
      'since then, they haven't usually not any longer always put everything
      well in order'   (Cinque 1999: 45)

However, this argument does not show that there are as many head positions available as there are adverbial projections. If one allows multiple specifiers, only two verbal heads can account for the entire distribution in (24). One position is the head position that the verb occupies and of which the preverbal adverbials are specifiers; the other position may be left empty and hosts all postverbal adverbials as specifiers.

(25) a. $[_{XP}$ ADV1 X$^\circ$ $[_{YY}$ ADV2 Y$^\circ$ $[_{ZP}$ ADV3 Z$^\circ$ $[_{UP}$ ADV4 U$^\circ$]]]]
      b. $[_{XP}$ ADV1 ADV2 X$^\circ$ $[_{YP}$ ADV3 ADV4 Y$^\circ$]]

Hence, the only way to distinguish between the two possible structures in (23) lies in the fact that in (23a) a particular formal feature [Asp$_{FREQ(1)}$] must be available to project Asp$_{FREQ(1)}$P. In (23b), by contrast, this feature does not have to be present. If it can be shown that English lacks particular formal features, this forms evidence for the existence of structures such as (23b). If, however, it cannot be proven that such features are absent, no empirical distinction can be made between (23a) and (23b). Hence the question of which structure in (23) is correct for a language like English depends completely on the question of whether the set of formal features is universal (UG-based) or based on L1 acquisition (and thus empty at the initial stage). Since the absence of formal features is decisive, the most plausible track to follow is to hypothesize that the set of formal features is non-universal, and therefore empty in UG. The reason for this is purely methodological: A hypothesis that takes all formal features to be part of UG predicts the availability of both (23a) and (23b), whereas the non-universal approach only allows (23b). If the predictions that the flexible hypothesis makes are correct, the correct structure for English must be the one in (23b).

The reader may already have noticed that the discussion above implicitly assumed that functional projection is reserved to formal features, i.e. only formal features are allowed to project. This is a standard assumption in the literature, which can be traced back to Giorgi & Pianesi (1997) and their Feature Scattering Principle:

(26)   *Feature Scattering Principle*
       Every feature can head a projection.

Although it is highly likely that syntactic operations can only access syntactic material (and thus only formal features and not semantic features), the fact that only formal features may project needs to be explained. I will do so after the discussion on flexible features in Section 4.5.3.

4.5.2 *The Flexible Formal Features Hypothesis*

Grammatical features are thought to constitute three categories: phonological features, formal features, and semantic features (Chomsky 1995). Phonological features are interpretable at the SM interface and semantic features are interpretable at the C-I interface. Formal features come in two kinds: interpretable and uninterpretable formal features. Interpretable formal features are also interpretable at the C-I interface, i.e. they carry semantic content, and are therefore also members of the set of semantic features. The sets of formal features and semantic features thus intersect. Uninterpretable formal features need to stand in a proper agreement relation with an interpretable formal feature in order to prevent the derivation from crashing at the interfaces.

(27)   Phonological features   Formal features   Semantic features

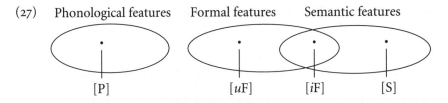

[P]   [*u*F]   [*i*F]   [S]

Suppose that the set of formal features is empty at the initial stage. L1 learners must then acquire which features are formal(ized) and which features are not. In other words, an L1 learner needs to have positive evidence that certain lexical elements carry formal features. Let us look again at the properties of formal features. Since they come in two kinds, we need to discuss the properties of both interpretable and uninterpretable features in order to see what property can act as a proper cue (in the sense of Lightfoot 1999) during language acquisition.

Interpretable formal features have two different properties: They are interpretable at LF and they can check uninterpretable features.[13] However, they are not recognizable as such for a language learner. Their first property is not decisive, since semantically speaking formal features are undistinguishable from non-formal semantic features ([F]s), as shown in (28).

(28) $||X_{[F]}|| = ||X_{[iF]}||$

Secondly, the fact that interpretable formal features are required to check uninterpretable features cannot trigger the acquisition of formal features either. A formal feature [*i*F] can occur without any problems in a sentence without any [*u*F]s. Only a [*u*F] cannot survive without the presence of a proper [*i*F]. However, this can only be acquired on the basis of negative evidence, which is virtually absent during L1 acquisition. Hence the properties of interpretable formal features can never lead to the acquisition of formal features as such.

Uninterpretable features, on the other hand, do give rise to cues. Let us look at the properties of uninterpretable features again, using the insights of Section 4.4. Uninterpretable formal features are semantically vacuous. Moreover they require the presence of an interpretable formal feature and they give rise to doubling effects, thus triggering syntactic operations such as Move and Agree. All these properties can be identified by a language learner. In fact, they all

---

[13] Feature checking here is used since it is the common term for the process that is going on here, described in Section 4.4. Checking thus means that a licensing requirement of an uninterpretable feature is fulfilled, thus leading no longer to ungrammaticality.

reduce to so-called doubling effects. Let us define doubling in the following way.

(29)   F exhibits a doubling effect iff the presence of a semantic operator Op_F is manifested overtly by more than one element in the morphosyntax.

Hence the presence of formal features can be acquired by L1 learners since the presence of uninterpretable features can be acquired. The presence of formal features in natural languages then immediately follows. Hence the following hypothesis can be formulated.

(30)   *The Flexible Formal Feature (FFF) Hypothesis*[14]
         A language has a formal feature [i/uF] iff it exhibits doubling effects with respect to F.

This means that a language only has a formal feature [i/uPAST] if past tense exhibits doubling effects with respect to past tense; a language only has a formal feature [i/uNEG] if negation exhibits doubling effects with respect to negation, and so on.

4.5.3 *Formal Features and Projection*

The proposal that only formal features are allowed to project still needs to be addressed. This follows from the observations made above: Formal features may give rise to doubling effects; semantic features do not (if they did they would have to be reanalyzed as formal features). Let us now see what the consequences are for formal features and projection. Let us take the following abstract functional projection:

(31)

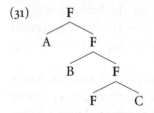

The reader may already have observed that projecting F exhibits a doubling effect with respect to F: A functional projection consists of multiple layers, each assigned a label that corresponds to the head. But obviously not all instances of F are semantic operators: A NegP, for instance, does not contain three or four negative operators; it contains only one. And (23a) only contains

---

[14] This hypothesis was first introduced in Zeijlstra (2008) in a slightly different form.

one adverbial, *often*, and not four elements to be interpreted as $Op_{AspFREQ(1)}$ (candidates being the specifier *often*, $Asp_{FREQ(1)}P$, $Asp_{FREQ(1)}'$, and $Asp_{FREQ(1)}^0$). The latter scenarios however would have been the case if semantic features were allowed to project. This explains why projection is restricted to formal features and not to semantic features.

The argument that functional projection only is allowed addresses some problems that have been mentioned in the literature regarding the necessity of functional projection, especially the apparent redundancy of feature doubling that is the case with Spec-head agreement (cf. 4). Given the fact each instance of Merge needs a label and that features provide such a label, redundancy occurs immediately. However, this redundancy is not problematic if it is motivated on independent grounds, which, arguably, is the case here. Formal features are needed in order to enable doubling effects so that conflicting interface conditions can be fulfilled in multiple optimal ways. Now, if these formal features create functional projections as a by-product, this instance of redundancy is no longer problematic. In fact redundancy in natural language straightforwardly follows from the Perfectness Hypothesis.

Thus far the FFF hypothesis has not been proven. It has only been demonstrated that formal features can be acquired, since uninterpretable features can be acquired (and therefore their interpretable counterparts can too) and that functional projection is subject to the presence/availability of formal features. But this makes the FFF hypothesis empirically testable. If it can be shown that if a functional F^0 is present cross-linguistically, F exhibits doubling effects, the FFF hypothesis is confirmed. If F^0s may be attested without giving rise to any doubling effect, except for projection, than the FFF hypothesis must be rejected, and the set of formal features is then likely to be part of UG instead of resulting from L1 acquisition.

A few words need to be said about the distinction between phrases and heads. In current minimalist reasoning, lexical items are not marked for head or phrasal status. This does not, however, imply that there is no difference between heads and phrases. The only difference is that X^0s, X-Bars and XPs should no longer be thought of as syntactic primitives, but as derived notions. As is well known, heads can be rephrased as having a property [−Max, +Min] and phrases as [+Max, −Min] (see Hornstein *et al.* 2005 for discussion). Consequently, relativized minimality effects (Rizzi 1990) can still be attested empirically (see Rizzi 2001; Starke 2001). Hence standard diagnostics for the distinction between heads and non-heads can still apply. Heads, for instance, do not allow movement of other heads across them (following Travis's 1984 Head Movement Constraint), and adjunction may only take place between two elements with identical syntactic status (heads adjoin to heads, phrases to phrases), as has been shown by many scholars (take Merchant 2006 as an example).

The fact that heads are empirically detectable, and the prediction that the FFF hypothesis makes, namely that formal features [i/uF] are acquired as a result of doubling effects and that only formal features are allowed to project, gives rise to the following templates for grammatical universals:

(32)   F^0 → overt doubling effects with respect to F

This template for typological universals can easily be explained. The FFF hypothesis accounted for the fact that it takes doubling effects with respect to F for the L1 learner to trigger the acquisition of formal features [i/uF]. Only formal features [i/uF] are allowed to project (given that projection is an instance of doubling). Hence, if a particular F^0 is overtly realized, it must have been analyzed as carrying a formal feature [i/uF] and thus there must have been doubling effects with respect to F in the language input.

Note that this template is unidirectional. It does not say that whenever there are formal features [i/uF] there must be an overt head F^0. It only says that if such a head is there, there must be doubling effects too.

The FFFH has not been tested for a wide range of domains, as of yet. However, the results that have appeared until now point in the direction of the FFFH. Let me briefly give two examples.

Negation has been long known to be a functional category that exhibits doubling effects. In many languages two morphosyntactically negative elements may give rise to a single semantic negation, a phenomenon known as Negative Concord (see Laka 1990; Haegeman & Zanuttini 1991, 1996; Ladusaw 1992; Haegeman 1995; Zanuttini 1997; Giannakidou 2000; de Swart & Sag 2002; and Zeijlstra 2004, amongst many others). In Zeijlstra (2004) it has been concluded on the basis of a large domain of languages that the FFFH prediction is correct for negation. Every language with a negative marker that is a syntactic head also exhibits Negative Concord.

Another domain is modality. Although many have argued that in languages modal auxiliaries occupy a syntactic projection of their own, as is the case in English, according to the FFFH these languages are expected to exhibit "Modal Concord" effects. In Zeijlstra (2008) it is shown that this prediction is correct. Modal Concord is indeed present in languages that have a particular modal head.

4.5.4 *Functional Structure Revisited*

Now that the balance has turned in the direction of flexible functional structure, the question immediately arises why must there be functional structure in the first place. In other words, why do some languages have NegPs, ModPs, AspPs, etc.? The answer to this question lies in the fact that each language needs to have some way to express a particular semantic operator. As has been discussed before, the fact that interface conditions may be conflicting leads to equally optimal strategies to express a semantic operator. From the C-I perspective, a structure as (33) would be required.

(33)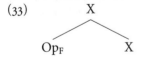

In this case no extra functional structure is required. Functional Application can be applied and the interpretation of the highest X follows directly from Op$_F$ and the lower X. Since F does not give rise to doubling effects that language will not contain any formal features [i/uF] and F can thus not project. This structure is reminiscent of (23b), repeated below for convenience.

(34)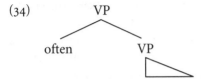

However, as explained before, SM preferences result in a preference for Spell-Out of multiple elements on the same node. This requires doubling effects and these doubling effects require the presence of formal features. Given the FFF Hypothesis, these formal features are only acquired as a result of doubling effects. Hence if the SM-biased strategies for expressing a semantic operator require additional structure, during L1 acquisition the relevant features will be formalized (i.e. analyzed as a formal feature). Given that formal features may project, the doubling effects required for the expression of semantic operators may lead to additional functional structure that is hosted by the required formal feature. Let me illustrate this with an example. The expression of negation can either be realized without formal features (DN languages) or with formal features (NC languages). Both expression strategies are equally economical, which explains why both are attested in natural language. If a negative marker is used to express the (presence of a) negative operator, this requires extra structure, resulting from merger with the negative marker. This is the case in both Yiddish and in Italian.

(35) Ikh hob *nit* gezen *keyn* moyz.   *Yiddish*
      I   have NEG seen N-   mice
      'I haven't seen any mice.'

(36) *Non* ha   telefonato a   *nessuno.*   *Italian*
       NEG has.3SG called   to N-body
      'He didn't call anybody.'

Let us assume for the sake of the argument that both negative markers carry
[*i*NEG] and both n-words [*u*NEG]. Then the presence of [*u*NEG] requires
merger of VP with the operator. VP is projected by V. Now nothing *a priori*
determines what the label of merger should be. Both V and [*i*NEG] are proper
candidates:

(37)   V/NEG

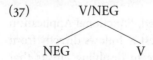

    NEG   V

Hence, languages vary with respect to the element that projects in these cases.
Italian *non* projects, and therefore exhibits X⁰ behaviour, yielding a NegP.
Yiddish on the other hand does not have its negative marker project and
therefore it is a specifier or adjunct of VP. The fact that different functional
projections are available, although this is not strictly necessary, simply follows
because nothing prevents it. What grammar does is require additional structure, but it does not impose any restriction on the label of the new structures.
Hence, languages will vary with respect to these labels.

4.6 Consequences for Parameters

Thus far, I have addressed three "imperfections" in natural language: uninterpretable formal features, dislocation effects, and flexible functional structure.
They have all received an explanation. I have argued that cross-linguistic
variation arises as a result of conflicting interface conditions. Furthermore, I
have argued that formal features are required to enable dislocation effects that
an SM-based expressing strategy for semantic operators would prefer. Finally,
I have argued that flexible functional structure is a result of the fact that only
formal features may project and that those formal features are only acquired if
necessary. By means of reasoning along these lines all grammatical differences
between languages seem to follow from the way that a semantic operator can
be expressed in different equally optimal ways. This has been addressed by the
Strongest Parametric Variation Hypothesis (SPVH), repeated below as (38):

(38) *The Strongest Parametric Variation Hypothesis* (SPVH)
      The Strongest Minimalist Thesis governs the entire range of parametric
      variation.

The question is now what the consequence of SPVH is for the status of parameters. As has already been addressed in the introduction, the innate status of parameters is not unproblematic. Under this approach postulating innate parameters in fact becomes unnecessary. The fact that languages can express semantic operators in different ways accounts for the existence of parametric choices. The first choice that an L1 learner must make in order to determine how a particular Op$_F$ is expressed is by determining whether a formal feature [i/uF] exists or not. This follows from the FFF Hypothesis. If not, the language learner does not have to acquire more syntactic information in order to express Op$_F$ in his/her grammar. If F on the other hand is formalized, new choices emerge: Which elements have [iF] and which have [uF]? Moreover, questions arise such as to when [i/uF] projects (i.e. on which item).

What is crucial, however, is that such questions impose themselves on language learners as a result of previous choices. Therefore those questions, i.e. those parameters, do not have to be assumed to be innate. Note that this view saves quite a lot of ballast in the sense that it does not encounter all the problems that innate parameters suffer from. On the other hand, it still limits the entire space of grammatical variation. Moreover, in its essence it is still very close to the two dominant perspectives on parameters: Baker's Parameter Hierarchy (Baker 2001) and the Borer–Chomsky conjecture (Borer 1984; Chomsky 1995).

The first perspective states that parametric variety is hierarchical. This means that a second parametric choice is only possible after setting the first parameter(s) in a particular way. Note that under the approach formulated above, this also follows. The only difference is that the hierarchy is not innate; it creates itself. Some choices require further choices, whereas some other choices do not require these further choices. The idea that parameters are not innate does not exclude them from being hierarchical with respect to each other.

The Borer-Chomsky conjecture states that parameters are reduced to properties of functional heads. Under the approach that I propose, parameters cannot be properties of functional heads in the first instance since functional heads are not part of UG. The "first" parameters reduce to properties of a semantic operator (Op$_F$). Only if these semantic operators have to be analyzed as carrying an interpretable formal feature ([iF]), elements carrying a formal feature [i/uF] may project. And only if they do, the language has a functional head F^0. After this procedure, things are similar since these heads can serve as a locus for more specified parameters, once again established in the input-driven manner outlined above. The rationale behind the Borer-Chomsky conjecture is that parametric variation reduces to lexical variation. This also follows from my proposal. Semantic operators are lexical items in the first place and thus parametric variation still reduces to lexical variation.

Hence, the main advantages of the above-mentioned perspectives remain. Parametric hierarchies are well motivated empirically, and are also predicted by the SPVH. The idea that parametric variation is lexical variation is also kept.

4.7 Conclusion

In this chapter I have concluded that Chomsky's SMT governs the entire range of parametric variation.

First, it has been shown how different economy conditions, applying at the SM and C-I interfaces, lead to different strategies for expressing semantic operators. A C-I-biased strategy uses different lexical items to express a particular semantic operator; an SM-biased strategy spells out markers of different semantic operations on one and the same lexical item. As a result doubling is needed in order to make those structures interpretable at LF.

Second, I have demonstrated that in order to license dislocation effects, (uninterpretable) formal features are needed, thus accounting for the existence of redundant material in grammar, a puzzle that has remained unsolved so far.

Third, I have shown that it is possible to describe functional structure in a flexible way. I have presented an empirically testable hypothesis, the FFF Hypothesis, which argues that formal features are syntactically flexible. According to this hypothesis, the set of formal features is empty in UG, and formal features are acquired as a result of doubling phenomena in the language input.

Fourth, the idea that formal features are acquired as a result of doubling effects explains why only formal features are allowed to project: Projection is an instance of doubling. The fact that only formal features may project, in combination with the syntactic flexibility of formal features, accounts for cross-linguistic variety with respect to functional structure.

Finally, the hypothesis that all grammatical variation follows from the Revised Strongest Minimalist Thesis provides a new perspective on parameters that maintains all the benefits of traditional parameters, namely that parametric variation is limited, hierarchically ordered, and lexically encoded, but that does not presuppose that parameters are innately present.

Of course the programmatic nature of this study leads to many open questions, and I am fully aware of the fact that many problems still need to be solved. On the other hand, I think the proposals formulated above solve many questions that have been problematic thus far. Moreover, the proposals formulated analyze many aspects of grammar in terms of interface conditions rather than pointing in the direction of UG, a desideratum in current minimalist reasoning.

5

Adjunction, Phase Interpretation, and Condition C*

PETR BISKUP

5.1 Introduction

As is well known, there is an adjunct-argument asymmetry with respect to reconstruction and Condition C (van Riemsdijk & Williams 1981; Lebeaux 1988; Speas 1990; Heycock 1995; Fox 1999, 2000; Chomsky 2004a; Stepanov 2000, 2001; Lasnik 2003). Consider the contrast in example (1), taken from Chomsky (2004a: 117):

(1) [$_{wh}$ Which [[picture [of Bill]] [that John liked]]] did he buy t_{wh}?

The R-expression *Bill* within the complement of *picture* cannot be coreferential[1] with *he*—it induces a Condition C violation—because it is not free.[2] In contrast, the R-expression *John* within the adjunct *that John liked* can be linked to *he*; no Condition C effect arises. Consider the Czech example (2), which is analogous to the English sentence (1). As demonstrated by the

---

* For helpful comments and discussion, I thank Klaus Abels, Uwe Junghanns, Andrew McIntyre, Gereon Müller, Marc Richards, an anonymous reviewer, and the audience at the *InterPhases* conference (Nicosia, Cyprus, May 2006). For grammatical judgements, I thank Jakub Dotlačil, Kristína Krchňavá, Denisa Lenertová, Hana Škrabalová, Jana Vejvodová. For improving my English, I thank Marc Richards. An earlier version of this contribution appeared as Biskup (2006b) and will appear as Biskup (forthcoming).

[1] By "coreference" I mean referential identity of two (or more) expressions. As usual, I mark coreference by coindexing. Referential identity can be obtained in two ways, by binding or by assigning the same semantic value from the discourse storage. In Section 3.3, I will show that this distinction plays an important role.

[2] Chomsky (1981: 184–5, 188) defines Binding Condition C as follows:

   (i) An R-expression is free.
   (ii) α is X-free if and only if it is not X-bound (with X replaced by A or Ā).
   (iii) α is X-bound by β if and only if α and β are coindexed, β c-commands α, and β is in an X-position.

coindexation, (2) behaves in the same way as its English counterpart with respect to Condition C.[3]

(2) Který obrázek   Karla$_1$, který měl Jirka$_2$rád, si *pro*$_{*1,2}$ koupil?[4]
    which picture-ACC of-Karel which liked Jirka-NOM self   bought
    'Which picture of Karel that Jirka liked did he buy?'

Two approaches have prevailed in recent years. The late merger approach—building on Lebeaux (1988)—is represented, for example, by Nissenbaum (2000), Stepanov (2000, 2001), or Fitzpatrick & Groat (2005). This approach is based on the different timing of adjunct merger and argument merger. Since adjuncts, in contrast to arguments, are not selected, they may be inserted into the structure acyclically. According to Stepanov (2000, 2001), adjuncts in fact must be introduced into the structure post-cyclically, that is, after all other processes are complete.

More concretely, after *wh*-movement of *který obrázek Karla* ('which picture of Karel') to SpecCP in (2), the relative clause *který měl Jirka rád* ('that Jirka liked') is merged with the copy of *obrázek Karla* ('picture of Karel') in SpecCP. Since *wh*-movement applies prior to the adjunction of the relative clause, the R-expression *Jirka* contained in the adjunct is not c-commanded by *pro* and Condition C is not violated. However, since arguments are merged cyclically, the DP *Karla* is merged as a complement of *obrázek* and consequently, it is c-commanded by *pro*. Later, given reconstruction of the restriction of the *wh*-operator with the R-expression *Karla* to its lower position, a violation of Condition C arises.[5]

The second approach is the cyclic merger analysis proposed by Chomsky (2004a) or Rubin (2003). This approach argues for strict cyclicity also in the case of adjunction. Specifically, in example (2), the relative clause *který měl Jirka rád* 'that Jirka liked' is adjoined to the NP *obrázek Karla* 'picture of Karel'

---

[3] I make the standard assumption that relative clauses are adjuncts. All relative clauses in this chapter are meant as restrictive. The grammatical status of some sentences is improved if the relative clause is interpreted non-restrictively. This is not surprising because non-restrictive relatives have many properties that are not typical for restrictives (it has been argued that non-restrictive relatives are generated separately from their host; that they are conjoined to the matrix clause; that they never form a constituent with their head etc.; see Bianchi 2002).

[4] For some speakers, coreference between *Karel* and the subject of the matrix clause is marginally possible if the overt pronoun *on* is used instead of *pro*. Czech is a *pro*-drop language and when the subject pronoun is overt, then it has a contrastive or emphatic function (*Mluvnice češtiny 3*, 1987). I will use *pro* in examples because it is the unmarked case.

[5] To account for reconstruction in cases like this, different strategies were used. For example, Lebeaux (1988) assumes that Condition C is an "everywhere" condition and Chomsky (1995) proposes the Preference Principle that forces the restriction of the *wh*-operator to be minimal. For discussion of differences between syntactic and semantic reconstruction, see Fox (1999, 2000) or Sternefeld (2001).

in its base position. This approach is based on the special status of adjunction and different types of merger. In contrast to the symmetrical set merger of two objects resulting in the set $\{\alpha, \beta\}$, adjunction of α to β, is realized as an asymmetrical pair-merge operation that results in the ordered pair $<\alpha, \beta>$. In this way, adjuncts are kept on a separate syntactic plane and hence they are exempt from standard c-command relations. Later, as part of the operation Spell-Out, adjunction is simplified by the operation Simpl(ification) that converts the ordered pair $<\alpha, \beta>$ into the set $\{\alpha, \beta\}$. Since Simpl applies where the relative clause adjunct is spelled out—that is, to the copy merged into SpecCP in (2)—and not to the (unpronounced) copy in the base position, the R-expression *Jirka* is not c-command-visible for *pro*. Therefore *Jirka* cannot be bound by *pro* and Condition C is obeyed. In contrast, since the R-expression *Karla* in (2) was set merged in the complement position of *obrázek*, it is c-command-visible for *pro* and Condition C is violated.

The remainder of this chapter is organized as follows. In Section 5.2, I will investigate different types of adjuncts in Czech and discuss how the cyclic and the late merger approach handle them. I will argue that there is a need to differentiate between clausal and non-clausal adjuncts with respect to coreference and Condition C. While non-clausal adjuncts containing a coindexed R-expression always produce a Condition C effect, clausal adjuncts with a coindexed R-expression can obviate Condition C effects. Coreference is possible if the clausal adjunct or the element containing it has a presuppositional status and if the R-expression is spelled out in the CP phase of the clausal adjunct. In Section 5.3, I will show that both the discussed approaches have problems with the data presented. I will argue that both clausal and non-clausal adjuncts are merged cyclically and that Condition C effects are not a uniform phenomenon. They can be induced by three different factors. I will argue that for coreference issues—as for reference issues—the correlation between the phase structure, tripartite quantificational structure and information structure of the sentence is relevant. R-expressions in the CP phase of clausal adjuncts can corefer with the coindexed pronoun because they are embedded enough in the structure and because they are interpreted as backgrounded in the CP phase. Then I will argue that the application of Condition C must be able to wait until the semantic interface of the highest phase in the sentence and that at least some pieces of information from the preceding phases cannot be forgotten. Conclusions will be drawn in Section 5.4.

5.2 Different Types of Adjuncts and Adjunct Merger

Here I will examine the behavior of different types of adjuncts with respect to Condition C effects and show that they behave differently. More specifically, I will show that it is necessary to distinguish between clausal adjuncts and non-clausal adjuncts. I will also demonstrate how the data are treated by the cyclic and late merger approach to adjunction.

5.2.1 Non-Clausal Adnominal Adjuncts

Let us begin with non-clausal PP adjuncts. I will deal here only with locative adjuncts, but what will be said holds for other non-clausal adnominal adjuncts as well. Consider example (3).

(3) * Kolik   knížek z   Pavlovy$_1$ police *pro*$_1$ přečetl?
     how-many books from Pavel's   shelf   read
     'How many books from Pavel's shelf did he read?'

To account for the Condition C effect in sentence (3), the R-expression *Pavlovy* within the adjunct should be c-commanded by the *pro* subject. Hence, there must be a lower position in the structure into which the restriction of the *wh*-operator containing the R-expression is reconstructed. This is naturally ensured if the adjunct is inserted into the derivation cyclically—in the base position of the object—albeit not by pair merge.[6]

It has been observed in the literature (Heycock 1995; Fox 1999, 2000; Witkoś 2003) that there is a correlation between bleeding Condition C, wide scope, and the presuppositional interpretation of the appropriate *wh*-phrase. Let us look at what happens when the presuppositional *wh*-phrase *který* 'which' or partitive *který z* 'which of' are used instead of non-presuppositional *kolik* 'how many' in sentence (3). Both *wh*-phrases presuppose the existence of a set of books on Pavel's shelf, hence one may assume that the restriction of the *wh*-operator does not reconstruct and Condition C effects do not arise. However, this expectation is not met, as demonstrated by example (4). We find the same pattern as in example (3). The adjuncts in both sentences in (4) show reconstruction behavior.

(4) a. * Kterou knížku z   Pavlovy$_1$ police *pro*$_1$ přečetl?
         which book   from Pavel's   shelf   read
         'Which book from Pavel's shelf did he read?'

---

[6] The control sentence (i) shows that the ungrammaticality of sentence (3) is due to the given coindexation. (3) is grammatical with non-identical indices or with two different R-expressions. Consider also the grammatical example (8) with the coindexed anaphor *své*, which shows that the problem lies in the R-expression.

(1) Kolik   knížek z   Pavlovy$_1$ police Jirka/*pro*$_2$ přečetl?
     how-many books from Pavel's   shelf Jirka-NOM read
     'How many books from Pavel's shelf did Jirka/he read?'

b. * Kterou z knížek z   Pavlovy₁ police *pro*₁ přečetl?
     which of books from Pavel's   shelf   read
     'Which of the books from Pavel's shelf did he read?'

Similarly example (5), which is a modified version of Fox's example (1999: 165), demonstrates that a Condition C effect arises regardless of whether 'many' has scope over 'decide' or 'decide' over 'many.'[7]

(5) * Kolik   lidí   z   Pavlova₁ města se *pro*₁ rozhodl
      how-many people from Pavel's city   self   decided
      najmout?
      hire
      'How many people from Pavel's city did he decide to hire?'

As shown in the following example (6), the information-structural status of the elements containing the adjunct does not play any role either with respect to reconstruction and Condition C. It does not make any difference whether the DP with the adjunct is topicalized (6a) or scrambled (6b), i.e. back-grounded; the R-expression *Pavlovy* embedded in the adjunct always yields a Condition C effect.

(6) a. * Tu knížku   z   Pavlovy₁ police *pro*₁ v pátek   přečetl.
          the book-ACC from Pavel's shelf   on Friday read
          'The book from Pavel's shelf, he read on Friday.'

     b. * V pátek   tu knížku   z   Pavlovy₁ police *pro*₁/on₁
          on Friday the book-ACC from Pavel's   shelf
          přečetl.[8]
          read
          'On Friday, he read the book from Pavel's shelf.'

If the DP with the locative adjunct stays in situ so that the R-expression contained in the adjunct is c-commanded by the coindexed pronoun, Condition C is, of course, violated, as demonstrated by example (7).

(7) *V pátek   *pro*₁ přečetl tu knížku   z   Pavlovy₁ police.
      on Friday   read   the book-ACC from Pavel's   shelf
      'On Friday, he read the book from Pavel's shelf.'

---

[7] The term *kolik* represents both parts of the English complex quantifier *how many* (for what number N are there N many). The two readings then can be paraphrased as follows:

(i) What is the number N, such that there are N many people from Pavel's city, such that he decided to hire them? (many > decide)
(ii) What is the number N, such that he decided to hire N many people from Pavel's city? (decide > many)

[8] The overt pronoun *on* is used to show that the scrambled element can precede the subject as well.

Thus, the data above suggest that non-clausal adnominal adjuncts merge cyclically, namely not by pair merge. This seems surprising if one takes into account the possibility of adjuncts merging late (as proposed by the late merger approach) or being c-command-invisible (as proposed by the cyclic merger approach). However, there is an argument from Binding Condition A that shows that non-clausal adnominal adjuncts indeed merge cyclically. The grammatical sentence (8) demonstrates that the adjunct with the anaphor *své* 'self' cannot be merged acyclically after *wh*-movement of the object; it must be merged in the c-command domain of the clausal subject.

(8) Kolik   knížek ze   své$_i$ police Pavel$_i$/pro$_i$ přečetl?
     how-many books from self shelf   Pavel-NOM read
     'How many books from his shelf did he read?'

Another argument supporting the cyclic merger analysis comes from examples like (9). The pronoun *jeho* 'his' contained in the adjunct can be bound by the quantifier *každému* 'everybody,' which suggests that the adjunct with the pronoun was merged with the direct object before its topicalization.

(9) (Nějakou) knížku   z   jeho$_i$ police *pro* každému dítěti$_i$
     (some)   book-ACC from his   shelf   every   child-DAT
     četla po večerech.
     read in evenings
     'A book from his shelf, she read every child in the evenings.'

To conclude this section, non-clausal adnominal adjuncts seem to behave like arguments. Condition C effects and other reconstruction phenomena suggest that non-clausal adnominal adjuncts are merged cyclically and that they reconstruct regardless of the presuppositional and information-structural status of the containing phrase. Thus, they pose a problem for both the discussed approaches because theoretically, one should get a grammatical sentence with an R-expression within a non-clausal adnominal adjunct (that is either c-command-invisible or late merged).

5.2.2 *Clausal Adnominal Adjuncts*

In the preceding section, we saw that with respect to Condition C, non-clausal adnominal adjuncts are always bad. What about clausal adnominal adjuncts? Sentence (2) demonstrates that relative clause adjuncts in Czech behave as their English counterparts. To illustrate this issue properly, let us have a look at more examples. First consider sentence (10), which is slightly degraded under the given coindexation. The clausal adjunct with the R-expression *Pavel* does not feed Condition C, which suggests that the relative clause does not have to be present or c-command-visible in the lower copy of the *wh*-phrase.

(10) ? Který argument, který Pavel₁ přednesl, *pro*₁ zuřivě
which argument which Pavel-NOM gave furiously
bránil?
defended
'Which argument that Pavel gave did he defend like fury?'

If the partitive presuppositional *wh*-phrase is used (11a), the adjunct also shows an anti-reconstruction behavior; but it seems that with the partitive *wh*-phrase coreference works a little better. However, if the *wh*-phrase is non-presuppositional as in (11b), i.e. it is a question only about the number of the arguments with the restriction reconstructed, the sentence is bad.

(11) a. ? Který z argumentů, které Pavel₁ přednesl, *pro*₁
which of arguments which Pavel-NOM gave
zuřivě bránil?
furiously defended
'Which of the arguments that Pavel gave did he defend like fury?'

b. ?* Kolik argumentů, které Pavel₁ přednesl, *pro*₁
how-many arguments which Pavel-NOM gave
zuřivě bránil?
furiously defended
'How many arguments that Pavel gave did he defend like fury?'

The sentence (10) becomes perfectly acceptable if the adverbial *taky* 'also'—an additive focus particle—is used, as in (12a). *Taky* presupposes a contextually given set of alternatives, to which the element associated with *taky* is added. In example (12a), it is the event *zuřivě bránil* 'defended like fury' that is added to the alternatives. Since the event of giving the arguments (*přednesl*) is introduced into the set of alternatives to the event (*zuřivě bránil*), and since the arguments were given by *Pavel*, coreference between both subjects *Pavel* and *pro* is necessary. Then, the meaning of sentence (12a) is: For which x, such that x is an argument that Pavel gave, does it hold that Pavel also defended x? That *pro* must indeed be coreferential with *Pavel* in this case is illustrated in sentence (12b), which is ungrammatical because of distinct subjects.[9] The presence of the additive adverbial in (12a) reduces the coreference possibilities, and in this way it improves the grammatical status of sentence (10).

[9] The focus particle *taky* may not be stressed because then the associated element would be *Jirka* and this would induce a set of alternatives to him.

(12) a. Který argument, který Pavel₁   přednesl, *pro*₁ taky
          which argument which Pavel-NOM gave   also
          zuřivě   bránil?
          furiously defended
          'Which argument that Pavel gave did he also defend like fury?'

      b. *Který argument, který Pavel   přednesl, Jirka   taky
          which argument which Pavel-NOM gave   Jirka-NOM also
          zuřivě   bránil?
          furiously defended
          'Which argument that Pavel gave did Jirka also defend like fury?'

The following example demonstrates that the information structure of the relative clause itself is an important factor in Condition C as well.[10] In sentence (13a), which minimally differs from (10), the R-expression *Pavel* stays in situ and is narrowly focused in the adjunct clause and coreference between *Pavel* and *pro* in the matrix clause is not possible. For *Pavel* to be a possible antecedent of *pro*, it must be backgrounded, as in (10).[11, 12]

(13) a. *Který argument, který přednesl Pavel₁,   *pro*₁ zuřivě
          which argument which gave   Pavel-NOM   furiously
          bránil?
          defended
          'Which argument that Pavel gave did he defend like fury?'

      b. *Který argument, který přednesl v pondělí   Pavel₁,   *pro*₁
          which argument which gave   on Monday Pavel-NOM
          zuřivě   bránil?
          furiously defended
          'Which argument that Pavel gave on Monday did he defend like fury?'

[10] Note that information structure can be recursive; see Krifka (1992); Partee (1992); Meinunger (2000); Ishihara (2004a, 2004b); Neeleman & Szendrői (2004).

[11] Compare van Riemsdijk & Williams (1981: 203), who show that the coindexed R-expression cannot be a focus NP:

(i)   a. Which picture that MARY gave to John₁ did he₁ want most desperately?

      b. * Which picture that Mary gave to JOHN₁ did he₁ want most desperately?

[12] The control sentence (i) shows that (13a) is grammatical with non-identical indices or with two different R-expressions.

(i)   Který argument, který přednesl Pavel₁,   Jirka/*pro*₂ zuřivě   bránil?
      which argument which gave   Pavel-NOM Jirka-NOM   furiously defended
      'Which argument that Pavel gave did Jirka/he defend like fury?'

As illustrated by sentence (13b), as part of wide focus *Pavel* cannot be the antecedent for *pro* either. The temporal adverbial *v pondělí* 'on Monday' and the subject *Pavel* can stay in the *v*P phase and be focused there and the sentence is still ungrammatical. Thus, the R-expression antecedent of the subject pronoun must be backgrounded in the adjunct clause. From now on, I will refer to this condition as the Background Adjunct Coreference Principle:

(14)   *Background Adjunct Coreference Principle* (1st version)
       Coreference between an R-expression within an adjunct clause and the
       subject pronoun in the matrix clause is possible only if the R-expression
       is backgrounded in the adjunct clause.

So far I have dealt with the information structure of the adjunct clause. Let us now look closer at the information structure of the matrix clause. In the preceding section I showed that non-clausal adjuncts induce a Condition C effect independently of the information-structural status of their host. It is fair to ask how it works in the case of clausal adjuncts. Consider the contrast between sentences (15a) and (15b), which are modified examples taken from Witkoś (2003: 77).

(15)   a.   ? Na Mariinu tetu,   kterou si Pavel₁   nepamatuje,
            to Marie's aunt-ACC which self Pavel-NOM NEG-remembers
            *pro*₁ reagoval s   hněvem.
                    reacted with anger
            'To Marie's aunt that Pavel does not remember he reacted with
            anger.'

       b.   * Na Mariinu tetu,   kterou si nepamatuje   Pavel₁,
            to Marie's aunt-ACC which self NEG-remembers Pavel-NOM
            *pro*₁ reagoval s   hněvem.
                    reacted with anger
            'To Marie's aunt that Pavel does not remember he reacted with
            anger.'

(15) shows that the adjunct clause contained in the topicalized PP can obviate a Condition C effect. And as in the previous sentences with *wh*-movement, (10) and (13), Condition C effects do not arise if the R-expression is backgrounded in the adjunct clause. But if the R-expression is focused in the adjunct clause,

the sentence is ungrammatical again.[13] The conclusion is obvious; what is critical for the grammaticality of the sentence is the information-structural status of the R-expression in the adjunct clause, not just the adjunct status of the relative clause or the information-structural status of the element containing the adjunct clause.

Both the cyclic merger and the late merger approach have a problem with these data because it is not clear what the information-structural status of the R-expression in the adjunct clause has to do with the timing of adjunct merger or with the type of adjunct merger.

If the adjunct clause with the coindexed R-expression is overtly c-commanded by the pronoun, the sentence is ungrammatical, as you can see in (16).

(16) * *pro*₁ reagoval s   hněvem na Mariinu tetu,   kterou si
      reacted with anger to Marie's aunt-ACC which self
      Pavel₁   nepamatuje.
      Pavel-NOM NEG-remembers
      'He reacted with anger to Marie's aunt that Pavel does not remember.'

According to Fitzpatrick & Groat (2005), late merger of adjuncts and derivational c-command[14] make interesting predictions for cases where the pronoun relevant for Condition C occurs in the DP containing the clausal adjunct. This is demonstrated in (17) by Czech paraphrases of Fitzpatrick & Groat's (2005: 5) examples.

---

[13] The same results are obtained with the adjunct clause contained in scrambled elements:

(i) a. ? Včera   na (tu) Mariinu tetu,   kterou si Pavel₁   nepamatuje,   *pro*₁
         yesterday to (the) Marie's aunt-ACC which self Pavel-NOM NEG-remembers
         reagoval s   hněvem.
         reacted with anger
         'Yesterday, to Marie's aunt that Pavel does not remember, he reacted with anger.'

    b. * Včera   na (tu) Mariinu tetu,   kterou si nepamatuje Pavel₁,   *pro*₁
         yesterday to (the) Marie's aunt-ACC which self NEG-remembers Pavel-NOM
         reagoval s   hněvem.
         reacted with anger
         'Yesterday, to Marie's aunt that Pavel does not remember, he reacted with anger.'

[14] Fitzpatrick & Groat (2005) follow Epstein *et al.* (1998) and Epstein (1999) and define derivational c-command as follows:

(i) A term X c-commands all and only the terms of a term Y with which it is merged. The terms of X are:

    a. X

    b. The terms of the daughters of X.

(17)   a.   * Která z jeho$_1$ tvrzení, že   Pavel$_1$ byl nemocný,
             which of his   claims   that Pavel-NOM was sick
             Marie   vyvrátila?
             Marie-NOM refuted
             'Which of his claims that Pavel was sick did Marie refute?'

       b.   Který z jeho$_1$ argumentů, které Pavel$_1$ považoval
             which of his   arguments   which Pavel-NOM considered
             za dobré, Marie   kritizovala?
             good   Marie-NOM criticized
             'Which of his arguments that Pavel considered to be good did
             Marie criticize?'

       c.   * Který z jeho$_1$ argumentů, které považoval za dobré
             which of his   arguments   which considered good
             Pavel$_1$,,   Marie   kritizovala?
             Pavel-NOM Marie-NOM criticized
             'Which of his arguments that Pavel considered to be good did
             Marie criticize?'

Sentence (17a) shows that the R-expression *Pavel* inside the complement clause induces a Condition C effect because the complement is merged cyclically prior to merger of *jeho* 'his'. In contrast, in sentence (17b), according to Fitzpatrick & Groat (2005), the adjunct clause *které Pavel považoval za dobré* 'that Pavel considered to be good' would be merged acyclically after *wh*-movement of the *wh*-phrase *který z jeho argumentů* 'which of his arguments.' This means that the adjunct was not present in the structure when the pronoun was merged; hence the R-expression *Pavel* contained in the adjunct is not derivationally c-commanded by the pronoun. Consequently, no Condition C effect arises. However, (17c) illustrates that in this case, too, the R-expression cannot be coreferential with the pronoun if the sentence does not observe the Background Adjunct Coreference Principle. Thus, the late merger approach with derivational c-command also cannot explain why adjunct clauses with a focused R-expression as in (17c) cannot avoid a violation of Condition C as in (17b). Since the coindexed pronoun in (17) is not a subject pronoun, I modify the Background Adjunct Coreference Principle as follows:

(18)   *Background Adjunct Coreference Principle* (2nd version)
       Coreference between an R-expression within an adjunct clause and a
       pronoun in the matrix clause is possible only if the R-expression is
       backgrounded in the adjunct clause.

The conclusion drawn from this section is that clausal adnominal adjuncts can—in contrast to non-clausal adnominal adjuncts—obviate Condition C effects. We have seen that factors such as the presuppositional status of the elements containing the adjunct clause or information-structural properties of the coindexed R-expression play a role in the availability of coreference between the R-expression in the adjunct clause and the pronoun in the matrix clause. We have also seen that there are Condition C data that pose a problem for the cyclic merger and late merger approaches.

5.2.3 *Non-Clausal Adverbial Adjuncts*

In this section, I consider the behavior of some adverbial prepositional phrases with respect to Condition C. It has been argued—see, for example, Bošković & Lasnik (1999), Ochi (1999*b*), Nissenbaum (2000), and discussion in Speas (1990) or Stepanov (2000, 2001)—that adverbial adjuncts, similarly to adnominal adjuncts, can or must be merged acyclically as well. However, it will be shown that non-clausal adverbial adjuncts, like non-clausal adnominal adjuncts, always produce Condition C effects.

Consider example (19) with the *wh*-moved temporal adverbial. Although, given the inherent presuppositional status of the *wh*-word *který* 'which,' the existence of a set of Pavel's vacations is presupposed, the sentence induces a Condition C effect.

(19)   * O   kterých Pavlových$_1$ prázdninách *pro*$_1$ líbal   Marii?
         during which   Pavel's   vacation   kissed Marie-ACC
         'During which of Pavel's vacation did he kiss Marie?'

As far as manner adjuncts are concerned, the ungrammatical sentence (20) suggests that the relevant part of the adverbial adjunct with the R-expression reconstructs and is c-commanded by *pro*, resulting in a violation of Principle C.[15]

(20)   * Kterým Pavlovým$_1$ způsobem *pro*$_1$ líbal   Marii?
         which   Pavel's   way   kissed Marie-ACC
         'In which way of Pavel's did he kiss Marie?'

The following examples show that topicalized adverbial adjuncts give the same results. It seems that they cannot be merged directly into the topicalized

---

[15] Sentences with a non-presuppositional *wh*-word are bad too; consider (i):

(i)   * Jakým Pavlovým$_1$ způsobem *pro*$_1$ líbal   Marii?
        what   Pavel's   way   kissed Marie-ACC
        'In what way of Pavel's did he kiss Marie?'

position;[16] they seem to be merged below the position of *pro*, then topicalized, and although spelled out in a position c-commanding the *pro*, they are still c-command-visible for the *pro*. This is demonstrated by (21) for temporal adverbials and by (22) for manner adverbials. Thus, examples such as these call Chomsky's (2004*a*) cyclic merger approach into question.[17]

(21)   * O   Pavlových$_1$ prázdninách *pro*$_1$ líbal   Marii.
          during   Pavel's   vacation   kissed Marie-ACC
          'During Pavel's vacation, he kissed Marie.'

(22)   * Pavlovým$_1$ způsobem *pro*$_1$ líbal   Marii.
          Pavel's   way   kissed Marie-ACC
          'In Pavel's way, he kissed Marie.'

Concerning the time of adjunction of these adverbial adjuncts, they might be merged acyclically, for example into a *v*P-adjoined position below scrambled elements, but this late merger would have to precede the merger to the topic position or *wh*-position.[18] And if their late merger also follows merger of the *pro* into SpecTP, it is not possible to employ the derivational c-command approach.

Reconstruction phenomena as to Condition A demonstrate that adverbial adjuncts are merged into the c-command domain of the subject and not directly into their surface positions. Consider example (23) with the topicalized temporal adverbial and (24) with the topicalized manner adverbial.

(23)   O   svých$_1$ prázdninách Pavel$_1$/*pro*$_1$ líbal   Marii.
          during   self   vacation   Pavel-NOM kissed Marie-ACC
          'During his vacation, Pavel / he kissed Marie.'

(24)   Tím svým$_1$ způsobem Pavel$_1$/*pro*$_1$ líbal   Marii.
          the self   way   Pavel-NOM kissed Marie-ACC
          'In his own way, Pavel / he kissed Marie.'

---

[16] Theoretically, they might merge there, but then one should account for why they lower, which is not easy under the standard assumption that adjuncts are not selected.

[17] (i) shows that the ungrammaticality of examples like (21) is due to the given coindexation. Consider also (23) with the coindexed anaphor *svých* showing that the problem lies in the R-expression.

(i)   O   Pavlových$_1$ prázdninách Jirka/*pro*$_2$ líbal   Marii.
        during   Pavel's   vacation   Jirka-NOM kissed Marie-ACC
        'During Pavel's vacation, Jirka/he kissed Marie.'

[18] Johnson (2003) uses the fact that adjuncts feed movement operations like *wh*-movement against Stepanov (2000, 2001), who proposes that adjuncts are merged into the structure after all other processes are complete.

The following examples with quantifier-bound pronouns also show that the adverbial adjuncts are not merged directly into their surface positions. Since the pronouns can be bound by the quantifier, (25) and (26) suggest that there is a lower copy of the adjunct c-commanded by the scrambled indirect object.

(25) O jeho$_1$ narozeninách *pro* každému dítěti$_1$ dali dárek.
      on his   birthday   every child-DAT gave present-ACC
      'On his birthday, they gave every child a present.'

(26) Tím jeho$_1$ způsobem *pro* každému dítěti$_1$ signalizovali
      the his way   every child-DAT signalled
      konec   hry.
      end-ACC game
      'In his own way, they signalled every child that the game ended.'

If the adverbial adjunct containing the R-expression occurs in a position c-commanded by the coindexed pronoun, a Condition C effect appears as well, as demonstrated by (27) and (28).

(27) * *pro*$_1$ líbal Marii   o   Pavlových$_1$ prázdninách.
           kissed Marie-ACC during Pavel's   vacation
      'He kissed Marie during Pavel's vacation.'

(28) * *pro*$_1$ líbal Marii   Pavlovým$_1$ způsobem.
           kissed Marie-ACC Pavel's   way
      'He kissed Marie in Pavel's way.'

To summarize this section, non-clausal adverbial adjuncts seem to always reconstruct and violate Condition C. In the case of *wh*-movement, Condition C effects arise independently of the referential status of the appropriate *wh*-word. While the acyclic merger approach is conceivable under certain (very restricted) conditions, Chomsky's (2004a) cyclic merger is not. With respect to the cyclic approach one has to ask how it is possible that adjuncts overtly c-commanding the pronoun—copies of which should be c-command-invisible—produce Condition C effects. In the case of the acyclic merger approach, one should ask why the late merger does not help adjuncts to avoid Condition C effects.

5.2.4 Clausal Adverbial Adjuncts

I showed above that clausal adnominal adjuncts can obviate Condition C. Therefore one can expect that the clausality of the adjunct plays a role in the case of adverbial adjuncts as well. Thus, in this section, I will test the prediction that there are cases where an R-expression within a clausal adverbial adjunct can be coreferential with the pronoun in the matrix clause. If you take a look at example (29), you can see that this prediction is met.

(29) Než   Pavel₁   odjel, *pro*₁ políbil Marii.
      before Pavel-NOM left   kissed Marie-ACC
      'Before Pavel left, he kissed Marie.'

If the R-expression *Pavel* is c-commanded by *pro*, as in example (30), the sentence is ungrammatical. Condition C effects can be obviated only when the adjunct clause is preposed (backgrounded) as in example (29). That the temporal adjunct is backgrounded in (29) is evidenced by the felicitous context question *Co se stalo, než Pavel odjel?* 'What happened before Pavel left?' and the infelicitous question *Kdy políbil Marii?* 'When did he kiss Marie?', given that the question-answer correlation helps to determine information structure; see Sgall, Hajičová, & Buráňová (1980), Büring (1997), Erteschik-Shir (1997), Meinunger (2000), Engdahl (2001), and Drubig (2003), among others.

(30) * *pro*₁ políbil Marii,   než   Pavel₁   odjel.
           kissed Marie-ACC before Pavel-NOM left
      'He kissed Marie before Pavel left.'

The availability of coreference between the R-expression within the temporal adjunct and the pronoun in the matrix clause depends on the position of the adjunct clause in the sentence and, as in the case of relative clause adjuncts, on the Background Adjunct Coreference Principle. Consider the ungrammatical example (31), in which the R-expression *Pavel* is focused in the temporal adjunct.[19, 20]

---

[19] The generalization also holds in the case of other types of predicates and clausal adjuncts. Consider (i) with a transitive predicate and a manner adjunct:

(i) a. Tím, že   Pavel₁   políbil Marii,   *pro*₁ potrestal Jitku.
         the   that Pavel-NOM kissed Marie-ACC   punished Jitka-ACC
         'Pavel punished Jitka by kissing Marie.'

     b. * Tím, že   Marii   políbil Pavel₁,   *pro*₁ potrestal Jitku.
          the   that Marie-ACC kissed Pavel-NOM   punished Jitka-ACC
          'Pavel punished Jitka by kissing Marie.'

     c. * *pro*₁ potrestal Jitku   tím, že   Pavel₁   políbil Marii
               punished Jitka-ACC the   that Pavel-NOM kissed Marie-ACC
          'Pavel punished Jitka by kissing Marie.'

[20] The control example (i) shows that the ungrammaticality of (31) is due to coindexation.

(i) Než   odjel Pavel₁,   Jirka/*pro*₂ políbil Marii.
     before left Pavel-NOM Jirka   kissed Marie-ACC
     'Before Pavel left, Jirka/he kissed Marie.'

(31)   * Než   odjel Pavel$_1$,   *pro*$_1$ políbil Marii.
        before   left   Pavel-NOM   kissed   Marie-ACC
        'Before Pavel left, he kissed Marie.'

The coindexed R-expression must also be backgrounded in those cases where it is not the subject of the adjunct clause. Compare the grammatical sentence (32a) with the bad sentence (32b), which differ only in the information-structural status of the object; in (32a) *Pavel* is backgrounded and in (32b) it is focused.

(32)   a.   Poté, co   Pavla$_1$ vyhodili z   práce, *pro*$_1$ začal pít.
          after   that   Pavel-ACC   fired   from job   began   drink
          'After Pavel was fired from his job, he began to drink.'

       b.   * Poté, co   vyhodili z   práce Pavla$_1$,   *pro*$_1$ začal pít.
          after   that   fired   from job   Pavel-ACC   began   drink
          'After Pavel was fired from his job, he began to drink.'

The same is true also in those cases where the coindexed pronoun is not the subject of the matrix clause, as illustrated by the contrast in example (33).

(33)   a.   Poté, co   Pavla$_1$ vyhodili z   práce, táta   ho$_1$
          after   that   Pavel-ACC   fired   from job   father-NOM   him
          začal   bít.
          began   maltreat
          'After Pavel was fired from his job, his father began to maltreat him.'

       b.   * Poté, co   vyhodili z   práce Pavla$_1$,   táta   ho$_1$
          after   that   fired   from job   Pavel-ACC   father-NOM   him
          začal   bít.
          began   maltreat
          'After Pavel was fired from his job, his father began to maltreat him.'

So, clausal adverbial adjuncts spelled out in a position c-commanded by the pronoun produce a Condition C effect. This fact is in line with the cyclic merger approach and goes against the acyclic merger (of the adjunct clause with *v*P after merger of *pro* into SpecTP) with derivational c-command. The acyclic merger approach without the derivational definition of c-command is possible; it will correctly derive ungrammatical sentences, again assuming adjunction to *v*P and *pro* in the specifier of TP. When clausal adjuncts are preposed, a Condition C effect appears when the Background Adjunct Coreference Principle is not observed. This is a problem for the cyclic merger approach with its c-command-visibility analysis. The acyclic merger approach (at least its loose types) can solve this ungrammatical situation arguing that in the appropriate cases, the adverbial adjunct is merged cyclically and then preposed. This, however, cannot account for the dependency between the position and information-structural status of the R-expression in the adjunct clause and the occurrence of Condition C effects.

5.3 Theoretical Consequences and Analysis

In this section, I sum up the empirical arguments against the cyclic merger approach and the acyclic merger approach. Then I will argue that both clausal and non-clausal adjuncts are merged cyclically and that Condition C effects are not a uniform phenomenon. I will also discuss the distinction between clausal and non-clausal adjuncts and specify conditions under which an R-expression contained in a clausal adjunct can corefer with the coindexed pronoun. Finally, I will discuss the place of application of Condition C.

5.3.1 *The Cyclic and Acyclic Approach and Empirical Problems*

It has been shown that there is a distinction in the behavior of non-clausal and clausal adjuncts. Whereas non-clausal adjuncts—regardless of whether they are adnominal or adverbial—always produce a Condition C effect, clausal adjuncts of both types can obviate Condition C effects under certain conditions. Thus, a theory of adjunction that tries to treat all adjuncts uniformly runs into difficulties.

Let us first have a look at Chomsky's (2004a) cyclic merger approach. Since according to this approach, all adjuncts are always merged by the pair-merge operation—in contrast to the set merger of arguments—making them c-command-invisible until Spell-Out, it cannot differentiate between the behavior of clausal and non-clausal adjuncts.

Another problem of Chomsky's approach (2004a) is that the operation Simpl(ification), which converts the ordered pair into a set and thus makes adjuncts c-command-visible, applies where the adjunct is spelled out. This predicts that lower copies of the moved adjunct do not induce a Condition C effect. However, this prediction is not true, as was demonstrated by non-clausal adjuncts or clausal adjuncts contained in a non-presuppositional element.

Chomsky's approach also does not give an explanation for the dependency between the availability of coreference and the position and information-structural status of the R-expression in clausal adjuncts.

Rubin's proposal (2003) faces the same problems as Chomsky (2004a) because he suggests that adjuncts are headed by a functional head

Mod(ification) and all phrases headed by this head are subject to the pair-merge operation, which brings about the same consequences as Chomsky's approach (2004*a*).

Chomsky also discusses instances of extraposed adjuncts and relative clause adjuncts and argues that adjuncts are always spelled out where their hosts are; consider (34).

(34)   In $<\alpha, \beta>$, α is spelled out where β is.

$$\text{(Chomsky 2004}a\text{: 119)}$$

However, there is a counter-argument to this claim, namely discontinuous noun phrases in Slavic languages, Latin, German, and other languages (see Bošković 2005; Fanselow & Ćavar 2002). As demonstrated by the following example, Spell-Out of the topicalized adjunct *z Pavlovy police* 'from Pavel's shelf' can be dissociated from Spell-Out of its host *dvě knihy* 'two books' in the *v*P phase.

(35)   [Z   Pavlovy police]$_1$ *pro* přečetl dvě knihy t_1.
          from Pavel's   shelf   read   two books-ACC
          'He read two books from Pavel's shelf.'

I now turn to the acyclic merger approach. As already mentioned in *n.* 18, Stepanov's proposal (2000, 2001) according to which adjunction must follow all non-adjunct mergers has problems with the fact that adjunction feeds other types of movement, as was pointed out by Johnson (2003). Stepanov (2000, 2001) tries to avoid the problem of *wh*-adjuncts arguing that *wh*-adjuncts are in fact selected and consequently have to be merged cyclically. However, other problems with adjuncts that can reconstruct, for example, topicalized non-clausal adjuncts, still remain.

In the other acyclic merger approaches (the Lebeaux-style 1988 approaches), adjuncts are just given the possibility of being merged late. This predicts that adjuncts should be able to obviate a Condition C effect. But, as mentioned above with respect to Chomsky's approach (2004*a*), this is not corroborated by the data. Non-clausal adjuncts never obviate Condition C effects and clausal adjuncts only do so if they are presuppositional or contained in a presuppositional element and obey the Background Adjunct Coreference Principle. So, these regularities also pose a problem for the Lebeaux-style approaches.[21]

The acyclic approach with derivational c-command (Fitzpatrick & Groat 2005) faces the same problem. For example, it predicts, contrary to fact, that

---

[21] These regularities would probably pose a problem also for Kayne's (2002) movement approach, where the pronoun and its antecedent start as one constituent.

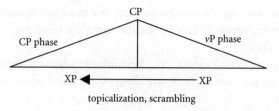

FIGURE 5.1 Backgrounded and specific interpretation of moved elements

a relative clause adjunct containing a focalized R-expression can be merged into the DP with the relevant possessive pronoun acyclically and thus avoid a Condition C violation.

5.3.2 *Cyclic Merger*

Since non-clausal adjuncts—no matter whether adverbial or adnominal— always produce a Condition C effect and since they exhibit reconstruction effects with respect to Condition A and quantifier binding, I assume that they are merged cyclically. In fact, they might be merged acyclically, but, as already discussed in Section 5.2.3, this would have to be before their further movement or movement of the element containing them. And if derivational c-command is assumed, it would also have to be before merger of the relevant c-commanding pronoun (or the c-commanding subject for Condition A phenomena or the c-commanding quantified phrase in the case of quantifier binding). Unless there is a necessity to accept this analysis, I will pursue the cyclic merger analysis.[22]

Before moving on to clausal adjuncts, let us specify more closely the theoretical framework. In Biskup (2006*a*) it is demonstrated that phrases moved to the CP phase—scrambled or topicalized—are interpreted as backgrounded and get a specific interpretation (see Fig. 5.1). The specificity can be epistemic, partitive or generic. I propose that this is driven by the interface requirement that backgrounded specific elements are linearized and interpreted in the CP phase in scrambling languages like Czech.

Therefore, building on Diesing (1992), Partee (1992), and Chomsky (2000, 2001, 2004*a*, 2008), I argue that there is a correlation between the phase structure, tripartite quantificational structure and information structure of

---

[22] Although adjuncts are taken to be merged cyclically, this is not to say that adjuncts generally cannot be generated in the left periphery of the sentence. As pointed out to me by an anonymous reviewer, Cecchetto & Chierchia (1999) argue that Italian clitic left-dislocated PPs are base-generated in the left periphery. According to them, given chain binding at LF, a Condition C violation is due to the clitic (or a theta grid element) coming from the lower part of the sentence. In Section 5.3.3, I show that clausal adverbial adjuncts can be externally merged in the left periphery of the sentence.

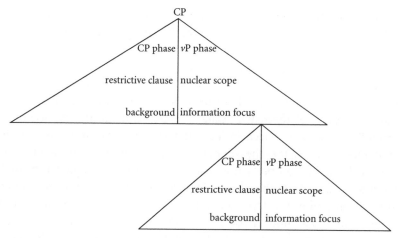

Figure 5.2 FIGURE 5.2 Recursivity of phase, quantificational, and information structure

the clause. Thus, at the semantic interface, the *v*P phase (the elements in the phase) is interpreted as the nuclear scope of the quantificational structure and the domain of information focus. The CP phase is interpreted as the domain of the restrictive clause and the domain of background. And this structure can be recursive (see Partee 1992, Krifka 1992, Meinunger 2000, Neeleman & Szendrői 2004, and Ishihara 2004*a*, *b*), as schematized in Fig. 5.2.

Now, let us look at clausal adjuncts. We have seen that they can avoid Condition C effects under certain conditions. This is possible in the case of the presuppositional status (inherently presuppositional *wh*-phrases or backgrounded elements) of the clausal adjunct or the element containing it and the backgrounded information-structural status of the relevant R-expression. In addition, the clausal adjunct cannot be spelled out in a position c-commanded by the coindexed pronoun.

Thus, there are two basic points of view. Either clausal adjuncts are merged cyclically similarly to non-clausal adjuncts, and then it is necessary to account for why in the appropriate cases they do not induce a Condition C effect; or they are merged acyclically in the cases where they do not produce a Condition C effect and cyclically in the cases where they do.[23]

---

[23] This reasoning is relevant to relative clause adjuncts. To clausal adverbial adjuncts, it is relevant only under the assumption of derivational c-command because late merger of clausal adverbial adjuncts is taken to merge these adverbials to the same position as cyclic merger. So, in the cases of obviating a Condition C violation, adverbial adjuncts would be merged into the structure after merger of the coindexed pronoun and then preposed. Another option would be to assume that the preposed clausal adverbial adjuncts that do not induce Condition C effects are merged directly to their overt position; see discussion below.

Let us pursue the second possibility for the moment. Recall that obviating a Condition C violation is dependent on the Background Adjunct Coreference Principle. According to the phase-based model proposed above, sentences are sent to the interfaces phase by phase and the CP phase is interpreted as background and the *v*P phase as focus. So, for the Background Adjunct Coreference Principle to be able to filter out the inappropriate cases at the semantic interface of the matrix clause CP phase, it must know where the relevant R-expression has been spelled out in the adjunct clause. More specifically, it must know whether the coindexed R-expression checks the appropriate feature with the EPP property responsible for movement to the CP phase in the adjunct clause. Note that the case where the R-expression is not present in the background of the acyclically merged (and then moved in the case of adverbial adjunct) adjunct clause and where consequently this R-expression, not being in accordance with the Background Adjunct Coreference Principle, induces a Condition C effect, is indistinguishable from the cases where the adjunct clause with the R-expression in focus is merged cyclically and then moved.[24] Thus, if one wants to keep the original idea of two different mergers and not to have these two types of Condition C effects, it would be necessary to eliminate the cases where adjuncts having the R-expression in focus are merged acyclically. This means that the derivation should know already, before merger of the adjunct clause, which R-expression (if there are more than one) should corefer and know its information-structural status to be able to decide whether the adjunct clause will be merged cyclically (if the R-expression is to be focused) or acyclically (if backgrounded). In addition, in the case of relative clause adjuncts, the derivation should know before merger of the adjunct whether its prospective host is presuppositional or not. Thus, given this look-ahead complication and the fact that the first point of view is theoretically more attractive—there is only one type of adjunct merger and consequently, only one type of merger generally, the cyclic one—I will follow the first point of view.

There is in fact an additional possible analysis, which is based on the assumption that merger of adjunct clauses is always acyclic. Condition C effects then would have to be ascribed to the (independent) Background Adjunct Coreference Principle. However, there are a few arguments against this hypothesis, and against the possibility of acyclic merger generally.

If we assume only acyclic merger for clausal adjuncts, we again have two types of merger—the cyclic one for non-clausal adjuncts and the acyclic one

---

[24] The first case involves just assigning the same semantic value but the second one also involves binding; see discussion in Section 5.3.3.

for clausal adjuncts—which, given the reductionism of Occam's Razor, undermines this proposal.

In Section 5.2.2, I demonstrated by example (11b), repeated below as (36), that the R-expression *Pavel* contained in the adjunct clause merged into the non-presuppositional *wh*-phrase produces a Condition C effect. Since the antecedent *Pavel* is backgrounded in the adjunct clause, the ungrammaticality of this sentence cannot be accounted for just by violation of the Background Adjunct Coreference Principle. However, it is naturally explained if the restriction of the *wh*-phrase containing *Pavel* reconstructs and hence violates Binding Condition C. It then follows that the adjunct clause cannot be merged acyclically.[25] If one holds the loose acyclic merger position, that is, that the adjunct clause in cases like (36) is merged cyclically and then moved with its host, then one needs to account for why the cyclic merger with preposing takes place just in cases of non-presuppositional *wh*-phrases.

(36) ?* Kolik   argumentů, které Pavel₁   přednesl, *pro*₁
         how-many arguments   which Pavel-NOM gave
         zuřivě   bránil?
         furiously defended
         'How many arguments that Pavel gave did he defend like fury?'

Further support for the cyclic merger analysis can be found if one considers quantifier-bound pronouns. *Pro* contained in the relative clause adjunct can be bound by the quantifier *každý* 'everybody' in example (37). This suggests that there is a lower copy of the *pro* c-commanded by the matrix clause subject.

(37) Kolik   argumentů, které *pro*₁ považoval za dobré,
         how-many arguments   which   considered good
         každý₁   přednesl?
         everybody-NOM gave
         'How many arguments that he considered to be good did everybody give?'

A potential argument against cyclic merger of clausal adjuncts might be sentence (17b), for convenience repeated below as (38). Recall that according to Fitzpatrick & Groat's approach (2005), the relative clause adjunct is merged acyclically after *wh*-movement of *který z jeho argumentů* 'which of his

---

[25] Degree questions represent another argument of this type. According to Heycock (1995), degree questions have an interpretation similar to the non-referential interpretations of amount questions (as in (36)). Since the R-expression within the adjunct clause contained in *wh*-moved degree predicates shows reconstruction effects, the clausal adjunct cannot be merged acyclically; see example (40) below.

arguments.' Therefore, given the derivational definition of c-command, there is no Condition C effect.

(38) Který z jeho₁ argumentů, které Pavel₁   považoval
      which of his   arguments which Pavel-NOM considered
      za dobré, Marie   kritizovala?
      good   Marie-NOM criticized
      'Which of his arguments that Pavel considered to be good did Marie criticize?'

To avoid this problem, one can analyze the relative clause *které Pavel považoval za dobré* 'that Pavel considered to be good' as an adjunct to *jeho argumentů* 'his arguments.' This means that the relative clause picks out from the modified NP—the set of his arguments—the ones that Pavel considered good. Then the derivation continues merging it with the preposition *z* (of) and so on. This analysis is supported by the fact that the following example (39) with the demonstrative pronoun *těch* is fully ok, which shows that the pronoun *jeho* can be a modifier and does not have to be the head D in sentence (38).

(39) Který z těch jeho₁ argumentů, které Pavel₁   považoval
      which of the his   arguments which Pavel-NOM considered
      za dobré, Marie   kritizovala?
      good   Marie-NOM criticized
      'Which of his arguments that Pavel considered to be good did Marie criticize?'

To sum up, both clausal and non-clausal adjuncts are merged cyclically. Since obviating a Condition C effect by clausal adjuncts embodies an obvious regularity, in the following section we will look more closely at this issue.

5.3.3 *Coreference and Condition C*

In this section, I argue that Condition C effects are not a uniform phenomenon. There are three different factors in Condition C effects: the Background Adjunct Coreference Principle, the antilocality requirement on coreference, and Condition C itself. I will show that Condition C effects in the case of clausal adjuncts can be attributed to Condition C or the Background Adjunct Coreference Principle and that Condition C effects in the case of non-clausal adjuncts can be attributed to Condition C or the antilocality requirement on coreference.

I have shown that not reconstructing the phrase containing the adjunct clause is a prerequisite for avoiding a Condition C violation, but I have not said much about how Condition C works. It was illustrated by example (36) (repeated from (11b)) and other examples in Section 5.2.2 that the presuppositional status of the *wh*-word in the *wh*-phrase containing the adjunct is crucial for avoiding a Condition C violation. Heycock (1995) argues that the referential status of the noun phrase within *wh*-moved degree predicates to which the relative clause is adjoined is important for Condition C as well. Consider the contrast in example (40), where (40a) with the relative clause adjoined to the non-specific indefinite is ungrammatical, whereas sentence (40b), where the relative clause is adjoined to the definite noun phrase and therefore not reconstructed, is grammatical.

(40) a. * [How afraid of some question Gore$_1$ hasn't prepared for]$_2$ do you think he$_1$ is t_2?

   b. [How afraid of the people Gore$_1$ insulted years ago]$_2$ do you think he$_1$ is t_2 now?

(Heycock 1995: 564–5)

Recall that I also argued in Section 5.2.2 that presupposition triggers, such as certain focus particles, can force the pronoun in the matrix clause and the R-expression in the adjunct to be coreferential.

   The generalization emerging from the clausal-adjunct data in Sections 5.2.2 and 5.2.4 is that for coreference to be possible, the R-expression in its overt position may not be c-commanded by the pronoun. Here, Chomsky's proposal (2004a) is right in that the place of Spell-Out plays an important role in Condition C. This observation is reminiscent of Lebeaux (1988: 148):

(41) If a, a name, is contained within a fronted adjunct then Condition C effects are abrogated; otherwise not.

The question arises why the overt position is so important. I have already argued that in scrambling languages like Czech, the place of Spell-Out of elements is narrowly associated with their interpretation and information-structural status; this was schematized in Fig. 5.1 and Fig. 5.2. A closer look at the grammatical examples with clausal adjuncts in Section 5.2.2 and 5.2.4 reveals—if we abstract away from the *wh*-examples—that the adjuncts, or the elements containing them, not overtly c-commanded by the pronoun are in fact backgrounded, that is, topicalized or scrambled.[26] Since backgrounding implies presuppositionality, the consequence is obvious. The R-expression does not reconstruct below the coindexed pronoun and therefore it does not

---

[26] As I show below, some clausal adverbial adjuncts can be merged directly to their left-peripheral position, but it changes nothing with respect to their backgrounded status, given the model proposed here.

violate Binding Condition C. Thus, the backgrounded or presuppositional status of clausal adjuncts or the elements containing them helps them not to reconstruct and so not to violate Condition C. More specifically, the anti-reconstruction behavior and the backgrounded status of the adjunct clause is due to the checking of the appropriate feature with the EPP property in the CP phase. If there is no LF, as Chomsky (2004a) proposes, reconstruction (the interpretation of the appropriate copy) takes place at the semantic interface. The presence of the checked feature always signals the place of interpretation of the appropriate element, as already mentioned in the case of the backgrounded R-expression, and is relevant to both Condition C and the Background Adjunct Coreference Principle. Thus, the presence of the checked feature on the adjunct means that at the semantic interface, the higher copy of the adjunct—that is, the copy in the matrix clause CP phase—will be interpreted.

This, however, is not the whole story. In the case of clausal adjuncts, one also has to take into account the second factor in Condition C effects. So, if the phrase containing the adjunct clause or the adjunct itself is presupposed and the R-expression does not violate Condition C, one has to ask whether the R-expression in the adjunct clause observes the Background Adjunct Coreference Principle, that is, whether the R-expression is spelled out in the CP phase of the adjunct clause. As in the case of the interpretation of the adjunct clause at the semantic interface, it is crucial whether the R-expression checks the appropriate feature in the CP phase (whether it is topicalized or scrambled), but now it is the CP phase in the adjunct clause. If this is the case, then, given the proposed model, the R-expression is interpreted in the CP phase at the semantic interface, that is, as backgrounded, and consequently coreference is possible. Then the situation with the coreferential R-expression and pronoun—with the adjunct clause interpreted in the matrix clause CP phase and the non-c-commanded R-expression interpreted in the adjunct CP phase—looks like Fig. 5.3.

The idea behind the Background Adjunct Coreference Principle is that R-expressions focused in the adjunct clause cannot be coreferential with the matrix clause pronoun because discourse maintains referential continuity (see Reinhart forthcoming). This means that only "old," "known" (backgrounded) elements are possible antecedents of pronouns.

What is the relation between the Background Adjunct Coreference Principle and Condition C? According to Junghanns (2002) and Lenertová (2008), certain left-peripheral adverbial clauses are externally merged to the matrix CP; compare also Iatridou (1991), who argues that at least certain types of clausal adjuncts can be generated in the left periphery. If this is true for

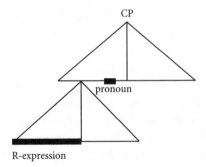

FIGURE 5.3 Coreferential pronoun and R-expression

sentences (29) and (31), repeated here as (42a,b), then the contrast between
them and the ungrammatical status of sentence (42b) cannot be accounted for
by a violation of Condition C, that is, by reconstruction of the R-expression
Pavel into a copy position c-commanded by the coindexed *pro*.

(42) a. Než   Pavel₁   odjel, *pro*₁ políbil Marii.
          before Pavel-NOM left   kissed Marie-ACC
          'Before Pavel left, he kissed Marie.'

      b. * Než   odjel Pavel₁,   *pro*₁ políbil Marii.
          before left Pavel-NOM   kissed Marie-ACC
          'Before Pavel left, he kissed Marie.'

It was pointed out by Junghanns (2002) and Lenertová (2008) that the CP-
external left-peripheral adverbial clauses—in contrast to internal adverbial
clauses, which are moved to a lower left-peripheral position from a clause-
internal position—cannot serve as hosts for clitics.[27] Since the clitic *se* must
be preceded by an additional element in (43a) and cannot directly follow
the adjunct clause (43b), the temporal adjunct is merged directly with the
matrix CP.

(43) a. Než   Pavel   odjel, rozhodl se   políbit Marii.
          before Pavel-NOM left   decided self kiss-INF Marie-ACC
          'Before Pavel left, he decided to kiss Marie.'

      b. * Než   Pavel   odjel, se   rozhodl políbit Marii.
          before Pavel-NOM left   self decided kiss-INF Marie-ACC
          'Before Pavel left, he decided to kiss Marie.'

Applying this to (42), there is no position c-commanded by the matrix subject
to which the R-expression embedded in the adjunct can reconstruct; therefore

---

[27] Czech clitics are of Wackernagel type (second-position clitics).

the ungrammaticality of sentence (42b) cannot be accounted for by a Condition C violation. This means that the ungrammatical status of (42b) results only from the violation of the Background Adjunct Coreference Principle, which shows that the Background Adjunct Coreference Principle is independent of Condition C. This does not pose a problem, because coreference (as assigning the same semantic value) and binding are two different linguistic procedures; see, for example, Reinhart (2000, forthcoming) or Reuland (2001).

I argued in Section 5.2.4 that the R-expression in the right-peripheral adjunct clause cannot be coreferential with the pronoun in the matrix clause because *pro* c-commands it, hence Condition C is violated. I showed that if the adjunct clause is preposed, that is, interpreted as backgrounded, the R-expression can corefer with *pro* if it observes the Background Adjunct Coreference Principle. I also showed that the Background Adjunct Coreference Principle holds in cases where the coindexed R-expression is not the subject of the adjunct clause and in cases where the coindexed pronoun is not the subject of the matrix clause. Now the question arises as to what happens if the R-expression occurs in a right-peripheral adjunct clause and the coindexed pronoun occurs in a position not c-commanding the R-expression. Since Condition C and the Background Adjunct Coreference Principle are two independent principles, as I argued above, one expects that the availability of coreference will depend only on the Background Adjunct Coreference Principle when Condition C is not relevant in this case. To test this prediction, let us consider example (44).

(44) a. * *pro*₁ vzal si   Marii   poté, co   Pavel₁   odešel
           took self Marie-ACC after that Pavel-NOM left
       z   práce.
       from job
       'He married Marie after Pavel left his job.'

   b. *pro*₁ vzal si   Marii   poté, co   *pro*₁/Jirka₂   odešel
       took self Marie-ACC after that   Jirka-NOM left
       z   práce.
       from job
       'He married Marie after he/Jirka left his job.'

   c. ? Že si   *pro*₁ vzal Marii,   bylo ohlášeno   poté, co
       that self   took Marie-ACC was announced after that
       Pavel₁   odešel z   práce.
       Pavel-NOM left   from job
       'That he had married Marie was announced after Pavel left his job.'

d. * Že si *pro*₁ vzal Marii   bylo ohlášeno   poté, co
    that self   took Marie-ACC was   announced   after   that
    odešel z   práce Pavel₁.
    left   from job   Pavel-NOM
    'That he had married Marie was announced after Pavel left his
    job.'

Sentence (44a) is ungrammatical because the adjunct clause is merged within the *v*P phase and interpreted there at the semantic interface, hence the R-expression is c-commanded by the coindexed pronoun and Condition C is violated. The control sentence (44b) demonstrates that the problem indeed lies in the coindexed R-expression. That the adjunct clause is interpreted in the *v*P phase of the matrix clause is confirmed by the fact that it is interpreted as focus: (44b) is appropriate in the context *Kdy si vzal Marii?* 'When did he marry Marie?' but cannot occur in a context where the adjunct information is already known, for example, *Co bylo poté, co odešel z práce?* 'What happened after he left his job?'. In the modified sentence (44c), where the adjunct clause is also merged within the *v*P phase of the matrix clause and interpreted there— the adjunct clause is interpreted as focus and can be construed only as a temporal modifier of the matrix clause *bylo ohlášeno*—there is no c-command relation between *pro* in the subject clause and the coindexed R-expression in the adjunct clause. Therefore a Condition C violation cannot arise here and since the R-expression obeys the Background Adjunct Coreference Principle, coreference is possible, as schematized in Fig. 5.4. As expected, if the R-expression is focalized in the adjunct clause (see again Fig. 5.4, hence the Background Adjunct Coreference Principle is violated), the sentence becomes ungrammatical (44d). This shows that the structural position of the adjunct clause is not relevant to the Background Adjunct Coreference Principle; it does not play a role whether the adjunct clause occurs (and is interpreted) in the CP phase (as in (42)) or in the *v*P phase (as in (44)).

Example (44c) with the coindexed pronoun in the subject clause also shows that the Background Adjunct Coreference Principle should be loosened. The coreferential pronoun does not have to occur only in the matrix clause. Thus,

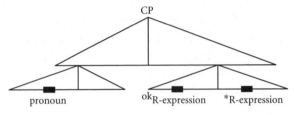

FIGURE 5.4 Coreferential possibilities of R-expressions in the adjunct clause

the final version of the Background Adjunct Coreference Principle is stated in (45).

(45)   *Background Adjunct Coreference Principle* (final version)
Coreference between an R-expression within an adjunct clause and a pronoun in a clause distinct from the adjunct clause is possible only if the R-expression is backgrounded in the adjunct clause.

If the final version of the Background Adjunct Coreference Principle is correct, then the distance between the coindexed pronoun and R-expression should not play a role. This seems to be the case, as illustrated by example (46), where the coindexed pronoun occurs in the complement clause embedded in the subject clause. In (46a), with the backgrounded R-expression, coreference is possible, but in (46b), where the R-expression is focalized, coreference is not possible.

(46)   a.   ? Že pro_2 tvrdila,   že   si pro_1 vzal   Marii,   bylo
that   claimed   that   self   took   Marie-ACC   was
ohlášeno   poté,   co   Pavel$_1$ odešel   z   práce.
announced   after   that   Pavel-NOM   left   from   job
'That she had claimed that he had married Marie was announced after Pavel left his job.'

    b.   * Že pro_2 tvrdila,   že   si pro_1 vzal   Marii,   bylo
that   claimed   that   self   took   Marie-ACC   was
ohlášeno   poté,   co   odešel   z   práce   Pavel$_1$.
announced   after   that   left   from   job   Pavel-NOM
'That she had claimed that he had married Marie was announced after Pavel left his job.'

Some sentences theoretically can violate both Condition C and the Background Adjunct Coreference Principle, for example a focused R-expression within a clausal adjunct contained in a non-presuppositional element that is moved from a position c-commanded by the coindexed pronoun to a non-c-commanded position; see (47a). It is not a trivial question whether this type of sentence is ruled out by the Background Adjunct Coreference Principle, by Condition C, or by both. However, it seems that the Background Adjunct Coreference Principle is at work in (47a), too, because according to some speakers, (47a) is worse than example (47b), where the R-expression is backgrounded, hence the Background Adjunct Coreference Principle is not violated.

(47)   a.   * Kolik   argumentů, které   přednesl Pavel$_1$,   pro$_1$
             how-many arguments which   gave   Pavel-NOM
             zuřivě   bránil?
             furiously defended
             'How many arguments that Pavel gave did he defend like fury?'

       b.   ?* Kolik   argumentů, které   Pavel$_1$ přednesl,
             how-many arguments which   Pavel-NOM gave
             pro$_1$ zuřivě   bránil?
             furiously   defended
             'How many arguments that Pavel gave did he defend like fury?'

One may ask whether the Background Adjunct Coreference Principle really holds only for adjunct clauses or whether it can also be used in the case of arguments. Example (48) shows that arguments behave differently. Although the sentence is an ideal case with respect to the availability of coreference—the R-expression is backgrounded in the complement clause and the clause itself is backgrounded (moved to the CP phase of the matrix clause)—coreference is not possible. Thus, in contrast to clausal adjuncts, it does not help that the R-expression is separated from the coindexed pronoun by the clausal boundary, and it is still necessary to distinguish between arguments and adjuncts.[28]

(48)   * Že   Pavel$_1$ políbil Marii,   pro$_1$ nám říkal včera.
         that Pavel-NOM kissed Marie-ACC   us   told   yesterday
         'He told us yesterday that Pavel had kissed Marie.'

Let us now turn to the difference between clausal and non-clausal adjuncts. I argued in the preceding section that there is a correlation between the phase structure, tripartite quantificational structure and information structure of the clause and that this structure can be recursive. A look at Fig. 5.3 reveals that R-expressions in clausal adjuncts are one level more deeply embedded in the structure than the coindexed pronoun in the matrix clause, and than R-expressions in non-clausal adjuncts. Thus, it is the CP phase boundary that makes it possible for R-expressions in clausal adjuncts (if they obey the Background Adjunct Coreference Principle), in contrast to non-clausal ones, to be coreferential with the coindexed pronoun. A look at Fig. 5.4 reveals

---

[28] Given the selectional difference between arguments and adjuncts, one may propose that reconstruction in the case of arguments is necessary, which has the consequence that Binding Condition C is violated. Since I argue that reconstruction (the place of interpretation) is dependent on semantic properties (presuppositionality, backgrounding) of the appropriate elements—which should hold also in the case of arguments—interpretation of more copies is necessary (on this topic, see, for example, Safir 1999 or Sportiche 2005). Since this chapter primarily concerns adjuncts, I leave this issue open to further research.

that the R-expression is two clausal boundaries away from the pronoun and that the R-expression in example (46) is even three clausal boundaries away from the coindexed pronoun. Therefore it is not surprising that both cases are grammatical with the given coindexation. Thus, there is an antilocality phenomenon in coreference issues; compare the discussion about the depth of embedding of the relevant antecedent in van Riemsdijk & Williams (1981), Speas (1990), Huang (1993), and Müller (1995a). Under the assumption that coreference can be established by accessing the discourse storage at the semantic interface (Reinhart 2000, forthcoming; Reuland 2001; Partee 2004) so that the appropriate pronoun receives a value from the discourse storage, I propose that the too local elements—the R-expressions contained in non-clausal adjuncts—are not established enough in the discourse storage to serve as possible antecedents in Czech.

Since derivations are sent to interfaces phase by phase, the discourse storage can also be filled in a phase-by-phase fashion. Consequently, one might expect that it is a phase boundary that makes the R-expression established enough for the pronoun at the semantic interface. However, example (49) with a vP-phase boundary between the R-expression and the coindexed pronoun demonstrates that this idea of phase-based disjoint reference does not work. Note that since there is no c-command relation between the pronoun and R-expression, the ungrammaticality of (49) cannot be due to a violation of Condition C. Thus, the relevant boundary is the CP phase, and not generally every phase.

(49)   * Jana   a   jeho$_1$ sestra   přečetli včera
       Jana-FEM-NOM and his   sister-NOM read   yesterday
       knížku   z   Pavlovy$_1$ police.
       book-ACC   from Pavel's   shelf
       'Jana and his sister read a book from Pavel's shelf yesterday.'

Speas (1990: 50–2), building on Lebeaux (1988), argues against the embedding analysis, using sentences like (50a,b), where the R-expression is embedded equally. She argues that there is a distinction between "theta-marked adjuncts," which are VP-internal and must be present at D-structure, and "non-theta-marked adjuncts," which are VP-external and are not present at D-structure. Since the locative adjunct in (50b), her (59b), is a theta-marked adjunct, it produces a Condition C violation. In contrast, the adjunct denoting temporal location in (50a), her (59a), is not theta-marked, and does not violate Condition C.

(50)   a.   In Ben$_1$'s office, he$_1$ is an absolute dictator.

       b.   * In Ben$_1$'s office, he$_1$ lay on his desk.

However, no such distinction is found in the Czech equivalents in (51). Both types of non-clausal adjuncts make the sentence ungrammatical, as expected when no clausal boundary is present.

(51)   a.   * V   Benově₁   kanceláři *pro₁*   je   absolutní   diktátor.
           in   Ben's   office   is   absolute   dictator

     b.   * V   Benově₁   kanceláři *pro₁*   ležel   na   stole.
           in   Ben's   office   lay   on   desk

I now argue that it is not just the depth of embedding of the syntactic structure that is crucial for the locality phenomena with non-clausal adjuncts. Consider the ungrammatical sentence (52), with the R-expression embedded in a number of prepositional phrases. This example also shows that the impossibility of coreference is not due to the precedence relation between the coindexed pronoun and R-expression, as one might think looking, for example, at (49). And if prepositional phrases are phases, then (52) is also an argument against phase-based disjoint reference.

(52)   * Kterou   knížku   na   polici   u   stolu   vedle   Pavlovy₁
      which   book-ACC   on   shelf   near   table   next-to   Pavel's
      postele *pro₁*   přečetl?
      bed   read
      'Which book from the shelf near the table next to Pavel's bed did he read?'

In what follows I show that it is generally the CP boundary that is relevant to the availability of coreference and not the type of the adjunct immediately containing the R-expression itself. Both the clausal (53a) and non-clausal (53b) adjuncts are adjoined to the same host, hence the different behavior of clausal and non-clausal adjuncts has nothing to do with the host. And as expected, the clausal adjunct containing the backgrounded R-expression does not produce a Condition C effect, but the non-clausal adjunct does. If it were the case that the type of the adjunct itself is the decisive factor in the availability of coreference, then one would expect the non-clausal adjunct containing the R-expression to always produce a Condition C effect. However, this is not the case, as illustrated by the grammatical sentence (53c), where the non-clausal adjunct is embedded in the adjunct clause.

(53)   a.   Tu   knížku,   kterou   má   Pavel₁   na   polici, *pro₁*
        the   book-ACC   which   has   Pavel-NOM   on   shelf
        nemá   rád.
        NEG-likes
        'The book that Pavel has on his shelf, he does not like.'

b. * Tu knížku   na Pavlově₁ polici *pro*₁ nemá rád.
    the book-ACC on Pavel's   shelf   NEG-likes
    'The book on Pavel's shelf, he does not like.'

c. Tu knížku,   kterou na Pavlově₁ polici viděli všichni, *pro*₁
    the book-ACC which on Pavel's   shelf   saw   all
    nemá rád.
    NEG-likes
    'The book that everyone saw on Pavel's shelf, he does not like.'

Now there are two factors that can induce Condition C effects in the case of non-clausal adjuncts: Condition C itself and the antilocality requirements on coreference. As in the case of clausal adjuncts, one would like to know more about the relation between the two principles. In languages like English, non-clausal adjuncts can avoid a Condition C violation; see (54) taken from Huang (1993: 106). Its Czech counterpart is ungrammatical, as demonstrated in (55). If one wants to keep the idea that there is only one type of merger— the cyclic one—and that languages do not differ in this respect, then one has to conclude that the Czech example does not violate Condition C but rather the antilocality requirement on coreference. Recall also example (49), where the ungrammaticality of the sentence cannot be due to the violation of Condition C. This means that Czech non-clausal adjuncts containing an R-expression, too, can avoid a Condition C violation, but given the organization of grammar (coreference principles), the pronoun cannot be coreferential with the coindexed R-expression, that is, it cannot get the same semantic value at the semantic interface. So, I argue that the difference between languages lies in coreference possibilities (discourse procedure), rather than in merger possibilities or binding principles.

(54)   Which pictures near John₁ does he₁ like most *t*?

(55)   * Které obrázky   vedle Johna₁ *pro*₁ miluje nejvíc?
       which pictures-ACC near John   likes   most

Let us say a bit more about where Condition C applies. We have seen that Condition C—concretely, reconstruction—is sensitive to interpretation, similarly as is coreference (assigning the same semantic value). More specifically, it is sensitive to the information-structural and presuppositional properties of adjuncts or elements containing them. Then it is obvious that Condition C cannot apply prior to the semantic interface. And we have seen that it holds for adjuncts or elements containing them appearing in the CP phase of the matrix clause. Hence, Condition C must be able to wait until the semantic interface of the highest phase in the sentence.

Sometimes, Condition C is able to span a derivation across several phases. Consider the following sentence with the adnominal adjunct spelled out in the first phase and the pronoun present in the highest phase in the sentence. This goes against the claim (Chomsky 2000, 2001, 2008) that once information has been spelled out, it cannot be accessed in further computation. For arguments that the derivation cannot forget the preceding phases, see also Cecchetto (2004), Marušič (2005), von Stechow (2005), or Boeckx & Grohmann (2007).[29]

(56) * *pro*$_1$ myslel, že Pavel   říkal, že Honza   četl
            thought that Pavel-NOM said   that Honza-NOM read
      knížku   z   Petrovy$_1$ police.
      book-ACC from Petr's   shelf
      'He thought that Pavel said that Honza read a book from Petr's shelf.'

Another argument against "forgotten" phases comes from the coreference behavior of R-expressions contained in clausal adjuncts. I have shown that they can be coreferential with the matrix clause pronoun only if they are backgrounded, that is, moved to the CP phase of the adjunct clause. Thus, when the CP phase of the matrix clause is sent to the semantic interface and the coindexed pronoun is interpreted, the piece of information about the appropriate R-expression—whether it has checked the relevant features in the CP phase of the adjunct clause—must still be accessible.

Recall that I showed in (44c) that the pronoun contained in the subject clause, which was moved to its overt subject position from the verbal object position, can be coreferential with the R-expression within the adjunct clause. So, at the time when the subject clause CP phase with the pronoun is sent to the semantic interface, it has no relation to the adjunct clause, which possibly has not been derived yet. This means that the interpretation of the pronoun has to wait for the R-expression and the phase cannot be forgotten. If the phase with the appropriate pronoun could be forgotten, then it would not be clear why in cases like this the pronoun is not disjoint in reference from elements in other phases.

5.4 Conclusion

In this chapter I have investigated four types of adjuncts with respect to Condition C and coreference: (non-)clausal adnominal adjuncts and (non-)clausal adverbial adjuncts. I have shown that there is a distinction between clausal and

---

[29] This means that the economy effect of phases does not concern memory, but the size of the workspace.

non-clausal adjuncts. While non-clausal adjuncts always produce Condition C effects, clausal adjuncts can obviate Condition C effects. I have argued that the Condition C data cannot be accounted for by acyclic merger of adjuncts (e.g. Lebeaux 1988) or by the special status of adjunct merger (e.g. Chomsky 2004a). I have argued that all adjuncts are merged cyclically and Condition C effects are not a uniform phenomenon. They can be induced by three different factors: by the violation of Condition C itself, by the violation of the Background Adjunct Coreference Principle in the case of clausal adjuncts, or by the violation of the antilocality requirement on coreference in the case of non-clausal adjuncts. I have argued that for Condition C and coreference issues, the correlation between the phase structure, tripartite quantificational structure, and information structure of the sentence is relevant. The R-expressions in clausal adjuncts, in contrast to R-expressions in non-clausal adjuncts, can corefer with the coindexed pronoun because they are always at least one CP boundary away from the pronoun in the structure. And they can corefer with the pronoun only if they are spelled out in the CP phase of the clausal adjunct, because then they are interpreted as backgrounded, in conformance with the Background Adjunct Coreference Principle. This means that information about the R-expression cannot be forgotten and must be accessible to later phases.

Part II
Articulatory Issues

6

Non-Simultaneous Spell-Out in the Clausal and Nominal Domain*

FRANC LANKO MARUŠIČ

6.1 Introduction

Phases have interface realities, that is, they are propositional elements at the LF interface and have certain phonetic independence at the PF interface (Chomsky 2004a, 2005). These interface units are created by Spell-Out, the operation shipping syntactic structure to the two interfaces. Spell-Out applies cyclically and as a result we get multiple interface units. Whatever gets shipped to the interfaces at one go is a unit at the relevant interface. By looking at the PF and LF properties of various syntactic objects and checking what kind of units they are, we can determine their phasal composition (cf. Matushansky 2003).

In this chapter, I will show that apart from CP and vP, other projections behave as phases as well. What interests us most is that certain projections behave as phases at one, but not both interfaces, that is, certain projections correspond to phonetic units, but are not propositional. There are also others that are propositional, while at the same time lack the expected PF independence. In particular, non-finite TP (or whatever is the top projection of an embedded non-finite clause) has no PF independence but is at the same time a propositional element. Unaccusative or raising vP does not pass PF phase tests, but turns out to be a projection where a raised quantifier can get interpreted. In the nominal domain, DP/KP (or whatever is the top projection of the noun phrase) is not a propositional element but has very

* This chapter is partially based on my Ph.D. dissertation, which I finished in Stony Brook in December 2005. I owe a lot to my dissertation committee (Richard Larson, Dan Finer, John Bailyn, and Marcel den Dikken) for their comments, interest, support, and for forcing me to make things clearer both to them and to me. I would also like to thank Carlos de Cuba, Rok Žaucer, the anonymous reviewers, and Kleanthes Grohmann, the *InterPhases* conference organizer (Nicosia, Cyprus, May 2006), for comments, suggestions, judgements, support, etc.

obviously PF independence (it is a most intuitive phase, yet most intuitive only in the PF sense). An internal projection of the noun phrase, e.g. NP or NumP, does not have PF independence but behaves as a projection where quantifiers get interpreted. It is therefore an LF phase.

Interestingly, this is exactly the phasal composition we need in order to derive the two most obvious phenomena where the locus of interpretation differs from the locus of pronunciation: total reconstruction (of indefinites in raising constructions) and quantifier raising. Namely, if at some point in the derivation, the structure built thus far gets spelled out to one but not to the other interface, whatever was meant for the other interface but was not spelled out to this interface remains in the derivation and can even move further as the derivation progresses. If a partially spelled out constituent does indeed move further, it ends up being spelled out to the other interface at a later point in some other position. As a result, the position of an element would differ from one interface to the other. In case of raising verbs, since they are phases only for the LF interface, the PF part of the embedded subject can move to the matrix clause (to get case etc.), but its LF part gets spelled out inside the lower clause. This results in the subject being pronounced within the matrix clause yet at the same time interpreted inside the embedded clause, which is known as total reconstruction. The opposite is true of the DP/KP. The entire noun phrase gets spelled out to the PF interface, but it does not get spelled out to the LF interface. Thus the LF part of the nominal can participate in the derivation and LF-related features can move from inside the DP/KP. This would give us a syntactic object pronounced at some low position while interpreted higher in the structure, which is what we call covert movement (quantifier raising being a very clear and uncontroversial case of it).

What we get is thus a completely derivational account of total reconstruction and quantifier raising, which explains the two phenomena with the same mechanism.[1]

Phases are stages or cycles of the derivation at the completion of which the complement of the phase head is sent to the two interfaces. Spell-Out is said to be simultaneous to the two interfaces. This is the most straightforward and the most restricted possibility. It is also the only symmetric possibility. However, if phases represent units at the interfaces, and if this is the only way units are created, then this answer is quite clearly wrong. We have on the one hand compounds, which are semantically complex but phonologically simple expressions, and on the other hand idioms, which are phonologically complex

---

[1] Actually, this is already done by the copy theory of movement, but its explanation is not ideal for other reasons discussed below and in more detail in Marušič (2005).

but semantically simple expressions (complexity is here measured in the number of internal units).

I explore the possibility of having Spell-Out occurring independently to a single interface. This would mean that, at the point of Spell-Out, only some features of the structure built thus far would get frozen and shipped to an interface. Since lexical items are composed of three types of features, semantic, phonetic, and formal ({S,P,F}), if only one type gets frozen the other two can still take part in the derivation. For example, if the complement of a certain head is only spelled out to LF but not PF (let us call this an *LF-only phase*), its completion would freeze all the features that must end up at LF, but not those that are relevant for PF. Then, at the next (full) phase, when the derivation reaches e.g. *v*P, the structure ready to be shipped to PF would be twice the size of the structure ready to get shipped to LF, since part of the structure has been already shipped to LF at the earlier LF-only Spell-Out. Non-simultaneous Spell-Out to the two interfaces is not a new idea. It has already been proposed by Megerdoomian (2003), Felser (2004), Bobaljik & Wurmbrand (2003) (an earlier version of Bobaljik & Wurmbrand 2005), and Marušič & Žaucer (2006). It is also hinted at in Sauerland & Elbourne (2002) and offered as a possibility but rejected in Matushansky (2003).

One obvious but so far unmentioned problem comes to mind if one accepts non-simultaneous Spell-Out. A phase boundary is not only the point where the completed phase is spelled out, but also the point where a new phase starts. If the points of the LF and PF Spell-Out differ, does it mean the starting points of new phases also differ? Since a phase is defined as a complete cycle, including the subarray and the derivation, having completely independent phases would suggest completely independent subarrays consisting of PF-only or LF-only related material/features. But that would suggest the matching of PF and LF is a result of pure coincidence, which seems plainly wrong. After all, simultaneous Spell-Out is presumably the normal way things work; it is non-simultaneous Spell-Out that is exceptional. I am assuming that lexical items (and other elements in the numeration) comprise sets of the three kinds of features discussed earlier {S,P,F}. Therefore, all features enter the derivation at the same time, simply because of the nature of the lexicon. That is to say, if a lexical item consists only of semantic and formal but no PF features (e.g. the null verbs of e.g. Marušič & Žaucer 2005; see also reference cited there) or the other way around (having PF features, but no LF features), then the PF and LF numerations would indeed differ. However, this would not be through phase mismatch, but rather a consequence of the feature make-up of the specific lexical items. PF and LF portions of the structure would still both be shipped to their respective interfaces at the point of Spell-Out; it is just that the amount of spelled-out material would diverge.

Assuming the lexicon consists of lexical items of the form {S,P,F}, as explained above, numeration and its subarrays cannot consist of exclusively LF/S or exclusively PF/P features. Every subarray of the numeration is both a PF and an LF subarray, and therefore starts both a PF and an LF phase.

It also seems natural to say that by the time the derivation reaches the point of Spell-Out, the subarray must be emptied. In other words, when new elements enter the derivation in a new subarray, no old ones should remain.[2] If, at the point of Spell-Out, the derivation is not shipped to both interfaces, one could say that the phase is not really completed. Perhaps in this case the lower subarray could still provide items for the derivation, but then the lower subarray also would not have been emptied. Thus, it seems that even at the point where only a partial phase is completed, the subarray must be completely empty. Assuming it is empty, then, of course, the new phase must bring in items relevant for both interfaces (both S and P features). Thus, any partial phase acts as a starting point for both phases.

Notice that it does not matter how much material is being shipped to the interfaces at the point of Spell-Out, since a phase regularly accepts items that joined the derivation in a previous phase and moved up. In the case of an LF-only phase, the next PF phase would spell out structure constructed from two subarrays, corresponding to the two LF phases. Thus, if we accept non-simultaneous Spell-Out, phases still remain parallel and have a one-to-one correspondence; it is just that in some cases they do not spell out to both interfaces simultaneously.[3]

In this view, when a phase is said to be either PF-only or LF-only, it is actually the Spell-Out mechanism that is non-simultaneous, so that at the point of Spell-Out the structure is only transferred to one of the two interfaces. Only the Spell-Out is LF or PF-only, not the entire phase.

6.2 Phases in the Clausal Domain

In the phase theory (Chomsky 2004a, 2005, 2008), the standard idea is that the two phases in the clausal domain are CP and active *v*P. I will provide evidence

---

[2] Assuming we have a single active memory location for subarrays, one might say that the old items from the previous subarray get simply overwritten.

[3] See Marušič (2005) for a longer discussion of this mechanism and a detailed explanation of the workings of non-simultaneous Spell-Out. Various issues come to mind once we step off the beaten track, which is what I am doing here, but in the interest of space I cannot address all of them in this chapter.

that suggests unaccusative *v*P is also a partial phase, one that spells out only to LF. Another phase that spells out to LF alone is non-finite TP (or whatever is the topmost projection in non-finite clauses). Whether non-finite TP is a phase because finite TP is also a phase or because of something else (e.g. some phase-sliding mechanism, as proposed in Gallego 2006*a*) is a question I will not address here.

I am assuming a much richer clausal structure then just CP-TP-*v*P. When I propose that some projection is a phase because it matches to a proposition at the LF interface, I am actually saying that there is some projection around TP that becomes a proposition when shipped to the LF interface. At the same time, when the interpretation of a quantifier reveals that some projection is a phase edge, I do not mean that the very same projection is headed by the phase head whose complement gets spelled out to the LF interface. Rather, I want to say that there is a projection in the area whose complement gets spelled out to LF and whose head attracts quantifiers so that they can get interpreted and possibly move further. The two projections should obviously be one above the other. That is, the projection that is mapped to a proposition is the complement of the quantifier-attracting head. The exact identity of such projections is not important for present purposes.

6.2.1 *Non-Finite TP*

As shown in Marušič (2007, 2008), non-finite clausal complements lack a CP projection. Without a CP projection these constructions lack a strong phase between the two clauses. I will show here that the non-finite clausal complement is nevertheless a phase, but that it is only an LF/semantic phase. That is, the complement is spelled out to LF once it is completed. Then I will show that the same chunk of structure is not spelled out to PF at the same time.[4]

(i) LF phasehood
Just like finite clausal complements, non-finite clausal complements denote propositions. Propositions are the LF reality of phases (Chomsky 2000 *et seq.*).

---

[4] I am ignoring the question of the exact identity of the topmost projection in non-finite clauses. Wurmbrand (2001) claims there are at least four different types of non-finite clauses. Following her, restructuring infinitives could be only VPs. I am simplifying and label the topmost projection a TP, even though Wurmbrand (2007) claims non-finite clauses specifically do not have TP at all. But TP is used only as a label. As I have explained above, I am assuming a richer structure, so that what I am talking about here is a projection in the TP/IP region. The projection we are talking about could also be the matrix verb taking a clausal complement and inducing a phase (cf. Bobaljik & Wurmbrand 2003). Actually, it would be a projection below the matrix verb, the projection mediating between the clausal complement and the verb.

Non-finite clausal complements are opaque/intensional—an indefinite inside a non-finite clausal complement can have non-specific interpretation, a non-denoting term would not yield falsity of the entire sentence, etc. (all these properties are obviously related to the semantic type of the non-finite clause). For example, there need not be any specific Finn that Vid decided to marry for sentence (1a) to be true; Vid simply decided that he will marry a Finn, but does not know yet whom. In addition, in (1b), a non-denoting term in the complement does not necessarily yield falsity. Similar examples can be given for every other type of non-finite complementation.

(1)　a.　Vid se　je　sklenil　poročiti　z　eno Finko.[5]
　　　　　Vid REFL AUX decided marry-INF with a　Finn
　　　　　'Vid decided to marry a Finn.'

　　　b.　Vid se　je　sklenil　poročiti　z　vampirko.
　　　　　Vid REFL AUX decided marry-INF with vampire
　　　　　'Vid decided to marry a female vampire.'

We can also find supporting evidence for the claim that there is an LF phase under the matrix verb if we check the interpretation of universal quantifiers inside embedded non-finite clauses. Since the scope position of a universal quantifier is standardly taken to indicate the edge of an (LF) phase (QR, being a syntactic movement, has to proceed through phase edges where it can also take scope), finding an example where the quantifier gets interpreted inside the scope of the matrix verb should show that the embedded clause is an LF phase, and that it has an LF phase edge (cf. Legate 2003*a*, 2003*b*, and Sauerland 2003, among others). As shown in (2a), the universal quantifier can be understood inside the scope of the matrix verb, since the sentence has the interpretation under which Vid forgot to close all the windows, but did manage to close some. Similarly in (2b), the universal quantifier can take scope under negation, which is understood inside the scope of the matrix predicate *odločil* 'decide.' What Janez decided is not to close all windows, but to leave some of them open. In this last case, the universal quantifier gets scope in between the matrix verb and negation (his decision is about every window, not about each individual one).

(2)　a.　Vid je　pozabil zapreti　vsa okna.　　　　　　*forgot* > ∀
　　　　　Vid AUX forgot　close-INF all　windows
　　　　　'Vid forgot to close all windows.'

---

[5] Examples that are not in English are in Slovenian.

b. Janez se je odločil ne zapreti vsa   *decide > not > ∀*
Janez REFL AUX decided not close-INF all   ∀ > *not*
okna.
windows
'Janez decided not to close all windows.'

Since the universal quantifier in (2b) is understood inside the scope of negation, it might be argued that it is actually interpreted at the *v*P phase rather than at the phase immediately under the matrix verb. But as said, (2b) also has the interpretation where the universal quantifier is inside the scope of the matrix verb but outside of the scope of negation. For this particular interpretation, the quantifier gets interpreted in between the verb and negation. This argues for the existence of a phase edge, in particular for the existence of an LF phase edge that closes off the embedded clause. We can also avoid the *v*P phase, if we use an unaccusative verb in the non-finite complement. In this case the quantifier must be put in an adjunct position. Regardless of the lack of *v*P, a quantifier can still be interpreted inside the scope of the matrix verb, as in (3). Since there is supposedly no other phase (assuming an adjunct by itself is not a phase), the non-finite TP (or some projection just above it) has to be the projection where the quantifier gets interpreted.

(3) Meta je sklenila priti   vsako soboto.   *decided > ∀*
Meta AUX decide arrive-INF every Saturday
'Meta decided to arrive on every Saturday.'

In addition, if the lower clause consists of more than just the embedded VP and *v*P (which can easily be shown with adverbs that are part of the embedded clause, as in (4)), then it makes perfect sense to include all the functional projections of the lower clause in the semantic computation of the lower clause, rather than in the computation of the matrix clause. As mentioned, the entire complement clause expresses a proposition, not just the lowest *v*P inside. It expresses a proposition regardless of the type of verb inside the complement clause. Even if the complement has an unaccusative verb (which does not have a *v*P phase), the complement still corresponds semantically to a proposition, and as such is a perfect candidate for an LF Spell-Out unit.

(4) Peter je sklenil (bolj) pogosto obiskovati babico.
Peter AUX decided (more) often   visit-INF   grandmother
'Peter decided to visit grandmother (more) often.'

ECM constructions, as in (5), are typically analyzed as not having the CP projection, since the subject from the embedded clause can get case from the matrix verb. Thus, if we can interpret a DP in the region between the verb and the embedded negation, it would have to be in SpecTP. To illustrate, in the crucial interpretation of (5), the embedded subject takes scope over the embedded object, which in turn takes scope over negation. It should be possible to paraphrase this reading as "John expects that there is someone for whom it is true that for all classes, he will not attend them." The embedded subject of the example (5) can definitely be understood *de dicto*, suggesting it is interpreted inside the lower clause. Since the embedded object can be interpreted inside the scope of the indefinite and outside of the scope of negation (assuming QR goes through phase edges), the embedded object must be in the phase edge in the lower SpecTP (in the lower specifier).

(5)   John expects some student not to attend all classes. $\exists > \forall > not$

There are arguments for claiming finite TP is also a phase (contra Chomsky 2000 *et seq.*, following Uriagereka & Martin 1999, Sauerland & Elbourne 2002; cf. Grohmann 2000). TP is a projection that maps to a proposition, which becomes quite obvious if one looks at modals. The sentences in (6) are ambiguous between root and epistemic interpretation of the modal.

(6)   a.   You must be in the University Café right now.

      b.   Every Stony Brook student must be in the University Café right now.

      c.   A Stony Brook student must be in the University Café right now.

Root modal interpretation of (6a) is typically paraphrased as '*you have the obligation to be in the University Café right now.*' The epistemic modal interpretation, on the other hand, is commonly paraphrased as *it is a necessary assumption that you are in the University Café right now.* The two paraphrases already suggest a difference between the two modals with respect to the scope of the subject. Whereas the root modal takes narrow scope with respect to the subject, the epistemic modal takes wide scope. In simplified logical notation, (6c) would get the following two interpretations, $\exists x \, \square \, [Px]$—there is an x such that it is necessary that P(x) is true—for the root and $\square \, \exists x \, [Px]$—it is necessary that there is an x such that P(x) is true—for the epistemic reading. Assuming the subject is always positioned in SpecTP, the difference has to come from the position of the modal. Indeed, the two modals are argued to be located in two different functional projections, the epistemic ModP is higher than TP while the root ModP is lower (e.g. Cinque 1999, 2004*b*; Butler 2003).

Kratzer (1981, 1991) analyzes both modals as propositional operators (they combine with a proposition to give a proposition) quantifying over possible worlds. This is most clearly seen for epistemic modals that are commonly said to take scope over the whole sentence. Butler (2003), building on Kratzer's analysis, claims that modals scope over any propositional element. Thus, if we accept that there are two strong phases, we get two modals: root modals that scope over the *v*P proposition and epistemic modals that scope over the TP. Although Butler does not take TP to be a phase, it seems that he should, after all, he is paralleling TP and *v*P. He claims that (epistemic) modality is bound to the CP phase. The complement of C, for him the TP is the semantic unit. But instead of saying something similar is true for *v*P as well, he puts another CP between TP and *v*P. Whatever the exact workings of his analysis are, the parallel we are seeking between *v*P and TP has been established. Both projections have the same status for Butler; neither is a phase, but they still both match to a proposition, which would mean they are both units at LF Spell-Out.

Thus we seem to have an LF phase where we would not expect any, since I have shown that there is no CP in non-finite complement clauses. Uriagereka & Martin (1999) and Sauerland & Elbourne (2002) claim that finite TPs are also phases. If this is true, arguing non-finite TP is a phase seems natural. Bobaljik & Wurmbrand (2005) claim verbs taking a non-finite clausal complement induce agreement domains, which are also loci of quantifier interpretation. In an earlier version of their paper (Bobaljik & Wurmbrand 2003) they call them LF-only phases. Regardless of where the phasehood comes from, the crucial question now is whether these phases are really LF-only phases, or are they complete phases (both PF and LF). I will now look at PF-phase diagnostics and show that these LF phases do not have the properties of PF phases.

(ii) PF phasehood

As mentioned earlier, following Marušič (2008), non-finite embedded clauses do not have a CP projection. This means that they lack a strong phase. However, we saw earlier that LF diagnostics showed there is nevertheless a phase in between the two clauses. We now turn to the phonological properties of non-finite complementation.

Assuming phonological positioning of clitics, clitics move to the second position inside the relevant prosodic unit. Clitics climb from non-finite clauses in Slovenian (cf. Golden 2003; Marušič 2008), therefore there is no PF boundary between the two clauses that would block their fronting. However, there are some refined tests available for PF phasehood. Matushansky (2003), following Legate (2003*a*, 2003*b*), gives three types of diagnostics for PF phases: *nuclear stress rule application*, *movement*, and *isolability*.

A PF phase, the point at which structure is sent to the PF component, should be the locus of the Nuclear Stress Rule application (cf. Cinque 1993). The Nuclear Stress Rule is a phonological rule that gives the nuclear stress to the rightmost lexical element in the structure. It is reasonable to assume it applies to a structure when it is shipped to PF; that is, at every (PF) phase. Thus every PF phase brings another application of the nuclear stress rule. Finite clausal complements seem to have two intonational phrases with a pause in between the two clauses and main stress on the rightmost lexical word of each clause, as shown in (7a) (sentences have to be pronounced with neutral intonation for this to be observable). This is not the case in non-finite complementation, where the entire sentence is most naturally pronounced as a single intonational phrase with only one main sentential stress, (7b,c). Since non-finite clauses also lack CP, one could imagine this lack of nuclear stress is a direct consequence of the lack of a CP phase.

(7) a. Peter je   včeraj   povedal **Meti**, da   bo   prišel na zabavo
         Peter AUX yesterday told   Meta   that AUX come   to party
         sam.
         alone
         'Peter told Meta yesterday that he will come to the party alone.'

     b. Peter je   včeraj   sklenil priti   danes k nam na
         Peter AUX yesterday decided come-INF   today to us   to
         zabavo.
         party
         'Peter yesterday decided to come today to us for a party.'

     c. Peter je   včeraj   Meti ukazal priti   danes k nam
         Peter AUX yesterday Meta ordered come-INF today to us
         na **zabavo.**
         to party
         'Peter yesterday decided to come today to us for a party.'

If a phrase is a phase, then it should also be available for movement. In particular, it should participate in various types of (potentially) PF movements. Matushansky concludes that, according to this diagnostic, TP is not a PF phase. She notes that TP does not participate in "movement-like structures that may not involve purely syntactic movement" (Matushansky 2003: 10). As shown in (8a), CP can be extraposed, but TP cannot (8b). Similarly, (8c) shows that TP cannot be topic left-dislocated (while CP and DP can be). The same is true of pseudo-clefting, as shown in (8d) ((8) from Matushansky 2003: exx. (19), (20), (23)).

(8) a. It surprised Ron [$_{CP}$ that Hermione was interested in someone else].

b. *It surprised Ron [$_{TP}$ Hermione (to) be interested in someone else].

c. *[Hermione (to) be interested in Viktor], who could imagine it.

d. *What Goneril seemed was [$_{TP}$ to fear King Lear].

Additionally, Slovenian sentences with non-finite complement clauses allow a kind of multiple scrambling presented in (9) (note that Slovenian is an SVO language). The kind of scrambling shown in (9) is only allowed within a sentence/clause. Normally, only one element can scramble over a finite CP, but in cases where more than one can scramble, they must form a constituent and appear leftmost. Thus, both (10d), with the fronted constituent following the matrix subject, and (10e), with two elements from the embedded clause surrounding the intervening matrix subject, are bad. No such restrictions hold for scrambling within a single clause.

(9) Medveda je   že   včeraj   po   gozdu brez   puške
     bear   AUX already yesterday around forest without gun
     iskal Peter.
     search Peter
     'Peter looked for a bear in the forest without a gun already yesterday.'

(10) a. Janez pravi, da je Meta pozabila iti   včeraj
          Janez says   that AUX Meta forgot   go-INF yesterday
          domov.
          home
          'Janez says that Meta forgot to go home yesterday.'

b. Domov, pravi Janez, da je Meta pozabila iti
    home   says Janez that AUX Meta forgot   go-INF
    včeraj.
    yesterday

c. Pozabila iti   domov pravi Janez, da je Meta
    forgot   go-INF home says Janez that AUX Meta
    včeraj.
    yesterday

d. *Janez pozabila iti   domov, pravi, da je Meta
    Janez forgot   go-INF home   says   that AUX Meta
    včeraj.
    yesterday

    e. *Domov Janez včeraj   pravi, da je Meta iti
       home   Janez yesterday says   that AUX Meta go-INF
       pozabila.
       forgot

Very clearly, the kind of reordering in (9) is not available in (10). This reordering or multiple scrambling is available in non-finite complementation basically to the same degree as it is in simple monoclausal sentences—anything can appear anywhere.[6]

(11a) is a basic sentence with neutral word order. The embedded clause (written in bold) follows the matrix verb. The other examples in (11) have scrambled word order, with the differences between them being simply stylistic.

(11)   a. Peter je   včeraj   v gostilni pozabil **povabiti Vida na**
         Peter AUX yesterday in pub   forgot invite-INF Vid to
         žur.
         party
         'Yesterday in the pub, Peter forgot to invite Vid to the party.'

     b. **Vida** je   Peter **na žur** včeraj   v gostilni **povabiti**
         Vid AUX Peter to party yesterday in pub   invite-INF
         pozabil.
         forgot

     c. **Na žur** je **Vida** Peter včeraj   v gostilni **povabiti**
         to party AUX Vid Peter yesterday in pub   invite-INF
         pozabil.
         forgot

     d. **Na žur** je Peter **Vida** včeraj   v gostilni **povabiti**
         to party AUX Peter Vid yesterday in pub   invite-INF
         pozabil.
         forgot

     e. **Vida** je   **na žur** Peter včeraj   v gostilni **povabiti**
         Vid AUX to party Peter yesterday in pub   invite-INF
         pozabil.
         forgot

     f. Peter je   **povabiti Vida na žur** včeraj   v gostilni
         Peter AUX invite-INF Vid to party yesterday in pub
         pozabil.
         forgot

[6] I am not using any adverbs in these cases, since they have a more fixed linear order.

g. **Povabiti** je **Vida na žur** Peter včeraj v gostilni
   invite-INF AUX Vid to party Peter yesterday in pub
   pozabil.
   forgot

h. **Povabiti** je **Vida** Peter **na žur** včeraj v gostilni
   invite-INF AUX Vid Peter to party yesterday in pub
   pozabil.
   forgot

i. **Povabiti** je Peter **na žur** včeraj v gostilni pozabil
   invite-INF AUX Peter to party yesterday in pub forgot
   Vida.
   Vid

j. **Povabiti** je Peter včeraj v gostilni pozabil **Vida na**
   invite-INF AUX Peter yesterday in pub forgot Vid to
   žur.
   party

   ...

This largely unconstrained reordering is semantically vacuous, as shown in (12), where the pronoun can be bound by the originally c-commanding quantifier regardless of where the pronoun ends up being scrambled to, even if it is pronounced in a position that should in principle be c-commanding the quantifier (that is, if this reordering is syntactic). Multiple scrambling is also insensitive to principle C (cf. Marušič 2005).

(12) a. [Vsak bolan otrok]$_i$ je ukazal sestri **prinesti kosilo v**
        every sick child AUX ordered sister bring-INF lunch in
        njegovo$_i$ **sobo.**
        his room
        'Every sick child ordered his sister to bring lunch to his room.'

   b. **Kosilo** je ukazal sestri **v njegovo**$_i$ **sobo prinesti** [vsak bolan otrok]$_i$.

   c. **V njegovo**$_i$ **sobo** je sestri **kosilo** ukazal **prinesti** [vsak bolan otrok]$_i$.

   d. **V njegovo**$_i$ **sobo** je [vsak bolan otrok]$_i$ sestri **kosilo prinesti** ukazal.

      ...

Multiple scrambling could not be a simple syntactic left-dislocation, since then we might expect it to be available out of non-finite clauses as well; in particular, we would expect sentences (10d,e) to be acceptable, just like the comparable (11d) and (11f), contrary to fact. Multiple scrambling is acceptable only with special intonation, and is subject to total reconstruction. Sauerland &

Elbourne (2002) argue that only PF movements totally reconstruct (cf. Aoun & Benmamoun 1998). Following this view, multiple scrambling is not syntactic, but rather an instance of PF movement. If multiple scrambling is PF movement, it is most reasonably limited to a PF unit, and since PF units are created by (PF) phases, we can conclude that there is no PF phase in between the matrix and the embedded non-finite clause. If that is the case, then Slovenian non-finite clauses do not get spelled out to PF.

Matushansky also discusses isolability as a potential diagnostic for PF phases. If a certain phrase can be pronounced alone, outside of its proper place in a sentence, then it is a good candidate for PF phasehood. Following this diagnostic, non-finite clausal complements should be PF phases. As shown in (13), a non-finite clausal complement can be pronounced in isolation (both in English and Slovenian). However, as shown in (14) (from Matushansky 2003), this diagnostic does not always show PF phases. What is pronounced in isolation in (14) is neither *v*P nor TP, the two potential phases in the relevant region.

(13) a. (Peter ti je ukazal oditi v cerkev.) — Oditi   v   cerkev?
                                                   go-INF in church
           '(Peter ordered you to go to church.) — To go to church?'

      b. (Peter se je odločil kupit avto.) — Kupit   avto?
                                               buy-INF car
          '(Peter decided to buy a car.) — To buy a car?'

(14) Alice didn't leave. — Didn't leave? What do you mean, didn't leave?

In addition, TP is the typical locus of the EPP feature, also called by Chomsky (2005, 2008) *the edge property*, allowing items from inside the phase to evacuate to its edge to remain active. TP is also the projection where agreement with *phi*-features takes place, again suggesting TP should be a phase, just like *v*P is the locus of Acc case assignment (and agreement with the object).[7] These properties are all properties of finite T, but here, we are talking about non-finite TP; that is, a TP that does not assign Nom case[8] and may not even have the EPP (its EPP is not visibly checked). In other words non-finite TP does not display two of the prominent features of a phase head. As discussed in Marušič (2005) (and also by many others), Case and (the standard) EPP are both properties associated with PF phases. Not having either suggests that the projection is not a phase for the PF interface. Since I have shown that non-finite complement clauses are propositional elements, and the location where

---

[7] Chomsky (2008) acknowledging these properties claims they are all inherited from the phasal C.

[8] For the Icelandic facts from Sigurðsson (1991) and Slavic facts from Franks (1995) and Marušič *et al.* (2002, 2003) I want to say that (at least) the Nominative case on the depictives and floating quantifiers in these cases is an instance of default case.

quantifiers can take scope, I have argued that they are phases for the LF inter-face. Thus, we can conclude that non-finite TP is a locus of non-simultaneous Spell-Out, where structure only gets spelled out to LF, but not to PF.

6.2.2 *Unaccusative/Raising vP*

Active *v*P is standardly considered a phase. On the LF side, *v*P is consid-ered a propositional element, since this is the projection where argument structure (which is clearly something relevant for the LF interface) is com-pleted. Notice that argument structure is completed also at the level of raising and unaccusative *v*P. No projection higher than (unaccusative) *v*P introduces new arguments. Therefore, clearly in terms of the LF interface, both active and unaccusative *v*P are comparable. However, in terms of Case assignment, things are different. Case is a condition for the PF interface, and therefore Case assignment could be seen as a property of PF phase edges (edges where struc-ture gets spelled out to the PF interface). With respect to Case assignment, the two *v*Ps have an obvious difference. Active *v*P assigns accusative case to the internal argument, while unaccusative *v*P does not.

(i) LF phasehood

Sauerland (2003) argues for the existence of an intermediate scope position in raising constructions, claiming the matrix *v*P in raising constructions is a phase (contra Chomsky 2001). His claim is based on sentences like (15), where the universal quantifier falls under the scope of negation yet still binds the pronoun. This shows that it has to be interpreted higher than the internal object of the raising verb, and at the same time lower than negation. According to Sauerland, the only such position is *v*P of the matrix-raising predicate. Positions where raised quantifiers can take scope are phase edges, since quan-tifiers, when raising from within a lower phase have to move through them. Assuming that reconstruction does not involve a special operation like LF lowering (as in May 1985), every position through which a quantifier is moved is an edge position of the lower phase.

(15)   Every child$_i$ doesn't seem to his$_i$ father to be a genius.   *not* > ∀ > *his*

A slightly different test can be constructed that seems to work also with other raising predicates like *likely*. Notice that the test also works without a universal quantifier binding a pronoun if we use floating quantifiers. The presence of the floating quantifier between negation, shown in (16a), and the raising predicate already suggests that the DP has moved through a position in that area (following Sportiche 1988), suggesting there is a phase edge position in between negation and the matrix verb; i.e. raising *v*P. In addition, the universal quantifier in (16b) is also interpreted under negation and has wide scope with respect to the raising predicate, so it is interpreted in the Spec*v*P position. The same is true of (16c). This should mean that the *v*P above *likely* is indeed a phase edge for the LF interface. This means that structure gets spelled out to the LF interface at the (unaccusative) *v*P stage.

(16) a. Children$_i$ don't all seem to their$_i$ parents to be smart.

  b. Our children don't all seem to be in the room.

  c. Austrians aren't all likely to be placed among the top 10.

On the basis of reconstruction facts, Legate (2003*a*) also claims that passive, unaccusative, and raising *v*Ps are phases, since *wh*-movement proceeds through them, allowing parts of the *wh*-word to be interpreted in *v*P. Thus we have another reason to posit LF phasehood of the raising *v*P.

These arguments are not flawless. For example, if one accepts Zanuttini's (1997) analysis that negation raises to a position above TP where it gets interpreted, then the position where the universal quantifier gets interpreted to get the desired reading of (15) and (16) need not be Spec*v*P. Consequently, we do not have any reason to posit the intermediate position in the specifier of the raising *v*P through which the quantifier moved. Nothing of what I want to show here depends on the raising *v*P having or not having the status of a non-simultaneous phase. I will continue to assume raising *v*P is a partial phase, but it might as well be different.

(ii) PF phasehood

The preceding arguments have all been arguments for an LF Spell-Out, since they are concerned with the positions at which items get interpreted. As the first evidence against a simultaneous PF Spell-Out, I submit cases of long-distance agreement in English raising constructions. As shown in (17), the DP inside the embedded non-finite clause agrees with the matrix T. We have seen that there is an LF phase boundary between the position of a DP inside the lower clause and the matrix T, namely the embedded TP, and therefore there cannot be any agreement with LF-related features. But since the DP has also PF-related plural features, and since agreement is indeed observed, we can conclude that the DP and T must be PF phasemates.

(17) There seem to be mosquitoes all around me.

Raising *v*P does not have the typical properties of PF phases. Of the three tests for PF phases, I will only use (PF) movement tests here, since the other two are more controversial. Taking Matushansky's (2003) paradigm of not clearly syntactic movements, we can test each type of movement with raising verbs. Doing so, we see that raising *v*Ps cannot participate in pseudo-clefting, (18b–d), predicate fronting, (19b–e), or *though*-constructions, (20b).

(18) a. What Goneril did was [$_{vP}$ blind Gloster].

   b. * What there was was [$_{vP}$ seem to be a man in the garden].

   c. * What there was was [likely to be a man in the garden].

   d. *? What somebody was was [likely to be in the garden].[9]

(19) a. Mary said she would kick her, and [kick her] she did.

   b. * Jill said John'd be likely to be inside and [likely to be inside] he was.

   c. * John said Bill'd seem to be tired and [$_{vP}$ seem to be tired] Bill did.

   d. * John said Bill'd be believed to be able to drink 4 beers in 10 minutes, and [$_{vP}$ believed to be able to drink 4 beers in 10 minutes] he was.[10]

   e. * Bill said someone'd be likely to be inside and [likely to be inside] somebody was.

(20) a. [$_{vP}$ Marry her lover] though Juliet did, the results were disastrous.

   b. * [$_{vP}$ Seem to be tired] though Mary did, she still had to work.

These data show that raising *v*Ps are not units at the PF interface, and that nothing gets spelled out to the PF interface when a raising *v*P is completed. Accepting the arguments suggesting raising *v*Ps are LF interface units, we have found another case of a non-simultaneous Spell-Out.

6.3 Phases in the Nominal Domain

6.3.1 *DP/KP (The Topmost Nominal Projection)*

It is commonly assumed that DP is a phase. Upon closer examination however, it turns out that it is actually a deficient phase, since it clearly represents a unit at the PF interface, but at the same time it does not represent a proposition, and thus does not constitute a semantic (LF) phase. A quantifier does not constitute a natural semantic constituent with the NP restriction alone regardless of the way we analyze quantification. In both the relational (Larson 1991) and the clausal (Sportiche 1997) views of quantifiers, the semantic unit of the quantifier includes both its restriction (the NP) and its scope

---

[9] (18d) is said to be marginal in case there is a definite *somebody*. With wide scope of the indefinite, (18d) might be a case of a control equivalent of the raising construction.

[10] There is some disagreement regarding the ungrammaticality of this example.

(the rest of the clause). Unless we put a pronominal representing the scope in the specifier of the DP, as in Larson (1991), the top level projection of the quantified noun phrase does not form a semantic phase/unit.[11]

(i) LF phasehood

Matushansky (2003) cites two tests for LF phases: (a) *phases have the status of a "proposition*," and (b) *QR and successive cyclic wh-movement can target edges of phases*. The first test is fairly clear and easy to make. Propositions are syntactic objects with the semantic type <t>, while DPs are never of the semantic type <t>. Lack of an LF phase/Spell-Out with the second test was most clearly shown by Sauerland (2005). He claims DP is not a scope island, and that quantifiers from inside the DP in inverse scope-linking constructions never end up taking scope at the DP level (cf. e.g. Larson 1985). If quantifiers never take scope at the DP edge, then this should mean DP is not an appropriate scope position for quantifiers, which in turn means DP has no LF phase edge.

Sauerland's arguments come from inverse scope-linking constructions in which a quantified noun phrase (QNP) that is embedded inside another QNP takes scope higher than the QNP it is embedded in. So, although the structure is something like [QNP1 [QNP2]], the interpretation ends up being QNP2 > QNP1. To give an example, the embedded QNP *every linguist* in (21) can take scope over *one book*, which results in the interpretation that Tom read not only one book, but several. In other words, for every linguist, Tom read one book by this linguist.

(21)   Tom read [$_{DP}$ one book by [$_{DP}$ every linguist]].

The main question at this point in these examples is, where exactly does the embedded QNP *every linguist* take scope, outside or inside the DP? The standard answer so far (e.g. Larson 1985) has been that it always takes scope inside the DP, but just outside of the quantifier. Sauerland argues against this view, and shows that an embedded QNP can indeed take scope outside the main DP. But before we go into his main arguments, let us first review his main background assumptions. Sauerland looks at inverse scope-linking constructions in the object position of an intensional verb. Since there are three quantificational elements, great care is needed to determine which element

[11] A reviewer points out that deverbal nominals clearly involve argument structure and are typically argued to be propositional. If the completion of argument structure and propositionality is evidence of LF phasehood, then noun phrases like *John's paintings of Mary* should be LF phases. But notice that as shown in Section 6.3.2, there is evidence for a DP-internal LF phase that could possibly be equated with the one just mentioned. Note further that DP's LF phasehood is challenged not by the semantic properties of the noun inside DP, but rather by the semantic properties of the quantifier. If *John's* is the determiner in *John's picture of Mary*, then the issue remains, but since nominals like *all Leonardo's paintings* are also available, we can still argue the entire DP is not a phase in these cases for the same (quantification-related) reason just like any other quantified noun phrase.

takes scope over another one. As Sauerland points out, indefinites are good for testing narrow scope with respect to an intensional verb. A sentence like (22) has two readings, corresponding to the two relative scopes of the indefinite and the intensional verb.

(22)   Jon wants to marry someone from Valencia.

On one reading, marrying anyone from Valencia would satisfy Jon (e.g. Jon does not know anyone from Valencia, so he does not have the desire to marry anyone in particular, but believes that Valencian girls are really beautiful, since he heard it from a friend). In this case the indefinite takes scope under the intensional verb. On the other reading, there is someone from Valencia (e.g. Jessica Serrano), such that Jon wants to marry her. On this reading (as is obvious from the paraphrase), the indefinite takes scope over the intensional verb. Note that wide scope of the indefinite is sometimes argued to arise from reasons other than QR, but since indefinites will be used to determine narrow-scope, this is not really important.

Plurals, on the other hand, are good for testing wide scope relative to an intensional verb. In (23), there are again two readings. The narrow-scope reading of the plural DP *these two women from Nicosia* is true in a situation where John wants to marry both women we are talking about. The wide-scope reading, on the other hand, is true in a situation where John wants to marry either of the two women, but not both of them. This second reading is said to require QR of the plural DP over the intensional verb. That this is really related to QR is shown by example (24), which is according to Sauerland necessarily understood with the narrow scope (CP blocks QR, so that the plural is always under the intensional verb), so that it is only true in a situation where Sue desires that John marries twice.

(23)   John wants to marry these two women from Nicosia.

(24)   Sue desires that John marry these two women from Nicosia.

(cf. Sauerland 2005: 305)

Putting the proposed wide and narrow scope tests together, Sauerland constructs an example with a plural DP inside an indefinite DP. The point is to separate the two parts of the DP (the embedded QNP2 and the main QNP1) with the help of an intervening intensional verb. Since indefinites are easy to test for narrow scope and plurals for wide scope, QNP2 should be a plural and QNP1 an indefinite. This kind of DP is observed in (25). As Sauerland argues, the embedded QNP2 *these two countries* in (25a) can take scope not only higher than *someone*, but also higher than *want*. At the same time, *someone* takes narrow scope with respect to *want* (example (25) from Sauerland 2005: 306, ex. (8)).

(25)   a.   Sue wanted to marry someone from these two countries.

     b.   'For these two countries, there's someone that Sue wanted to marry.'   *two > someone > want*

     c.   'Sue's wish: for these two countries, marry someone from that country.'   *want > two > someone*

     d.   'For these two countries, Sue had the desire to marry someone from that country.'   *two > want > someone*

(25d) should not exist if the embedded QNP2 takes scope inside the DP, yet this is the salient reading in a context where Sue writes in a personal ad that she is looking for a Japanese or Canadian man to marry. Comparable facts are found in Slovenian. (26) indeed has the interpretation that Sue wanted to marry only once and that she did not care whom she married as long as that person was from one of the two countries she specified.[12]

(26)   Marija je   hotela poročit nekoga iz   teh   dveh držav.
      Marija AUX wanted marry   someone from these two   countries
      'Marija wanted to marry someone from these two countries.'

Sauerland suggests that the DP-internal QNP2 never takes scope at the DP edge. Since scope-taking is a determining factor for (LF) phase edges, not being able to take scope at the DP edge means that the DP edge is not an (LF) phase edge.

    A different argument showing that DP is not a scope island can also be produced. If contained QNPs can only scope at the edge of the containing QNP, then we have a strong prediction in the case where a contained QNP embeds another QNP. I have in mind something like the examples in (27), sketched in (28).

(27)   a.   some exit from [every freeway in [a large California city]]

     b.   every book by [some author from [some Eastern European country]]

---

[12] At the same time an indefinite under an intensional verb can be understood non-specifically, parallel to (22), and a plural can scope wider than the intensional verb, parallel to (23), (i). Additionally, when QR is impossible (e.g. out of finite clausal complements), such reading is also impossible, (ii).

(i)   Rok si   danes želi it na ta   dva hriba. Ali   na Krn ali pa na Žrd.
    Rok REFL today wish go on this two hills   either on Krn or else on Žrd
    'Rok wishes to go to these two mountains today. Either Krn or Žrd.'

(ii) #Želi si   da bi   danes šel na ta   dva hriba. Ali   na Krn ali na Žrd.
    wish REFL that COND today go on this two hills   either on Krn or on Žrd
    'He wishes that he would climb these two hills today. Either Krn or Žrd.'

(28) $[_{QP1}$ Q1 $[_{NP1}$ ... $[_{QP2}$ Q2 $[_{NP2}$ ... $[_{QP3}$ Q3 $[_{NP3}$ ...]]]]]]

In these cases, DP-only scoping predicts that QP3 can not QR directly to QP1, eliminating the possibility for the scope order in (29). It also predicts other scope orderings to be impossible, but I will limit myself to this one.

(29)   *QP3 > QP1 > QP2

This prediction does not bear out. (30), with three QNPs, one inside the other, is obviously multiply ambiguous. In a situation where Vili is a building manager and has to take care of several buildings, the interpretation of the QPs in their base order refers to no key, since a door can only be located in one house (in a case where he has only one house, this would be different). But even the predicted interpretation, with the order QP1 > QP3 > QP2, (30b), is not the most salient reading, nor is it the most pragmatically reasonable. The most salient, natural, and pragmatically acceptable reading is the reading given in (30c), where the most embedded QP3 takes scope over the main QP1. According to this sequence of quantifiers, what Vili got is a master key for each building he takes care of.

(30)   a.   Viliju   sem dal   en   ključ za vsa vrata v vseh njegovih
              Vili   AUX give one key   for all door in all   his
              stavbah.
              buildings
              'I gave Vili a key for all doors in all his buildings.'

        b.   Vili got a master key that opens all doors for each house.

        c.   Vili got a single master key for all the doors in all his houses.

Just like the facts from Sauerland (2005), presented above in (25), the Slovenian facts in (30) also show that DP is indeed not a scope island. Following Sauerland, I will extend this finding to claim QR never targets the DP edge, meaning that DP is not an LF phase (does not spell out to LF).

(ii) PF phasehood
Matushansky (2003) shows that, in the case of DP, PF and LF diagnostics actually produce contradictory results. LF diagnostics, on the one hand, show that DP is not a phase, while PF diagnostics, on the other hand, show that it is. Of the three PF tests Matushansky uses, we will skip *isolation* because of its previously mentioned problems.

We will first have a look at movement structures that possibly do not involve purely syntactic operations. One such case is extraposition. Since it only applies to *v*Ps and CPs and not to DPs (there is possibly a syntactic reason for that), it is not useful in our case. Topic left-dislocation, on the other hand, a possible test for the same effect, applies to DPs and CPs, but it does not work with *v*Ps, (31) (examples (31) through (35) are from Matushansky 2003: 10–11).

(31)   a.   [$_{CP}$ That Hermione was interested in someone else], who could imagine it?

     b.   [$_{DP}$ Hermione's interest in someone else], who could imagine it?

     c.   [Hermione be interested in Viktor], who could imagine it?

Clefting, as in (32), does not apply to *v*Ps, but it again applies to both CPs and DPs.

(32)   a.   It's [$_{CP}$ that Desdemona was faithful] that Othello doubted.

     b.   It's [$_{DP}$ Desdemona's faithfulness] that Othello doubted.

Pseudo-clefting applies to both uncontroversial cases, *v*P and CP, and it also works with DPs, as in (33). As shown in Section 6.2.3, pseudo-clefting also does not apply to raising *v*Ps, providing evidence that they are not PF phases.

(33)   a.   What King Lear said was [$_{CP}$ that Cordelia was no longer his favorite daughter].

     b.   What Goneril did was [$_{vP}$ blind Gloster].

     c.   What Regan listened to was [$_{DP}$ Goneril's suggestions].

Predicate fronting is not really applicable to CPs, because it only applies to predicates (and CPs are not predicates), and although (34a) is only given a question mark in Matushansky (2003), my informants claim it is much worse than that.

(34)   a.   ? Juliet promised that she would marry Romeo, and [$_{CP}$ that she would marry Romeo] her parents didn't think/know.

     b.   Goneril said she would pluck out Gloster's eyes, and [$_{vP}$ pluck out his eyes] she did.

     c.   Regan is called the villain of the play and [$_{DP}$ the villain of the play]$_i$ she is t_i.

Though-constructions also exclude CPs, possibly for the same reason; CPs are not predicates. They apply freely to *v*Ps and DPs, (35).

(35)   a.   [$_{vP}$ Marry her lover] though Juliet did, the results were disastrous.

     b.   [$_{DP}$ The villain of the play]$_i$ though Regan is t_i, I still like her best.

It seems thus, that movement diagnostics confirm the PF phasehood of DPs. The results are not completely unanimous with respect to the other phases, but there seem to be (syntactic) explanations for each case where a diagnostic does not apply. If DP is a PF interface unit, it is probably sent out to PF when the DP phase is completed.

Just like movement diagnostics, the Nuclear stress rule also provides evidence for the PF phasehood of DPs. The Nuclear stress rule assigns stress to the rightmost stress-bearing element in a PF phase (cf. Legate 2003*b*; Cinque 1993). It assigns primary stress to the rightmost element in the object DP in (36a) and to the preposition left behind when this rightmost element moves out in (36b), suggesting that DP is a unit on which nuclear stress rule applies.

(36)   a.   Balthasar disliked rumors about **Justine**.

(Matushansky 2003: 12–13)

        b.   Who did Balthasar dislike rumors **about**?

Since DPs pass all the proposed PF diagnostics for phases,[13] we can safely conclude that DP is a PF phase (see Matushansky 2003 for more discussion and skepticism). Thus, we have shown that a DP spells out to PF but not to LF, meaning DP is a PF but not an LF phase.

6.3.2 *DP-Internal Phase (Matushansky 2003; Svenonius 2004)*

Matushansky (2003) also argues that there is a DP-internal projection (below the quantifier) that is of semantic type $<t>$, but it is less clear whether this projection is also a phase. This projection, which is also a QR landing site, has to be under the projection of the article. This is clearly seen in example (37) (from Matushansky 2003: 6), where the NPI *any* has to QR in order to be interpreted, yet cannot QR higher than the article (either to an IP-adjoined position or to a higher projection inside the DP) or else the NPI would not get licensed (nor would we get the appropriate interpretation). According to Matushansky, this node possibly, but not necessarily, corresponds to the escape hatch for QR of degree operators, which is presumably SpecNumP (cf. Svenonius 2004).

(37)   No student from any foreign country was admitted.

---

[13] With movement, this is less obvious because of the large number of potentially relevant movement operations, but nevertheless, DPs pass a comparable amount of movement diagnostics as the two most uncontroversial phases, CP and *v*P.

6.4 Coming from the Other End

As noted in the introduction, Reconstruction is a case of an item being pronounced higher than where it is interpreted. We can explain this phenomenon
by saying that the item was spelled out to LF prior to its Spell-Out to PF.
Covert movement, on the other hand, can be seen as an event of Spell-Out
to PF happening prior to Spell-Out to LF. In both cases, the location where an
item is interpreted is not the same as the location of its pronunciation. We will
now see that in order to derive these two phenomena using non-simultaneous
Spell-Out, we need non-simultaneous phases in exactly the locations where
we posited that they are.

6.4.1 *Total Reconstruction*

The clearest instantiation of reconstruction is total reconstruction. Unlike
partial reconstruction, total (or radical) reconstruction reconstructs the entire
phrase from its surface position (where it is pronounced) to its base position
(where it is interpreted).

A typical example is given in (38), where although the subject DP *someone
from Stony Brook* is pronounced higher than the predicate *likely*, it can still
be interpreted lower than the predicate. For the sentence in (38) to be true,
there need not be anyone specific from Stony Brook who has the property of
being likely to be in The Country Corner (the local Armenian restaurant). This
narrow-scope interpretation of the indefinite in (38) simply means that there
is above chance (or hugely above chance) likelihood/probability that there is
someone from Stony Brook University at the moment in The Country Corner
(maybe because this is one of the few good places around Stony Brook).[14]

(38)   Some SBU student is likely to be in The Country Corner right now.

On the copy theory of movement (Chomsky 1995), this result can be achieved
by interpreting the lower copy of the moved subject and by pronouncing the
higher copy. However, deleting a created copy is an unwanted backstep in the
derivation (some further problems are discussed by Sauerland & Elbourne
2002). Sauerland & Elbourne (building on a proposal by Aoun & Benmamoun
1998) avoid these problems by proposing PF movement of the subject. Their
analysis, however, wrongly predicts that reconstructing DPs will not interact

---

[14] See Lasnik (1998) for the view that A-movement does not reconstruct suggested by examples
like (i). I follow Bobaljik & Wurmbrand (1999) and Boeckx (2001) and assume that only indefinites
reconstruct in raising constructions.

(i)   Every coin is 3% likely to land heads.
        $\neq$ It is 3% likely that every coin will land heads.   (Lasnik 1998: 93)

syntactically with the matrix clause. For example, purely phonological movement of *scissors* in (39) should not trigger matrix plural agreement, just like the group-denoting plural DP *a northern team* does not (when it is interpreted inside the scope of *likely*), (39–41).

(39) a. Scissors *is/are likely to be in the drawer. *likely* > ∃

    b. There *is/are likely to be scissors in the drawer. *likely* > ∃

(40) a. A northern team is likely to be in the final. *likely* > ∃

    b. There is likely to be a northern team in the final. *likely* > ∃

(41) a. A northern team are likely to be in the final. ∃ > *likely*

    b. *There are likely to be a northern team in the final.

Sauerland & Elbourne claim group names, being morphologically singular (like *a northern team*) only trigger plural agreement when they are also interpreted inside the matrix clause, because plural agreement is triggered by the semantic plural feature [mereology]. If this feature is spelled out inside the lower clause, there is nothing to trigger plural agreement with, so we get default singular agreement in (40), when the DP is interpreted low. A possible AGREE relation must therefore be blocked by another (LF) phase in between the matrix TP and the embedded subject position in SpecTP. As argued above, this is the partial phase of the raising *v*P, which only spells out to LF, just like the non-finite TP.

Sauerland & Elbourne's analysis although explaining total reconstruction away with PF movement, does not really provide any mechanism for PF movement itself. I propose a revised version of their proposal. In particular, I derive an understanding of the kind of "PF movement" they discuss as syntactic movement of isolated P(honological) & F(ormal) features. Because there are LF-only phases at certain points in the derivation, P features remain available for further movement, even after the S features were spelled out. Thus, whatever is interpreted low can still move on and get pronounced higher.

If non-finite TP and raising *v*P are LF-only phases, we can give total reconstruction a completely derivational analysis. Once the matrix *v*P is completed, the entire lower TP, including its specifier, spells out to LF. This means all the LF-related features of the entire TP are inaccessible for any further derivation, but all the PF-related and formal features, on the other hand, remain active in the derivation. This syntactic object (composed of PF and formal features) later checks the EPP of the matrix clause and triggers plural agreement in (39). Since the subject gets shipped to LF inside the lower clause, it takes narrow scope with respect to the matrix predicate *likely*. But since it does not get shipped to PF at the same time, it can move to the matrix subject position, where it gets pronounced. Therefore no special mechanism is required to choose which copy of the moved argument is interpreted by LF and which by PF.

The derivation presented in (42) starts off with a simple intransitive (unergative) verb merging with v, the first phase, and its subject, (42a). DP then moves to the non-finite SpecTP, which is an LF-only phase, (42b). When elements from the next phase merge in, the S side of the complement of T becomes inaccessible, (42c). The embedded TP and the matrix v are both partial phases, only spelling out to LF. So that when the matrix T is merged in, only the P & F part of the DP in the lower SpecTP are accessible and move up to satisfy the matrix EPP, (42d) (F features trigger movement while the P features pied-pipe). The difference between the P and the S part of the derivation resulted from the presence of the two deficient phases (non-finite TP and the raising vP). The difference in the size of the spelled-out phase is erased with any new phase (e.g., the root C) merged into the structure. The derivation results in (42e).

(42) a. *S* $[_{vP} DP v \ [_{VP} V \quad]]$
         P $[_{vP} DP v \ [_{VP} V \quad]]$
      b. *S* $[_{TP} DP \quad T \quad [_{vP} \quad v \qquad]]$
         P $[_{TP} DP \quad T \quad [_{vP} \quad v \qquad]]$
      c. *S* $[_{vP} v \ [_{VP} V \ [_{TP} DP \quad T \quad$ —*spelled out*— $]]]$
         P $[_{vP} v \ [_{VP} V \ [_{TP} DP \quad T \quad [_{vP} \quad v \qquad]]]]$
      d. *S* $[_{TP} \quad T \quad [_{vP} v \quad$ ——— *spelled out*——— $]]$
         P $[_{TP} DP_i \ T \quad [_{vP} v \ [_{VP} V \ [_{TP} t_i \quad T \ [_{vP} \quad v \qquad]]]]]$

e. *S-interpretation:*	$V \ [_{TP} DP \dots$
P-interpretation: DP	$V \dots$

In the crucial step, (42d), the P-features of DP that remained visible due to the lack of PF phases move to the edge of the TP phase. They have thus split from the S-features of the same DP, which were already spelled out to LF as part of the embedded TP phase. At the end, the P-features get pronounced higher than where their S-counterparts get interpreted. With the interpretation being lower than pronunciation, DP appears to have reconstructed.[15]

---

[15] As explained in Section 6.2.3, the status of the raising vP being an LF(-only) phase is controversial. Note that total reconstruction can just as well be derived if the raising vP turns out not to be a (LF) phase. To do that we would need some other assumptions, which I unfortunately do not have enough space to introduce and explain. The reader is directed to Marušič (2005) for further discussion of these and related issues.

6.4.2 *Quantifier Raising*

Covert movement presents standard phase theory with a serious challenge. If phase boundaries freeze all syntactic movements, nothing should escape. If something does escape, such movement can only be an instance of purely LF movement. But covert movement is typically argued to be syntactic. Chomsky (2005, 2008) cites Nissenbaum's (2000) "solution," which takes the difference between *covert* and *overt movement* as a difference in timing between Spell-Out and move. If movement to the edge applies prior to Spell-Out, movement is overt. If Spell-Out applies prior to movement to the edge, movement is covert. With the standard assumptions that Spell-Out is simultaneous, and that Spell-Out creates uncrossable boundaries, there should not be any movement after Spell-Out, therefore, there should not be any covert movement. Nissenbaum assumes Spell-Out is not simultaneous to both interfaces, but rather that only phonological features get spelled out to PF cyclically, while the others remain in the derivation on its way to LF. In such a system, his solution makes perfect sense, but for us it is unacceptable. Another possible analysis, assuming copy theory of movement, deletes the lower LF copies and the upper PF copies created by movement (e.g. Bobaljik 1995). This analysis is not preferred since it returns the derivation to a previous stage, it involves an undoing operation. (In addition it lacks a convincing way of determining which copy is to be deleted at which interface. Knowing the two interfaces are not related such mechanism seems impossible.)

But covert movement can be understood coherently in terms of non-simultaneous Spell-Out. We can view it as an instance of a syntactic object that was previously spelled out to PF and now participates in the derivation with its as yet unspelled-out S & F features. As for the location of such a partial phase, the general account must lie in our analysis of DP structure. Quantifier-raising is a property of (strong) quantifiers, a subgroup of DPs, therefore it seems reasonable to look into the internal structure of the DP for the source of its movement. What we need seems to be a top projection of the DP that would not spell out to LF, so that the LF-related features of the DP could move covertly, but that the same projection would at the same time spell out to PF. This is exactly what we have seen to be the phasal composition of DPs. As we said, DP is a phonological/PF phase, but not a semantic/LF phase. When DP gets merged into the structure, there are no differences between the position of the S, P, and F features of the DP, but when the next phase is introduced, the DP's internal structure becomes PF-invisible.

Crucially, the highest phase inside a DP with a strong quantifier, labeled KP in (43) (following Bittner and Hale 1996), is not an LF phase, as argued by Matushansky (2003) and Sauerland (2005). Whenever the KP spells out to PF, since it is only a PF phase, its LF-related features (S) are not removed from the derivation (like their PF correspondent features) and can move further. Here again I should stress that when I say that KP is a phase and that it gets spelled out to PF, I actually mean that there is a projection on top of the DP/KP whose complement spells out to PF, and whose head and specifier obviously do not.

(43)   *quantificational nominal phrase*

Spells out to LF

$[_{KP}$ K $[_{DP}$ D $[_{NP}$ N]]]

Spells out to PF

Now we need to make a bit of a detour before we present a sample derivation. The separation of Spell-Out to the two interfaces makes us think what other properties associated with phases can be seen as interface-specific. One typical edge property is the EPP feature. Van Craenenbroeck & den Dikken (2006) argue EPP is actually a PF condition. We would think this makes it a property of the PF phase. No counter-arguments to this reasoning seem to exist. The only identified LF-only phases so far, the non-finite TP and the raising vP, most likely do not have the (classic) EPP. Note that it is impossible to determine where the typical subject of the non-finite clause PRO is located (and even if we could, if EPP is indeed a PF condition, how can a null subject satisfy it?). In addition, as Bošković (2002*a*) argues, expletives do not move, therefore in a sentence like (44), there is nothing in the embedded SpecTP, suggesting the embedded T does not have the EPP.

(44)   There is likely to be someone in the seminar room.

If having the (observable) EPP is a property of the PF phase edge, what is the property of the LF phase edge? I propose that just like there is an observable EPP (observable at the surface level, i.e. PF), there is also an EPP_{LF}, which has roughly the same function at the other interface. It allows LF-moved phrases to be accessible for further derivation. Just like the presence of a [+WH] feature determines the scope of a *wh*-word, we seem to need a feature-marking scope in the clause. I propose that scope is marked with the presence of a [+Quant] feature in the TP (or any other phase projection except CP). Note that [+Quant] and EPP_{LF} are not necessarily two different features. This feature then attracts the (LF part of the) quantifier, which thus appears to have covertly moved to the edge of the clause. The [+Quant] feature actually attracts [+Q], a formal feature of the quantifier.

With the basic assumptions presented, we can have a look at a sample derivation in (45). We start the derivation with a prefabricated KP in which, as discussed, the maximal projection is a PF-only phase, (45a). When the KP is merged with the verb in (45b), only the S & F-features of the quantifier are visible. The lower NP phase has the active edge, but again only for S & F-features. P-features of the complement of the KP phase are inaccessible, and P-features of the lower phase NP are already spelled out at this point. When the next higher phase, *v*P, merges in, the S & F-features of *DP* are visible, but not its P-features. Only KP and K are P-visible at *v*P, (45c). Thus only S & F-features of the DP can move up (the relevant F feature is attracted by the EPP$_{LF}$ or the scope-marking feature of the *v*P, while the S features move along). When the derivation reaches TP, the S & F-features of the quantifier are still accessible since they are located at the edge of the *v*P phase. They get attracted to the quantificational probe (the scope-marked projection which I assume here is simply TP, where the EPP$_{LF}$ is located), where they also move to, (45e). Thus we end up with the quantified object DP being interpreted higher than the subject, yet at the same time, pronounced lower, inside the VP, (45f).

(45) a. S $[_{KP}[_{DP} D [_{NP} N \quad]]]$

      P $[_{KP}[_{DP} D [_{NP} N \quad]]]$

    b. S $[_{vP} V [_{KP}[_{DP} D [_{NP} N \quad]]]]$

      P $[_{vP}V [_{KP}\text{—spelled out—} \quad]]$

    c. S $[_{vP}[_{DP} D[_{NP} N]]_i v$ $[_{vP} V [_{KP} \quad t_i \quad]]]$

      P $[_{vP}$ v $[_{vP} V [_{KP}\text{—spelled out—}]]]$

    d. S $[_{TP} KP T [_{vP}[_{DP}D[_{NP}N]]$ v $\text{—spelled out—}]]$

      P $[_{TP} KP T [_{vP}$ v $\text{—spelled out—}]]$

    e. S $[_{TP}[_{DP}D[_{NP}N]]_i[_{TP} KP T[_{vP} \quad t_i \quad v \quad \text{—spelled out—}]]]$

      P $[_{TP}$ $[_{TP} KP T [_{vP}$ v $\text{—spelled out—}]]]$

f. *S-interpretation*	$DP_{OBJ} DP_{SUBJ}$
P-interpretation	$KP_{SUBJ} KP_{OBJ}$

I am largely ignoring the partial reconstruction facts observed with QR and *wh*-movement. As shown in (46a–c), parts of the moved *wh*-phrase behave as if they are interpreted in the base position of the *wh*-phrase.

(46) a.   [Which picture of himself$_i$]$_k$ did John$_i$ like t$_k$.

    b.   [Which of each other$_i$'s friends]$_k$ did they$_i$ remind t$_k$ that he saw Bill.

    c. * [Which one of John$_i$'s friends]$_k$ did he$_i$ see t$_k$?

    d.   * He$_i$ saw every one of John$_i$'s friends.

    e.   * He$_i$ showed Mary every picture that John$_i$ took on his last trip.

Note that this is not the actual restriction of the quantifier but rather some even smaller part of the restriction. Restriction is typically interpreted where the quantifier is, as shown with the necessarily false (47a), where the non-denoting term gets interpreted inside of the matrix clause, and the possibly true (47b), where—on the narrow scope—reading the non-denoting "unicorn" gets interpreted inside the embedded clause.

(47)   a.   # Which unicorn is likely to be approaching?

      b.   A unicorn is likely to be approaching.

But since the restriction can be composite, parts of it behave as if they are interpreted low, reflexives can bind subject that appear lower than the *wh*-word, (46a), and names inside the restriction are subject to principle C violation caused by the pronoun that only c-commands the *wh*-trace, (46c). Notice that the same facts hold also for complements of quantifiers. Not everything gets QRed to a higher position where they could escape Principle C violation, (46d,e), etc.[16]

Partial reconstruction facts are indeed very intriguing and a theory that claims to be able to explain total reconstruction should have something to say about them too. At the present stage I can only hint at a possible solution. Note that there is a DP-internal phase, which only spells out to the LF interface. This partial phase could in principle be responsible for the reconstruction of parts of the DP. Obviously things are not as trivial since DP-internal parts can be interpreted in any position where the DP moved through. But note that a DP-internal part cannot attach to the main clausal structure by itself, since it needs the outer DP structure. This is problematic also for the (more or less) standard approaches using the copy theory of movement. Maybe in order for the DP-internal part to get interpreted at any of the positions the DP moved through, some sort of reprojection is needed (Hornstein & Uriagereka 2002). Since this is a special operation, it can apply at any given point in the structure, so that wherever it applies that is the location where the restriction will be interpreted.

---

[16] In a way, the existence of QR suggests that a sentence like *a girl saw every picture of herself* would have the reading where for every picture with a girl, there would be a girl that saw that picture. This reading is impossible. This might be an instance of scope freezing and I have nothing to add here. The fact that an example with a quantifier parallel to (46c) (e.g. *Someone sent him$_i$ to everyone of John$_i$'s friends*) is bad suggests that the complement of the quantifier does get interpreted low.

6.5 Conclusion

We have derived two apparently different phenomena (total reconstruction and quantifier raising) without any backtracking to earlier stages in the derivation. This is a very welcome result in the quest for a purely derivational theory. As it was shown, both phenomena are just a consequence of the phasal composition of the non-finite clauses and of the DP, both of which involve non-simultaneous Spell-Out to the interfaces.

With a way of understanding QR and total reconstruction, we can combine the two phenomena and derive the other reading of indefinites in raising constructions. I am assuming indefinites are ambiguous between true indefinites and strong quantifiers. If an indefinite is understood as a strong quantifier, it can QR to the matrix TP, just like other quantifiers can. So the fact that a sentence like (38) is ambiguous between a matrix and an embedded reading of the subject is no more surprising than the fact that (48) has the wide-scope reading of the universal (Boeckx 2001 claims examples like (48) have only the wide-scope reading).

(48)   Everyone is likely to feel embarrassed if Slovenia wins the world cup.

Further discussion of these cases, including a discussion of whether and why sentences like (48) are not ambiguous is given in Marušič (2005).

7

A Phonological View of Phases*

KAYONO SHIOBARA

7.1 Introduction

When first characterizing "phase," Chomsky (2000) states, based on the minimalist view of the grammar, that a phase should be "a natural syntactic object SO, an object that is relatively independent in terms of interface properties" (2000: 106). Among the two interfaces, the focus has been on the "meaning side," and such SOs have been taken to be the closest syntactic counterparts to a proposition, CP and *v*P. In Chomsky (2001), he further argues that "the choice of phases has independent support: these are reconstruction sites, and have *a degree of phonetic independence*" (2001: 12, italics are mine). This chapter focuses on the "sound side" of the two interfaces, and considers potential advantages of the phonologically based approach to phases. I show that the phonological view of phases calls for left-to-right (as opposed to bottom-up) structure-building in the computational component, and brings a conceptually welcome consequence that the grammar is shaped in response to external conditions on the interfaces, namely conditions on parsing.

7.2 Phases and Syntax-PF Mapping

7.2.1 *Multiple Spell-Out of Phases*

The notion of phase was introduced in Chomsky (2000), in the course of discussion on why raising is ever possible if Merge preempts Move. In (1) for example, at the embedded clause *α*, there are two options to satisfy the EPP feature of the embedded T, to merge *I* or to move *a proof*. If Merge is more

* I thank an anonymous reviewer and the audience at the *InterPhases* conference (Nicosia, Cyprus, May 2006) for valuable comments, and Christopher Tancredi for insightful comments and discussion and stylistic improvements. Any remaining errors or inadequacies are my own.

economical than Move, the latter option should not be available and hence it is wrongly predicted that (1a), not (1b), is derived.

(1) a. *I expected [$_a$ _ to be a proof discovered].

b. I expected [$_a$ a proof to be _ discovered].

Chomsky (2000) solves this problem by proposing that derivation proceeds by phase: At each stage of the derivation, a subset lexical array LA$_i$ is extracted, placed in active memory (the "workspace"), and submitted to the computation. He takes a phase of a derivation to be a syntactic object SO derived in this way by choice of LA$_i$, and argues that LA$_i$ contains an occurrence of C or of *v*, determining clause or verb phrase. That is to say, a phase is a CP or *v*P. According to this view, the word *I* is not included in the LA$_i$ for the embedded clause in (1b), and hence there is no option of merging *I* at this point.

The assumption here is that derivation is strictly cyclic, and as a conceptually welcome consequence, computational complexity is reduced with each stage of the derivation accessing only part of LA.

In Chomsky (2001) the role of phases becomes more significant and is extended to a cycle of Spell-Out into the phonological component. This means that the phonological cycle proceeds essentially in parallel with the syntactic cycle. This contrasts with the Extended Standard Theory (EST)-based system which has only a single position for Spell-Out. Let me schematically illustrate single Spell-Out and multiple Spell-Out.

(2) a. *Single Spell-Out*   b. *Multiple Spell-Out*

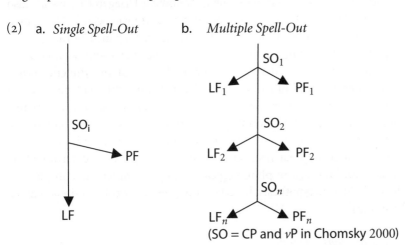

(SO = CP and *v*P in Chomsky 2000)

In (2a), at some point in the computation to LF, there is an operation Spell-Out that applies to the syntactic object SO$_i$ already formed. Spell-Out strips away from the SO$_i$ those elements relevant only to PF, leaving the residue of the syntactic structure, which is mapped to LF. The subsystem that maps the SO$_i$ to PF is called the phonological component, and the pre-Spell-Out computation is called the overt component whereas the post-Spell-Out mapping to LF is called the covert component.

In contrast to the single Spell-Out approach in (2a), in (2b) Spell-Out may apply more than once. According to recent work by Chomsky, Spell-Out domains are associated with derivational cycles of narrow syntax, i.e. phases, and the domain of a phase head is transferred to the phonological component when the phase is completed (Chomsky 2001: 13, 2004a: 108). By this assumption, only the specifier(s) of a lower phase head and the phase head itself remain accessible to further syntactic operations. This is formulated as the Phase Impenetrability Condition (PIC).

(3)   At the phase ZP containing phase HP, the domain of H is not accessible
      to operations, but only the edge of HP.   (Chomsky 2004a: 108)

In effect, the edge of HP belongs to the ZP phase for the purpose of Spell-Out, under the PIC.

Around the same time as Chomsky introduced the notion of phase, multiple Spell-Out was independently proposed elsewhere by Uriagereka (1999b). Uriagereka proposes that Spell-Out is just another rule, which applies as many times as required. He argues that it will apply whenever the terminals fail to command one another. Weinberg (1999), following Uriagereka (1999b), also assumes that Spell-Out applies whenever two categories cannot be joined together by the Merge operation. She applies her theory incorporating multiple Spell-Out to parsing. Notice here that Uriagereka and Weinberg, as well as Chomsky (2000), define the unit of Spell-Out in syntactic terms. In this chapter, I would like to look at phases from a different perspective: from the PF side of the grammar. Given that a phase defines not merely a derivational cycle but a phonological cycle of Spell-Out, why not define it in phonological terms? Furthermore, it should be more minimalist, i.e. part of virtual conceptual necessity, if the size of phase is determined by interface conditions, e.g. in phonological terms. I formulate this proposal as the Prosodic Phase Hypothesis, based on my previous works (Shiobara 2004, forthcoming).

(4)   *Prosodic Phase Hypothesis*
      A syntactic object SO is spelled out as a prosodic object PO.

The model of the grammar illustrated in (5) represents this PF-based view of phases.

(5)   *Multiple Spell-Out under the Prosodic Phase Hypothesis*

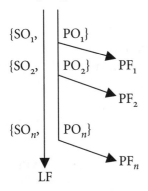

In (5), syntactic structure and prosodic structure are built independently of, but in parallel with, each other, and a certain SO-PO pair, whose size is subject to parameterization, is spelled out into the phonological component and mapped to PF. On the LF side, I take a conventional view that syntactic structure is mapped to LF all at once, as in the EST-based model in (2a) (though this assumption is not necessary or sufficient, and I will discuss the possibility of cyclic mapping to LF in 7.3.3).

Next, I will show how the multiple Spell-Out model in (5) is implemented; in particular, how SOs and POs are paired in the course of syntactic derivation and sent to the phonological component.

7.2.2 *Left-to-Right Derivation by Prosodic Phase*

I argue that the Prosodic Phase Hypothesis in (4), schematically represented in (5), is most naturally implemented if we assume left-to-right (L-to-R) derivation in the computational component (Shiobara 2004, forthcoming). Let us look at examples to see how L-to-R derivation allows a syntactic object SO to be spelled out as a prosodic object PO into the phonological component iteratively.

In English, a CP carries its own intonational contour (marked as Φ below) in the default case, as is shown in (6).[1] In L-to-R derivation, syntactic constituency as well as prosodic constituency are read off from the same structure,

---

[1] Obviously, a modification is necessary for marked cases where, for example, focus or focal intonation is involved (see Shiobara 2004).

but at different stages of derivation, as is shown in (7) (Phillips 1999; Shiobara 2004, forthcoming). (Terminal elements that belong to one prosodic word are connected with hyphens, and prosodic units are shaded.)

(6)   a.   [$_{CP_1}$ This is [$_{NP_1}$ the cat   [$_{CP_2}$ that caught [$_{NP_2}$ the rat
           [$_{CP_3}$ that stole [$_{NP_3}$ the cheese...

      b.   [$_{\Phi_1}$ This is the cat]   [$_{\Phi_2}$ that caught the rat]
           [$_{\Phi_3}$ that stole the cheese]...   (Chomsky & Halle 1968: 372)

(7)   *Left-to-right structure-building*

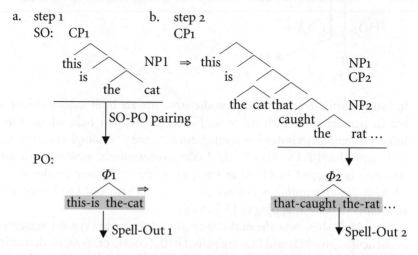

If we take an SO-PO pair whose PO is phonologically identified as an intonational domain to be a phase in English (for reasons to be discussed in 7.3.2.2), all the elements dominated by CP1 (= Φ_1) are spelled out at step 1, and then all the elements dominated by CP2 (= Φ_2) are spelled out at step 2.[2] Note that there is no constituent that corresponds to Φ_1 at step 2 any more, but this is not a problem because the elements in Φ_1 are already spelled out and do not have to be accessed any more. In (7), we can see that Spell-Out defines linear order and intonational phrasing without any additional mechanism: What is spelled out first precedes what is spelled out next; and what is spelled out corresponds to a prosodic unit, namely an intonational phrase (IntP), by definition. Thus, we do not have to look back at what is already spelled out to linearize the syntactic objects that are spelled out iteratively. Let me schematically

---

[2] For SO-PO pairing, I assume unidirectional mapping from a syntactic object to a prosodic object. In the L-to-R structure-building, the right edge of a CP should be identified as the point when the lexical requirements of the heads are saturated, the details of which cannot be fully shown here due to space limitation. (But see 7.3.2.2 and Shiobara 2004 for the details.)

summarize the multiple Spell-Out model under the Prosodic Phase Hypothesis in English.

(8)   *Multiple Spell-Out under the Prosodic Phase Hypothesis in English*

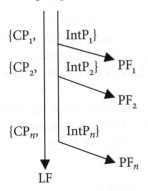

In contrast, if we assume bottom-up structure-building, neither linear order nor prosodic phrasing is trivially determined by Spell-Out.

(9)   *Bottom-up structure-building*

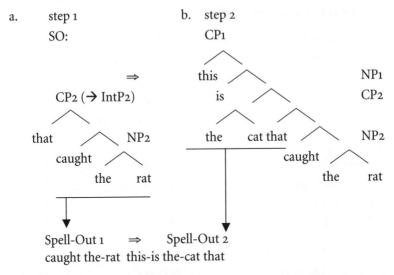

According to the Phase Impenetrability Condition in (3), at the CP2 phase level, the domain of the head C, *caught the rat*, is spelled out, and then at the CP1 phase level, the higher elements, *this is the cat that*, are spelled out. Then, we need an additional phonological mechanism to ensure that what is spelled out first is placed *after* what is spelled out next, which is dubbed the "Assembly Problem" by Dobashi (2003: 25). (See also Uriagereka 1999*b*: 256 and Tokizaki

2006: 2–3 for related discussions.) In order to place what is spelled out at the first phase level after what is spelled out at the higher phase level, the elements that have already been spelled out must still be active at the later phase level. This partially cancels out the reduction of computational burden at least in the phonological component, and is hence an unwelcome result. Moreover, the Spell-Out unit does not correspond to any prosodic unit so yet another phonological mechanism needs to be in charge of prosodic phrasing, despite the fact that syntactic phrasing and prosodic phrasing are closely (though not one-to-one) related (cf. *n.* 2).

In Japanese, a head-final language with (arguably) overt V-raising (Koizumi 2000; Ishihara 2000), if we assume bottom-up derivation, the elements which are supposed to be spelled out together are not even string-adjacent, e.g. *neko-ga*, and *toraeta* in (11b).

(10) a. [CP Neko-ga [vP tNP nezumi-o tV] toraeta].
          cat-NOM   rat-ACC   caught
          'A cat caught a rat'

     b. [Φ₁ Neko-ga] [Φ₂ nezumi-o toraeta].

(11) *Bottom-up structure-building*

      a. *step 1*   b. *step 2*

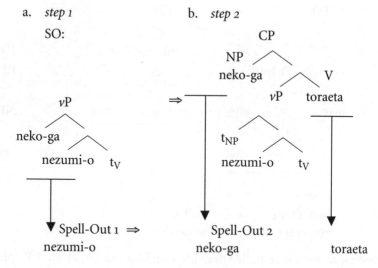

In Japanese, the left edge of a syntactic phrase corresponds to the left edge of a prosodic domain with its own tonal shape, namely a major phrase (MaP) (McCawley 1968; Selkirk and Tateishi 1991), and in (10) the object NP *nezumi-o* and the V *toraeta* form a prosodic unit together (which I mark as

Φ for consistency with English). Then, we need an additional phonological mechanism which guarantees that the object NP that is spelled out first is prosodically phrased together with the V, but not with the subject NP, although the V and the subject NP are spelled out together at the next higher phase level.[3] Thus, if we assume bottom-up derivation, we need additional mechanisms of linearization as well as prosodic phrasing in the phonological component. With L-to-R derivation, both of them come out free as a consequence of SO-PO pairing: Terminal elements are ordered when they get spelled out as SO-PO pairs (which I regard as phases here), in the same order in which they get merged into SOs or POs; and a phase, by definition, always has a prosodic correspondent. Let me schematically summarize the multiple Spell-Out model under the Prosodic Phase Hypothesis in Japanese.[4]

(12) *Multiple Spell-Out under the Prosodic Phase Hypothesis in Japanese*

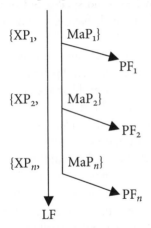

Thus far, we have seen that L-to-R derivation is better than bottom-up derivation in that linearization and prosodic phrasing fall out of the mechanism of multiple Spell-Out of the prosodically determined phase. At this point, a brief comparison with other linearization models is in order. In

---

[3] Furthermore, if Kayne's (1994) Linear Correspondence Axiom (LCA) is in charge of linearization, it should be the case that the object NP ends up in a higher position than the V to derive the object-V order, and this needs to stipulate a sort of object-raising in Japanese. See the discussion on LCA that follows shortly.

[4] So far, I have only discussed intonational phrases in English and major phrases in Japanese, based on empirical evidence that they play crucial roles as phases in syntax-PF mapping (cf. 7.3.2.2 below). Other prosodic units such as prosodic words and phonological phrases should have their significances as prosodic objects, but the point here is that they are irrelevant to Spell-Out and hence do not constitute phases.

the minimalist program, for example, Chomsky (1995) adopts Kayne's (1994) Linear Correspondence Axiom (LCA) for the purpose of linearization, and assumes that the LCA applies only in the phonological component (1995: 334–7). That is to say, Chomsky limits the LCA's place to the PF side of the grammar, though Kayne's original version of the LCA is a formal condition on syntactic phrase markers. Chomsky's version is more minimalist than Kayne's in that linearization is taken to follow from interface conditions, because it is the articulatory-perceptual (AP) system that requires that the derived syntactic objects must be linearized after all. However, it is not obvious exactly how LCA works in the phonological component. Furthermore, its implementation becomes less clear when derivation proceeds by phase because SOs are mapped to PFs iteratively by multiple Spell-Out, not all at once. I have shown that one way to approach this issue is to postulate L-to-R structure-building in the computational component: in L-to-R derivation, terminal elements are merged into an SO, paired with a PO, and spelled out into the phonological component and linearized, all of which happens from left to right.

Regarding Chomsky's reasoning for proposing CPs and *v*Ps as phases with independent interface properties (see Section 7.1), Epstein & Seely point out that the syntactic definition of a phase is problematic because it requires a computational look-ahead: "how can we know that they are relatively independent *at the interface* if Spell-Out applies *before* the interface is reached, and without access to interface properties?" and "why should PF care about the propositional content of what is spelled out?" (Epstein & Seely 2002*a*: 78). Under the PF-based approach to phases proposed in this section, prosodically identified SO-PO pairs act as units of Spell-Out. This way, the amount of look-ahead decreases, because the PF interface requirement directly determines the size of an SO-PO pair that is spelled out into the phonological component, e.g. PO = IntP in English and PO = MaP in Japanese.

7.3 Supporting Left-to-Right Derivation

7.3.1 *External Support for Left-to-Right Derivation*

7.3.1.1 *Parallelism with Parsing Mechanism*   The first argument for left-to-right (L-to-R) derivation comes from its parallelism with a language performance mechanism, namely, parsing. Recall that Kayne's (1994) LCA in itself does not determine whether Spec-Head-Comp or Comp-Head-Spec is the base order, and Kayne refers to "the asymmetry of time" to choose the former over the latter (Kayne 1994: 38, see also Uriagereka 1999*b*: 254 for relevant discussion). This choice is naturally made by L-to-R derivation since L-to-R is indeed the way time flows. That is to say, linear order is determined in the computational component and L-to-R derivation mimics the way terminal elements are "parsed" online, and hence can be regarded as a natural extension of the parsing mechanism (in line with Phillips's 1996 "Parser Is Grammar" view, see also Phillips 2003, 2005; Kempson *et al.* 2001; O'Grady 2005). Moreover, a phase as a computational cycle is reminiscent of a "chunk" as a performance unit (Gee & Grosjean 1983; Abney 1991).

Furthermore, in L-to-R derivation, terminal elements are merged at the right edge of the present structure. (See e.g. Schneider 1999 for detailed illustrations of L-to-R structure-building in the computational component.) This sort of right-attachment is independently motivated by, and closely related with, the parsing preferences, e.g. "Right Association" in Kimball (1973), "Late Closure" in Frazier (1978), and "Recency" in Gibson (1991).

The above-mentioned parallelism between the computational mechanism and the parsing mechanism is much in accordance with the minimalist spirit in that the grammar is shaped by external requirements. It partly bridges the gap between grammar/competence and performance, and contributes to providing a principled explanation for why the grammars are the way they are (in line with e.g. Hawkins 1994, 2004; Chomsky 2001, 2005, 2008; Uriagereka 1999*b*: 276; Shiobara 2004, 2007; O'Grady 2005).

7.3.1.2 *Reducing Computational Complexity*   A major conceptual motivation for the phase when it was proposed was that it reduces computational complexity (see 7.2.1). The Phase Impenetrability Condition (PIC) in (3) (repeated below) allows only the edge of a phase (= the specifier and the phase head) to be accessed and hence spelled out at the next higher phase level.

(3)   At the phase ZP containing phase HP, the domain of H is not accessible to operations, but only the edge of HP.   (Chomsky 2004*a*: 108)

However, the reference to "the edge" seems to obscure the significance of phase as a defining unit of the computational cycle. In other words, the specifier and the phase head do not seem to be a conceptually natural unit in the sense that they do not necessarily form a syntactic or prosodic constituent. In bottom-up derivation, the specifier and the head could be at the left edge, or the right edge, or both, of a phase, depending on whether the given language is head-initial (e.g. English, see (9)) or head-final (e.g. Japanese, see (11)).[5]

---

[5] See Fuß (2007) for empirical problems of separately spelling out the domain on the one hand, and the head and the specifier on the other.

L-to-R derivation solves this problem, because what is spelled out always forms a constituent at the stage when it is spelled out. Moreover, the locality effect captured by the PIC may be reinterpreted in L-to-R derivation without any additional problem: In L-to-R derivation, it is always the "right" edge of a phase that is accessible to the next computational cycle (say, the rightmost terminal element or the node that (immediately) dominates it, cf. Shiobara 2004). This is again independently supported by parsing preferences captured by e.g. Kimball's (1973) Right Association (see 7.3.1.1).[6]

7.3.2 *Internal Support for Left-to-Right Derivation*

7.3.2.1 *Syntactic Constituency*   On a purely syntactic basis, Phillips (1996, 2003) argues that the changes in constituent structure over the course of L-to-R derivation offer a natural account of cases where different constituency tests yield different results in English (see also Pesetsky 1995 for such examples). For example in (13), V′-fronting suggests that the V and the following elements should form a constituent and hence have a left-branching structure like (14a), whereas binding of the NP *each other* by the NP *them* suggests that the latter should be in a higher position than the former, resulting in a right-branching structure like (14b), where (*give*) is a copy of the V (*give*).

(13) a. John wanted to give books to them in the garden, and [ᵥ′ give the books to them in the garden] he did on each other's birthdays.

  b. John wanted to give books to them, and [ᵥ′ give the books to them] he did in the garden on each other's birthdays.   (Phillips 2003: 40)

(14) a. V′-fronting   b. Binding

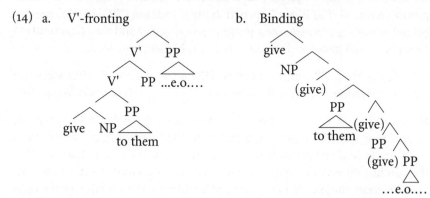

---

[6] Going back to the example in (1) that provided empirical support for phase-based derivation, recall that cyclic derivation by phase provides an answer to the question of why raising as in (1b) is ever possible if Merge preempts Move. In the context of L-to-R derivation, the question is reinterpreted as how leftward movement is implemented in an L-to-R manner. This requires a separate paper and readers are referred to e.g. Richards (2002b) and Aoshima *et al.* (2004), for analyses of leftward movement in L-to-R derivation.

L-to-R structure-building would yield only the right-branching structure like (14b), but during the course of the derivation, the V and its following elements always form a constituent. For example, at the point where PP *to them* is merged, the elements *give the books to them* form a constituent.

(15)

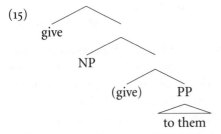

Therefore, apparent inconsistency of the results of V'-fronting and binding is accommodated and hence accounted for by L-to-R structure-building. This provides a convincing argument that derivation proceeds incrementally in an L-to-R manner.[7]

Coordination tests constitute another piece of evidence for L-to-R derivation in the syntax. It is well known that coordination is a liberal diagnostic of constituency, allowing coordination of many strings that do not seem to form constituents under traditional phrase-structure analyses. If we assume incremental structure-building, the liberality of the coordination test is predicted: Since the two conjuncts in coordinated structures are almost string-adjacent (separated only by the conjunction such as *and*), the first conjunct does not lose its constituency at the point when the conjunction is merged (Phillips 2003: 47–51). Consider the following example:

(16) [These cats [saw [these rats]]]

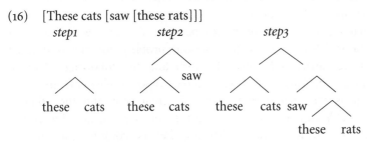

(17) step 1 [these cats]

    a. [These cats] and [those dogs] saw these rats.

    b. These [cats] and [dogs] saw these rats.

---

[7] In addition, Richards (2002b) argues that L-to-R (or what he calls Top-Down) derivation yields a better account of multiple (*wh-*)dependencies cross-linguistically, and Terada (2002) explains syntactic properties of thematic relations in terms of Top-Down structure-building. These provide additional internal (e.g. syntactic) support for L-to-R derivation.

(18)   step 2 [[these cats] saw]

    a.   [These cats saw] and [those dogs ate] these rats.

    b.   These cats [saw] but [ignored] these rats.

    c.   *These [cats saw] but [dogs ignored] these rats.

(Shiobara 2004: 82)

Let us take the step 2 in (18), for example. At this point, the second conjunct can target either the *NP–V* sequence *these cats saw* as in (18a), or just the V *saw* at the right edge as in (18b), because both of them are syntactic constituents. However, the *N–V* sequence *cats saw* cannot be coordinated with the same type of sequence, because the noun and the verb do not form a constituent. Note that the *NP–V* sequence in (18a) is no longer a constituent in the final structure (at step 4), but this is not a problem since it is a constituent at step 3 when the conjunction *and* gets merged. A sentence like (18a) represents the case of Right Node Raising, and its liberality has been problematic to traditional phrase structure analyses where a subject and a verb do not form a constituent. L-to-R derivation in the syntax offers a natural account for Right Node Raising.

How liberal coordination can be is further seen in the following example.

(19)   Other Canadian provinces either have now, or are being asked to develop the enforcement tools necessary to ensure there are no viola-tions of the Canada Health Act.   (*Vancouver Sun*, 5 December 2003)

The coordinator *(either) or* coordinates the verbs, and the DP *the enforce-ment...* appears in the sentence-final position. An interesting fact is that the adverbial element *now* intervenes between the first verb *have* and the coordinator. This gives rise to a serious problem for any traditional phrase structure analyses because the verb and the following adverbial should form a constituent, and two different types of elements are coor-dinated: One is the verb *have* and the adverbial *now*, and the other is only the verbal elements *are being asked to develop*. Again, this is not problematic for L-to-R derivation, because the first conjunct *have now* is a constituent at the point when the coordinator *or* gets merged into the structure.

7.3.2.2 *Phonologically Conditioned Linearization and Contraction*   Let us turn to phonological phenomena that might provide supporting arguments for a phonological view of phases. Certain types of word-order alternations are known to show a cluster of properties as stylistically marked constructions or rearrangements, such as (apparent) optionality and acceptability judgements that are often gradient and subject to variation between speakers. Due to such properties, they have been sometimes swept away from the "core" syntactic component into the phonological component (Chomsky 1995: 324–6). So-called heavy NP shift may be such rearrangement. It is not totally unreasonable to regard heavy NP shift as a phonological phenomenon because it is influenced by phonological factors such as prosodic weight or prominence (Zec & Inkelas 1990; Zubizarreta 1998; Shiobara 2001, 2004). In other words, heavy NP shift exemplifies phonologically conditioned linearization. I argue that heavy NP shift as such constitutes supporting evidence for the PF-based approach to phases and hence for L-to-R derivation.[8]

Under a theory of transformational grammar, the *V–NP–PP* order in English is usually taken as canonical and the alternative *V–PP–NP* order is derived from the canonical order via the operation of heavy NP shift. The distinction between the two orders is based on, for example, native speakers' intuition and frequency of occurrence in texts (Hawkins 1990, 1994). For expository purposes, I call the *V–NP–PP* order in English non-shifted order, and the alternative *V–PP–NP* order shifted order. The property of interest is that non-shifted and shifted orders exhibit different prosodic patterns. First, in a broad-focus context as indicated by (20A) below, the felicitous sentence exhibits the non-shifted *V–NP–PP* order with the default intonation pattern, where the whole sentence (CP) corresponds to one intonational phrase (IntP) (Chomsky & Halle 1968; Nespor & Vogel 1986). This is shown in (20B1). On the other hand, the shifted *V–PP–NP* order in (20B2), when possible at all, exhibits a marked intonation pattern where the rightmost NP forms its own IntP (Zec & Inkelas 1990; Rochemont & Culicover 1990: 105; Zubizarreta 1998: 149). The shifted order is judged to be infelicitous in a broad-focus context, but it improves for some speakers (as indicated with $\sqrt{}$/#) when the rightmost NP becomes *heavy* by containing a larger number of words as in (20B2'), or contains extra prosodic prominence (e.g. focal stress, indicated by upper case letters) as in (20B2").

(20)   A: What happened yesterday?

       B1:   [$_\text{IntP}$ Meg donated novels by Mishima to the library].

       B2:   #[$_\text{IntP}$ Meg donated to the library] [$_\text{IntP}$ novels by Mishima].

---

[8] A phonologically based approach could be extended to not only similar kinds of linearization such as scrambling, Right Node Raising, and Gapping (cf. Chomsky 1995: 324), but also linearization of a head and its dependents, which seems to be also phonologically conditioned, at least partially. See e.g. Shiobara (2004) for scrambling in Japanese, Féry and Hartmann (2005) for Right Node Raising and Gapping in German, and Donati & Nespor (2003) for VO/OV order cross-linguistically.

B2': $^{\checkmark/\#}$[IntP Meg donated to the library] [IntP her old and precious collection of novels by Mishima].

B2": $^{\checkmark/\#}$[IntP Meg donated to the library] [IntP novels by MISHIMA] (but not those by MURAKAMI).

These examples suggest that the prosodic property, namely weight, of the NP determines which order is possible and which order is not. The non-shifted order is prosodically unmarked in that it exhibits the default intonation pattern, whereas the shifted order is prosodically marked in that the rightmost NP must be prosodically heavy enough to form its own IntP.

Having seen the prosodic difference between the non-shifted order and the shifted order, I argue that the marked prosody associated with heavy NP shift falls out of L-to-R derivation and the V-initiality of English, and formulate this in terms of a rightward movement operation in (21) (cf. Shiobara forthcoming).

(21)   *Rightward movement*
       As soon as an unexpected verbal dependent is selected from the Numeration, create and merge a trace of an expected dependent right before the unexpected dependent is merged.

In the case of English heavy NP shift we saw in (20), the V *donate*, by its lexical selectional property, expects an NP dependent first, and then a PP dependent, in the course of L-to-R derivation. In light of (21), if a PP comes right after the V, a trace of an NP is created and merged before the PP, as is illustrated in (22).

(22)

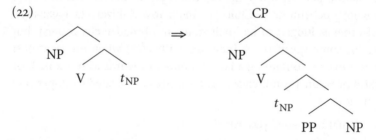

In the non-shifted order, such a trace-creating process does not apply because the verbal dependents show up and get merged in an expected manner. This way, prosodic markedness associated with heavy NP shift is captured by the presence of syntactic movement, which follows from the fact that a V comes before its dependent(s) (i.e. V-initiality) in English, as well as the claim that derivation proceeds from left to right.

Furthermore, assuming the general mapping condition that a CP is paired with an IntP in the default case in English (e.g. when no focal stress is involved) in (23) (cf. Section 7.2.2, *n*. 1), we can account for the marked prosody of the shifted order in terms of multiple Spell-Out by phonologically defined phases.

(23)   A CP is mapped to an IntP in English.

By (23), we can derive the fact that the sentence-final NP in the shifted order is spelled out on its own and forms an independent IntP. This is because when the PP is merged, the lexical selectional property of the V *donated* is satisfied and hence the whole structure is identified as a proposition, CP. The conditions in (21) and (23) account for the marked prosody of rightward movement in general: for example, it is known that a rightward dislocated element creates its own IntP as well (Nespor & Vogel 1986: 188).

Now we can formulate the condition on heavy NP shift in purely phonological terms:

(24)   The rightmost IntP must be prosodically heavy, by containing a large number of prosodic words or prosodic prominence.

The point is that the prosodic weight of the lastly spelled-out PO is the key property to determine whether heavy NP shift is allowed or not in English. An assumption here is that the size of a Spell-Out unit is an IntP in English, which captures the fact that the rightmost NP in the shifted order forms its own IntP. The prosodic condition on heavy NP shift is not easy to accommodate in any syntactically based approaches to phases with bottom-up derivation.[9, 10] Given the condition in (24), optionality of heavy NP shift should arise only when the NP is heavy enough to form its own IntP, and the gradient acceptability associated with heavy NP shift is attributable to the gradient nature of prosodic factors such as phonetic realization of prominence (Ladd 1986: 329).[11]

[9] Let me note that although I argue that English heavy NP shift is phonologically conditioned, the present phonologically based approach to phases differs from any representational approaches to syntax-phonology mapping such as Truckenbrodt's (1995, 1999), in that my approach is grounded in a strictly derivational view of the computational component.

[10] Recently there have been insightful analyses of various phonological phenomena in terms of cyclic derivation by phase with bottom-up derivation, e.g. Dobashi (2003), Kahnemuyipour (2004), Selkirk (2006*b*), and Kratzer & Selkirk (2007), to name a few. Unlike L-to-R derivation, however, they have to postulate their own mechanisms of linearization and prosodic phrasing (see 7.2.2).

[11] The significance of L-to-R derivation in accounting for English heavy NP shift is further emphasized when it is compared with the linearly equivalent operation in Japanese, i.e. VP-internal

Another phonological phenomenon that might argue for L-to-R derivation is found in phonological contraction. Given the fact that contraction may happen between two elements that do not seem to form a constituent under standard phrase-structure theories, such as (25)-(29), O'Grady (2005: ch. 8) argues that contraction argues for L-to-R derivation and that "contraction of the string XY is most natural when X combines with Y without delay" (O'Grady 2005: 139).

(25)   subject + auxiliary/copula

    a.   They'll (< They will) leave soon.

    b.   He's (< He is) here.

(26)   semi-auxiliary + *to*
    They hafta (< have to) go.

(27)   modal auxiliary + *have*
    They shoulda (< should have) gone.

(28)   auxiliary + *not*
    They don't (< do not) need that.

(29)   *wh*-word + auxiliary
    Who's (< Who is) Mary talking to?

Under standard bottom-up approaches, the contracted elements in (25)–(29) are not sisters. For example, in (29) the *wh*-word is in the specifier position of CP and the auxiliary is in the head C. Under the L-to-R approach to syntactic derivation, however, the two adjacent elements are always sisters at the point when the second element is merged.[12] Therefore, phonological contraction exemplified by (25)–(29) provides another argument for L-to-R derivation in the computational component.

7.3.3 *An LF View of Left-to-Right Derivation*

In this chapter, my focus has been on the sound side of the two interfaces, viewing the computational component from a phonological perspective. For

scrambling. We have seen that L-to-R derivation predicts the marked prosody associated with English heavy NP shift in terms of the rightward movement rule in (21). This contrasts with the Japanese equivalent, VP-internal scrambling, where such prosodic markedness is absent. L-to-R derivation can also account for this, because Japanese is head-final and the rightward movement rule in (21) is not applicable. We can take the absence of prosodic markedness in Japanese VP-internal scrambling as the reflection of the absence of syntactic movement in it. See Shiobara (2004, forthcoming) for details.

[12]   Of course, all the adjacent elements cannot undergo contraction. See O'Grady (2005: ch. 8) for what the restrictions on contraction are.

the LF side, I have taken the conventional view that the mapping from syntax to LF applies once (see (5), reproduced below).

(5)   *Multiple Spell-Out under the Prosodic Phase Hypothesis*

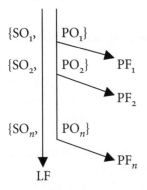

There may or may not be covert movement after the last mapping to PF. After all, sentential meaning is calculated on the LF from bottom up in a compositional way.

However, we might also assume that mapping to LF is multiple (cf. Epstein & Seely 2002a, 2006). If so, SO-PO pairs should be mapped to LF iteratively. This can be illustrated as (30).

(30)   *Multiple Spell-Out to PF and LF under the Prosodic Phase Hypothesis*

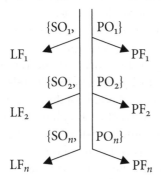

A phenomenon which might argue for this kind of multiple mapping to LFs and PFs is found in scope interpretation in Japanese. Japanese allows two intonation patterns for the same string, and in (31) below for example, the shaded elements form a phonological unit corresponding to the *wh*-scope of the sentence (Ishihara 2003; Kitagawa 2005: 320, brackets represented are based on bottom-up structure-building).

(31) a. [$_{CP}$ John-wa [$_{CP}$ Mary-ga nani-o   tabeta-ka]
          John-TOP   Mary-NOM what-ACC ate-COMP
          shirabeteiru-no]
          checking-Q
          'Is John checking what Mary ate?'

      b. [$_{CP}$ John-wa [$_{CP}$ Mary-ga nani-o tabeta-ka] shirabeteiru-no]
          'What is it that John is checking if Mary ate?'

Assuming bottom-up structure-building, the scope crosses the embedded CP boundary in (31b) and does not correspond to any syntactic constituent. In L-to-R derivation, on the other hand, it does form an SO when the rightmost element (the matrix Q –*no*) is merged.[13]

This suggests that L-to-R derivation by phonologically determined phases may also be adequate for the mapping from syntax to LF, presumably where *wh*-scope is calculated. Note that it is always *possible* to manipulate the syntactic structure and make what is spelled out together a constituent, but the question is whether such an operation is conceptually natural or not. At present, I know of no bottom-up analysis where the shaded element forms a syntactic constituent in (31b).

7.4 Conclusion

Focusing on the sound side of the two interfaces, this chapter considered potential advantages of the phonological approach to phases. One of the major consequences of the phonologically based definition of phase as a unit of Spell-Out was to postulate left-to-right (L-to-R) structure-building in the computational component, which has independent conceptual motivations in the following respects. First and foremost, L-to-R is the way terminal elements are produced or processed online in performance. Locality of the computation is reduced to the inherent property of L-to-R structure-building that it only refers to the right edge in a similar way as parsing. L-to-R structure-building in the syntax is also empirically supported by syntactic and phonological data, and possibly by scope phenomena related to the syntax-LF mapping.

L-to-R derivation by prosodic phases shifts a certain burden of linearization from the phonological component alone to the computational component, in that syntactic objects are merged from left to right in the way they are

---

[13] One thing still needed to be considered is how to semantically include the subject NP *Mary-ga* and the topic NP *John-wa*, which are also in the scope of Q in (32b). (Thanks to Satoshi Oku for pointing this out to me.) On the LF side, this problem could be solved by adopting the VP internal subject hypothesis, but its effect on PF is still to be worked out.

linearized. Therefore, although it is a minimalist interface-based approach to phases pursued in this chapter that calls for L-to-R structure-building in the computational component, L-to-R structure-building in itself may be taken as a revival of classical phrase-structure theories (e.g. Chomsky 1965), where a particular language has a set of phrase-structure rules which specify immediate dominance relations and linear precedence relations in the form of rewrite rules. Needless to say, the present proposal needs to undergo further testing and gain empirical motivations in order to show that this revival is a meaningful one.

8

A Dynamic Approach to the Syntax-Phonology Interface: A Case Study from Greek*

ANTHI REVITHIADOU & VASSILIOS SPYROPOULOS

8.1 Introduction

In this chapter, we investigate the consequences of the *Multiple Spell-Out Hypothesis* (henceforth, MSOH; Uriagereka 1999*b*; Chomsky 2000 *et seq.*) for prosodic constituency based on evidence from Greek phrasing. More specifically, our focus of investigation falls on the phrasing of clitic-doubled DP objects and that of subjects. The basic idea in the MSO program is that certain pieces of structure abandon the main syntactic computation before its completion and thus, become inaccessible to further computation. Consequently, such *derivational cascades* can be argued to be independently processed at the PF interface, predicting an isomorphism between syntactic and prosodic *islands*, i.e. opaque domains for the application of both syntactic and phonological rules.

The MSO program raises some important issues regarding the flow and processing of information between the components of grammar. Most interface theories tacitly assume a serial, unidimensional model of intermodular

* This contribution builds on some of the ideas developed in previous work (Revithiadou & Spyropoulos 2003, 2005). We wish to thank Kleanthes Grohmann and an anonymous reviewer for their insightful comments. We also wish to thank Juan Uriagereka, Elisabeth Selkirk, Caroline Féry, Mary Baltazani, Dimitris Papazachariou, and Marc van Oostendorp for providing useful feedback on earlier versions of this contribution, and Michalis Georgafentis for proofreading the final draft. We owe special thanks to the audiences of the following conferences: *IP 2003 on Prosodic Interfaces*, University of Nantes (March 27–29, 2003, *NELS* 35, University of Connecticut (October 22–24, 2004), *InterPhases*, University of Cyprus (May 18–20, 2006), as well as the attendees of the *Leiden Phonology Reading Group*, Leiden University/ULCL (February 12, 2004), the *SLALS Linguistic Seminars*, University of Reading (February 3, 2004), and the *Linguistic Colloquium*, University of Potsdam (February 15, 2006) for making valuable suggestions and comments. All errors are of course our own.

interaction[1] according to which a *mapping* is defined as "repackaging" of the output information of one module, so as to become a proper input to the other. For instance, Selkirk's (1986 *et seq.*) *End-Based Theory* (also extended by Truckenbrodt 1995, 1999) is a representative example of such a phonology-free syntax approach: Spell-Out takes place after the completion of the whole syntactic derivation (Chomsky 1981, 1995; Chomsky & Lasnik 1993). The output of syntax then becomes an input to the phonological component which, crucially, has limited sensitivity to syntactic information: Only edges (left/right) of X-bar constituents are visible to the mapping rules.[2] In other words, phonology is blind to syntactic relations such as head/complement, c-command, sisterhood, and so on. Differences in mapping between languages are due to parametric variation with respect to the X-bar level and the relevant edges (cf. Selkirk & Shen 1990).[3] However, serial models of interface become elusive with more elaborate structures which include non-cyclic syntactic elements that are added later in the syntactic structure, such as adjunct clauses, adverbs, and left-dislocated elements (Lebeaux 1988; Stepanov 2001).

MSO, on the other hand, is by design a non-linear model of syntactic derivation that calls for a parallel mode of interaction between the grammatical components. In this respect, it offers a new insight in the way syntax feeds phonology. In fact, we propose that certain syntactic chunks are spelled out independently from the rest of derivation and are parsed into separate phonological phrases (henceforth, p-phrase or ϕ).[4] To be explicit, we assume that

---

[1] For a bi-directional approach see Inkelas (1989) and Zec & Inkelas (1990).

[2] Selkirk (1995) argues that only lexical categories (not functional ones) and their projections are visible to the mapping rules. Moreover, empty categories and their projections do not project p-phrase boundaries (Nespor & Vogel 1986).

[3] Selkirk (2000), based on McCarthy & Prince's (1993) *Generalized Alignment*, proposes constraints on edge alignment of syntactic phrases with p-phrases (ϕ) such as the following:

(i) a. ALIGN-XP,L:Align (XP,L;ϕ, L)
        For each XP, there is a ϕ, such that the left edge of XP coincides with the left edge of ϕ.

    b. ALIGN-XP,R:Align (XP,R;ϕ, R)
        For each XP, there is a ϕ, such that the right edge of XP coincides with the right edge of ϕ.

Truckenbrodt (1995, 1999) also adds the WRAP-XP constraint in (ii):

(ii) WRAP-XP: Each XP is contained in a phonological phrase.

Cross-linguistic variation arises from different rankings of the respective constraints. Some indicative examples of various p-phrasings are given in

(iii)   [V   NP   PP]$_{VP}$ *syntactic string*
    a. [ ]ϕ [ ]ϕ [   ]ϕ p-phrasing due to high ranking of ALIGN-XP,L
    b. [   ]ϕ [   ]ϕ p-phrasing due to high ranking of ALIGN-XP,R
    c. [   ]ϕ p-phrasing due to high ranking of WRAP-XP

[4] See also Kahnemuyipour (2004); Adger (2007); Selkirk (2006a,b); Kratzer & Selkirk (2007), among others.

the rules of phonology proper (i.e. rules inducing changes in the phonological pattern) do not make direct reference to syntactic constituents but rather to units of the *Prosodic Hierarchy*.[5] Moreover, we take the p-phrase to be the primary prosodic constituent that mediates in the syntax-phonology interface, because it shows systematic, although not always isomorphic, relation to syntactic structure. In this chapter, evidence for the existence of such a constituent in Greek comes, primarily, from sandhi rules and, secondarily, from fill-word template requirements and intonation.

The isomorphism or the lack of it between the edges of p-phrases and the edges of syntactic constituents plays a central role in this contribution. We show that rephrasing, driven by the need of p-phrases to achieve a prosodically well-formed size, is a favored restructuring process in Greek but not for every input string. We argue that certain syntactic islands, the islandhood of which is a direct consequence of their status as derivational islands, reflect their islandhood at the phonological level as well by resisting restructuring. The existence of multiple phrasing options for a given syntactic string has long been acknowledged in the literature (Nespor & Vogel 1986; Ghini 1993, among others). More recently, studies on phrasing in Romance (Sandalo & Truckenbrodt 2001; Prieto 1997, 2005; Elordieta *et al.* 2003, 2005; D'Imperio *et al.* 2005; Elordieta 2007) and other languages (Hirose 1999, 2003 for Japanese; Jun 2003 for Korean) have underlined the relevance of notions such as branchingness, weight balancing, and length of phrasing. Such prosodic size constraints, called collectively here *binarity constraints*, assess the wellformedness of a constituent of a particular level of prosodic structure C^i in terms of the number of the constituents of a particular level C^{i-1} that it contains (Selkirk 2000). The innovation of this chapter, however, relies on the fact that the (non-)isomorphism between syntactic and prosodic structure is sometimes derived from the derivational history of a syntactic string and, more specifically, from the way syntactic pieces of information are assembled.

Prosodically driven restructuring will also prove to be a valuable diagnostic in the investigation of the different derivational status of clitic-doubled objects and subjects. It is exactly this difference that supports a distinction between two different implementations of Spell-Out and, consequently, calls for a revision of the standard MSO model.

The remainder of this chapter is organized as follows. Section 8.2 presents the specifics of the MSOH and sets the stage for the discussion that follows. Section 8.3 examines the syntactic and prosodic islandhood of preverbal

---

[5] There is ample empirical motivation for the existence of prosodic constituency in the literature. See, among others, Selkirk (1978, 1980, 1981, 1984); Nespor & Vogel (1986); Hayes (1989).

and postverbal clitic-doubled DP-objects. Furthermore, it lays out the main proposal, namely, that clitic-doubled DP-objects are syntactic and prosodic islands as a result of their being derivational islands. Section 8.4 discusses an alternative approach to the prosodification of adjuncts. Section 8.5 addresses the issue of preverbal Greek subjects, which raise problems for the standard MSO architecture. Section 8.6 proposes a revised version of MSOH, which draws a distinction between two different implementations of Spell-Out, and explores its effects for the PF interface. Section 8.7 concludes this contribution.

8.2 Derivation, Cyclicity, and the Multiple Spell-Out Hypothesis

The Minimalist Program (Chomsky 1993 *et seq.*) constitutes a radical shift to a derivational approach to language. In such an approach, explanation of linguistic phenomena is provided by an independently motivated local generative procedure, the *derivation* (see also Uriagereka 1998, 2002*a*; Epstein & Seely 2002*a*). Moreover, there are no syntactic levels of representation, except for the interfaces with the Conceptual-Intentional system (LF) and the Articulatory-Perceptional system (PF). The *derivation* is a strictly cyclic and minimally local procedure which is linked with the interfaces by means of the operation Spell-Out.

In the recent developments of the Minimalist Program (Uriagereka 1999*b*, 2002*a*; Chomsky 2000, 2001; Epstein & Seely 2002*a*) and, especially in the MSOH, the role of strict cyclicity has been capitalized. The main assumption of the MSOH is that Spell-Out is able to apply iteratively sending pieces of syntactic derivation to PF and LF. The MSO architecture is depicted in (1):

(1)   Lexicon ⟶ syntactic operations

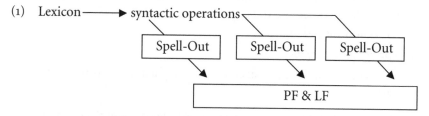

Spell-Out is, therefore, proposed to apply at the end of a derivational cascade. The application of Spell-Out destroys the internal structure of the cascade, so that it behaves as a single object for the purposes of the rest of derivation. As a consequence, the derivation is divided into derivational domains/cascades, each one with its own derivational history. These derivational domains define syntactic cycles within the strict limits of which syntactic operations apply; cross-cycle relations and operations are strictly forbidden (see also Nunes &

Uriagereka 2000). This prohibition takes the form of the *Principle of Strict Cyclicity* (PSC) stated in (2).

(2)   *Principle of Strict Cyclicity* (PSC; Uriagereka 1999*b*: 274)
      All syntactic operations take place within the derivational cycles of cascades.

The interesting question that emerges at this point is whether MSOH has certain implications for the interfaces. As a consequence of the derivational architecture, we propose that it does so and that PSC should extend to the interfaces in the form of the *Generalized Principle of Strict Cyclicity* (GPSC). More specifically, we claim that derivational domains/cascades define also phonological and interpretative cycles, in the domain of which phonological and interpretative operations apply. This is because these cascades reach PF and LF as separate units and are, therefore, independently processed by the operations of these components.

(3)   *Generalized Principle of Strict Cyclicity* (GPSC)
      All syntactic, phonological and interpretative operations take place within the derivational cycles of cascades.

Focusing on the implications of the MSOH for the syntax-phonology interface, we further propose that the products of each application of Spell-Out are mapped onto separate prosodic constituents. More specifically, we argue that, since these derivational cascades reach PF as individual units, they are independently processed and thus, are mapped onto separate p-phrases. This leads to the prediction that no phonological rule (i.e. sandhi) can relate elements of different derivational cascades, even if all the conditions for the application of such a rule are otherwise respected. This prediction, which stems from the GPSC, is encapsulated in (4):

(4)   *PF Corollary of GPSC*
      The edges of a derivational cascade are aligned with a p-phrase boundary.

Delving more into the issue of what constitutes a natural definition of a derivational cascade, we first encounter Chomsky's (2000 *et seq.*) definition in terms of *phases*. Phases are theoretically postulated as subarrays at the Numeration and coincide with the CP and the *v*P constituents, as these objects are propositional in nature. Spell-Out in such a system is triggered by the computational requirement that the checked features be deleted, so as to be unavailable for the rest of derivation. The PSC in Chomsky's system takes the form of the *Phase Impenetrability Condition* (PIC):

(5) *Phase Impenetrability Condition* (PIC; Chomsky 2001: 13)
     For strong phase HP with head H the domain of H is not accessible
     to operations outside HP; only H and its edge are accessible to such
     operations, the edge being the residue outside H, either Specifiers (Specs)
     or elements adjoined to HP.

In practice, PIC implies that Spell-Out applies at the domain of a phase upon
its completion. Thus, the phase system predicts that for an SVO structure there
are three Spell-Out domains: (i) the VP upon the completion of *v*P phase, (ii)
the IP upon the completion of the CP phase, and (iii) the root Spell-Out that
finalizes the structure.

(6)

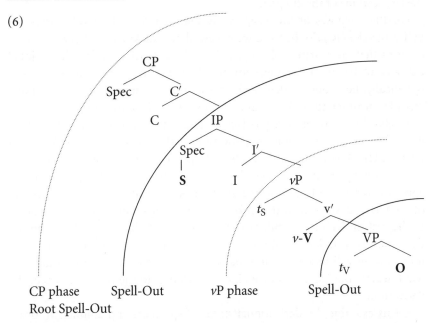

CP phase   Spell-Out   *v*P phase   Spell-Out
Root Spell-Out

Given now our assumptions about the impact of MSO on the PF interface,
which is stated as the *PF Corollary of GPSC* in (4), the phase system predicts
the following prosodification of an SVO structure:

(7) Spell-Out of VP → [O]ϕ
     Spell-Out of IP → [SV]ϕ
     → [SV]ϕ [O]ϕ

Such an approach may be taken to independently derive phonological phrasing based on the products of each application of Spell-Out.[6] Nevertheless,

---

[6] See Dobashi (2003) for a proposal along these lines and Elordieta (2007) for an overview.

the predicted phrasing of the SVO string is not the only pattern attested in the languages of the world and more crucially not even in the same language (e.g. English; Selkirk 2000). One may assume that the attested patterns are the result of rephrasing processes taking place at the PF in order for certain binarity or perhaps other constraints to be satisfied (see the discussion in Section 8.1). Crucially, such an assumption undermines the predictive power of the model, in the sense that at the end it is PF that ultimately decides on what constitutes an optimal phrasing of a string. More importantly, it entails abandoning the notion of isomorphism, at least as we know it, between the grammatical components. We will return to the issue of phase Spell-Out in the last sections of the chapter.[7]

For the purposes of this chapter, we mainly follow the model proposed by Uriagereka (1999*b*), because we believe that it makes some very clear predictions that are worth exploring. Uriagereka chooses to define derivational cascades in terms of the mechanisms of phrase-structure building.[8] More specifically, he proposes that Spell-Out applies at the end of a derivational cascade, in order to make its linearization possible according to the *Linear Correspondence Axiom* of Kayne (1994). These derivational cascades are thus defined in terms of continuous application of Merge and are called *Command Units* (CU). When such a CU is about to get incorporated into a derivation in progress by means of a discontinuous application of Merge, Spell-Out applies and sends it to PF for linearization. As a result, the internal structure of the CU is destroyed so that it behaves as a single object for the purposes of the rest of derivation and, crucially, for the interfaces as well. When the derivation is completed and sent to PF by another application of Spell-Out, linearization will ignore the internal structure of the CU as non-visible and will linearize the CU as a single object in relation to the other objects of the derivation.

Let us examine the derivational status of specifiers and adjuncts in order to understand how exactly the derivation proceeds. Such elements constitute separate CUs that are connected with the rest of the derivation by means of a discontinuous application of *Merge*. As such, they qualify as derivational cascades which are forced to be independently spelled out. Thus, by the

---

[7] It should be mentioned that the phase model of Spell-Out has been proposed by a number of researchers to correctly derive sentential stress and the intonational phrasing of a clause, by mapping phases onto specific prosodic constituents such as Major or Intonational phrases (Ishihara 2003; Kahnemuyipour 2004, 2005; Kratzer & Selkirk 2005, among others).

[8] See Johnson (2003) for a proposal that also defines derivation and derivational cascades in terms of the phrase-structure-building algorithm.

PSC (2) they are predicted to be syntactic islands (deriving the *Condition on Extraction Domains* (CED) effects; see Nunes & Uriagereka 2000), and, significantly, by the GPSC (3) they are predicted to be prosodic islands as well. To exemplify, the derivation of the structure $[_\varepsilon \ \varepsilon \ [_a \ [_\gamma \ \gamma \ \delta] \ [_a \ a \ \beta]]]$, which contains the syntactic object $K = \{_\gamma \{\gamma, \ \delta\}\}$, an adjunct or a Specifier, is as follows:

(8)   The derivation of a structure $[_\varepsilon \ \varepsilon \ [_a \ [_\gamma \ \gamma \ \delta] \ [_a \ a \ \beta]]]$
        cascade1 (CU1) $= \{_\gamma \{\gamma, \ \delta\}\} \rightarrow$ Spell-Out 1
        cascade2 (CU2) $= \{_\varepsilon \{\varepsilon, \ \{_a \{\{_\gamma \ \} \ \{_a \{a, \ \beta\}\}\}\}\}\} \rightarrow$ Spell-Out 2

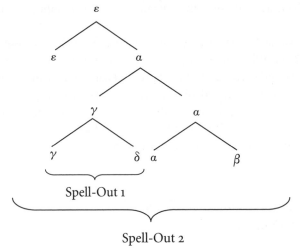

Crucially, (8) predicts that no phonological operation can relate any of the elements (γ, δ) of the object K with an adjacent element of the rest of the derivation (i.e. $\varepsilon, \ a$), and that the only available phrasing is (9a):[9]

(9)   a. $[\ldots \varepsilon \ ]\phi \ [\ \gamma \ \delta \ ]\phi \ [\ a \ \beta \ ]\phi$
        b. $^*[\ldots \varepsilon \ \gamma \ ]\phi \ [\ \delta \ ]\phi \ [\ a \ \beta \ ]\phi$
        c. $^*[\ldots \varepsilon \ \gamma \ \delta \ ]\phi \ [\ a \ \beta \ ]\phi$

---

[9] An anonymous reviewer raises the question as to why ε being simplex is not able to prosodify together with $K = \{_\gamma \{\gamma, \ \delta\}\}$, since it is able to c-command it. We believe that the answer lies in the fact that ε does not belong in the same CU as K, because it does not combine with it by means of a continuous application of Merge. Notice that ε merges with $[_a \ [_\gamma \ \gamma \ \delta] \ [_a \ a \ \beta]]$ and not with K itself. In addition, recall that K being a CU is forced to independently spell out before it merges with the structure. If by GPSC and its PF Corollary a CU is mapped onto its own closed phonological constituent, then there is no way that ε can prosodify together with K.

    d. $*[\dots \varepsilon \gamma]\phi [\delta \alpha \beta]\phi$

    e. $*[\dots \varepsilon]\phi [\gamma \delta \alpha \beta]\phi$

    f. $*[\dots \varepsilon]\phi [\gamma]\phi [\delta \alpha \beta]\phi$

    g. $*[\dots \varepsilon \gamma \delta \alpha \beta]\phi$

Such a model therefore assumes an isomorphism between the syntactic and the phonological islandhood of a chunk as a result of its derivational history. That is, the mapping algorithm is sensitive to the syntactic derivation, in the sense that derivational cascades are mapped onto independent phonological phrases, despite the dynamics of the mapping system itself.

In what follows, we will review significant evidence from the prosodification of OclV(S) and clVO(S) structures in Greek which shows that the syntax-phonology interface is indeed sensitive to the products of syntactic derivation. More specifically, the clitic-doubled object, which constitutes a peripheral adjunct element, is shown to be mapped onto a separate phonological phrase that, contra to the predictions of the mapping system, does not comply with binarity and, more significantly, it resists restructuring.

8.3 The Syntactic and Prosodic Islandhood of Clitic-Doubled DP-Objects

8.3.1 *Preverbal Clitic-Doubled DP-Objects*

8.3.1.1 *Syntactic Status*   Preverbal clitic-doubled objects have been shown to be peripheral elements, base-generated as adjuncts to the MoodP or to the CP, and coindexed with the clitic in order to license their features and theta-role (Philippaki-Warburton 1987 *et seq.*):[10]

(10)   *to axláði*   *to*   *éfaye*   *o*   *kóstas*
        the pear-ACC it-ACC eat-PAST.3SG the Kostas-NOM
        'As for the pear, Kostas ate it.'

---

[10] Alternatively, it has been proposed that clitic-doubled objects occupy the Specifier position of a Topic Phrase (Tsimpli 1990; Alexiadou 1997; Roussou 2000). Since this has no major effect on our discussion (both adjuncts and Specifiers constitute island domains), we will consider the TopicP analysis as a notational variant of the adjunct analysis, for the purposes of this chapter, and we will not try to evaluate them.

(11)

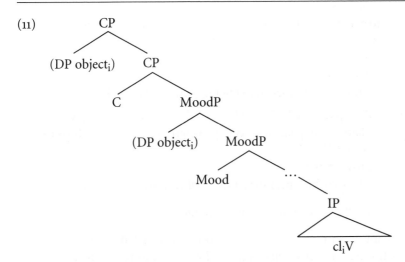

Their peripheral status is indicated by the fact that they are not arguments and constitute left-dislocated topics (Philippaki-Warburton & Spyropoulos 1999; Philippaki-Warburton *et al.* 2004).[11] As such, these elements can never be focused:[12]

(12) * TO AXLÁÐI   to   éfaγe   o   kóstas
      the pear-ACC it-ACC eat-PAST.3SG the Kostas-NOM
      'It is the pear that Kostas ate it.'

That they are base-generated adjuncts is indicated by the fact that they can appear outside weak islands (Tsimpli 1990). Compare (13a) with the ungrammatical (13b) which contains a wh-phrase moving out of a weak island:

---

[11] See also Anagnostopoulou (1994) and Giannakidou (2000) among others.

[12] It has been reported (Philippaki-Warburton & Veloudis 1984; Giannakidou 2000) that the emphatic *kanénas* 'no one' can be clitic-doubled in constructions such as:

(i) **kanenós**   ðén tu   arési   i   kakometaxírisi
     no one-GEN NEG him-GEN like-3SG the maltreatment-NOM
     'Nobody likes being treated badly.'

It is important to clarify that the stress prominence exhibited by *kanénas* derives from its lexically associated emphatic stress (indicated with boldface in example (i)). Giannakidou (2000) also convincingly shows that such elements should not be syntactically treated as preposed foci. The most crucial piece of evidence comes from the fact that when they do become foci, the clitic-doubling option is unavailable:

(ii) *KANÉNAN   ðén ton   íða
      no one-ACC NEG him-ACC see-PAST.3SG
      'NOBODY I saw.'

(13) a. to axláði$_i$ ðé   mu   ípan   [pjós   to$_i$
        the pear-ACC NEG me-GEN tell-PAST.3PL who-NOM it-ACC
        éfaγe]
        eat-PAST.3SG
        'As for the pear, they didn't tell me who had eaten it.'

   b. *ti$_i$ /pjó   axláði$_i$ ðé   su   ípan   [pjós
        what/which pear-ACC NEG you-GEN tell-PAST.3PL who-NOM
        éfaγe t_i]?
        eat-PAST.3SG
        '*What/which pear didn't they tell you who had eaten?'

More crucially, these elements exhibit CED effects:

(14) *pjanú$_i$ mu   ípes   óti [$_{DP}$ to axláði t_i] to
       who-GEN me-GEN tell-PAST.2SG that the pear-ACC   it-ACC
       éfaγe   o   kóstas?
       eat-PAST.3SG the Kostas-NOM
       'Whose did you tell me that Kostas ate the pear?'

All these facts indicate that preverbal clitic-doubled objects constitute independent derivational cascades and exhibit syntactic islandhood. They are thus predicted to be independently spelled out, before they merge with the rest of the structure, and to constitute prosodic islands, too.[13]

8.3.1.2 Prosodification

(i) Evidence from sandhi rules

It has been shown on the basis of intonational evidence that preverbal clitic-doubled objects are mapped onto an independent p-phrase or intonational phrase (i-phrase) (Baltazani & Jun 1999; Baltazani 2002). Here, we provide additional support for this conclusion from sandhi phenomena. In (15), we provide a representative list of sandhi rules that provide cues for p-phrase breaks.

(15) *sandhi rules at the level of p-phrase in Greek*
   a. *t-voicing*
       t → d/ [... V__V]ϕ
       e.g. /θélo̲ ta kulurákja/ → [θélo *d*a kuluráca]
       '(I) want the cookies.'

---

[13] Unlike other languages, such as Germanic, Greek topicalization does not involve scrambling (see (13)), so that the surface position of the topic element cannot be due to either syntactically or phonologically motivated (Féry 2007) movement.

b. *s-voicing*
   s → z / [... ___ C[+cont, +voi], m, n]ϕ
   e.g. /meɣálos máɣos/ → [meɣálozmáɣos]   'big magician.'

c. *C-degemination*
   C_i → Ø / [... [...___]PrW [C_i...]PrW]ϕ
   e.g. /ásximos satrápis/ → [ásximoçsatrápis]   'ugly satrap.'

d. *V-degemination*
   V_i → Ø / [... [...___]PrW [V_i...]PrW]ϕ
   e.g. /káni italiká/ → [kánçitaliká]   '(s/he) learns Italian.'

e. *nasal-stop assimilation*
   [+nas] → [α p.a.] / [... ___ C[-cont, α p.a.]...]ϕ
   [− cont] → [+voi] / [... [+nas] ___...]ϕ
   e.g. /éxun palépsi/ → [éxuᵐbalépsi]   '(they) have wrestled.'

For the purposes of our discussion, we focus on t-voicing, s-voicing, vowel degemination, and nasal-stop assimilation. In general, sandhi rules are blocked between the clitic-doubled object and the following constituent, suggesting that the clitic-doubled object forms a separate p-phrase. This is illustrated by the examples in (16) and (17), which render the orders *DP-object clV DP-subject* and *DP-object DP-subject clV*, respectively.

(16)   DP-object clV DP-subject

   a. *to axláði to éfaɣe o kóstas*
      the pear-ACC it-ACC eat-PAST.3SG the Kostas-NOM
      [tØ axláði]ϕ [to éfaje o kóstas]ϕ
      'As for the pear, Kostas ate it.'

   b. *tis próves mas/sas tis klíni*
      the rehearsal-ACC.PL us/you-ACC.PL them-ACC.PL arrange-3PL
      o pános
      the Panos-NOM
      [tis próves]ϕ [mas/sas tis klíni o pános]ϕ
      'As for the rehearsals, Panos arranges them for us/you.'

   c. *tus amán tus parakoluθún ta peðjá*
      the A.M.A.N. them-ACC.PL watch-3PL the kid-NOM.PL
      [tus amán]ϕ [tus parakoluθún ta peðjá]ϕ
      'As for the A.M.A.N. (group), the kids watch them.'

(17) DP-object DP-subject clV

    a. *tin ániksi̱*   i̱   kátja   tin   aɣapá
        the spring-ACC the Katia-ACC it-ACC love-3SG
        [tin ániksi]ϕ [i kátça tin aɣ apá]ϕ
        'As for the spring, Katia loves it.'

    b. *ton aléko*   o   baᵐbás   ton   misí
        the Aleko-ACC the dad-NOM him-ACC hate-3SG
        [ton aléko]ϕ [o baᵐbás ton misí]ϕ
        'As for Alex, dad hates him.'

As is obvious from the above examples, sandhi rules provide additional evidence for the independent p-phrasing of clitic-doubled objects. More specifically, in (16a), t-voicing, a rule that voices an intervocalic *t*, fails to apply between the clitic-doubled object and the clitic, although its structural conditions are met. Similarly, in (16b), s-voicing, which is initiated before a voiced fricative or a nasal, is blocked between the object and the following clitic. In (16c), nasal-stop voicing assimilation is also blocked between the clitic-doubled object and the following clitic. Moreover, in (17a–b), vowel degemination is not enforced between the clitic-doubled object and the DP-subject. We conclude, therefore, that the syntactic islandhood of clitic-doubled objects is matched with prosodic islandhood as well. This is further supported by the fact that they exhibit resistance to rephrasing, which constitutes a popular restructuring procedure at the level of p-phrasing.

(ii) Evidence from wellformedness constraints on phrasing
Revithiadou (2004*a,b*, 2005) argues that the End-based mapping algorithm for Greek is {Right, XP}, translating to the ranking: ALIGN-XP,R ≫ ALIGN-XP,L. However, on the basis of a corpus of 204 declarative sentences (elicited by four native speakers—three female and one male—and produced with neutral sentence stress), she shows that there is a strong preference for p-phrases to be binary. This is particularly enforced when the subject (S) is light (smaller than two feet) and the VP is heavy (larger than two feet). The examples below illustrate both available phrasing options:

(18) [DP Det N] [IP V [VP *t*V [DP Det N] [PP P DP]]]
    to   fós̱   ðíni̱   i̱sxí   sti   mixaní
    the light-NOM give-3SG power-ACC to-the machine-ACC
    'The light gives power to the engine.'

    a. [to fós]ϕ [ðínØ isçí]ϕ [sti mixaní]ϕ   *end-based mapping*

    b. [to fóz ðíni]ϕ [isçí sti mixaní]ϕ   *binarity-based mapping*

(19) [$_{DP}$ Det N] [$_{IP}$ V [$_{VP}$ t_V [$_{DP}$ Det N] [$_{PP}$ P DP]]]
      o   páno<u>s</u>   <u>ð</u>íni   efxé<u>s</u>   me kártes
      the Panos-NOM give-3SG wish-ACC.PL with card-ACC.PL
      'Panos sends wishes with cards.'

    a. [o pános]ϕ [ðínØ efçés]ϕ [me kártes]ϕ *end-based mapping*

    b. [o pánoz ðíni]ϕ [efçéz me kártes]ϕ *binarity-based mapping*

The blocking of s-voicing and vowel degemination between the DP-subject and the V in (18a) and (19a), respectively, suggests that the respective constituents belong to separate phrases. Moreover, in (18a), the VO string forms a p-phrase, since vowel degemination applies between the V and the object, i.e. *ðínØ isçí*. In (19a), s-voicing is blocked between the DP-subject and the V, suggesting that they phrase separately, whereas the deletion of the high vowel /i/ before the more sonorous /e/ between the V and the object, *ðínØ efçés*, suggests that these two constituents phrase together.

The data in (18b) and (19b), on the other hand, reveal that a second algorithm, which evaluates p-phrases on the basis of prosodic weight, is in force. In fact, the (b)-phrasings are preferred over the (a)-phrasings, especially in normal to rapid speech rates. The driving force for (b)-phrasings is binarity. In (18b) and (19b), the V joins with the DP-subject into a binary p-phrase, that is, a p-phrase that consists of two Prosodic Words (*PrW, ω*). Likewise, the two complements are combined together into a second binary p-phrase, thus yielding a balanced and symmetrical i-phrase: {[$\omega\omega$]ϕ [ω ω]ϕ}i-phrase.

Binarity is achieved only when a constraint such as (20),[14] which regulates what the minimal size of a p-phrase needs to be, outranks the syntax-phonology interface constraint: BIN^{min} ≫ ALIGN-XP,R.

(20) *prosodic binarity*
               (Selkirk 2000, based on Itô & Mester 1992, 1995; Ghini 1993)

    a. BIN^{min}: A p-phrase must consist of at least two PrWs.

    b. BIN^{max}: A p-phrase must consist of at most two PrWs.

To summarize, weight balancing and prosodic branchingness constraints constitute the driving force for the partition of sentences into prosodic units that show no respect to syntactic boundaries. A phrasing mechanism that assigns primary role to prosodic wellformedness (21a) naturally stands in a rivalry

---

[14] Elordieta *et al.* (2005) propose a parametric size constraint which calculates prosodic heaviness in terms of syllables, prosodic words or levels of syntactic branchingness, depending on the language. Such parametric constraints, however, raise serious theoretical problems since a basic tenet of *Optimality Theory* (Prince & Smolensky 1993) is that constraint-reranking, and not different parameter settings, is the primary source of cross-linguistic variation.

relationship with the end-based mapping (21b) that requires a hand-in-hand cooperation between phonology and syntax.

(21) *p-phrasing algorithms*

   a. *edge-based algorithm*: alignment ≫ binarity

   b. *binarity-based algorithm*: binarity ≫ alignment

Interestingly, binary phrasings are not an option for the sentences in (22). Clitic-doubled DPs consisting of a single prosodic word are not liable to the balancing forces of the binarity-based algorithm and they resist restructuring.

(22) a. *to axláði to éfaɣe o kóstas tis*
         the pear-ACC it-ACC eat-PAST.3SG the Kostas-NOM the
         ánas
         Anna-GEN
         'As for the pear, Anna's Kostas ate it.'

   a′. [to axláði]φ [to éfaje o kóstas tis ánas]φ

   a″. *[to axláði do éfaje]φ [o kóstas tis ánas]φ

   b. *tin ániksi i kátja tin éxi aɣapísi*
         the spring-ACC the Katia-ACC it-ACC have-3SG love
         'As for the spring, Katia has loved it.'

   b′. [tin ániksi]φ [i kátça tin éçi aɣapísi]φ

   b″. *[tin ániksØi kátça]φ [tin éçi aɣapísi]φ

To conclude, blocking of sandhi rules and resistance to binarity indicate that preverbal clitic-doubled objects form independent phrases and hence prosodic islands.

8.3.2 *Postverbal Clitic-Doubled DP-Objects in clVO(S) Constructions*

8.3.2.1 *Syntactic Status*   Postverbal objects in clVO(S) constructions exhibit different syntactic properties from objects in VO(S) structures, which are unquestionably arguments. Thus, it has been argued that clitic-doubled objects in clVO(S) constructions are peripheral elements to the *v*P domain, adjoined to either *v*P or VP (Philippaki-Warburton *et al.* 2004; Georgiafentis 2004):[15]

---

[15] Alternatively, they have been proposed to constitute Specifiers in an internal Topic projection (Georgiafentis 2004):

(i) [IP to éfaɣe [iTopicP to axláði [vP o kóstas tv tCL]]]

(23) a. to   éfaγe   to axláði   o   KÓSTAS
          it-ACC eat-PAST.3SG the pear-ACC the Kostas-NOM
          'As for the pear, it was Kostas that ate it.'

      b. [IP to éfaγe [vP to axláði [vP o kóstas tV tCL]]]

The peripheral status of clitic-doubled DP-objects in clVO(S) is indicated by
the fact that, unlike DP-objects in VOS structures, they cannot be focused.

(24) a. éfaγe   [TO AXLÁÐI]FOC o
          eat-PAST.3SG the pear-ACC   the
          kóstas (answer to 'What did Kostas eat?')
          Kostas-NOM
          'Kostas ate THE PEAR.'

      b. *to   éfaγe   [TO AXLÁÐI]FOC o kóstas
          it-ACC eat-PAST.3SG the pear-ACC   the Kostas-NOM
          'As for the pear, Kostas ate it.'

Furthermore, clitic-doubled objects in clVOS constructions constitute islands
for extraction from within (CED effects) (25a). Notice again the difference
from objects in VOS constructions (25b):

(25) a. *pjanúᵢ   mu   ípes   óti to   éfaγe
          who-GEN me-GEN tell-PAST.2SG that it-ACC eat-PAST.3SG
          [DP to axláði tᵢ] o   kóstas?
              the pear-ACC the Kostas-NOM
          'Whose did you tell me that Kostas has eaten the pear?'

      b. pjanúᵢ   mu   ípes   óti éfaγe
          who-GEN me-GEN tell-PAST.2SG that eat-PAST.3SG
          [DP to axláði tᵢ] o   kóstas?
              the pear-ACC the Kostas-NOM
          'Whose did you tell me that Kostas has eaten the pear?'

We conclude that clitic-doubled objects in clVO(S) constructions qualify as
derivational cascades. Therefore, they are predicted to exhibit, on the one
hand, similar prosodic behavior as preverbal clitic-doubled objects in OclV(S)
constructions, and, on the other hand, different prosodic properties from DP-
objects in VO(S) constructions.

8.3.2.2 *Prosodification*   In order to figure out the prosodic behavior of
DP-objects in the constructions under investigation, we designed eight declarative sentences of the clVO(S) order, differing in the size of the DP-object.
These sentences were compared with respect to their prosodic pattern to eight
declarative sentences of the VO(S) order. Five subjects, three female and two

male, ranging in age from 22–30 years old, participated in the experiment. All subjects were speakers of Standard Greek and unaware of the exact purposes of the experiment. They were given a total of sixteen randomized target sentences displaying mixed VOS and clVOS patterns interspersed with eight fillers. All twenty-four sentences were rendered with DP-subject focusing,[16] which was elicited with the help of questions, as indicated by the sample dialogues in (26)–(27). Prosodically light (L) and heavy (H) structures for Vs and Os were used, so that all possible combinations could be represented in the sentences, namely, LLX, HHX, LHX, HLX (where X stands for the focused subject). The subjects were told to read the sentences in conversational style without being given any specific instructions regarding the phrasing. Sentences were recorded on a Maranz PMD 660 digital recorder with an AKG C547 BL microphone and were analyzed using PRAAT (Boersma & Weenink 2006).

(26) pjí   (a) éfaɣan   / (b) to   éfaɣan   to axláði?
     who-NOM.PL eat-PAST.3PL/   it-ACC eat-PAST.3PL the pear-ACC
     'Who ate the pear?'

   a. LLX, VOS
      éfaɣan   do axláði   TA PEÐJÁ
      eat-PAST.3PL the pear-ACC the kid-NOM.PL
      'THE KIDS ate the pear.'

   b. LLX, clVOS
      to   éfaɣan   to   axláði   TA PEÐJÁ
      it-ACC eat-PAST.3PL the pear-ACC the kid-NOM.PL
      'As for the pear, THE KIDS ate it.'

(27) pjí   θa (a) simeostólizan /(b) to   simeostólizan
     who-NOM.PL FUT decorate-PAST.3PL /   it-ACC decorate-PAST.3PL
     to   próto   árma?
     the first-ACC vehicle-ACC
     'Who would have decorated the first vehicle with flags?'

   a. HHX, VOS
      θa simeostólizan   to próto   árma   TA
      FUT decorate-PAST.3PL the first-ACC vehicle-ACC the
      PEÐJÁ
      kid-NOM.PL
      'THE KIDS would have decorated with flags the first vehicle.'

---

[16] This way we dispense with the problem of postfocal de-accentuation, which disqualifies (cl)V-focusing as an informative case study.

  b. <u>HHX, clVOS</u>

      θa   to   simeostólizan   to   próto   árma
      FUT   it-ACC   decorate-PAST.3PL   the   first-ACC   vehicle-ACC
      TA   PEÐJÁ
      the   kid-NOM.PL
      'As for the first vehicle, THE KIDS would have decorated it with flags.'

The results of the experiment verify the hypothesis that postverbal clitic-doubled objects constitute prosodic islands in the sense that they never phrase together with the verb. More specifically, in VO(S) orders, the V and O are phrased together, [VO]φ, if both are light, but are grouped into separate p-phrases, [V]φ [O]φ, if both are heavy. Both p-phrasings are illustrated in (28a) and (28b), respectively. Particularly in the latter example, the HH constituents are organized into two equally balanced p-phrases, indicating that prosodic minimality considerations, such as binarity, are in control of their size.

(28)   *p-phrasings of VOS orders*

  a. <u>LLX, VOS</u>

      [éfaɣan   *do* axláði]φ   [TA PEÐJÁ]φ
      eat-PAST.3PL   the   pear-ACC   the kid-NOM.PL
      'THE KIDS ate the pear.'

  b. <u>HHX, VOS</u>

      [θa   simeostólizan]φ   [to   próto   árma]φ
      FUT   decorate-PAST.3PL   the   first-ACC   vehicle-ACC
      [TA PEÐJÁ]φ
      the   kid-NOM.PL
      'THE KIDS would have decorated the first vehicle with flags.'

Evidence for the proposed p-phrasings comes mainly from the application of sandhi rules, the prosodic templates of fill-words and partly from intonation. Starting from sandhi rules, nasal-stop assimilation applies between the verb *éfaɣan* and its complement *to axláði* in (28a), indicating that the two constituents are phrased together. The same rule is blocked in (28b), because both the heavy verb *θa simeostólizan* and its branching complement *to próto árma* independently comply to binarity and hence, form independent p-phrases. This sentence contrasts with (29) where nasal-stop assimilation applies because the prosodically light Vs and Os phrase together:

(29)   éspaɣa<u>n</u>   <u>ta</u> pjáta   I   NÍFES
      break-PAST.3PL   the   plate-ACC.PL   the   bride-NOM.PL
      [éspaɣan *da* pçáta]φ [I NÍFES]φ
      'THE BRIDES were breaking the plates.'

On the other hand, the examples in (30) clearly show that the postverbal clitic-doubled object in clVOS orders does not incorporate into the p-phrase of the clV, strikingly at the expense of binarity. Sandhi rules, such as nasal-stop assimilation, for instance, which otherwise would have applied, are blocked. Consequently, the p-phrasing is consistently [clV]ϕ [O]ϕ, for constructions with both light and heavy Vs and Os.

(30)   *p-phrasings of clVOS orders*

  a. <u>LLX, clVOS</u>
    [to éfaɣan]ϕ [to axláði]ϕ [TA PEðJÁ]ϕ
    it-ACC eat-PAST.3PL the pear-ACC the kid-NOM.PL
    'As for the pear, THE KIDS ate it.'

  b. <u>HHX, clVOS</u>
    [θa do simeostólizan]ϕ [to próto árma]ϕ
    FUT it-ACC decorate-PAST.3PL the first-ACC vehicle-ACC
    [TA PEðJÁ]ϕ
    the kid-NOM.PL
    'As for the first vehicle, THE KIDS would have decorated it with flags.'

The next piece of evidence comes from fill-words such as *ré, re sí, moré*, and parentheticals, e.g. *léj* '(s/he) says', *as púme* 'let's say', and so on, which in Greek are placed after the first p-phrase of the i-phrase: {[...]ϕ ___ [...]ϕ ...}i-phrase. The fill-words are inserted after the clV constituent, i.e. clV]ϕ ↓ [OS, suggesting that in clVO(S) orders the object does not belong to the initial p-phrase, as illustrated in (31a). Furthermore, they follow the VO constituent in VO(S) strings, i.e. VO]ϕ ↓ ..., provided that both the V and O are light. This is shown in (31b) where the V and the object, driven by the need to achieve binarity, combine into one p-phrase. (Cf. examples (31a′–b′) where the fillers occur after the heavy verb.)

(31)   *fill-words in VOS and clVOS orders*

  a. [to éfaɣan]ϕ *léj* [to axláði]ϕ [TA PEðJÁ]ϕ
    it-ACC eat-PAST.3PL say-3SG the pear-ACC the kid-NOM.PL
    'As for the pear, let's say, THE KIDS ate it.'

  a′. [to éxun simeostolísi]ϕ *léj* [to próto
    it-ACC have-3PL decorate   say-3SG the first-ACC
    árma]ϕ [TA PEðJÁ]ϕ
    vehicle-ACC the kid-NOM.PL
    'As for the first vehicle, let's say, THE KIDS have decorated it with flags.'

b. [éfaɣan   *do* axláði]$_\phi$ *léj*   [ta peðjá]$_\phi$
    eat-PAST.3PL the pear-ACC say-3SG the kid-NOM.PL
    'THE KIDS, let's say, ate the pear.'

b'. [éxun   simeostolísi]$_\phi$ *léj*   [to próto   árma]$_\phi$
    have-3PL decorate   say-3SG the first-ACC vehicle-ACC
    [ta peðjá]$_\phi$
    the kid-NOM.PL
    'THE KIDS, let's say, have decorated with flags the first vehicle.'

The evidence presented above establishes beyond doubt that the object is phrased differently in clVOS and VOS orders. More specifically, like their preverbal counterparts, postverbal clitic-doubled objects constitute prosodic islands in the form of independent p-phrases. The prosodic and syntactic islandhood of these elements is an immediate consequence of their status as derivational cascades, which are assembled in their own derivational workspace, and are independently spelled out and processed by PF.

Intonation offers promising insights into the issue of prosodic islandhood of clitic-doubled objects. Baltazani & Jun (1999) and Baltazani (2002) claim that initial as well as medial clitic-doubled objects display the exact same intonational pattern. We reached the same conclusion in a provisional study of the intonational phrasing of the preverbal and postverbal clitic-doubled objects (see Fig. 8.1 and Fig. 8.2).[17]

Figures 8.1 and 8.2 lead us to the following observations: First, both the preverbal and the postverbal clitic-doubled object form a p-phrase each with a L* pitch accent and a H-. Second, a phrase accent marks the right p-phrase boundary of the clV string, regardless of whether it precedes (Fig. 8.1) or follows (Fig. 8.2) the clitic-doubled object.[18] In VOS constructions, the H- marks the end point of the p-phrase that contains the VO string. Contrast Fig. 8.1 and Fig. 8.2 with Fig. 8.3. In short, the objects in clVOS and OclVS orders form independent p-phrases with a L* pitch accent and a H-, whereas the object in VOS orders phrases together with the verb. The end result once again points to the expected direction: Clitic-doubled objects are wrapped into their own phrase.

---

[17] We wish to thank Mary Baltazani for analyzing these sentences for us.

[18] This accent can either be H- or L-, depending on the speaker. In Greek, narrow focus such as o *kóstas* is signaled with a H*+L nuclear pitch accent followed by a L-L% (Arvaniti & Baltazani 2000).

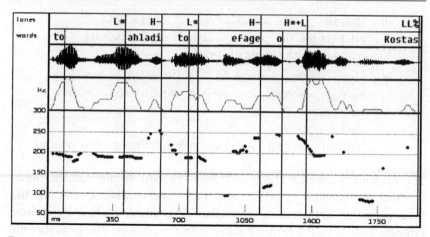

FIGURE 8.1 Intonational pattern of OclVS order with focus on S: to axláði to éfaɣe o KÓSTAS

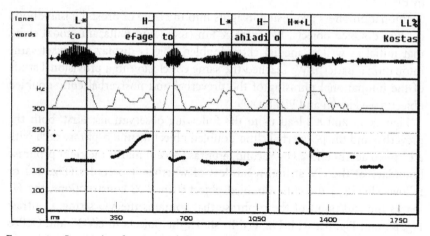

FIGURE 8.2 Intonational pattern of clVOS order with focus on S: to éfaɣe to axláði o KÓSTAS

8.3.3 *Syntactic Derivation and the Prosodification of Clitic-Doubled DP Objects*

So far we provided both syntactic and phonological evidence for the island-hood of clitic-doubled objects regardless of their position within the sentence. Syntactically, these elements are not arguments and this explains why they cannot be focused. Moreover, they constitute islands for extraction from

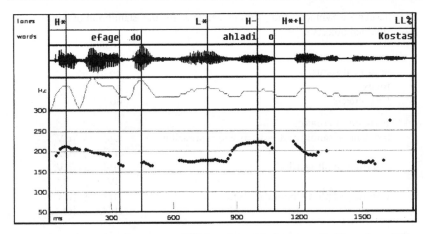

FIGURE 8.3 Intonational pattern of VOS order with focus on S: éfa*y*e do axláði o KÓSTAS

within, exhibiting CED effects. These syntactic properties suggest that clitic-doubled objects constitute independent derivational domains. This means that they are assembled at their own derivational workspace and merge with the rest of the structure by means of a discontinuous application of Merge. Following Uriagereka's analysis, such a merging takes place after an application of Spell-Out has driven their derivation to PF. Spell-Out destroys the internal structure of the clitic-doubled object and turns it into a derivational island. The PSC (2) then accounts for the syntactic islandhood of clitic-doubled objects: Spell-Out makes the material inside the clitic-doubled object inaccessible for further computation.

In addition, there is substantial phonological evidence from sandhi rules, fill-word templates, and intonation that clitic-doubled objects behave as phonological islands as well: They map onto a separate p-phrase, regardless of the phrasing of the rest of the derivation, and fail to prosodically incorporate with the rest of the structure, showing an otherwise unexplained resistance to the binary groupings triggered by the performance-based algorithm.

Table 8.1 summarizes the syntactic and prosodic evidence put forward so far in support of the matched syntactic and prosodic islandhood of clitic-doubled objects.

Putting these facts together, we conclude that there is an isomorphism between the syntactic and the phonological islandhood of clitic-doubled object which can be straightforwardly explained when we consider the derivational status of such elements. Being non-cyclic and independently spelled out, they become a derivational island for both the syntactic derivation

TABLE 8.1 Syntactic and prosodic evidence for the islandhood of clitic-doubled objects

SYNTACTIC EVIDENCE	
argument status	no
focus	no
CED effects	no
PROSODIC EVIDENCE	
blocking of sandhi and resistance to rephrasing	O]ϕ ↓ [clV...
	clV]ϕ ↓ [O...
insertion of fill-words	O]ϕ ↓ [clV...
	clV]ϕ ↓ [O...
insertion of phrase boundary tone	O]ϕ ↓ [clV...
	clV]ϕ ↓ [O...

and the prosodic structure. Thus, the prosodic behavior of clitic-doubled objects in Greek offers robust evidence for the representational effects of the derivation at the interfaces. The existence of such effects was originally suggested by Uriagereka (2002*a*: 10–12) and, in Section 8.2, it is stated in the form of GPSC (3) and its PF Corollary (4). Such a principle clearly predicts that a derivational island is an island for all components and it defines domains into which relevant operations are restricted to apply. To exemplify our proposal, we provide the derivation and the prosodification of the OclVS structure (32) in (33). The point of interest is the prosodic break between the clitic-doubled object and the clV constituent. All things being equal, the same analysis can be extended to clVOS orders.

(32)   to   axláði   to   éfaγe   o   kóstas
       the   pear-ACC   it-ACC   eat-PAST.3SG   the   Kostas-NOM
       'As for the pear, Kostas ate it.'

(33)   CU1: {to axláði} → Spell-Out1: [to axláði]ϕ
       CU2: {to éfaγe o kóstas} → Spell-Out2: [to éfaγe o kóstas]

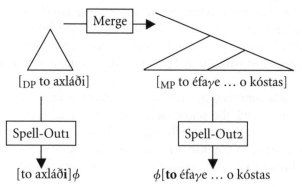

8.4 An Alternative Account to the P-Phrasing of Adjuncts: Truckenbrodt's "Dominance" Approach

Research on the area of the syntax-phonology interface and, especially on p-phrasing, has very little to state about the peculiarities characterizing the phrasing of non-cyclic elements such as adjuncts. Truckenbrodt (1995) builds up a proposal for the p-phrasing of adjuncts, based on Chomsky's (1986a, 1993) definition of dominance (34):

(34) *Dominance* (Chomsky 1986a: 7)
      A is dominated by B only if A is dominated by every segment of B.

Based on this definition, he assumes that adjuncts (a) are segments and (b) are not dominated by the category they adjoin to. This has two important consequences for the p-phrasing of adjuncts: First, because they are segments, they can p-phrase *together* with the host category and, second, because they are not dominated by the category they adjoin to, they can phrase *separately* from the host category. Let us exemplify this point with an abstract example.

Assume a language like Greek, where WRAP-XP is high ranked and, more specifically, outranks ALIGN-XP,R. According to Truckenbrodt's proposal the adjunct structure depicted in (35) results in two possible p-phrasings: (36a) and (36b). In (36a), the end-based mapping algorithm maps the higher XP onto a p-phrase, thus rendering the p-phrasing [α XP]ϕ. This is because WRAP-XP demands elements genuinely inside of an XP to be wrapped into a single p-phrase. In (36b), the same mapping algorithm maps α and the lower XP onto separate p-phrases, i.e. [α]ϕ [XP]ϕ, because α is not dominated by the category it adjoins to. That is to say, WRAP-XP does not care whether elements adjoined to XP and outside of the (lower) XP, in the relevant sense, are wrapped in with the material genuinely inside of XP.

(35) *p-phrasing of an adjunct*

```
              XP
           ╱      ╲
        α           XP
     to axláði    to éfaγe
```

(36) a. [$_{XP}$ α XP]
          [   ]ϕ

      b. [$_{XP}$ [α]   XP]
          [   ]ϕ [   ]ϕ

Since Wrap-XP cannot definitively decide on the two outputs, we conclude that in Greek Align-XP,R, which is ranked below Wrap-XP, decides in favor of the fine-grained p-phrasing in (36b). So far, Truckenbrodt's account derives the empirically attested pattern (36b), but faces a rather important empirical problem: It cannot preclude the inclusion of the adjunct into the p-phrase of the XP in Greek preverbal clitic-doubled objects. Recall that in Greek, prosodic binarity vigorously interacts with the syntax-phonology interface constraints, and dramatically affects the prosodification of the input string. In Section 8.3.1.2 (ii), we have shown that Bin^{min} crucially dominates Align-XP,R, thus predicting p-phrasing (36a) not only to occur, but to also be the preferred output in cases where α is subminimal, i.e. it consists of a single PrW. This expectation, however, is not borne out since, as shown above, initial clitic-doubled objects do not rephrase with the clV.

To account for that, a proponent of the domination account needs to invoke additional machinery, perhaps in the form of parochial alignment constraints (e.g. Align-Adjunct, L/R, ϕ, L/R) which would map elements of specific syntactic status, i.e. adjuncts, onto certain phonological units. Given that these constraints are high-ranking, they would guarantee that the relevant constituents will not rephrase with the remaining string. There is no doubt that employing such constraints in the analysis would have the desired effect of mapping adjuncts onto their own closed phonological units. However, an analysis along these lines offers no principled reason to explain why the forcefulness of these alignment constraints—expressed by means of high-ranking—is intimately related with the specific syntactic status of certain elements. On the other hand, our approach not only manages to predict the attested p-phrasing patterns and to exclude the non-attested ones, but also enjoys the merit that such an interface mapping is the result of the independently established principles and operations of the computational system itself, without having to resort to poorly motivated structure-specific mechanisms and constraints.

8.5 A Problematic Case: Greek Preverbal Subjects

It has been established that preverbal DP-subjects in Greek do not occupy an EPP Specifier position, but are rather adjoined either to the IP domain (MoodP) or to the CP domain (Philippaki-Warburton 1987, 1989; Alexiadou & Anagnostopoulou 1998; Spyropoulos 1999; Spyropoulos & Philippaki-Warburton 2002), and are coindexed with a *pro* in the relevant theta position. According to Uriagereka's (1999*b*) definition of derivational cascades as CUs, Greek preverbal DP-subjects in SVO constructions qualify as derivational cascades and are thus expected to be independently spelled out, exhibiting both syntactic and prosodic islandhood. However, this prediction is not borne out. First, preverbal DP-subjects in Greek are not islands, in that they allow for extraction from within (Spyropoulos 1999, 2003; Kotzoglou 2005):

(37) [pjanú   maθití]ᵢ   mu   ípes   [CP óti [DP-subj i
      who-GEN student-GEN me-GEN tell-PAST.2SG   that   the
      mitéra tᵢ]   paraponéθike   sto   ðiefθindí]]?
      mother-NOM complain-PAST.3SG to-the headmaster-ACC
      'The mother of which student did you tell me complained to the headmaster?'

Second, when preverbal DP-subjects are light, they comply to binarity:

(38) to fós   ðini   isxí   sti   mixaní
      the light-NOM give-3SG power-ACC to-the machine-ACC
      'The light gives power to the engine.'

   a. [to fós]φ [ðinØ isçí]φ [sti mixaní]φ   *end-based mapping*

   b. [to fóz ðini]φ [isçí sti mixaní]φ   *binarity-based mapping*

(39) o kóstas   mázeve   eljés   kalamón
      the Kostas-NOM harvest-PAST.3SG olive-ACC.PL Kalamata-GEN.PL
      'Kostas was harvesting Kalamata olives.'

   a. [o kóstas]φ [mázevØ eljés kalamón]φ   *end-based mapping*

   b. [o kóstaz mázeve]φ [eljés kalamón]φ   *binarity-based mapping*

The syntactic and prosodic non-islandhood of Greek preverbal subjects indicates that, although they constitute independent CUs, they do not behave as derivational cascades. This renders Uriagereka's (1999*b*) definition of derivational cascades in terms of CUs problematic. It also shows that Spell-Out need not be triggered by the requirements of PF linearization according to Kayne's (1994) Linear Correspondence Axiom, as originally suggested by Uriagereka (1999*b*).

8.6 Revising the Model

8.6.1 *The Derivational Status of Subjects*

A cross-linguistic examination of the syntactic islandhood of subjects underlines the significance of the problem at the theoretical level. In general, preverbal subjects constitute islands from extraction from within, an observation that has been stated as the *Subject Condition* (Chomsky 1973). Huang's

(1982) *Condition on Extraction Domains* unified the *Subject Condition* and the *Adjunct Condition*, and the Barriers framework (Chomsky 1986a) offered a unified analysis of the corresponding facts (namely, the non-availability for extraction from within subjects and adjuncts) as a combinatory result of the *Subjacency Condition* and the *Empty Category Principle*. Uriagereka's (1999b) Multiple Spell-Out system offers a minimalist account of CED as an effect of derivational islandhood: Subjects and adjuncts, being non-complements, are forced to be independently spelled out and thus no extraction is permitted from inside them (Nunes & Uriagereka 2000).[19]

However, a unified account of the Subject and the Adjunct Conditions seems to be unjustified, because, although extraction out of adjuncts is universally banned, there are languages that permit extraction out of (preverbal) subjects (e.g. Basque, Greek, Japanese, Russian, Turkish, Hungarian, Serbo-Croatian, Latin). Based on these observations, Stepanov (2001) suggested that the Subject and the Adjunct Conditions should be dissociated and that extraction out of subjects and adjuncts should be treated differently. More specifically, he suggested that adjuncts are islands by virtue of their being merged late in the derivation, following the well-known observation of Lebeaux (1988), whereas it is the derived position of subjects that makes them opaque to extraction. Stepanov follows Takahashi's (1994a) ideas on movement and argues that extraction out of subjects is blocked because of PF requirements on chain linearization, a minimalist variant of the *Freezing Principle* by Wexler & Culicover (1980). Based on Spyropoulos' (2003) observations that the minimalist variants of the Freezing Principle are too deep a cut—mainly because they incorrectly disallow a number of permissible extractions out of subjects, Kotzoglou (2005) proposes an interesting revision of the model. More specifically, he builds on the ideas on *Chain Reduction* requirements (Nunes 2004) and *Anti-Locality* (Grohmann 2003) in order to propose that the islandhood of the subject is regulated by the number of copies of the moving element surviving in a phase. Putting aside the technical details, these proposals share the intuition that subjects do not constitute derivational islands in the sense of Uriagereka (1999b). Their islandhood is regulated instead by independent principles of the computational system and crucially not because these elements are spelled out independently from the main derivation. Thus, subjects, unlike adjuncts, seem to belong to the main clausal skeleton, i.e. the main derivational workspace of the clause.

---

[19] See also Johnson (2003).

8.6.2 *The Revised Proposal and the Status of Spell-Out*

On the basis of the Greek case study of clitic-doubled objects and preverbal subjects, we are now in the position to revise our proposal. We maintain that the effects of the *Generalized Principle of Strict Cyclicity* refer to derivational cascades. However, derivational cascades are now defined as the chunks that are assembled and processed in their own derivational workspace, and are spelled out and processed by the interfaces independently from the main derivation. In short, derivational cascades are only these chunks that exhibit rigid and universal syntactic islandhood and loose connectivity with the main derivation.

According to the revision proposed here, adjunct modifiers qualify as derivational cascades because (a) they exhibit rigid and universal islandhood and (b) they have been independently argued to be loosely connected with the main derivation (Lebeaux 1988; Pietroski & Uriagereka 2002). Subsequently, they are also expected to exhibit prosodic islandhood in terms of forming their own p-phrase and resisting rephrasing.[20] Subjects, on the other hand, belong to the main clausal skeleton, as indicated by the fact that their islandhood is neither rigid nor universal. This is further reinforced by the observation that subjects rarely show prosodic islandhood even in languages that respect the *Subject Condition*. For instance, in Italian and European Portuguese preverbal subjects constitute syntactic islands (extraction out of them is not banned) but not prosodic, in the sense that they either phrased with other elements of the clause (European Portuguese; Elordieta *et al.* 2003) or are subject to rephrasing (Italian; Nespor & Vogel 1986; Ghini 1993).

Let us now return to Greek and the distinction between preverbal subjects and clitic-doubled objects. The problem arises since the widely accepted analysis of preverbal subjects considers them as left-dislocated elements doubled by a null subject element in the main derivation. Such an analysis implies that there is a structural similarity between preverbal subjects and clitic-doubled objects (compare the relevant structures in Sections 8.3.1.1, 8.3.2.1, and 8.5). Nevertheless, clitic-doubled objects do not allow extraction from within and resist prosodic rephrasing; preverbal subjects, on the other hand, allow for extraction from within and are able to rephrase. Consequently, their difference as far as the syntactic and the prosodic islandhood calls for an explanation.

Although we are still in search of a more conclusive answer to this issue, we have sufficient evidence to contemplate a hypothesis that preverbal subjects are a part of the clausal skeleton, whereas clitic-doubled objects are not. The latter elements constitute a kind of a peripheral modifier similar in status with

---

[20] For a preliminary study which verifies this prediction in Greek see Féry & Skopeteas (in progress).

overt arguments in polysynthetic languages (Baker 1996; see the discussion in Spyropoulos 1999, 2001). There are good reasons to believe that these elements have a different derivational status: First, clitic-doubled objects can never appear in an argument position (see the discussion in Sections 8.3.1.1 and 8.3.2.1 and the references cited therein), whereas subjects can do so in VS(O) constructions (see Philippaki-Warburton 1989; Alexiadou & Anagnostopoulou 1998; Alexiadou 1999, among others). Second, preverbal subjects can be focused (41a); clitic-doubled objects can never be focused (40).

(40) *clitic-doubled objects*

    a. *to   éfaγe   [TO AXLÁÐI]$_{FOC}$ o   kóstas
        it-ACC eat-PAST.3SG the pear-ACC   the Kostas-NOM
        'It is the pear that Kostas ate it.'

    b. *[TO AXLÁÐI]$_{FOC}$ to   éfaγe   o   kóstas
        the pear-ACC it-ACC eat-PAST.3SG the Kostas-NOM
        'It is the pear that Kostas ate it.'

(41) *preverbal subjects*

    a. [O KÓSTAS]$_{FOC}$ éfaγe   to axláði
        the Kostas-NOM eat-PAST.3SG the pear-ACC

    b. éfaγe   [O KÓSTAS]$_{FOC}$ to axláði
        eat-PAST.3SG the Kostas-NOM the pear-ACC

    c. éfaγe   to axláði   [O KÓSTAS]$_{FOC}$
        eat-PAST.3SG the pear-ACC the Kostas-NOM
        'KOSTAS ate the pear.'

We may, therefore, speculate that preverbal subjects retain some of their argument properties, something that has already been suggested by Horrocks (1994). Furthermore, it is sensible to also assume that this is closely related to the nature of the doubling element as well as the satisfaction of visibility conditions (see Spyropoulos 1999, 2001). In the case of preverbal subjects, the doubling element is considered to be either a *pro* or the agreement morpheme itself. In the case of clitic-doubled object, it is an overt clitic pronoun. This overt clitic may be considered to be able to fully satisfy the relevant argument requirements, whereas the null-subject elements can do it only partially, permitting the overt subject to share with it the argument role. We leave the issue of formal expression of these intuitions and speculations open to further research.

We believe that this distinction has serious repercussions for the status of Spell-Out. We mentioned in Section 8.2 that Spell-Out is an operation that ships certain parts of derivation to the interfaces and hence destroys their internal structure so that they are no longer accessible to computation. There are two ways to implement the derivational effects of Spell-Out. Uriagereka (1999b) draws a distinction between *radical* and *conservative* Spell-Out. Radical Spell-Out not only destroys the internal structure of the derivational chunk, but it also wipes it out so that it behaves as a single element for the purposes of the rest of the derivation. Conservative Spell-Out, on the other hand, destroys the internal structure of the derivational chunk, but preserves its items linearized as a list. We claim that this distinction is crucial and is intimately related to GPSC. Radical Spell-Out incorporates the GPSG and defines derivational cascades, whereas conservative Spell-Out only defines the syntactic cycles that can take place within the limits of a derivational cascade. This means that radical Spell-Out not only ships parts of derivation to the interfaces, but also forces the interfaces to exhaustively process them. In contrast, conservative Spell-Out ships strings away from the derivation, but does not force the interface to exhaustively process them at once.

We take this idea one step further and propose the following. Radical and conservative Spell-Out are cover labels for the interface procedures that are associated with Spell-Out, which is viewed as an operation that merely ships material away from the syntactic derivation and destroys its internal structure. PF immediately processes this material by linearizing it and assigning to it higher order prosodic structure, i.e. p-phrasing.[21] This kind of processing constructs only a partial phonological representation and defines conservative Spell-Out. P-phrasing and sentential stress are finalized at root Spell-Out, i.e. after the whole derivation is completed (see also Kratzer & Selkirk 2007), when core PF constraints (e.g. binarity and heaviness constraints) can take effect. This final PF processing defines radical Spell-Out.

Putting together the elements of our proposal, we claim that the derivation of a sentence proceeds in a cyclic fashion following a clausal skeleton which includes the predicate, its arguments, and all the relevant functional categories. This constitutes the main derivational workspace. Since derivation is a strictly cyclic procedure, Spell-Out may apply inside this main derivational cascade, defining cycles in the form of either Chomsky's phases or Uriagereka's specifiers. Crucially, such a conservative Spell-Out permits the spelled-out strings to communicate at the interfaces, because they have not been erased and their elements survive at the interface together with the elements of other spelled-out chunks that belong in the same derivational workspace. That is, as far as the syntax-phonology interface is concerned, such strings are still

---

[21] See *n.* 4.

visible and open to the restructuring mechanisms that take place at PF in order to ameliorate their prosodic make-up. In parallel to the main derivation, adjunct modifiers may also be formed at their own derivational workspace. These elements constitute independent derivational cascades and, upon their completion, they are radically spelled out, so that, when they join the main derivation, they have already been processed at the interfaces and wiped out. No communication across their boundaries is possible any more, since these cascades are completely opaque and their elements totally invisible. It is the opaqueness of these cascades that derives the effects of GPSC.

The behavior of Greek clitic-doubled objects as opposed to that of preverbal subjects offers ample support to the proposed architecture. With the clitic undertaking the argument function, clitic-doubled objects are peripheral elements and constitute derivational cascades. They are thus radically spelled out before they join the main derivation and their rigid syntactic and prosodic islandhood derives from their derivational status. Preverbal subjects, on the other hand, belong to the main derivation.[22] They are thus subject to the syntactic cycles defined by the application of the conservative Spell-Out. Their syntactic islandhood is regulated by the principles of the computational system, which in this case permit the extraction from within. Their prosodification is subject to the independently justified principles and algorithms of the mapping procedure of the syntax-phonology interface, which correctly derive the attested patterns.

8.7 Conclusion

This contribution explores the empirical scope of the MSOH with particular emphasis on the syntax-phonology interface. More specifically, we have shown that the interface is sensitive to differences in the processing of syntactic material, in that it reflects—via p-phrasing—the derivational status of cascades. Empirical justification for the assumption that the derivational dynamics of MSO has a representational effect at the syntax-phonology interface was provided from Greek clitic-doubled objects in both clVO(S) and OclV(S) strings. Such elements constitute derivational cascades that are independently processed by the PF. Future research should reveal the limits of this isomorphism, if any. In other words, it should explore whether more instances of

---

[22] In more recent work (Spyropoulos & Revithiadou 2007), we capitalize on the syntactic and prosodic non-islandhood of preverbal Greek subjects and propose that these elements are not left-dislocated, as it is usually assumed, but rather they occupy an EPP Spec. Thus, being EPP elements, preverbal subjects belong to the main clausal derivation and their non-islandhood derives from their derivational status.

prosodic islandhood (expressed as avoidance of prosodic restructuring or failure to satisfy prosodic binarity restrictions, and so on) coincide with syntactic cascades that are independently spelled out, and vice versa.

Our research also centered on what exactly qualifies as a derivational cascade. For this reason, we discussed the syntactic and prosodic non-islandhood of preverbal DP-subjects in Greek. We have argued that, at first sight, the observed type of isomorphism creates problems for the standard MSO model and calls for its refinement. We provided sufficient argumentation that the Greek case study offers the required empirical verification for the distinction between two different implementations of Spell-Out, which has already been technically drawn in Uriagereka (1999b). To be precise, we argued that, unlike clitic-doubled objects which are adjuncts that are separately assembled and fed to the interfaces, Greek subjects exhibit enough argument properties to be kept within the derivational workspace of the clausal skeleton. This entails that they are still visible to other elements of the same derivational workspace and hence susceptible to the laws of prosodic restructuring. Technically, this implies a split in the implementation of Spell-Out between a radical and a conservative type, exactly as theoretically suggested by Uriagereka (1999b). The extension proposed here is that only the latter incorporates the GPSC and has consequences for the interface. To conclude, the revised version of MSOH advanced here makes specific predictions for the syntax-phonology interface since prosodic islandhood should always match rigid and universal syntactic islandhood that results from radical Spell-Out.

Future research should be directed to further exploring the type of syntactic dependencies established between certain elements and the main derivational cycle.

9

Spelling Out Prosodic Domains: A Multiple Spell-Out Account*

YOSUKE SATO

9.1 Introduction

This chapter proposes a general syntax-prosody mapping hypothesis couched within the recent derivational model of syntactic computation known as the Multiple Spell-Out Hypothesis, or MSO (Uriagereka 1999*b* and Chomsky 2000, 2001, 2004*a*, 2008; see also Epstein *et al.* 1998). This hypothesis, which uniquely maps mid-derivational complex objects in syntax to prosodic domains at the PF component, correctly demarcates a set of structural domains within which a variety of prosodic alternations across languages are found and possible. Specifically, the proposed syntax-prosody hypothesis, couched within Uriagereka's version of the MSO model, makes correct predictions about possible domains within which Taiwanese tone sandhi, French liaison, Gilyak lenition, and Kinyambo high tone deletion are found. However, a certain pattern of soft consonant mutation across CP vs TP boundaries in Welsh poses an apparent problem to the proposed analysis because Uriagereka's system would not be able to draw a distinction pertinent to the Spell-Out operation between these two categorial nodes. I argue that this problem receives a straightforward explanation once the proposed hypothesis is expanded to incorporate another version of the MSO model known as Phase Theory (Chomsky 2000 *et seq.*), in particular the notion of CP phase.

* I am very grateful to the following people as well as anonymous reviewers for critical comments and valuable discussion on earlier versions of this contribution: David Adger, Andrew Carnie, Noam Chomsky, Kleanthes Grohmann, Heidi Harley, Scott Jackson, Yoshiaki Kaneko, Simin Karimi, Richard Kayne, Howard Lasnik, Dave Medeiros, Masaru Nakamura, Masayuki Oishi, Takashi Toyoshima, and Juan Uriagereka. I also thank Charles Lin and Shaio-hui Chan for the Taiwanese data, as well as Sumayya Racy and her native consultants for the French data. This work was supported by the Fulbright Fellowship. None of those people is responsible for any remaining errors in this chapter, which are entirely my own.

I also argue for the necessity of incorporating the notion of *v*P phase into the proposed analysis based on the interaction of *wh*-traces with consonant mutation in Welsh and the lack of consonant mutation across *v*P boundaries in Irish. These results suggest that a derivational system of syntax that combines Uriagereka's and Chomsky's dynamic models would be needed to ensure proper access to phonology from syntax and vice versa.

This chapter is organized as follows. In Section 9.2, I outline the MSO model proposed by Uriagereka (1999*b*). In Section 9.3, I propose a general syntax-prosody mapping hypothesis within the model which maps a spelled-out domain to a prosodic domain. This hypothesis yields three universal predictions concerning the domains in which phonological alternations are possible. I show that these predictions are indeed borne out by a wide range of phonological alternations across languages such as tone sandhi in Taiwanese, liaison in French, lenition in Gilyak, and high tone deletion in Kinyambo. In Section 9.4, I turn to soft consonant mutation in Welsh and point out that the present analysis couched within Uriagereka's MSO system cannot derive the TP/CP difference with respect to mutation in this language. I claim that this difference naturally falls out once Chomsky's (2000 *et seq.*) notion of CP phase is incorporated into the mapping hypothesis. I also show that a certain interaction of *wh*-traces with consonant mutation in Welsh as well as the absence of the mutation across *v*P boundaries in Irish can be construed as supporting the existence of *v*P phase if the present analysis is correct.

9.2 Uriagereka's (1999*b*) Multiple Spell-Out Model

Uriagereka's (1999*b*) MSO model originates from the minimalist desire to keep the so-called "Base Step" and dispense with the "Induction Step" of the Linear Correspondence Axiom proposed by Kayne (1994), as defined in (1a) and (1b), respectively.

(1) *Linear Correspondence Axiom* (Uriagereka 1999*b*: 252)

    a. Base Step: If α asymmetrically c-commands β, α precedes β.

    b. Induction Step: If γ precedes β and γ dominates α, α precedes β.

This theoretical stance leads to the claim that the linearization procedure as in (1a) can function only with uniformly right-branching structures in syntactic derivation. In other words, the procedure will not suffice when two internally complex, left-branching structures are merged. Consider a hypothetical configuration in (2).

(2) *Complex Specifiers and Adjuncts*

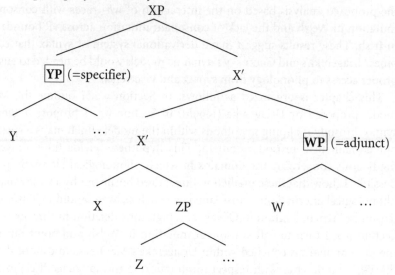

In this configuration, the head X merges with the uniformly right-branching structure ZP to form a larger syntactic object X′ (or XP in the Bare Phrase Structure Theory of Chomsky 1995). The Base Step in (1a) suffices to determine that the terminal X precedes the terminal Z (and those contained within its sister). A problem arises when the X′ merges with another internally complex, left-branching phrase such as WP and YP in (2). The Base Step in (1a) will not suffice to determine linear ordering of the terminals within the lower X′ (i.e. X, Z, and those contained within ...) relative to those contained within WP (i.e. W and those contained within ...) because there is no asymmetrical c-command relation between the terminals contained within the two phrases. The same problem arises when the higher X′ merges with another left-branching phrase YP.

To avoid this conceptual problem, Uriagereka proposes that at the point when two internally complex, left-branching structures are merged, syntactic derivation spells out one of the complex structures to the PF component. After this Spell-Out, the complex object reenters the derivation as a kind of "frozen giant lexical compound" whose phrase structure status is as simplex as words like *book, chair,* and *desk*. In other words, all specifiers and adjunct phrases must be spelled out early in this derivational system for the purposes of linearization if they contain left-branching structures. Let us illustrate this system with the configuration in (2). Before WP or YP merges with the rest of the tree, it undergoes early Spell-Out and gets flattened into an ordered sequence of strings in accordance with the Base Step in (1a). After the relative ordering between the terminals within WP and YP is fixed, the two structures are reintroduced into the syntactic derivation as a simplex numeration item so that the Base Step can determine the relative order of this word with respect to the terminal elements contained within the other complex phrase. See also Johnson (2003, 2004), who proposes a related version of Uriagereka's idea that adjuncts and specifiers, both analyzed as adjoined elements, undergo early Spell-Out for the PF component and get renumerated into the syntactic derivation as a derived numeration item.

This MSO model straightforwardly derives left-branch conditions such as the Condition on Extraction Domains (Huang 1982), as illustrated in (3a–b).

(3) *Condition on Extraction Domains*

   a. *Which book did [$_{DP}$ a critic of t] meet you at the conference?

   b. *Which book did you go to class [$_{PP}$ before she read t]?

The DP in (3a) and the PP in (3b) correspond to YP and WP in the configuration in (2), respectively. Since the DP and PP here are left-branching specifier and adjunct phrases respectively, they undergo early Spell-Out to the PF component and reenter the syntactic derivation as a frozen renumerated item. Accordingly, extraction out of this frozen item into another derivational cascade becomes impossible in the same way that k cannot be extracted out of the word *book*.[1]

It is to be noted at this point that in Uriagereka's MSO model, the status of a syntactic object as specifier or adjunct does not entail that it is subject to early Spell-Out. Given the natural minimalist assumption that Spell-Out is a costly, last-resort operation, as are other computational steps, that only applies to an

---

[1] Richard Kayne (p.c.) points out the qualitative difference in unacceptability between subject island cases as in (3a) and adjunct island cases as in (3b), stating that the former is felt to be ten times as bad as the latter. Uriagereka's MSO model, which derives subject and adjunct islands in exactly the same way as a consequence of early Spell-Out, has little to say in accounting for this qualitative difference. One view suggested by this qualitative difference would be that attempts to unify the subject and adjunct conditions are empirically incorrect. This view is not necessarily correct. One could argue that subject extraction involves movement from a separate cascade while adjunct extraction involves this kind of movement plus late/postcyclic Merge in the sense of Lebeaux 1988. This additional operation would incur a more severe violation in the computational component. I thank Heidi Harley (p.c.) for suggesting the line of argument made here.

Another potential problem with Uriagereka's (1999*b*) model comes from the observation that extraction from within an adjunct is universally ill-formed whereas languages like Japanese allow extraction from within a subject. Recent work as in Stepanov (2001), for example, claims that the subject and adjunct conditions should be dissociated, suggesting that adjuncts form closed domains due to their late/postcyclic Merge while subjects become opaque for extraction due to their derived position as proposed in the Freezing Principle of Wexler & Culicover (1980). Strictly speaking, however, in Uriagereka's model, subject extraction could be only apparent in that it does not involve movement like adjunct extraction. For example, it could be created by a bound null pronoun that fills the subject position in languages like Japanese which allow this option. If so, the difference in acceptability between subject and adjunct extraction in languages like Japanese might be attributable to some other independent factors.

otherwise non-linearizable syntactic object (Uriagereka 1999*b*: 256), a simplex specifier or adjunct *cannot* be spelled out to the PF component. To illustrate, consider a hypothetical configuration in (4).

(4)   *Simplex Specifiers and Adjuncts*

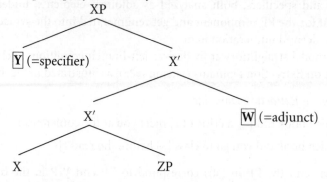

In this configuration, the specifier Y and the adjunct W, each being a terminal node, need not, hence cannot be spelled out due to the Last Resort nature of the operation Spell-Out because both Y and W can enter into an asymmetric c-command relation with the rest of the configuration for the purposes of the linearization based on the Base Step in (1a) without being spelled out. This "loophole" correctly derives the fact that a simplex subject or adjunct itself can be a target of extraction as in (5a,b), in contrast to (3a,b).[2]

(5)   *Simplex Subjects and Adjuncts*

   a.   Who do you think [DP *t*] loves Tom?

   b.   How do you think Mary solved this math problem [Adv *t*]?

The movement of the subject *who* and the adjunct *how* is licit in these examples because their simplex composition prohibits them from undergoing early Spell-Out, thereby keeping them in the syntactic derivation so that the required movement operations can ensue.

To summarize, Uriagereka's (1999*b*) MSO model assumes that all left-branching structures, including specifiers and adjuncts, must undergo early Spell-Out to the PF component for the purposes of linearization. This model correctly derives several well-known constraints on movement as in Huang's (1982) Condition on Extraction Domains as an automatic consequence of its derivational system. I have also noted that a simplex specifier and adjunct structure is immune from early Spell-Out due to the Last Resort nature of the Spell-Out operation.

---

[2] The same point applies to cases where complex subjects and adjuncts are extracted wholes as in *which man that Bill likes left Tucson yesterday*? *Wh*-movement is licit in this example under Uriagereka's system since it does not involve extraction *out of* a subject position.

9.3 The Syntax-Prosody Mapping Hypothesis

The central idea pursued in this chapter is that dynamically split derivational models of syntax as in Uriagereka's (1999*b*) MSO model should have well-defined repercussions in constraining possible domains of phonological rule application under a certain conception of the minimalist design of language. Given the Strong Minimalist Thesis (Chomsky 2000 *et seq.*) that language is an optimal solution to interface conditions, it is natural to expect that independent mid-derivational syntactic objects defined in a derivational model of syntactic computation should correspond to separate derivational cascades that reach the PF component independently. Under this view, the maximally general hypothesis about the interface of syntax with the PF component will take the following form.

(6) *The Syntax-Prosody Mapping Hypothesis*
     The spelled-out domains are mapped to prosodic domains at PF.

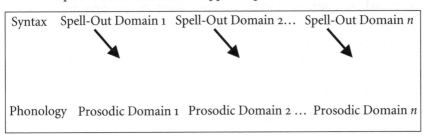

This hypothesis states that a spelled-out domain in syntax corresponds to a prosodic domain at PF within which phonological alternations are possible in natural languages. Suppose that a phonological alternation exists between two elements, trigger and target, in a language. The proposed hypothesis predicts that this alternation should be found between the two elements only if they are within the same prosodic domain; in other words, this alternation cannot happen across two different prosodic domains. This is illustrated in (7a,b).

(7) *Possible Domains for Phonological Alternations*

  a.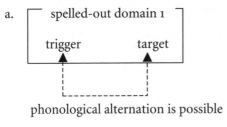

      phonological alternation is possible

b.

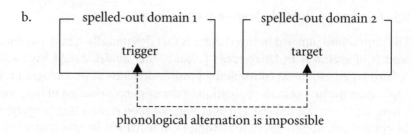

phonological alternation is impossible

In (7a), the target of a phonological alternation is contained within the same spelled-out domain as the trigger of the alternation; hence the alternation should be possible between the trigger and the target. By contrast, the same alternation should not be able to apply between the two elements in (7b) because they are contained within two different spelled-out domains.[3]

Consider now what predictions Uriagereka's MSO model makes regarding possible prosodic domains in human language. Recall that all and only left-branching syntactic objects, including complex specifiers and adjuncts, undergo early Spell-Out. This means that the two mid-derivational objects are mapped to prosodic domains at PF in accordance with the mapping hypothesis in (6). Thus, we have three universal predictions in (8a–c).

(8) *Predictions of the Mapping Hypothesis under Uriagereka's MSO Model*

    a. A head and its complement form a single prosodic domain.

    b. A left-branching specifier/adjunct structure forms an independent prosodic domain from the head and complement to which it is adjoined.

    c. A simplex specifier/adjunct structure is included in the same prosodic domain as the head and complement to which it is adjoined.

---

[3] This hypothesis is proposed in Sato (2006*a*, 2006*b*). There it is argued that it provides a unified account of nuclear sentence stress placement both within English and across languages as well as the core properties of English contraction (*wanna*-contraction, auxiliary contraction, and pronominal cliticization). Other researches have independently come to similar conclusions, applied to different data. Kahnemuyipour (2004) provides a derivational account of nuclear stress rules within the Phase Theory of Chomsky (2000, 2001, 2004*a*, 2008). See also Arregi (2002, 2003) for a related derivational account of nuclear sentence stress. Dobashi (2003) proposes a similar hypothesis for phonological phrasing within the Phase Theory. Uriagereka (1999*b*: 262–5) himself points out that the interface hypothesis of this sort receives empirical support from focus spreading, pauses/parenthetical expressions, phonological association of certain function items to the lexical heads, and the cliticization of determiners to their preceding heads in Galician. Johnson (2002, 2004) develops a similar idea from focus spreading within a Multiple Spell-Out model similar to the one pursued in Uriagereka (1999*b*).

In the following section, I demonstrate that these three predictions are borne out by a wide variety of facts concerning tone sandhi in Taiwanese, liaison in French, lenition in Gilyak, and high tone deletion in Kinyambo.

9.4 Tone Sandhi, Liaison, Lenition, and High Tone Deletion

In this section, I demonstrate that the three predictions made above in (8a-c) are indeed borne out by facts concerning tone sandhi in Taiwanese, liaison in French, lenition in Gilyak and high tone deletion in Kinyambo.

9.4.1 *Tone Sandhi in Taiwanese*[4]

Tone sandhi refers to the phonological alternation in which the citation tone of a syllable changes into some other tone when followed by another syllable with a different lexically listed tone. This alternation can be formulated in a rule-based format as in (9) (Chen 1987: 113).

(9)   *Tone Sandhi Rule*
       $T \rightarrow T' /\_\_$ within a tone group
          Key: T = base tone, T' = sandhi tone

Tone sandhi in Taiwanese is governed by the set of fully productive rules shown in (10) (Simpson & Wu, 2002: 72).

(10)   *Tone Sandhi Change in Taiwanese*[5]
       (tone... changes to tone...)
       $1 \rightarrow 7$
       $2 \rightarrow 1$
       $3 \rightarrow 2$
       $4 \rightarrow 8$ when the syllable ends in p/t/k;
          $\rightarrow 2$ when the syllable ends in a glottal stop
       $5 \rightarrow 7$ (southern Taiwan)
              3 (northern Taiwan)
       $6 \rightarrow 1$
       $7 \rightarrow 3$
       $8 \rightarrow 4$ when the syllable ends in p/t/k;
          $\rightarrow 3$ when the syllable ends in a glottal stop

---

[4] This section owes a great deal to the pioneering work by Simpson & Wu (2002) and Wu (2004) on Taiwanese tone sandhi. All the data in this section are from these works unless otherwise noted.

[5] Wu (2004: 84) characterizes the eight tones in the following way: the 1st: high-level 3–5, the 2nd: high-falling 5–1, the 3rd: low-falling, the 4th: low-entering tone (a syllable with a final stop), the 5th: contour-tone 2–4, the 6th: high-falling 5–1, the 7th: mid-level 3–3, the 8th: high-entering. Tones 2 and 6 are phonologically identical.

For example, the contrast between (11a) and (11b) shows that a syllable with tone 3 changes into the one with tone 2 when it is followed by any syllable with some lexical tone, not just by the neutral tone.

(11) *Examples of Tone Sandhi in Taiwanese*

    a. **khi3** pak8kiang1 → **khi2** pak8kiang1   (Tone sandhi)
        go Beijing   go Beijing
        'go to Beijing'

    b. **zau2** a-NT → **zau2** a-NT   (No tone sandhi)
        run already   run already
        'already run'   (Simpson & Wu, 2002: 72)

The observation made by Simpson & Wu (also Wu 2004) that is crucial to the present chapter is that there are three syntactically definable domains in which tonal change is found and possible. First, the head-complement configuration licenses tone sandhi, as shown in (12a–b).[6]

(12) *Head-Complement Configuration*
    a. V-NP$_{object}$ b. P-NP
        be• [lng•pun• chhe•]   **tui•** [goan• lau•pe•]
        buy two-CL   book   to my   father
        'buy two books'   'to my father'
                                 (Simpson & Wu 2002: 73)

Second, tone sandhi does not occur between a head and its internally complex specifier, as shown in (13). In this example, the final syllable of the word *goan•lau•pe* 'my father' does not undergo tone sandhi when followed by the verb *u•* 'have'. In the same way, tone sandhi is not possible between a head and its internally complex adjunct, as shown in (14); the last word *khi* 'go' does not change its tone despite its being followed by *A•hui* 'A-hui', a word with non-neutral tone.

(13) *Head-Specifier Configuration*

    [$_{DP}$ goan• lau•pe] u• lng• chhing• kho•
       my   father have two thousand dollar
    'My father has two thousand dollars.'   (Charles Lin, p.c.)

(14) *Head-Adjunct Configuration*

    [$_{CP}$ na•si A•sin m• khi], A•hui ma• be• khi.
       if   Asin NEG go   A-hui also NEG go
    'If Asin is not going, Ahui will not go.'   (Simpson & Wu 2002: 74)

---

[6] From now on, I use the symbol • to indicate the occurrence of tone sandhi. A syllable followed by this dot undergoes tone sandhi.

Finally, when a specifier or adjunct element is a simplex, non-branching lexical item, we have tone sandhi between the element and its following head. This is shown in (15)–(16).

(15)   *Simplex Specifier (Subject Pronouns)*

   Wa•/Li•/Yi•/Wun•/Lin•/Yin•   jim• ji-jia• kao.
   I/You (sg)/He (She)/We/You (pl)/They kiss this-CL dog
   'I/You (sg)/He (She)/We/You (pl)/They kiss this dog.'
                                                (Shiao-hui Chan, p.c.)

(16)   *Simplex Adjunct (Adverbs)*[7]

   Wa•-e pe•bu za• kun.
   I-GEN parent early sleep
   'My parents sleep early.'   (Shiao-hui Chan, p.c.)

In these examples, the subject pronoun and manner adverb undergo tone sandhi when followed by a word with non-neutral tone even though they occupy specifier and adjunct positions.

Importantly, the three structural configurations noted above exactly correspond to the spelled-out domains under Uriagereka's (1999*b*) MSO model. The head-complement configuration licenses tone sandhi between a head and its complement because they are contained within the same spelled-out domain. A tone sandhi cannot occur between a head and its internally complex specifier or adjunct element because the two objects are contained within two different spelled-out domains. The fact that a specifier and adjunct *can* undergo tone sandhi with its following head only when they are simplex also naturally falls out; as we have seen in Section 9.3, the Last-Resort nature of Spell-Out as a computational process prevents them from undergoing Spell-Out. As a result, they are contained within the same spelled-out domain as the head. In this way, the three predictions of the hypothesis in (6) are fully borne out by facts concerning Taiwanese tone sandhi.

9.4.2 *Liaison in French*

French liaison is another sandhi phenomenon in which a normally silent consonant is pronounced before a vowel-initial element in certain structurally definable configurations. For example, the normally silent consonant /z/ of the first word *des* 'some' is pronounced when it is immediately followed by

---

   [7] I assume that *za* 'early' is attached to the VP. This is an assumption that needs further empirical investigation. However, since the adverb is a simplex word, the claim still holds that the simplex composition has a derivational role to play in calculation of tone sandhi at the PF component. Thanks to an anonymous reviewer for this question.

the vowel-initial word *ennuis* 'troubles.' This liaison does not occur when the same word is followed by the consonant-initial word *problèmes* 'problems.'[8]

(17)   *French Liaison*

    a.   des ∩ ennuis '(some) troubles'

    b.   des/problèmes '(some) problems'

French liaison can be stated in a rule-based format as in (18).

(18)   *French Liaison*

$$[-\text{sonorant}] \rightarrow \emptyset / \_\_\_ \# \left\{ \begin{array}{c} [+\text{consonant}] \\ \# \end{array} \right\}$$

                                                                                     (Selkirk 1974: 579)

This is a rule of final obstruent deletion. This rule states that a consonant is deleted before the sequence of ## (two word boundaries) or of # followed by a consonant-initial word. To illustrate, consider the following examples.

(19)   a.   des ∩ ennuis   '(some) troubles'

        b.   dans ∩ une sale   'in a room'

        c.   Paul nous ∩ appelle.   'Paul is calling us.'

        d.   Les garcons/enragent.   'The boys are getting mad.'

        e.   Les immigrés/envoyaient/des lettres/à leurs familles.

           'The immigrants were sending letters to their families.'

                                                             (Selkirk 1974: 580)

In the examples in (19a-c), liaison is found between a deter-miner/preposition/clitic pronoun and a major category item. The rule maintains the final consonant because liaison in each example is found before a single word boundary as in *des # ennuis, dans # une # salle,* and *nous # appelle* according to the conventions outlined in Chomsky & Halle (1968). In the examples in (19d,e), on the other hand, there is no liaison between the subject DP and the verb or between the verb and the first object DP or between the first DP object and the second PP object. The rule in (18) deletes the final consonant in these examples even if it precedes a vowel at the beginning of the following word because in each example the final word of the left-hand category is separated from the first word of the right-hand one by a sequence of double word boundaries as in *## Les # garcons ## enragent ##* and *## Les # immigrés ## envoyaient ## des # lettres ## à # leurs # familles ##* according to Chomsky and Halle's formalism. For the same reason, the rule

---

[8] The symbol ∩ indicates that a consonant followed by that symbol has undergone liaison while the slash / indicates that a consonant followed by that symbol has not undergone this alternation.

in (18) also accommodates the fact that sentence-final consonants are never pronounced in any of the above examples because of the existence of double word boundaries, as in *## Les # garcons ## enragent ##* for (19d). Selkirk (1972, 1974) proposes the following generalization on this sandhi phenomenon.

(20) *Selkirk's Generalization*
       A liaison context exists between an inflected X and its complement, both dominated by X'.   (Selkirk 1974: 581)

This generalization states that the target word can undergo liaison when it is followed by its complement. Thus, the determiner *des* 'some' in (17a) enters in a liaison context with its following word *ennuis* 'troubles' because this structure instantiates the head-complement structure. In this subsection, I show that the generalization in (20) can be maintained in its slightly revised form under the more recent conception of phrase structure known as Bare Phrase Structure of Chomsky (1995).[9]

   Consider first the head-complement configuration. This configuration creates a liaison context, as shown in (21a–e). To take (21b), for example, the verb *mangeait* 'was eating' undergoes liaison when it is followed by the indefinite article *une* 'a'.

(21) *Head-Complement Configuration*

      a. des ∩ ennuis   '(some) troubles'   D-NP

      b. mangeait ∩ une pomme   'was eating an apple'   V-DP

      c. des mois féconds ∩ en événements   '(some) months full of events'
          A-PP

      d. dans ∩ une sale   'in a room'   P-DP

      e. prêt ∩ à partir   'ready to leave'   A-CP
                                    (Selkirk 1974: 580, 582, 584)

---

[9] As Richard Kayne (p.c.) points out, syntactic environments on French liaison have been commonly held to be divided into three classes (obligatory, optional, or impossible). Selkirk (1974: 581) claims that the so-called "optional" environments come into play only when conversations become formal, as in an elevated speech style, and, as a result, liaison is never found in the relevant environments in normal conversation. She proposes an adjustment rule which converts the sequence of a double ## into a single # to account for a number of otherwise exceptional cases of liaison observed in an elevated speech. The purpose of this chapter is to see whether the proposed analysis can correctly demarcate the set of possible and impossible domains of French liaison, not to propose a theory of (non-syntactic) conditions on the alternation. Accordingly, I leave this important issue on the obligatoriness/optionality of French liaison aside. See Selkirk (1972) for more discussion on this issue. All the data in this subsection come from Selkirk (1974) unless otherwise noted.

One crucial argument for the generalization comes from examples like (22a,b) and (23a,b), which show a curious correlation of the presence/absence of liaison with a particular semantic interpretation.

(22) *Correlation of Liaison with Semantic Interpretation*

    a. un marchand de draps/anglais
        'a merchant of English sheets'
        OR 'an English merchant of sheets'

    b. un marchand de draps ∩ anglais
        'a merchant of English sheets'
        NOT 'an English merchant of sheets'   (Selkirk 1974: 583)

(23) *Correlation of Liaison with Semantic Interpretation*

    a. Les masses sont fidèles/à Rome.
        'The masses are faithful to Rome.'
        OR 'The masses are faithful in Rome'

    b. Les masses sont fidèles ∩ à Rome.
        'The masses are faithful to Rome.'
        NOT 'The masses are faithful in Rome.'   (Selkirk 1974: 585)

In (22a), where liaison is not found between *draps* 'sheets' and *anglais* 'English', two interpretations are available. In one interpretation, the sentence-final adjective *anglais* 'English' modifies *draps* 'sheets' and yields the reading "A merchant of English sheets." In the other interpretation, the adjective modifies the non-adjacent noun *marchand* 'merchant' and yields the reading "an English merchant of sheets." This semantic ambiguity disappears when liaison occurs between *draps* and *anglais*, as shown in (22b). In this sentence, the only interpretation available is "a merchant of English sheets" where *anglais* modifies its immediately preceding nominal *draps*. The same correlation between the presence/absence of liaison and semantic interpretation is also observed in the examples in (23a,b). In (23a), which does not have liaison between *fidèles* 'faithful' and *à* 'to, in,' the PP *à Rome* can be interpreted as either the complement or the adjunct of the adjective, yielding the two readings noted. In (23b), on the other hand, liaison takes place between the verb and the preposition. In this case, the only interpretation available is "The masses are faithful to Rome," where the preposition *à* is interpreted as the complement of the adjective *fidèles* 'faithful.'

This correlation between phonology and semantics is predictable by generalization such as the one in (20) under the Bare Phrase Structure Theory of Chomsky (1995). Specifically, the example in (22a) without liaison is associated with either the structure in (24a) or the structure in (24b) whereas the example in (22b) with liaison is associated only with the structure in (24a).

(24)

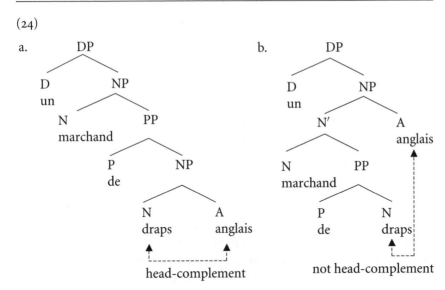

a. head-complement   b. not head-complement

In the example in (22a), the optionality of liaison between *draps* 'sheets' and *anglais* 'English' suggests that the two words may or may not stand in the head-complement relation. Thus, the example is either associated with (24a) or (24b). This structural ambiguity yields the semantic ambiguity. In the example in (22b), the occurrence of liaison between the two words suggests that they must stand in the head-complement relation, and (24b) is the only structure that satisfies this structural requirement. Thus, the example has the unambiguous reading "A merchant of English sheets." The same story holds for the similar pair of examples in (23a,b).

Note that this account crucially rests on the Bare Phrase Structure Theory. It has been widely assumed before the advent of this theory that modifier expressions like *anglais* 'English' are the sister of the N′ that dominates *draps* 'sheets.' In this pre-minimalist conception, then, the two elements would not stand in the head-complement relation. In other words, the head-complement relation that is relevant to determining liaison contexts is purely structural, not selectional in any way as in the X′ Theory. Only in the Bare Phrase Structure Theory that does not recognize bar levels as a primitive notion in phrase structure do *anglais* and *draps* occur within the purely structural head-complement configuration. The proposed account for the correlation of liaison with semantic ambiguity thus provides indirect support for the Bare Phrase Structure Theory.

The following examples of liaison might be a problem for the generalization in (20) because the verb, the target of liaison, does not appear to stand in the head-complement configuration with its following manner adverb, the trigger of liaison, under the standard conception of phrase structure.

(25) a. Gramsci correspondait ∩ assidûment avec sa belle-soeur.
          'Gramsci corresponded assiduously with his sister-in-law.'

      b. Marie caressait ∩ affectueusement sa fille.
          'Marie affectionately caressed her daughter.'

                                              (Selkirk 1974: 587)

(26) a. Il regardait ∩ avec plaisir cette emission.
          'He watched that program with pleasure.'

      b. Il parlait ∩ avec hésitation de leur faillite.
          'They spoke of their failure with hesitation.'

                                              (Selkirk 1974: 587)

There are a number of recent analyses that allow us to maintain the generalization (20) in face of these examples. I mention one possible analysis here. Larson (1990) and Stroik (1990) propose that manner adverbs are base-generated as sisters of the verb. I maintain, following Larson (1988: 347–50) (see also Carnie 1995, 2000), that the V′ dominating the main verb and the adverb undergoes reanalysis as V, which in turns moves into the *v* head. Under this analysis, the relevant part of the structure of (25a) will be as in (27).[10]

(27) *The Structure of (25a)*

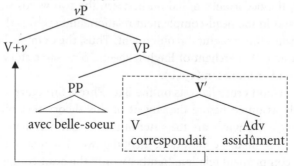

In this structure, the verb *correspondait* 'corresponded' stands in the head-complement relation with the manner adverb *assidûment* 'assiduously.' The same analysis applies to (25b) and (26a,b).[11]

---

[10] Another account is PP/DP extraposition. I will not go into details of this alternative account in this contribution.

[11] David Adger (p.c.) raises the question of how the present analysis could derive the order V + *pas* + the adverb in the negative counterparts to (26a,b) given in (ia,b).

(i) a. Il ne regardait pas avec plasir cette emission.
         'He did not watch that program with pleasure.'

     b. Il ne parlait pas avec hesitation de leur fallite.
         'They did not speak of their failure with hesitation.'

So far, we have seen that the head-complement relation provides a liaison context in French, consistent with the original generalization made by Selkirk (1972, 1974). This result is exactly what is predicted by the syntax-prosody mapping hypothesis couched within Uriagereka's (1999*b*) MSO model, which claims that the head and its complement are contained within the same spelled-out domain. Consider now whether liaison occurs between a head and its specifier/adjunct. Some constructions that instantiate the specifier-head relation are given in (28a,b).

(28) *Specifier-Head Configuration*

    a. Donnez ces lunettes/à Marcel.
        'Give these glasses to Marcel.'

    b. Ils voulaient changer des métaux/en or.
        'They wanted to change metals into gold.'   (Selkirk 1974: 584)

(28a) is a double object construction, which is analyzed as having the *v*-V configuration with the first and second objects base-generated in the specifier and complement of the lower V under recent analyses, as shown in (29) (see Larson 1988; Pesetsky 1995; Harley 1995, 2003). (28b) is a resultative construction that can be analyzed as having a similar structure as the double object construction with the direct object base-generated in the specifier of the PP headed by the secondary resultative predicate, as shown in (30) (see Carrier & Randall 1992; Radford 1997).

(29) *The Structure of (28a)*

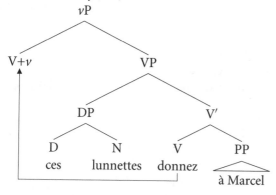

However, these examples are judged to be awkward by French native consultants of Sumayya Racy (p.c.). They point out that the two examples above were at the very limits of acceptability. For them, it is somewhat distressing to put *pas* between the V and PP and the V + PP needs to be treated as a unit to the exclusion of the negative element. The reanalysis process proposed in the text is meant to capture this intuition.

(30)   *The Structure of (28b)*

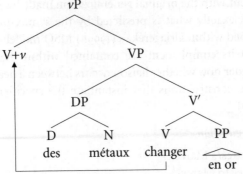

In (29), *lunettes* 'glasses' cannot undergo liaison before *à* 'to' since the two words are not in the head-specifier configuration. In the same way, in (30), the trigger (*changer* 'change') and the target (*métaux* 'metals') are not in the head-complement relation, which blocks liaison between these two elements. Notice here that the trigger and target of liaison in the examples in (28a,b) instantiate the head-complex specifier configuration. This configuration is what the proposed mapping hypothesis in (6) predicts not to be a possible liaison context because a complex specifier undergoes early Spell-Out and is processed at the PF component separately from the rest of the derivation. The proposed analysis also predicts that liaison should be impossible between a head and the last word of a complex adjunct since the latter forms an independent prosodic domain from the domain that contains the head. This prediction is also borne out by examples as in (31), whose rough syntactic representation is shown in (32).

(31)   *Head-Adjunct Configuration*
Je réfléchissais/avant de répondre.
'I was reflecting before answering.'   (Selkirk 1974: 588)

(32)   *The Structure of (31)*

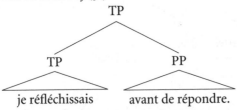

In this structure, liaison is not observed between *réfléchissais* 'was reflecting' and *avant* 'before' because the latter is contained within the spelled-out domain (PP) that is processed separately from another spelled-out domain (TP) that contains the main clause *je réfléchissais* 'I was reflecting.'

Finally, the proposed hypothesis makes a prediction that liaison should be possible between a head and its specifier or adjunct only when the latter is simplex. Interestingly, this prediction is also indeed borne out by examples as in (33)–(35). The examples here are provided by Summaya Racy (p.c.).

(33)   *Complex vs Simplex Subjects*

    a. Les garcons/étaient grands.
       'The boys were big.'

    b. Nouns ∩ allons. Vous ∩ allez.
       'We go.'/'You go.'

(34)   *Complex vs Simplex Indirect Objects*

    a. Donnez/un gateau à Marcel.
       'Give a cake to Marcel.'

    b. Donnez ∩ en à Marcel.
       'Give some of it to Marcel.'

(35)   *Complex vs Simplex Adjuncts*

    a. Marie le caressait/aussitôt qu'elle le voyait.
       'Marie caressed it as soon as she saw it.'

    b. Marie le caressait ∩ aussi.
       'Marie caressed it too.'

The examples in (33a,b) show that the subject undergoes liaison before the verb only when it is a simplex, non-left-branching element. The same effect of the simplex vs complex composition of the target onto the presence/absence of its liaison is also observed in the contrast between (34a) and (35a), on the one hand, and (34b) and (35b), on the other.[12]

To recap, I have demonstrated that the three predictions of the proposed syntax-prosody mapping hypothesis couched within Uriagereka's (1999*b*) model are confirmed by a range of data concerning French liaison. In the next

---

[12] A natural question to address here is why the adverb *aussi* should not precede the VP *les caressait* in the example in (35b) by the Base Step in (1b), which dictates that the base order should be V + Adv + NP. In this particular example, the object clitic undergoes cliticization into the main verb. This PF cliticization then makes this amalgam count as a single terminal node for the purposes of the Linear Correspondence Axiom (Chomsky 1995; Sato 2006*b*). Alternatively, the VP remnant movement moves the V + DP across the adjunct adjoined to *v*/VP. The cliticization then derives to the correct word order clitic + DP + Adv in examples like (35b).

two subsections, I further show that facts regarding lenition in Gilyak and high tone deletion in Kinyambo provide additional preliminary support for the proposed analysis.[13, 14]

9.4.3 *Lenition in Gilyak*

Kenstowicz & Kisseberth (1979: 436–7) point out that in Gilyak, the initial obstruent of a word is voiced after nasals and spirantized after vowels, as shown in (36a-d) (see Krejnovich 1937 for the original source of data).

(36)   *Gilyak Lenition*

   a.   noun + noun

   q^hos   'neck'

   Ne xos   'otter neck'

   ves q^hos   'crow neck'

   b.   adjective + noun

   t↔f   'house'

   pilan t↔f 'big house'

   c.   pronoun + noun

   p↔x   'paint'

   N↔ N-bex 'our paint'

   d.   direct object + verb

   v↔kz-d^j 'throw away'

   ki v↔kz-d^j 'throw away shoes'

   Nas p↔kz- d^j 'throw away belt'

Kenstowicz & Kisseberth observe that these four configurations exhaust the contexts in which lenition is found in Gilyak. Importantly, all of these structures instantiate the head-complement relation between the trigger and target of lenition under the Bare Phrase Structure Theory (recall related discussion in Section 9.4.2.). Thus, the observed pattern of lenition in Gilyak provides additional preliminary support for the proposed mapping hypothesis.

---

[13] Guimarães (1998) has counter-evidence for the claim in this contribution that only a simple specifier/adjunct element can stand in a liaison context with its following element. He provides several cases of liaison that can involve left-branching structures in limited conditions and proposes a similar analysis to the one proposed here within the top-down derivational model. The relevant work was not available to me when I completed this work. I leave careful examination of the data concerning this claim discussed in Guimarães (1998) for another occasion. I thank Juan Uriagereka (p.c.) for pointing this out.

[14] An anonymous reviewer raises the question of how different the proposed derivational analysis is from previous prosodically based analyses of the prosodic phenomena discussed so far. In other words, the set of data could be and might have been explained in representational terms, by referring to notions such as branchingness of constituents. I disagree. There have been few analyses in representational terms that attempt to incorporate structural notions such as complement, adjunct, and specifier for the exploration of the syntax-phonology interface and see how far we can go without relying on prosody-theoretic notions or some correspondence rules between syntax and phonology. The present analysis is just one attempt to see whether a systematic, purely syntactic explanation can be achieved. The valuable exception is Cinque (1993). Furthermore, as we will see in Section 9.5, consonant mutation in Welsh is sensitive to the CP vs TP boundaries and the presence/absence of the *v*P boundary blocks mutation in Irish. No representational analyses have been proposed that map a particular syntactic category to a barrier to certain prosodic phenomena, and only the derivational analysis such as the one proposed here can accommodate the observed contrast.

9.4.4 *High Tone Deletion in Kinyambo*

Bickmore (1990) observes that a high tone in a word is deleted when followed by another word with the same tone within certain structural configurations.[15] One example of high tone deletion in this language is given in (37).

(37)　*Kinyambo High Deletion*

o-mu-k<u>a</u>ma	mukázi	(cf. omuk<u>á</u>ma 'chief' (in isolation))
chief	old	

　　'old chief'

　　　　　　　　　　　　　　　　　　　　　　　　　　　(Bickmore 1990: 9)

In this example, the high tone of the citation form of the word *omuk<u>á</u>ma* 'chief' is deleted before another word *muk<u>á</u>zi* 'old' whose second syllable contains high tone.

What is interesting for us about high tone deletion in Kinyambo is Bickmore's observation that the simplex vs complex composition of subject and indirect object is correlated with the presence vs absence of high tone deletion in them. Consider examples in (38a,b) and (39a,b).

(38)　*Simplex vs Complex Subject in High Tone Deletion*

　　a.　Abak<u>o</u>zi bákajúna.　　(cf. *abak<u>ó</u>zi* 'workers' (in isolation))
　　　　workers　they-helped
　　　　'The workers helped.'

　　b.　Abakozi bak<u>ú</u>ru bákajúna.　　(cf. *bak<u>ú</u>ru* 'mature' (in isolation))
　　　　workers mature they-helped
　　　　'The mature workers helped.'　　　　　　　(Bickmore 1990: 14)

(39)　*Simplex vs Complex Indirect Objects in High Tone Deletion*

　　a.　Nejákw<u>o</u>rech' á bak<u>o</u>z'
　　　　he-will-show　workers
　　　　émbwa.　　　　(cf. *nejákw<u>ó</u>recha* 'he-will-show' (in isolation))
　　　　dog
　　　　'He will show the workers the dog.'

　　b.　Nejákworech' ómukama w'ábak<u>ó</u>zi
　　　　he-will-show　chief　　　of workers
　　　　émbwa.　　　　(cf. *abak<u>ó</u>zi* 'workers' (in isolation))
　　　　dog
　　　　'He will show the chief of the workers the dog.' (Bickmore 1990: 15)

---

[15] Kinyambo has a total of three surface tones: High (á), Low (a), and Falling (áa). There is a maximum of one non-Low tone per noun. The non-Low tone never appears on the final syllable.

These examples show that when a specifier element such as subject and indirect object is simplex, its high tone is deleted; when it is complex, its high tone is maintained. Thus, the high tone deletion pattern in Kinyambo provides evidence for the proposed mapping hypothesis.[16, 17]

9.5 Consonant Mutation in Welsh and Irish and Phase Theory[18]

Consonant mutation refers to the phenomenon in which the initial consonant of the citation form of a word undergoes phonological replacements under certain syntactically definable configurations. The phonological effects of consonant mutation in Welsh are shown in (40), with one example given in (41).

(40)   *Welsh Consonant Mutation*

p → b   b → f   m → f
t- → d   d → dd   rh → r
c → g   g → NULL   ll → l   (Harlow 1989: 289)

(41)   *Welsh Consonant Mutation*

Gwenlodd   y   dyn **gi.**   (citation form = *ci* 'dog')
saw-PAST-3SG the man dog
'The man saw a dog.'   (Harlow 1989: 289)

In (41), the citation form of the word *ci* 'dog' undergoes consonant mutation into *gi*. I assume, somewhat controversially, that the trigger for consonant mutation in Welsh is an XP that immediately precedes the target (see Harlow 1989; Tallerman 1990, 1993, 2006; Roberts 1997, 2005 for detailed discussion on the possible trigger for consonant mutation in Irish). In this section, I examine several cases in which syntactic derivation crucially affects the presence vs absence of consonant mutation in this language.

One case concerns the observation made by Tallerman (1990: 405–6) (cf. U.I.G.C. 1976; Jones & Thomas 1977; Harlow 1989) that CP clauses, not TP

---

[16] One remaining problem with this analysis, of course, is why the inflected verb *nejákworech* 'he-will-show' loses high tone in its third syllable in (39b). The present analysis would wrongly predict that it should not lose its high tone because the indirect object is spelled out and mapped to a prosodic domain that excludes the inflected verb. I leave this problem for future study. Another surprising part in (39b) might be the lack of high tone deletion in *ómukama* 'chief,' whose citation form is *omukáma*. I maintain for the purposes of discussion here that the high tone deletion occurs in this example because it stands in a sisterhood relation with its following argument *w'ábakózi* 'of workers.'

[17] Kaisse (1985: ch. 7) examines a wide range of other sandhi rules—including syntactic doubling in Italian, tone sandhi in Mandarin Chinese and Ewe, and vowel shortening in Kimatuubi—and proposes a unified account of them that makes crucial reference to the structural notion of c-command. These alternations may be amenable to the proposed account. I leave careful examination of these facts for another occasion.

[18] I thank Andrew Carnie (p.c.) and Heidi Harley (p.c.) for directing my attention to the relevance of the present analysis to consonant mutation in Welsh and Irish.

clauses, constitute barriers for consonant mutation. Consider the following example.

(42) *Lack of Consonant Mutation across the CP Boundary*

Dywedodd [$_{NP}$ hi] [$_{CP}$ (y) [$_{IP}$ **bydd**   hi'n   prynu car
said-3SG   she   COMP will-be-3SG she-PROG buy   car
newydd]]
new
'She said (that) she will be buying a new car.'   (Tallerman 1990: 405)

In (42), we have an optional complementizer *y*. Irrespective of whether this complementizer is omitted or not, the finite verb in the embedded clause does not mutate even though it follows the potential trigger NP *hi* 'she' in the matrix clause (Tallerman 1990: 405). This absence of consonant mutation suggests that CP clauses serve as barriers to mutation. This conclusion receives further confirmation from examples as in (43a,b). The embedded clauses in these examples are CPs, as shown by the occurrence of the complementizers *tan* 'until' and *pan* 'when'.

(43) *Lack of Consonant Mutation across the CP Boundary*

a. Mi wnei   di aros [$_{NP}$ yma] [$_{CP}$ **tan/*dan**
     PRT will-do-2SG you stay   here   until
     ddo   i yn ol]
     will-come-1SG I back
     'You'll stay here until I come back.'
                (Jones and Thomas 1977: 139, cited in Tallerman 1990: 404)

b. Mi welais i [$_{NP}$ Huw] [$_{CP}$ **pan/*ban** gyrraeddais i]
     PRT saw-1SG I   Huw   when   arrived-1SG I
     'I saw Huw when I arrived.'   (Tallerman 1990: 405)

In these examples, the embedded complementizers do not undergo mutation even when preceded by the NP, which otherwise serves as trigger for consonant mutation.

Now, compare these examples with those in (44) and (45).

(44) *Consonant Mutation across the IP Boundary*

Dywedodd [$_{NP}$ yr anthro] [$_{IP}$ **fod** Gareth wedi colli'r bws]
said-3SG   the teacher   be Gareth PERF lose-the bus
                        (citation form *bod* 'be')
'The teacher said Gareth had missed the bus.'
                (U.I.G.C. 1976: 92, cited in Tallerman 1990: 405)

(45) *Lack of Consonant Mutation across the CP Boundary*

> *Dyweddodd [NP yr athro] [CP y   [IP **bod** Gareth wedi
> said-3SG   the teacher   COMP   be   Gareth PERF
> collo'r bws]]
> lose-the bus
> 'The teacher said Gareth had missed the bus.'   (Tallerman 1990: 406)

The data in (44) show that consonant mutation can be triggered across the IP boundaries when there is no position for complementizers. That there is no complementizer position in the complement of the verb "say" is supported by the fact that the complementizer *y* cannot occur with the non-finite form *bod*, as the ungrammaticality of (45) indicates. Based on these examples, it seems safe to conclude, following Tallerman (1990), that CPs, but not TPs, are barriers to consonant mutation in Welsh.

A natural question to ask at this point, of course, is what it is about CPs that makes them blockers for mutation. It is important to notice that Uriagereka's MSO model, which we have assumed so far, cannot answer this question because it does not draw any distinction between the two specific categorical nodes CP and TP that would be pertinent to Spell-Out. As we have seen in Section 9.2, Uriagereka's (1999*b*) framework assumes that Spell-Out is a costly, Last-Resort operation that is triggered for the purposes of linearization as in the Base Step in (1a), not in a way that is sensitive to the label of mid-derivational objects that syntactic computation will create along its way.

A straightforward explanation for this syntactic effect on the presence vs absence of consonant mutation is readily available under another version of the MSO model known as Phase Theory, as outlined in Chomsky (2000, 2001, 2004*a*, 2008). Like Uriagereka (1999*b*), Chomsky adopts the assumption that syntactic objects are sent off to the PF and LF components for phonological and semantic interpretation in a piecemeal fashion. The derivational points at which this transfer takes place are defined as phases, mid-derivational syntactic objects that contain an instance of v or C.[19] More concretely, once the vP and CP structures have been constructed, they undergo Spell-Out to PF and LF. Under the mapping hypothesis proposed in Section 9.3, which uniquely maps spelled-out domains to prosodic domains at PF, this means that CPs and vP should constitute domains at PF within which phonological alternations are possible. This expanded mapping theory therefore provides a principled

---

[19] Chomsky (2000, 2001, 2004*a*) assumes that only those verbs with "full argument structure," excluding passive and unaccusative verbs, have strong phase heads. However, I adopt the null assumption that every instance of v is a strong phase head. See Legate (2003*b*), however, for several semantic and phonological arguments that all instances of v, unaccusative or passive, constitute a strong phase in the sense of Chomsky.

explanation for the effect of the distinction between CP and TP on consonant mutation in Welsh. Consonant mutation does not occur in (42), (43a,b), or (45) because the trigger is separated from the target of the alternation by the CP boundary. This mutation does happen between the embedded auxiliary and the matrix NP in (44) because there is no CP boundary that separates the two.[20]

Furthermore, there is one argument of a different sort in Welsh that *v*P also plays a crucial role in defining a structural configuration for consonant mutation. Consider the following example of Welsh from Tallerman (1993) (as cited by Radford 2004: 405).

(46)   *Traces in SpecvP as Trigger for Consonant Mutation*

   Beth wyt ti   'n   **feddwyl** oedd gen I?
   what are you PROG thinking   was   with me
                                    (citation form = *meddwyl* 'think')
   'What do you think I had?'

Tallerman (1993) provides independent evidence that *wh*-traces trigger consonant mutation. In the example in (46), the embedded verb has undergone mutation so that the mutated form *feddwyl* 'think' is used instead of its citation form *meddwyl* 'think.' Given her assumption that *wh*-traces work as a trigger for mutation, a natural account for (46) is to suppose that movement of *beth* 'what' leaves its trace in the specifier position of the *v*P in the embedded clause (see also Willis 2000 for a different account). Thus, examples like (46) constitute one clear case of the syntax-phonology mapping in which consonant mutation confirms the existence of *v*P phase in Welsh (cf. *n.* 22).

As an anonymous reviewer points out, one might wonder whether there is any piece of independent evidence that *v*P also serves as blocker for consonant mutation just like CP does in Welsh. This question is reasonable given that Chomsky assumes that *v*Ps as well as CPs form strong phases. Though I could not come up with any data that bears on this question from Welsh itself, facts concerning consonant mutation in Irish, a related Celtic language, provide evidence that *v*P indeed serves as blocker for this phonological process.[21] Consider first examples in (47a,b).

---

[20] Bošković (2001) and Bošković & Lasnik (2003) also provide independent evidence that the C head creates intonational boundaries and blocks PF affixation.

[21] I am very grateful to Andrew Carnie (p.c.) for providing the data and idea presented here. See Carnie (2008).

(47)   *Irish Consonant Mutation*

    a.   an   Bheán **bhocht**   (cf. citation form = *bocht* 'poor')
        DEF.FEM woman poor
        'the poor woman'

    b.   Tá an   bheán **bocht.**
        is DEF.FEM woman poor
        'The woman is poor.'   (Andrew Carnie, p.c.)

In the example in (47a), the adjective undergoes lenition from its citation form *bocht* to *bhocht* after the word *bheán* 'woman.' In the example in (47b), however, this mutation does not happen to the same adjective despite the fact that it is immediately preceded by the same trigger. We can account for this apparent mysterious contrast between (47a) and (47b) once we assume that a vP boundary exists between the trigger and the target of lenition in (47b), not in (47a), as shown in (48).[22] This assumption is independently motivated by the observation that vP-adverbs such as *igconai* 'always' can be inserted between *bheán* 'woman' and *bocht* 'poor', as shown in (49) (see McCloskey 1996).

(48)   *Lack of Irish Consonant Mutation across vP Boundaries*

        Tá [$_{FP}$ an   bheán ... [$_{vP}$ **bocht**]]
                             ↓
                     blocker for mutation

(49)   *The position of vP-adverbs*

        Tá an   bheán i gcónaí bocht.
        is DEF.FEM woman always poor
        'The woman is always poor.'   (Andrew Carnie p.c.)

A similar argument can be made on the basis of the contrast between (50a) and (50b) in Irish.

(50)   *Irish Consonant Mutation*

    a.   dha phingin **dheas**   (cf. citation form = *deas* 'poor')
        two penny   poor
        'two poor pennies'

    b.   Tá dha phingin **deas.**
        is two penny poor
        'Two pennies are poor.'   (Andrew Carnie, p.c.)

---

[22] One hidden assumption here that needs independent support is that the A-movement trace of *an bheán* 'the woman' in Spec$v$P would not trigger consonant mutation.

As is well known in the literature on Irish (Stump 1988; see also Green 2007 and Wolf 2007), the word *dha* 'two' is peculiar in that it serves as a trigger for mutation to a non-adjacent element such as *dheas* 'poor' in (50a). This mutation does not apply between the same pair of target and trigger in the example in (50b). Again, this absence of mutation is naturally accounted for if we assume that the *v*P boundary exists between the two elements and blocks the mutation as a phase boundary, as shown in (51).

(51) *Lack of Irish Consonant Mutation across vP Boundaries*

Tá [$_{FP}$ dha phingin ... [$_{vP}$ **dheas**]]
           $\downarrow$
           blocker for mutation

To summarize, I have argued on the basis of the absence of the consonant mutation across CP and *v*P boundaries in Welsh and Irish that Chomsky's version of the MSO model known as Phase Theory should be integrated into the proposed syntax-prosody mapping hypothesis.

9.6 Conclusion

This chapter has proposed a general syntax-prosody mapping hypothesis within a recent derivational theory of syntax espoused by Chomsky (2000, 2001, 2004*a*, 2008) and Uriagereka (1999*b*). This hypothesis, which maps mid-derivational spelled-out domains to prosodic domains at the PF component, yields a number of universal predictions that have been indeed borne out by a variety of phonological alternations including tone sandhi in Taiwanese, liaison in French, lenition in Gilyak, high tone deletion in Kinyambo, and consonant mutation in Welsh and Irish. The overall result of this contribution strongly argues for the position that a derivational system of syntax that combines both Uriagereka's and Chomsky's models is needed for the proper access to phonology from syntax and vice versa.

Part III
Ordering Issues

10

Toward a Phase-Based Analysis of Postverbal Sentential Complements in German*

JIRO INABA

10.1 Introduction

In this chapter I will discuss the postverbal positioning of sentential complements in German. Specifically I will try to give an answer to the question of why sentential complements appear to the right of the verb (cf. (1)), although German is a verb-final language and other arguments (and adjuncts) accordingly show up to the left (cf. (2)):

(1) a. Wenn ich meiner Schwester erzähle [dass er gerne
         if   I   my   sister-DAT tell   [that he willingly
         Apfelwein trinkt]...
         apple-wine drinks]
         'If I tell my sister that he likes to drink apple wine...'

     b. ??/# Wenn ich meiner Schwester [dass er gerne Apfelwein
         trinkt] erzähle...

(2) a. Wenn ich meiner Schwester [die Wahrheit] erzähle...
         if   I   my   sister-DAT [the truth]   tell
         'If I tell my sister the truth...'

     b. * Wenn ich meiner Schwester erzähle [die Wahrheit]...

In order to elucidate the central problem of this peculiar property that the sentential complement exhibits concerning its positioning, I will concentrate

* For fruitful discussion and valuable comments, I would like to express my gratitude to the participants at the *InterPhases* conference (Nicosia, Cyprus, May 2006), especially to Kleanthes Grohmann, Ayesha Kidwai, Kayono Shiobara, and to the reviewers of this volume. Thanks also go to Eric Fuß, who discussed with me some important aspects of the ideas presented here.

the following discussion on the asymmetry between the preverbal nominal arguments, DPs, and the postverbal finite sentential complements, CPs, as shown above. I will eventually try to deduce the observed facts from the assumption that CPs, but not DPs, correspond to a separate Spell-Out domain which is sent to the interface levels successive-cyclically.

In the next section of this chapter, I will review a couple of previous analyses which handled the problem of postverbal positioning of sentential complements in German. In Section 10.3, I will lay out some theoretical assumptions concerning cyclic Spell-Out and linearization. Section 10.4 then offers an analysis for the positioning of nominal and sentential objects in German. In the ensuing section I will show how the proposed analysis can be extended to other relevant syntactic areas. In Section 10.6, I will comment on preverbal sentential objects in a couple of OV languages. The final section gives a brief summary of the discussion in this contribution.

10.2 A Review of Previous Analyses

In this section I will review some previous analyses which tried to give an account for the postverbal occurrence of sentential complements in German. The traditional and predominant one is the so-called movement analysis of extraposition, as proposed by Büring & Hartmann (1997) and Müller (1995b). These authors claim that all arguments in German are base-generated in a preverbal position and that CP complements are then extraposed and are right-adjoined to some maximal projection (say, to VP) during the derivation, which generates (1a) from (1b). As a trigger for this extraposition, Büring & Hartmann (1997: 28), for example, propose the following "filter":

(3)   Finite sentences may not be governed by V° or I°.

Starting from the OV structure, DP arguments stay in their base position (cf. (2)), whereas finite CPs are extraposed (cf. (1)) due to the filter (3).

The proposal along this line, however, faces both empirical and conceptual problems. Firstly, there is ample empirical evidence that the "extraposed" sentential complements,[1] which under the movement analysis at issue here should be located in some higher adjoined position, actually behave as elements that stay in their base position; see, among others, Webelhuth (1992), Bayer (1996), and a series of studies by Haider (e.g. 1995, 1997, 2000). Apart from that, the proposed filter, (3), is far from well motivated: (i) It is not clear

---

[1] In the present work, I occasionally use the term "extraposition" (or "extraposed") as merely referring to the postverbal positioning of the relevant element, without necessarily presupposing that it has actually moved rightward.

to what extent (or for which other languages) this constraint applies. (ii) No explanation is offered for the existence of such a filter. (iii) The theoretical status of "government" is not obvious within the current model, and even if we should follow Büring & Hartmann (1997) in working with such GB-theoretic notions, it seems conceptually odd to assume that an argument may not be governed (or L-marked) by the predicate which selects it; a structural configuration of this kind can be regarded as a typical one that should obtain between the selecting and the selected element. So long as all of these problems do not find a satisfactory answer, the strategy taken by Büring & Hartmann (1997) cannot be adopted as a solution to our problem at hand.

Another proposal is made by Zwart (1997). As opposed to Büring & Hartmann (1997), he assumes a uniform VO base structure; a so-called universal base hypothesis. A DP argument is then obligatorily moved leftward into a specifier position of some functional category (say, SpecAgrOP) in order to get its Case feature checked. CP arguments which do not have Case are, on the contrary, exempt from this movement and therefore stay in situ, namely in the right-hand sister position of the verb. The positional asymmetry between the DP and the CP is thus derived from the assumption that only the former is in need of Case checking, which leads to obligatory movement to the left.[2]

There are, however, a great number of arguments which speak against the universal base hypothesis and the analysis based on it. The crucial point is the assumption that all preverbal elements must have been moved out of the VP and are located in a higher derived position. This is the case not only for the DP complements, but also for PP arguments, predicates, and also for adjuncts. First of all, however, the motivation for such leftward movement is not always clear. In addition, there is no compelling evidence that preverbal arguments in so-called OV languages are necessarily situated in a derived position. On the contrary, they show the same kind of property typical of elements in the base position as the in-situ arguments in VO languages. For these and other problems incurred by the universal base hypothesis, see e.g. Gärtner & Steinbach (1994), Haider (1997, 2000), Fukui & Takano (1998), Bouchard (2002), M. Richards (2004), etc. In the face of such (in my opinion insurmountable) difficulties, the explanation for the postverbal CP arguments under this theoretical model cannot be adopted, however elegant it appears to be at first sight.

The two approaches reviewed so far start from a common base structure, respectively, for both DP and CP arguments, although the relative positioning

---

[2] Proposals in a similar spirit regarding the explanation of word order variation were already made in the 1980s by e.g. Travis (1984) and Koopman (1984).

is opposite; OV base in the movement analysis and VO base in the universal base hypothesis. Hubert Haider, who criticizes both of these strategies in a series of his work (see the literature cited above), postulates a base structure for languages like German in which DP and CP complements are licensed in the sister position of the selecting verb, but in different directions; DPs to the left and CPs to the right of the verb. I agree with Haider in that the strategies to derive one of the orders (VO or OV) from the other by way of movement face serious problems, especially from the empirical point of view. I will also make use of the insight behind his basic idea concerning the phrase structure, called Branching Constraint, in my own analysis below (see Section 10.4). So far as I see, what Haider asserts with respect to the different positioning of DP vs CP complements in the base structure, however, lacks independent motivation; there is namely offered no explanation why in an OV language like German CPs appear in the postverbal complement position.

Finally, an analysis proposed by Bayer (1996) will be introduced and discussed. He calls attention to the observation that the position of the complement clause relative to the governing verb is related to the position of the complementizer which heads the complement clause in question. Specifically, Bayer proposes what he calls "C-visibility":

(4)   Where CP is selected by V, its head tends to be linearly adjacent to V.

Actually, the relationship between the positioning of the complement clause and that of the complementizer of that CP has been already noticed in typological literature; see e.g. Kuno (1974), Grosu & Thompson (1977), Dryer (1980), Lehmann (1982), and Hawkins (1990, 1994). The generalization in (4) thus finds typological support. In the case of German, the CP in question appears to the right of the verb because the head C, which is realized e.g. as *dass* ("that"), appears in the left peripheral position of the CP.

In Bayer's analysis, the question remains as to at which level in the derivation the C-visibility, (4), should apply. Bayer is of the opinion that this condition obtains in the PF component (see e.g. Bayer 1996: 193, 243). As argued in Inaba (2007), however, this assumption is problematic. In addition, as Bayer himself acknowledges (1996: 193, 200), (4) is just a "descriptive generalization," for which no explanation is provided. One could, for example, ask why the relevant adjacency requirement does not hold between the head of the DP complement and the selecting verb in German; cf. [[$_{DP}$ D NP] V] vs *[V [$_{DP}$ D NP]]. As long as this special status of the CP complements is not motivated within Bayer's framework, their postverbal realization in German still remains a puzzle to be accounted for.

In this section, I reviewed some previous attempts to deal with the problem concerning the postverbal sentential complements in German. Crucially, the analyses starting from one base structure for all sorts of argument cannot be sustained. How the different underlying positioning of the DP vs CP complements, as Haider asserts it, can be motivated is yet to be pursued. A deeper explanation is called for also within the proposal by Bayer, whose empirical coverage, however, deserves attention; this point will be discussed further in Section 10.6.

10.3 Phase and Cyclic Spell-Out

In this section, I will lay out some basic assumptions which serve as the relevant theoretical devices in order to give a solution to the above-mentioned problem of this chapter. First of all, following the newer trend of the generative model (see e.g. Bobaljik 2002, M. Richards 2004), I assume that linear order of the constituents is determined after Spell-Out in the phonological component.[3] Another important aspect of the theory is the idea that Spell-Out from the syntactic into the phonological component (or the process of linearization) applies not at once for the whole sentence, but cyclically or by phase (see, among others, Uriagereka 1999*b*; Chomsky 2001; Grohmann 2003; Fox & Pesetsky 2005). The theoretical advantage behind this assumption is the "reduction of computational burden" (Chomsky 2001: 11f.): What has been spelled out to the interface levels need not be retained in the syntactic component any more (cf. also Chomsky 2000, 2008). I regard this concept of cyclic derivation as a natural consequence once a theoretical construct like a phase has been postulated.

What is in my opinion in need of careful examination, however, is the question of which syntactic categories should be sent to the interface levels as a unit or should be identified as a Spell-Out domain (SOD). Before going into the discussion, let us review how the concept of a phase was motivated in the first place. Chomsky assumes, crucially, that CP and *v*P are phases, while TP and DP are not:

(5)　The choice of phases has independent support: […] they have a degree of phonetic independence (as already noted for CP vs TP).

(Chomsky 2001: 12)

---

[3] Exactly speaking, Bobaljik (2002: 214) assumes that precedence is assigned to syntactic nodes at the point of Spell-Out. For the present purpose, it suffices for us to maintain the idea that linear ordering is not a matter of narrow-syntactic component. Also for the sake of simplicity, I do not mention the difference between Spell-Out and Transfer, as is explicated, for example, by Fuß (2007) and Grohmann (2007*b*); the same thing applies to PF or the phonological component and the sensorimotor system.

(6)   We have good reason, then, to regard *v*P and CP (but not TP) as phases.
      Why should these be the phases, and the only ones? Ideally, phases
      should have a natural characterization in terms of IC [= interface con-
      dition]: They should be semantically and phonologically coherent and
      independent. At SEM [= "semantic component"; J.I.], *v*P and CP (but
      not TP) are propositional constructions: *v*P has full argument structure,
      CP is the minimal construction that includes Tense and event struc-
      ture, and (at the matrix at least) force. At PHON [= "phonological
      component"; J.I.], these categories are relatively isolable (in cleft, VP-
      movement, etc.).   (Chomsky 2004a: 124)

Without discussion, let us accept Chomsky's assumption that the CPs constitute a phase, while it will be left open in this chapter whether (and/or under
which circumstances) the *v*Ps could also be qualified as a phase.[4]

What syntactic categories should then be sent to the interface levels as a
unit by means of cyclic linearization? Chomsky claims in this respect that the
complement (YP) of a phase head (H) is sent to Spell-Out at the level of HP
while H and SpecHP ("edge") are spelled out only after the next higher phase
(ZP) has been built (cf. e.g. Chomsky 2001, 2004a):

(7)

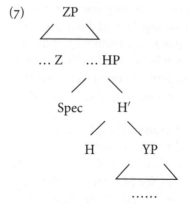

Chomsky (2004a: 108) says that the operation Spell-Out, especially the mapping onto the phonological component, "cannot be *required* to spell out PH
[= phase] in full, or displacement would never be possible." In order that the
edge position, e.g. SpecHP, can function as an "escape hatch" in the case of
successive cyclic movement out of a phase, the Spell-Out at the level of the

---

[4] Saito (2003a), for example, casts doubt on the status of a *v*P as a phase (see also the discussion in
Felser 2004). As for CPs, I agree with the opinion of Lee-Schoenfeld (2005: 252) that "[CPs] are phases
by all other criteria, and in everyone's system."

HP-phase must be able to keep the elements in SpecHP intact and send just the complement of the phase head, YP, into the phonological component.

At this point, I want to depart from Chomsky and assume that it is the phase itself that is sent to the interface levels by Spell-Out. Let us remember from (5) and (6) the original motivation for the phase and the idea of cyclic Spell-Out based on it: Once we postulate a theoretical apparatus, like the phase here, it is natural to relate the relevant operation, namely cyclic Spell-Out, directly to the phase itself and not to some part of it. Especially when the phonological independence is given as a justification for the phase (see (5) and (6)), it appears all the more plausible that the phase itself is sent to the PF component as a "relatively isolable" unit. To assume that the complement of the phase head constitutes a SOD seems to be a stipulation which would have to be extra motivated.

Chomsky claims, however, that the head and the Spec of a phase are, in a sense, not to be construed as residing within the phase, but are accessible from the next higher phase (cf. also N. Richards 2002*a*). I regard this idea per se as at least empirically supported, if we consider e.g. the cases like the selection of the head from the higher head. What I find problematic in Chomsky's formulation is the assumption that the elements in the edge (Spec and H in (7)) are separated from the complement (YP in (7)) when they are sent to the interface levels. If the elements in a single phase are not treated as a unit, it would contradict one of the basic ideas underlying the concept of a phase (cf. (5) and (6)). This conceptual problem is pointed out also by Bouchard (2002: 342f.). In addition, the special status of the edge is just stipulated in Chomsky's system, as discussed by Ko (2005).

There is moreover counter-evidence to Chomsky's assumption concerning the SOD from the empirical side as well. Fuß (2007) argues that the complementizer agreement in some West Germanic languages, which is represented as a relationship between C and T, should be better treated not as a (purely) syntactic operation, but rather as a postsyntactic or a phonological one (see also Ackema & Neeleman 2004 and Fuß 2005). This means that C and T are to be located in the same phonological domain.[5] If the argumentation by Fuß and the reasoning here are correct, it lends support to the assumption that both the elements in the edge of a phase and those in the complement of the phase head are sent to the phonological component as a unit.[6]

---

[5] In order to accommodate this observation into Chomsky's model of Spell-Out, whereby only the complement of the phase head is affected, Fuß (2007: 291) assumes "that the phonological component recompletes the phasal units previously disrupted."

[6] See however, M. Richards (2004: sect. 2.5), who points out the existence of a phonological boundary between a phase head and its complement.

It thus seems plausible to assume from a conceptual as well as an empirical standpoint that the phase corresponds to a SOD. This position is actually taken e.g. by Svenonius (2004), Fox & Pesetsky (2005), and Ko (2007). A potential problem that might arise from this assumption concerns the successive cyclicity of movement. That is, it is only by way of using the phase edge as an escape hatch that movement can take place out of a phase (cf. Chomsky 2001: 12, 44, 2004a: 125, and the literature cited there), and for that purpose, the elements in the edge should not undergo Spell-Out together with the elements within the complement of the phase head. Against this objection, I will sketch a possible solution. Let us assume that the Spell-Out of a phase Ph_1 takes place at the level of the next higher phase Ph_2, namely when Ph_2 has been completed. In case the elements in the edge of Ph_1 are to move successive-cyclically, this movement completes the higher phase Ph_2 by landing in its edge position, at which point the elements still within Ph_1 are spelled out. What underlies this idea seems to correspond to the following "guiding principle [...] for phases" proposed by Chomsky (2001: 13):

(8) Ph_1 is interpreted/evaluated at the next relevant phase Ph_2.

Chomsky adds here that "Spell-out is just a special case" of this "interpretation/evaluation." Although I cannot go into the details of the successive cyclicity of movement in this chapter, the idea represented in (8) is likely to be on the right track as a solution to the problem at hand.

In this section, I first introduced the idea of cyclic Spell-Out proposed in recent literature, where the syntactic unit called a phase plays a crucial role. I then tackled the problem of which syntactic category should be sent to the interface levels by the operation Spell-Out. Resorting to the basic insight behind the idea of the phase, I proposed, above all contra Chomsky, that the phase itself should be identified as a SOD which is sent to the phonological component where the word order is determined. In the next section, I will make use of this concept of cyclic linearization for the purpose of giving an explanation for the word-order facts in German presented in Section 10.2.

10.4 An Analysis for the Postverbal Sentential Complements in German

After presenting the relevant data to be explained and establishing the basic theoretical assumptions concerning Spell-Out, I will now in this section deal with the problem concerning the positioning of the sentential complements in German. For that purpose, we need some more precise characterization of the process of Spell-Out or linearization from the hierarchical syntactic structure.

Once we follow the idea of multiple or cyclic Spell-Out, a natural consequence is that Spell-Out, which results in the building of PF representations out of hierarchically organized syntactic objects, proceeds bottom-up, as is presupposed in the literature working within this model (cf. Section 10.3). This process is namely parallel to the building of syntactic structures by way of recursive Merge of lexical items. To be more concrete, let us assume that the process of linearization or Spell-Out of a whole clause begins with the lowest element on the (extended) projection line of the clause and its sister node. Because a clause, whether of the category CP or TP, is considered an extended projection of V (cf. Grimshaw 2000), the linearization proceeds from the matrix verb and its complement (see below).

We have taken it above that linearization, incurred by Spell-Out, occurs from the bottom and phase by phase; when a phase is encountered during the process of linearization, it is shipped to the phonological component, where it is linearized as a string to be pronounced. The question that now arises is how the object so spelled out is ordered in the phonological component with respect to the elements spelled out at other points in the derivation. Are the elements spelled out earlier realized (i.e. pronounced) earlier or later in the phonological component?

I take the position that a SOD that is sent to the phonological component earlier is realized later there and not the other way round. This is in line with the general architecture of syntactic structure advocated especially by Haider (see below) that elements that are more deeply embedded are in principle realized later (cf. also Kayne 1994). This way of correspondence between the hierarchical syntactic structure and the linear ordering of constituents, according to Haider (1994), enhances "effective parsing," and UG should provide some mechanism to this effect and not the other way round.

In Section 10.2, we shortly reviewed how Haider deals with the problem concerning the positioning of the DP and the CP complements in question. Although I regard his proposal per se as not satisfactory, I adopt the basic idea underlying it, which will be explicated shortly below. Because Haider's model is based on the traditional assumption that linear order is represented in the overt syntax, it has to be modified so as to be compatible with the framework adopted here that linear order is determined postsyntactically.

Let us now introduce the important proposal on which Haider's theory is based:

(9)　*Branching Constraint (BC)*
Projection-internal branching nodes of the (functionally extended) projection line *follow* their sister node.

　　　　　(Haider 2001: 75; cf. also Haider's other papers cited above)

I will not dwell on the definitions of each relevant terminology here, but only show what consequence is derived from this BC, which suffices for the purpose of this chapter. The crucial one is that a structurally higher constituent *in principle* precedes a lower one. In other words (Haider 1994: 13), "BC guarantees that (linear = temporal) *precedence* coincides with *c-command* on the projection line." Exactly in this point, the BC shares one important aspect of Kayne's (1994) Lexical Correspondence Axiom (LCA). The decisive difference from the LCA is that the BC allows for a head-final structure at the deepest level of the projection line, namely between the head and its complement. The direction in which a head licenses its complement is determined by a language-specific (or eventually by a category-specific) parameter. As an illustration, let us look at the following tree diagrams which represent the VP structure of a ditransitive verb in English (10) and German (11), respectively:

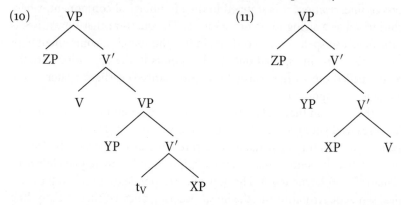

The verbal head licenses its complement to the right in English, whereas it does so to the left in German. The BC is thus a universally valid principle regulating the phrase structure. It is exempt from the shortcomings that the LCA has due to universal head-initiality of the base structure (cf. the literature cited in Section 10.2).

In order that Haider's proposal, as explicated above, will be compatible with the model of postsyntactic linearization adopted in this chapter, it requires a slight modification in its formulation. As an example, let us take up a syntactic structure like (12) in which only the hierarchical configuration should matter. For Haider, the ordering between XP and V is subject to parametric variation in the syntax, that is, the relevant directionality is determined at the beginning of the syntactic computation. This state of affairs can now be subsumed under the framework here if we postulate, along the lines of Bobaljik (2002), that the linear ordering between the lexical head, V, and its complement is established at the point of Spell-Out (see Section 10.3). As a result, we get, first of all, one of the phonological representations given in (13a), depending on the directionality of selection of the relevant head. As for the ordering on the higher levels of the projection, i.e. between V_1' and YP or between V_2' and ZP, we can say that the element on the projection line is always ordered after its sister node at the point of Spell-Out.[7] We thus get further PF representations as (13b) and (13c), where I give only the variant XP>V for the relationship between XP and V.

(12)

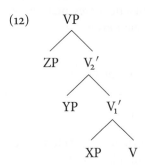

(13) a. PHON $<$ ... XP, V$>$ (or $<$ ... V, XP$>$)

  b. PHON $<$ ... YP, XP, V$>$

  c. PHON $<$ ... ZP, YP, XP, V$>$

At this point, it should be noted that the mechanism exemplified by way of (12) and (13) applies only in the case of linearization within a phase or a SOD. If XP is an independent SOD, it is sent to PF immediately, giving rise, first of all, to the phonological representation $<$ ... XP$>$.

Together with Haider and in opposition to Kayne (1994) we have assumed that the ordering between the head and the complement, e.g. between V and XP in (12), is variable depending on the language or on the category. For German we need, for example, rules like the following:

(14) C $>$ XP

(15) XP $>$ V

These have to be learned anyway during the process of language acquisition. My proposal above can thus be regarded as a natural consequence of Haider's model, which actually has a much wider empirical coverage in other areas of syntactic investigation. The theoretical advantage of my analysis as compared

---

[7] I thus take the BC to be operative not in the overt syntax, but in PF. This strategy is identical in spirit with Chomsky's (1995: sect. 4.8) proposal to "take the LCA to be a principle of the phonological component."

to Haider's is that we need not specify which syntactic category should correspond to XP in (15); as already discussed in Section 10.2, Haider would have to
resort to a caveat like "unless XP=CP" for which no explanation is offered by
him.

With these theoretical devices, which are either motivated independently or
restricted to the minimum, I will now demonstrate how the proposed mechanism captures the data to be explained. Let us first consider the sentential complementation in a sentence like (16). The abstract syntactic representations as
in (17) embody just a hierarchical and not a linear relationship between the
constituents:

(16)   wenn ich meiner Schwester erzähle [dass er gerne Apfelwein
        trinkt] (= (1a))

(17) $[_{CP_1}$ C $[_{TP}$ DP$_{Subj}$ T $[_{vP}$ v $[_{VP}$ DP$_{IO}$ $[_{V'}$ CP$_2$ V $]]]]]$

The process of linearization begins at the bottom of the projection line,
namely with the constituent consisting of V and its complement, CP$_2$, in this
case. Now, since this CP$_2$ constitutes an independent SOD, it is first sent to
the phonological component by itself. As a result, we get the phonological
representation as depicted in (18b):

(18)   a. $[_{CP_1}$ C $[_{TP}$ DP$_{Subj}$ T $[_{vP}$ v $[_{VP}$ DP$_{IO}$ $[_{V'}$ ~~CP$_2$~~ V $]]]]]$
        b.   PHON $< \dots$ CP$_2 >$

At the next phase level or the point of next Spell-Out, the whole sentence
is affected (cf. *n.* 4). In this case of intraphasal linearization, the constraint
corresponding to Haider's BC takes effect: The constituent on the projection line, i.e. V′, follows its sister node, DP$_{IO}$. As a consequence, V is linearized next, which is then followed by the DP$_{IO}$. In order to demonstrate
the mechanism more clearly, I depict the intermediate step of this intraphasal
linearization:

(19)   a. $[_{CP_1}$ C $[_{TP}$ DP$_{Subj}$ T $[_{vP}$ v $[_{VP}$ ~~DP$_{IO}$~~ $[_{V'}$ ~~CP$_2$~~ ~~V~~ $]]]]]$
        b.   PHON $< \dots$ DP$_{IO}$, V, CP$_2 >$

As concerns the functional heads v and T, if we follow the assumption that
they are never lexically occupied in German (see e.g. Haider 1993, 2005), the
linearization prescriptions for these categories are immaterial. Just for the sake
of concreteness, let us here accept the proposal by Haider (e.g. 2001) that non-
lexical functional heads are universally head-initial. With this assumption and
the rule (14), we finally get (20b):

(20)   a. $[_{CP1}$ ~~C~~ $[_{TP}$ ~~DP$_{Subj}$~~ ~~T~~ $[_{vP}$ ~~v~~ $[_{VP}$ ~~DP$_{IO}$~~ $[_{V'}$ ~~CP$_2$~~ ~~V~~ $]]]]]$

       b.   PHON $<$ C, DP$_{Subj}$, T, v, DP$_{IO}$, V, CP$_2$ $>$

The postverbal positioning of the CP complement, as shown in (16), is thus derived.

Let us next consider an example just with nominal objects:

(21)   wenn ich meiner Schwester [die Wahrheit] erzähle (= (2a))

(22) $[_{CP}$ C $[_{TP}$ DP$_{Subj}$ T $[_{vP}$ v $[_{VP}$ DP$_{IO}$ $[_{V'}$ DP$_{DO}$ V $]]]]]$

Here the verb and the direct object are linearized in a single Spell-Out cycle. In this case, the process of linearization of the head and the complement is subject to the language- or category-specific rule. As a consequence, they are sent to the phonological component with the order DP$_{DO}$ >V, according to (15) above:

(23)   a. $[_{CP1}$ C $[_{TP}$ DP$_{Subj}$ T $[_{vP}$ v $[_{VP}$ DP$_{IO}$ $[_{V'}$ ~~DP$_{DO}$~~ ~~V~~ $]]]]]$

       b.   PHON $<$ ... DP$_{DO}$, V$>$

The remaining process is identical to the one for the sentence (16) above.

10.5 Further Consequences

After demonstrating how the proposed analysis captures the observations to be explained, I will now show that it covers some other areas pertaining to relevant syntactic phenomena in German. The first one concerns the positioning of a finite sentential complement in the middle field. Some authors claim that a better result of acceptability yields when the sentential complement is located in a "scrambled" position rather than in its "base" position directly to the left of the verb (Bayer *et al.* 2005: 91; cf. also Brosziewski 1994 and Meinunger 2000):

(24)   (a)   Hans hätte   [dass Maria kommt]   vermutlich   bezweifelt.
             Hans had-SBJV [that Maria comes]   presumably   doubted
             'Hans would have presumably doubted that Maria will show up.'

       (b)   ?* Hans hätte vermutlich [dass Maria kommt] bezweifelt. (cf. (1b))

My analysis now predicts the (relative) well-formedness of the former variant. The structure for (24a) should look like the following:

(25)   ... $[_{VP2}$ CP$_i$ $[_{VP1}$ Adv $[_{V'}$ t_i V $]]]$

Because the CP in question is not in the complement position of the head at the point of Spell-Out any more,[8] it is linearized according to the concept of the BC assumed above: The projection line, VP_1 in (25), is realized following its sister node, CP_i, in the phonological representation. As a result, we get the linear order found in (24a).

Let us next take up some cases of infinitival complementation in German. As a vast amount of literature on this topic attests, infinitive complements (ICs) are classified either as coherent (non-sentential; restructuring) or incoherent (sentential; non-restructuring). Although ICs of control verbs can in principle appear either to the left or to the right of the matrix verb (cf. e.g. Grewendorf 1988; Bayer 1996), there is a tendency that incoherent ICs appear postverbally or in the "Nachfeld" (see e.g. Haider 1993; Wurmbrand 2001; and especially Bayer *et al.* 2005). Examples of these canonical positionings of ICs are given below:

(26) ... dass sie ihn   nicht zu stören wagt. (coherent)
         that she him-ACC not   to disturb dares
      '... that she does not dare to disturb him.'

(27) ... weil   der Junge   das Mädchen überredete
      ... because the boy-NOM the girl-ACC persuaded
      [es nicht zu kaufen]. (incoherent)[9]
      [it not   to buy]
      '... because the boy persuaded the girl not to buy it.'

Now there is almost a consensus in the literature that the incoherent ICs should be treated as a CP. Under this assumption, our linearization mechanism presented in the previous section yields the desired result that they usually appear postverbally, as shown in (27), just like the case of finite CP complementation already discussed. As for coherent ICs, some authors claim that they be better analyzed as VPs (cf. Fanselow 1989; Rosengren 1992; Wurmbrand 2001), others are of the opinion that there is no infinitival "complement" as such, but that the matrix and the embedded verb build a complex predicate (cf. Haider 1993, 2003; Kiss 1995). Whichever analysis one adopts, the coherent ICs are expected to show up in the preverbal position, namely in the middle field, due to the general prescription of the German

---

[8] For ease of exposition, I am making use of a trace here. Under the copy theory of movement, the CP in its base position is indeed spelled out as an independent SOD immediately and is realized in the rightmost position in PF. This CP, the foot of a scrambling chain, is not, however, pronounced there.

[9] The "intraposed" variant of this sentence is judged as marked by Kiss (1995: 33):

(i) ??... weil der Junge das Mädchen [es nicht zu kaufen] überredete.

V concerning linearization, i.e. XP>V (as already established as (15) in Section 10.4).

One problematic case seems to be the preverbal appearance of the IC of a non-restructuring matrix verb (cf. Bayer 1996: 216 and Wurmbrand 2001: 293):

(28)　a.　　... dass man　　uns　　[den Hans　　nur　Spanisch zu
　　　　　　　that one-NOM us-ACC [the　Hans-ACC only Spanish　to
　　　　　　　lehren] gezwungen hat.
　　　　　　　teach]　forced　　　has
　　　　　　　'... that they forced us to teach Hans only Spanish.'

　　　b.　%　... weil　　der Hans　　[der Maria　　nicht geholfen
　　　　　　　because the Hans-NOM [the Maria-DAT not　　helped
　　　　　　　zu haben] zutiefst bedauerte.
　　　　　　　to have]　deeply　regretted
　　　　　　　'... because Hans deeply regretted not to have helped Maria.'

Although this type of construction is taken up in the literature, it is clearly marked as compared to the "extraposed" variant and is actually rather limited in its occurrence: Bayer *et al.* (2005) present a result of their corpus research wherein only nine out of fifty-six control verbs embed their IC in the middle field at all. In all of these cases of intraposition, the matrix verb and the embedded infinitival verb are adjacent without fail, which is regarded as a necessary condition for the coherence of the IC. Furthermore, out of the above-mentioned nine control verbs, only one of them (namely *angeben* 'indicate') can be classified as a strictly non-restructuring verb in the sense of Wurmbrand (2001). From these observations it follows that the type of constructions as in (28), i.e. the intraposition or the preverbal positioning of the incoherent ICs, is a rather marked option which is in fact rarely attested. In order to give an account for the existence of it at all, one could assume a scrambling of the incoherent IC, which is actually visible in (28b), as we have established in the case of the marginal occurrence of the finite sentential complement in the middle field (cf. (24a)). Another alternative could be found in the assumption postulated by Bayer *et al.* (2005) that the intraposed ICs are not truly sentential or CPs, even when the matrix verb is not a restructuring verb. The possible preverbal occurrence of incoherent ICs as in (28) thus ceases to be a problem for my analysis.[10]

---

[10] A true problem arises, however, when we try to handle the data with the "extraposed" coherent ICs, the so-called third constructions. They are so peculiar in that the features of both coherence and incoherence are realized at once. For remarks concerning the special and exceptional status of this construction, see, among others, Höhle (1986), Wöllstein-Leisten (2001), Inaba (2007: ch. 4), and the literature cited there.

10.6 Notes on Strictly Head-Final Languages

Our phase-based (or more precisely, SOD-based) analysis of linearization, which was presented in Section 10.4 and further implemented in Section 10.5, presents itself as a rather strong hypothesis: The CP-complement that is directly selected by the verb in its sister position should be realized postverbally. One might well wonder at this point how the sentential objects in a strictly head-final language should be analyzed in which all sorts of arguments (can) appear in a preverbal position. Since it is impossible to discuss the data from all the relevant languages, I pick out just a few of them as a case study. In the relevant examples below, I follow the common convention to gloss the subordination markers that seem to functionally correspond to *that* in English as COMP, just for the sake of simplicity.

Bengali (and other relevant Indo-Arian languages) is basically a head-final language, but sentential complements introduced by the complementizer *je* appear to the right of the matrix verb, just as in German (cf. (29a)). Bengali now differs from German in that it has the possibility of embedding a finite sentential object in a preverbal position (cf. (29b); Bayer 1996, 1999, 2001):

(29) a.   chela-Ta Sune-che [je   [or baba   aS-be]].
           boy-CF   hear-PST [COMP [his father come-FUT]]
           'The boy has heard that his father will come.'

      b.   chela-Ta [[or baba   aS-be]   bole] Sune-che.
           boy-CF   [[his father come-FUT] COMP] hear-PST

Remember the condition of C-visibility proposed by Bayer (1996) from Section 10.2 above. Both of the sentences in (29) seem at first glance to provide further supporting evidence to this condition. There are, however, some reasons to doubt the complementizer status of *bole* and accordingly the CP status of the sentential object in (29b). Firstly, as Bayer (1999) establishes, the "final complementizer" in Bengali is derived from *verba dicendi* (like *say*).[11] This opens the possibility of treating *bole* as of the category V and consequently the sentential objects headed by it as a VP. Secondly, whereas the complementizer status of *je* (cf. (29a)) can be regarded as established in that it can also introduce an N-dependent clause just like the English *that*, it is not the case with *bole* (cf. Bayer 1999, 2001). Also as the "complementizer" of the sentential complement of a matrix verb, the distribution of *bole* is more restricted than that of *je* (cf. Bayer 2001); it is confined to a subset of predicates

---

[11] Actually, this is also the case in a variety of languages from different language families (cf. e.g. Hopper & Traugott 1993).

which can embed a *je*-clause. Rather, as its traditional term "quotative" implies (cf. also Singh 1980), the primary function of *bole* is "to set the preceding discourse in quotes" (Bayer 1999: 236, 2001: 13). Furthermore, Bayer (1999) actually points to the possibility that the final "complementizer" *bole* could be classified as a postposition (see also Singh 1980 for the postpositional usage of *bole*). As an indirect support to this assumption, Bayer (1999: 248) notes that "Bengali postpositions are generally derived from verbal participles."[12] Summarizing the discussion so far, we can conclude that the Bengali *bole* does not belong to the category C, at least not in the same sense as *that* or *dass*, but should rather be classified either as V or P. This assumption is also compatible with the observation that these categories in Bengali are head-final; the sentential complementation in question can thus be represented either as $[_{VP_1} [_{VP_2} [\ldots IP \ldots] [_{V_2} bole]] V_1]$ or as $[_{VP} [_{PP} [\ldots IP \ldots] [_P bole]] V]$.

Let us next turn to Persian, another OV language. Like Bengali, it has the option of realizing the sentential complement headed by the initial complementizer, *ke*, to the right of the matrix verb. Unlike in Bengali, however, the sentential complement including the same complementizer can appear preverbally (Öhl 2003: 182):

(30) a. Man mi-danam [ke   gorbe-ha shir   dust   darand].
          I   know   [COMP cats   milk friend have]
          'I know that cats like milk.'

      b. Man [[in   [ke   gorbe-ha shir   dust   darand]] ra]
          I   [[this [COMP cats   milk friend have]]   ACC]
          mi-danam.
          know

At first glance, a sentence like (30b) seems to contradict Bayer's condition on adjacency between V and C. A closer look at the example reveals, however, that the sentential complement in (30b) is equipped with a determiner (or a cataphoric pronoun; cf. Mahootian 1997 and Windfuhr 1987) and is additionally marked accusative. These facts suffice to attest to the DP status of the complement selected by the matrix verb here. Hence, there is nothing surprising about the positioning of the complement in (30b). The linearization process begins between the matrix verb and its DP complement. This DP selected by

---

[12] Ayesha Kidwai (p.c.) points out, however, that this is true only for a few locative or directional prepositions and that in such cases the NP complement is in genitive case, which does not apply to *bole*. Further research is needed in this area.

the verb appears to the left, as it is prescribed by the relevant parameter (i.e. XP>V) holding in Persian.[13]

Let us finally take up Japanese, a strictly head-final language. Among various elements that correspond to *that* in English, I will focus on *to*, which introduces a non-interrogative subordinate clause selected by a group of matrix verbs. A typical example is given below:

(31) Watasi-wa [Yuko-ga   keeki-o   tabeta to]   omou.
      I-TOP   [Yuko-NOM   cake-ACC   ate   COMP] think
      'I think that Yuko ate the cake.'

In spite of the familiar glossing of *to* as COMP, however, there are some grounds to doubt its status as a complementizer.[14] Firstly, the distribution of *to* as a complementizer is rather limited, as compared to *that* or *dass*, both of which are able to introduce not only all sorts of declarative clauses serving as a complement to a verb, but also a so-called complement clause of certain nouns. Furthermore, as opposed to the *that*-CP, a *to*-clause in Japanese cannot occur in the subject position (cf. Fukui 1995*b*). The most crucial difference between the "real" complementizer like *that* and the Japanese *to* in question seems to be that the latter basically functions as a marker of direct quotation. See, for argumentation in this direction, e.g. Nakau (1973), Wenck (1974), Shibatani (1978), Fukui (1995*b*), Suzuki (2000), and Öhl (2003).[15] Although I cannot go into the details of the characterization of *to* in this contribution, I regard Fukui's (1995*b*: 357) assumption as plausible "that Japanese lacks C with the same properties as the English complementizers." I consequently conclude that *to* in question here does not belong to the functional category C, as normally assumed owing to the analogy to the English *that*, and that correspondingly the *to*-clause should not be classified as a CP.[16]

---

[13] In order to make the mechanism proposed in Section 10.4 work, we need the technical implementation here that the linearization within the DP, which includes a CP, takes place directly after or at the same time as the linearization of V and DP.

[14] For example, Harada (1976) already puts forward the view that the *to*-clause as in (31) represents a case of NP complementation. Fukui (1995*a*) argues that *to* in question should be classified as a postposition (see, however, Mihara 1994 and Takezawa & Whitman 1998 for arguments against this view).

[15] Cf. Fukui (1995*b*: 355f.): "*that* and *to* have quite different properties, and that the basic function of *to* is largely, if not entirely, to introduce direct quotations." See also Suzuki (2000: 44): "[...] a *to*-marked complement shares many characteristics with an independent sentence. [...] along with the fact that *to* is not followed by the object marking particle *o*, [...] *to*-marked complements are not grammatically well-incorporated into the rest of the sentence." Furthermore, Shibatani (1978: 80f.) proposes that *to* be distinguished from the complementizers ("markers of complement clauses") and be better named a "marker of citation." Bayer (2001) holds a similar view for the Bengali *bole* discussed above.

[16] One could furthermore question the status of the relevant *to*-clause as a (primary) complement of the matrix verb. For discussion on this point, see Shibatani (1978: sect. 3.2), Suzuki (2000), and Inaba (2007: ch. 6).

In this section, I discussed cases of preverbal sentential objects from some (strictly) head-final languages. What is commonly regarded as a final complementizer in each language is actually not a complementizer,[17] but rather of the category P, V, or just a particle that marks quotation. The relevant sentential objects are accordingly not CPs, which would build an independent SOD, but are rather PPs, VPs, DPs, or eventually not complements in a strict sense (cf. *n.* 15 and 16). It then follows as a consequence of the theoretical model proposed in this chapter that the relevant sentential objects in these head-final languages, in which the instruction for linearization "XP>V" applies, are realized in a preverbal position.

10.7 Conclusion

In this chapter I discussed one of the long-standing problems of the German syntax, the postverbal positioning of the sentential object in this OV language. The analyses which start from a common base structure for all sorts of arguments and then derive one of the orders (OV or VO) from the other by way of movement cannot be sustained. Both the preverbal DP complement and the postverbal CP complement must be regarded as located in its base position, respectively. After modifying the original proposal made by Chomsky concerning cyclic Spell-Out based on the idea of the phase, I tried to deduce the different behavior between the DP and the CP complement in German from the assumption that only the latter constitutes a phase or an independent SOD. I proposed that the process of linearization proceeds bottom-up, just as the construction of the syntactic structure. A natural assumption along this line is that the earlier a constituent is spelled out, the later it appears in the PF representation, i.e. it is pronounced later. For the linearization of the head and its complement, a language- or a category-specific linearization rule is postulated which has to be learned anyway, while for the other levels of the projection line, Haider's BC holds, translated into the framework of postsyntactic linearization, according to which the constituent on the projection line is realized later than that within its sister node. As a consequence, we get the desired results concerning the positioning of the DP and the CP complements in German. While my analysis thus predicts a universal postverbal positioning of the CP complement which is located in the sister position of the verbal head, I claimed that this does not cause a problem for the preverbal sentential

---

[17] Ayesha Kidwai (p.c.) remarks that Malayalam has a subordination marker that fits all the diagnostics of a genuine complementizer and still requires obligatory preverbal positioning of its finite complement. If this observation is correct, that would make a counter-example to my generalization in the text. I leave the scrutiny into this point for future research.

objects in (strictly) head-final languages: I showed that they are not of the category CP (or eventually not really complements to the verb), but of some other category which is spelled out together with the verb, thus conforming to the general linearization pattern, XP>V, holding in these languages.

Before closing, I want to point out a typological relevance of the present research. It has been observed in the typological literature that in addition to uniformly verb-initial languages (e.g. English) and uniformly verb-final languages (e.g. Japanese) for both DP and CP complements, there are also German-type languages in which DPs appear preverbally and CPs postverbally (cf. Section 10.6). There seems to exist, however, no language with the opposite pattern, namely with postverbal nominal complements and preverbal sentential complements (cf. among others Dryer 1980). The analysis proposed in this chapter offers a theoretical explanation for this typological observation.

11

Right-Node Raising and Delayed Spell-Out [1]

ASAF BACHRACH & RONI KATZIR

11.1 Introduction

Across the Board (ATB) movement is generally subject to the same islands that constrain regular *wh*-movement: [2]

(1) * **Who**$_i$ did [a man who loves t_i dance], and [a woman who hates t_i go home]?

In (1) a *wh*-element is extracted from subjects within both conjuncts. Not surprisingly, the result is ungrammatical. We observe a systematic exception to this pattern: If the gaps corresponding to the extracted element are rightmost within both conjuncts, extraction is possible even across certain islands:

(2) **Which book**$_i$ did [John meet the man who wrote t_i], and [Mary meet the woman who published t_i]?

There is another construction involving coordination, Right-Node Raising (RNR; Ross 1967), that has long been known to be insensitive to conjunct-internal islands:

(3) [John met the man who wrote ___] and [Mary met the woman who published ___] **the recent bestseller about bats.**

[1] We thank Klaus Abels, Adam Albright, Karlos Arregi, Sigrid Beck, Johan van Benthem, Noam Chomsky, Michel DeGraff, John Frampton, Seungwan Ha, Irene Heim, Sabine Iatridou, Kyle Johnson, Ivona Kučerová, Idan Landau, Winnie Lechner, Alec Marantz, Andrea Moro, Alan Munn, Ad Neeleman, Maribel Romero, Tal Siloni, Raj Singh, Dominique Sportiche, Donca Steriade, Shoichi Takahashi, and the audiences of ECo5, MIT Ling-Lunch, Paris VIII, InterPhases, and the Hebrew University for valuable comments on this paper. Special thanks go to Danny Fox and David Pesetsky.

[2] For expository convenience we mark conjuncts with brackets, and material that is shared between conjuncts with boldface. We indicate leftward movement with indexed traces, and rightward movement with underscores. None of this should be taken to have any theoretical import.

In addition to island insensitivity, RNR shares with (2) the property that rightmost within each conjunct is a gap associated with the shared material. We will argue that these similarities are not accidental, and that (2) is an instance of RNR that has fed a subsequent operation of *wh*-movement. We will further argue that the interaction of RNR and *wh*-movement allows us to settle certain open questions about the structure of RNR. The remainder of this section reviews some of the known empirical puzzles of RNR and their implications on possible syntactic analyses. In Section 11.3 we present our new observations about the interaction of RNR and *wh*-movement. Combined with the facts discussed earlier, we show that the *wh*-movement facts argue for a multiple-dominance structure, an idea originally proposed by McCawley (1982) and defended more recently by Wilder (1999).

While multiple-dominance is required in order to account for the empirical facts, it cannot do so without a clear theory of locality. We develop our proposal, presented in Section 11.4, within the framework of the Minimalist Program, where locality, in the form of cyclic spellout, is a central notion, and where multiple dominance, in the form of Remerge, has been recently used as an account of movement. We observe, however, that current Remerge accounts of movement can be considerably simplified by taking complete dominance, rather than dominance, as the relevant notion for Spell-Out. Significantly, this simplification also makes the correct predictions about the interaction of RNR, *wh*-movement, and islands.

After describing how multiple-dominance structures are formed and spelled out, we turn to the question of how such structures should be linearized. In addition to general problems regarding the linearization of multiple-dominance structures, RNR exhibits a puzzling mix of strict linear-order requirements and extreme freedom. We show that as long as each node keeps track of the linearization of all the terminals that it dominates, we can use a weak linearization procedure that makes possible the required freedom, while the strict linearization requirements are taken care of by the independently needed Spell-Out mechanism. The full pattern of RNR, with and without *wh*-movement, is now predicted.

11.2 RNR Puzzles: A Short Survey

The literature contains three types of RNR analyses. ATB Movement (Postal 1974; Sabbagh 2007), phonological ellipsis (Hartmann 2000; Wilder 1997) and multiple dominance (McCawley 1982; Wilder 1999). In order to choose among the three, we need to answer two questions. The first question is whether

RNR depends on the existence of a syntactic host for the shared material (RN)[3] above the conjunction, or whether it remains *in situ*. The answer to this question will distinguish between the movement approach (which assumes a conjunction-external position) and both phonological ellipsis and multiple dominance approaches which do not require such position. To distinguish among the latter two approaches we need to answer the question of whether RNR is structurally identical to fully pronounced coordination structure, or whether there is a syntactic difference between the two. The phonological ellipsis account assumes that RNR and full coordination structures are syntactically identical, in the sense that each conjunct contains a separate instance of the RN, pronounced once in RNR and multiple times in full coordination. The multiple dominance account assumes that RNR is syntactically distinct from full coordination, since in RNR there is only one instance of the RN in the structure.[4]

As mentioned in the introduction, our answer to the first question will be that the RN remains *in situ*, and our answer to the second question will be that there is only one instance of the RN, shared between the two conjuncts. In the rest of this section and in Section 11.3 we will present data which address the two questions above. We will see that RNR is not sensitive to conditions on either leftward or rightward movement, posing a challenge to the idea that the RN moves above coordination; we will also see that the RN has scopal interactions that are unexpected under the view that each conjunct has a distinct instance of the RN. In Section 11.4.3 we will return to an important linear restriction on RNR that argues for a similar perspective on the two questions here.

11.2.1 *Islands*

RNR is insensitive to islands for leftward movement such as relative clause islands:

(4) [John met a man who wrote ___], and [Mary met a man who published ___] **a recent book about bats.**

Significantly, as mentioned above, ATB *wh*-movement does not share this property. Consider again (1) above, repeated here as (5):

---

³ Also known as Target, Pivot, and Right Node. We will usually refer to it as RN.

⁴ Movement accounts may differ regarding the answer to the second question, depending on the assumptions the particular account makes with respect to the general mechanism underlying ATB movement.

(5)   * **Who**$_i$ did [a man who loves t_i dance], and [a woman who hates t_i go home]?

The contrast between (4) and (5) suggests that RNR is not simply a mirror image of ATB. We return to this point when we discuss *wh*-extraction from RNR in Section 11.3.

11.2.2 *The Right-Roof Constraint*

Ross (1967) noticed that movement to the right is bounded by a highly restrictive locality condition. Heavy NP Shift (HNPS) demonstrates this restriction, often referred to as the Right-Roof Constraint (RRC).[5] A heavy NP may be dislocated to the right (6), but it can only cross local material on its way. In this example, the intervening *yesterday* originates within the same clause, and perhaps even the same verb phrase, as the heavy NP *the new headmaster*. When the intervening material is less local (7), HNPS is blocked.

(6)   Sam saw ___ yesterday **the new headmaster.**

(7)   * John claimed that Sam loves ___ yesterday **the new headmaster.**

As with the islands discussed above, RNR is not subject to the RRC:

(8)   [John claims that Sam loves ___], and [Mary claims that Sam hates ___] **the new headmaster.**

In (8), each conjunct contains two clauses, and the shared material is related to the most embedded position in each conjunct. A movement analysis for RNR has to explain how it is possible for rightward movement to escape two CPs (and at least as many cyclic nodes) in such cases.

11.2.3 *Non-Constituents and RNR Below the Word Level*

The insensitivity of RNR to islands and bounding conditions has been taken to suggest that the movement analysis is incorrect, and that the RN remains *in situ*. Additional support for this direction comes from an observation by Abbott (1976) that RNR can affect non-constituents (9). Moreover, as noted by Booij (1985), RNR sometimes operates below the word level (10), further complicating the task of a movement analysis.

(9)   [John borrowed ___], and [Mary stole ___] **large sums of money from the Chase Manhattan Bank.**

---

[5] Ross first used the term *upward boundedness*, introducing the term *Right-Roof Constraint* in subsequent lectures (Háj Ross and Alex Grosu, p.c.).

(10)   [His theory under-___], and [her theory over-___]**generates.**

(Sabbagh 2007)

One *in situ* approach to RNR analyzes the RN as appearing in each conjunct but being pronounced only within the rightmost one. All other instances undergo some kind of ellipsis. Such an approach has been argued for by Swingle (1995), Wilder (1997), and Hartmann (2000), among others. Island insensitivity, under this approach, is no longer a challenge since no movement takes place. Examples (9) and (10) are explained if we assume that non-constituents and word parts can be deleted.

11.2.4 *Exceptional Scope*

Treating the raising of the RN as illusory obviates many of the locality problems raised by RNR. However, evidence from Quantifier Raising discussed by Sabbagh (2007) suggests that the movement characterization of Ross (1967) is more accurate, at least as far as interpretation is concerned. Sabbagh notes that a quantifier in the RN can scope over elements that are too high for it if no RNR takes place.

(11)   a.   [John knows a man who speaks ___], and [Mary knows a woman who wants to learn ___] **every Germanic language.** ($\exists \succ \forall, \forall \succ \exists$)

b.   [John knows a man who speaks every Germanic language], and [Mary knows a woman who wants to learn every Germanic language]. ($\exists \succ \forall, *\forall \succ \exists$)

c.   John knows a man who speaks every Germanic language. ($\exists \succ \forall, *\forall \succ \exists$)

In (11a) the universal quantifier in the RN can scope over the indefinites *a man* and *a woman* inside the conjuncts. Pronouncing *every Germanic language* within each of the conjuncts (11b) does not allow the universal to scope over the indefinites. The tensed clauses inside each conjunct prevent QR, just as they would in a single conjunct version (11c).[6]

Other interpretive effects that seem to favor a movement analysis over an *in situ* approach are the ability of distributive and cumulative elements to take both conjuncts within their scope. The prominent reading of (12a) is that where the tunes that John hummed were different from the tunes that Mary whistled. Repeating *different tunes* within each of the conjuncts blocks this

---

[6] The focus of the current chapter is the effect of delayed Spell-Out on the phonological interface, and we will ignore the interpretative effects of RNR in much of what follows. In Bachrach & Katzir (2007) we propose an account of scope facts such as (11) that makes use of similar effects of delayed Spell-Out on interpretation at the semantic interface.

reading, as in (12b), which can only mean that the tunes that John hummed were different from each other and that the tunes that Mary whistled were different from each other. Similarly, the prominent reading of (13a) is that where the total of what John borrowed and of what Mary stole amounts to 3,000 dollars. This would be true, for example, if each took 1,500 dollars. Overt substitution blocks this reading, and (13b) can only mean that each of them took 3,000 dollars.

(12)   a.   [John hummed ___], and [Mary whistled ___] **different tunes.**

      b.   [John hummed different tunes], and [Mary whistled different tunes].

(13)   a.   [John borrowed ___], and [Mary stole ___] **a total of 3,000 dollars from the Chase Manhattan Bank.**

      b.   [John borrowed a total of 3,000 dollars from the Chase Manhattan Bank], and [Mary stole a total of 3,000 dollars from the Chase Manhattan Bank].

11.2.5 *Summary*

RNR is less local than movement usually is, and it can also target objects that do not undergo movement otherwise. At the same time, RNR exhibits semantic effects that are surprising if there is no syntactic difference between RNR and full coordination. In the following section we will present new data from the interaction of RNR with *wh*-movement. We will argue that the fact that RNR can sometimes feed *wh*-movement is an argument against the claim that the syntactic structure of RNR is identical to the structure of full coordination. Though at first sight it might seem that these new data support the existence of a syntactic position for the RN outside the conjunction, we will present further data which argue against this conclusion.

11.3 New Observations: RNR and Leftward Dislocation

11.3.1 *RNR Can Feed* wh-*Movement*

Consider again (4), repeated below:

(14)   [John met a man who wrote ___], and [Mary met a man who published ___] **a recent book about bats.**

We observe in (15) that a *wh*-phrase corresponding to the RN in (14) can appear on the left, even though each of the conjuncts contains a relative clause island (16).

(15)   **Which book**ᵢ did [John meet the man who wrote ___], and [Mary meet the man who published ___] t_i?

(16)   * Which bookᵢ did John meet the man who wrote t_i?

We describe (15) as *wh*-movement of the RN in (14). Our conclusion that the availability of RNR in (14) underlies the exceptional movement in (15) is supported by the fact that configurations where RNR is not available (17a) also do not allow for leftward ATB movement (17b):

(17)   a.   * [a man who loves ___danced], and [a woman who hates ___went home] **a book by Kafka**

         b.   * Which bookᵢ did [a man who loves t_i dance], and [a woman who hates t_i go home]?

In addition to extracting the whole RN (as in 15), it is also possible to extract only part of it, leaving overt material on the right:

(18)   **Which animal**ᵢ did John say that Mary knew [a man who wrote ___], and [a woman who published ___] **an encyclopedia article about** t_i?

(18) contains both RNR and *wh*-extraction from within the RN. Here, too, the conjuncts contain relative clause islands, making it unlikely that the *wh*-phrase was extracted before RNR applied to the remnant.

The interaction of RNR and *wh*- movement is particularly puzzling for the ellipsis account (where RNR is assumed to be syntactically identical to full coordination) since for such an account the island insensitivity of RNR is only illusory. By relegating RNR to the PF interface, they manage to avoid a modification of the general island and locality conditions of the grammar. But if RNR takes place after the syntactic derivation, it is hard to understand why (syntactic) *wh*-movement is exempt from certain islands precisely in those configurations that correspond to an RNR configuration. (18) also provides a straightforward argument against a linearization-based account of locality, where RNR is analyzed as rightward movement of a rightmost element, avoiding islands by virtue of being string-vacuous. A relevant case here is the analysis of Sabbagh (2007), who uses the linearization mechanism of Fox & Pesetsky (2005), together with a constraint on available landing sites on the right to derive the bounding conditions on RNR. The RN is linearized on the right edge of its immediate cyclic node, and then waits for the root to be merged. In the absence of intervening material, the RN can then right-adjoin to the root, ignoring all islands along the way. Crucially, in order to capture the generalization that RNR is restricted to the right most element in each conjunct (cf. Wilder 1999 and (62) here), the linearization of the RN to the right of the rest of all other conjunct-internal material is fixed. Nothing, after the first cycle is over, can move the RN to the left. But this is exactly what happens to the *wh*-phrase in (18).

11.3.2 *Islands that Never Go Away*

In the last section, we have presented data that argue against a linearization-based movement account of RNR. These data leave open the question of whether a different movement account could be made to work. In this section we present data that argue against movement accounts more generally. In recent minimalist literature, it is often observed that locality in grammar has two sources. One source are syntax-internal conditions such as Relativized Minimality (and related conditions on search). The other source are interface conditions which filter out certain derivations at Spell-Out. Foreshadowing the discussion of our proposal in the next section, we take relative clause islands to be Spell-Out islands, while effects such as Superiority are Relativized Minimality islands. A movement account of RNR would probably try to explain island bleeding (15, 18) as the consequence of the RN having moved to a position above the conjunction.[7] However, if the RN is syntactically above the conjunction, leftward extraction should, in principle, be exempt not only from Spell-Out islands, but also from Relativized Minimality islands internal to the conjuncts. This, however, is not the case. RNR does not bleed Relativized Minimality violations within the conjunction:

(19)   [Who cooked ___] and [who ate ___] **the black beans?**

(20)   * What$_i$ did [who cook t_i] and [who eat t_i]?

It is not clear how a movement account of RNR can distinguish between Relativized Minimality islands and Spell-Out islands.

11.3.3 *Islands Reappear*

We saw above that RNR is insensitive to islands, and that this insensitivity is (sometimes) inherited by subsequent overt movement (15) and covert movement (11a). Those examples, repeated here as (21) and (22) respectively, involve only islands within the conjuncts.

(21)   **Which book$_i$** did [John meet the man who wrote ___], and [Mary meet the man who published ___] t_i?

(22)   [John knows a man who speaks ___], and [Mary knows a woman who wants to learn ___] **every Germanic language.** ($\exists \succ \forall, \forall \succ \exists$)

As soon as we add an island above the coordination, it will restrict the movement of the RN just as it would restrict any other element.

---

[7] Or being base-generated there, as proposed to us by Noam Chomsky (p.c.).

(23) * **Which animal**_i does John know a reporter who made famous [a man who published ___] and [a woman who illustrated ___] **a book about** t_i?

(24) Some student made the claim that [John can speak ___], and [Mary can write ___] **every Germanic language.** ($\exists \succ \forall$, $*\forall \succ \exists$)

The relative clause modifying *a reporter* in (23) blocks the overt *wh*-extraction of the RN. The embedded tensed clause in (24) and the complex NP island containing it prevent the RN from taking scope over the existential quantifier.[8, 9]

11.3.4 *Interim Conclusion*

In the introduction we presented two main structural questions that we wanted to answer:

(25) a. Does RNR depend on an additional attachment site for the RN above conjunction (as in movement accounts)?

     b. Are there separate instances of the RN for each attachment site (as in PF-deletion accounts; the alternative is to attach the same instance multiple times into separate positions)?

The new data presented in this section allow us to answer both questions in the negative, thus narrowing down the range of possible analyses. Recall that one of the main obstacles facing movement accounts was the insensitivity of RNR to islands and other bounding conditions. To our knowledge, the only movement account to offer a solution to this problem is that of Sabbagh (2007), where the RN avoids islands by never having to cross overt phonological material after being linearized on the right. The observation that RNR can feed *wh*-movement is a counter-example to the most direct prediction of this approach. In addition, if RNR provided an attachment site above conjunction, we would expect all conjunct-internal locality conditions to disappear, contrary to fact. These observations add to the familiar facts from

---

[8] As mentioned above, the details of how the scope facts follow from the current framework are presented in Bachrach & Katzir (2007).

[9] The contrast between the insensitivity of RNR to islands below coordination and its sensitivity to islands above coordination is a problem not only for ATB and *in situ* analyses of RNR, but also for analyses in other frameworks. Categorial Grammars, for example, have offered accounts of RNR (Steedman 1987; Oehrle 1990; Morrill 2002) that are interestingly different from those discussed here. But there, too, a global choice must be made: Either islands interfere with composition, in which case no type will be created for the conjuncts and conjunct-internal islands will not allow RNR, or they do not interfere, in which case islands outside coordination will also cause no problem. Either way, the contrast cannot be accounted for.

the introduction regarding the possibility of using non-constituents and word parts as the RN. We conclude that there is, in general, no higher attachment site above conjunction.

As for the implications that the *wh*-movement facts have for the second question, notice that if there are separate instances of the RN, then an unpronounced copy in one conjunct allows a pronounced copy in a second conjunct to move across islands in a way that is unavailable for conjunction with two pronounced copies. It is not clear what kind of syntactic mechanism could account for this behavior. One of the main attractions of the PF-deletion approach was that it avoided the problem of island insensitivity by denying that movement takes place. The evidence from *wh*-movement lessens the appeal of this approach. This evidence adds to other problems for the multiple-instance approach mentioned in the introduction, such as the exceptional scopal effects. We conclude that RNR does not involve multiple instances of the RN.

11.4 Proposal

Combining our answers to the two structural questions in (25) we arrive at a structure in which the RN occurs once and is attached multiple times. However, while multiple dominance is the only approach that is compatible with the empirical facts, it does not, on its own, derive them. In particular, it is not clear why the fact that the RN is shared by the two conjuncts should exempt it from conjunct-internal islands. We will suggest that the islands to which the RN is immune are related to Spell-Out, and that the special behavior of the RN with respect to those islands is the result of the following principle:

(26)   Syntactic material is spelled out only when it is completely dominated.

The RN is shared between the two conjuncts. By (26), it will not be spelled out until the height of the coordination. This means that locality effects that depend on Spell-Out will not apply to the RN until that point.

As we will shortly see, (26) will not be specific to RNR; rather, it will be the result of general considerations regarding the construction of syntactic representations, the encoding of locality, and the mapping of structures onto linear strings. All of these considerations arise independently once multiple dominance is assumed. Our system, which we describe below, addresses these issues. We will propose to derive RNR from the interaction of three processes: (a) structure formation, (b) cyclic spellout, and (c) linearization. We develop our analysis within the minimalist framework, which already contains the means for the construction of multiple-dominance structures, discussed in

Section 11.4.1, and which incorporates cyclicity in the form of phases, discussed in Section 11.4.2. While our empirical concern remains RNR, much of the discussion will focus on general architectural issues, and in particular on *wh*-movement and locality within a multiple-dominance system. We show that current minimalist treatments of long-distance movement can be simplified by making Spell-Out sensitive to a properly defined notion of complete dominance, and that the pattern of interaction between RNR and *wh*-movement described in Section 11.3 can be derived without making any further assumptions. Our third component, linearization, which we present in Section 11.4.3, is a highly local process that applies independently of Spell-Out. Each node in the structure must satisfy certain linearization well-formedness constraints with respect to the nodes that it dominates.

11.4.1 *Merge*

The basic structure-building operation within the Minimalist Program (Chomsky 1995) is Merge, by which two syntactic objects, X and Y, are combined to form a new syntactic object, Z. For the simple case in which X and Y are disjoint, this is nothing more than a tree-forming operation. We follow Chomsky (2004a) in referring to this case as External Merge:

(27) $X, Y \implies$

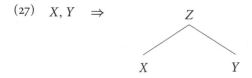

If Merge is not restricted to disjoint syntactic objects, we may remerge an object with a containing object. This operation, named Internal Merge in Chomsky (2004a), has been used to capture movement-like phenomena:

(28)

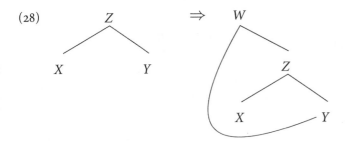

Applying Internal Merge results in structures where some nodes have more than one mother, a structural representation of movement that has already been proposed by Engdahl (1986). Other multiple-dominance structures have been used by McCawley (1982) to account for various discontinuous phenomena, including RNR. Within current Minimalism, it has been noticed by Citko (2005) that if Merge is a general structure-forming operation, it should apply not only between disjoint objects (External Merge) or between an object and a containing object (Internal Merge), but also across structures. We follow Citko in referring to this form of Merge as Parallel Merge:

(29)

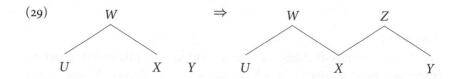

Parallel Merge makes possible a minimalist version of the multiple-dominance of RNR proposed by McCawley (1982, 1988), and argued for more recently by Wilder (1999):

(30)   John bought and Mary read a recent book about bats

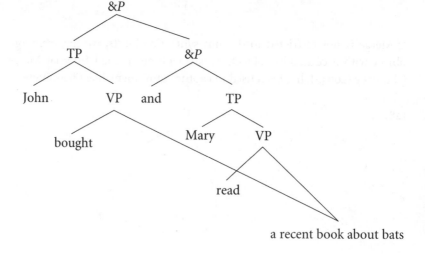

11.4.2 *Phases and Spell-Out*

11.4.2.1 *Spell-Out and External Merge*   Current Minimalism (Chomsky 2001, 2004*a*) posits a cyclic architecture (Bresnan 1971), in which the construction of syntactic structure is interspersed with non-syntactic operations, such as phonological or semantic interpretation. In minimalist terms, syntactic derivations are broken down into *phases*. At the end of each phase, an operation called *Spell-Out* sends the current syntactic structure to the phonological interface.[10] Phases are mediated by *phase heads*, syntactic categories that trigger the Spell-Out of their sisters. Structure that has been spelled out cannot be modified by subsequent operations. The relevant definitions from the literature (to be revised below) are summarized in (31)–(33):

(31)   **Spell-Out Domain (First Version):** The Spell-Out domain of a node X is the set of all nodes dominated by the sister of X.

(32)   **Phase Head (First Version):** A designated syntactic object that triggers Spell-Out of its Spell-Out domain after all of its specifiers have been merged. The phase head itself and all of its specifiers (the *edge* of the phase) are not spelled out until the next phase.

(33)   **Spell-Out:** A syntactic structure transferred to the interfaces is mapped onto an object that cannot be modified by further operations. In the case of the phonological interface, the resulting immutable object is a string.

11.4.2.2 *Some Concerns*   Spell-Out as just described is relatively straightforward to implement as long as structure is limited to trees, the output of External Merge. The tree is traversed in some order, usually the order in which it is constructed, and each terminal node is spelled out when its mother is spelled out. For copy theories of movement some additional machinery is required in order to ensure that only one copy will be pronounced within a chain. The Remerge theory of movement obviates the need for such mechanisms, since a chain consists of only one object. However, as has been observed (Frampton 2004; Fitzpatrick & Groat 2005), Remerge makes it difficult to define the relevant notion of Spell-Out in the first place. Since under Remerge there are no indexed copies or traces, the information required to distinguish the different occurrences of a node is no longer contained within the node itself:

---

[10] It is less clear what the result of Spell-Out is on the semantic side. We do not deal with semantic interpretation in this chapter, and so we will ignore the semantic results of Spell-Out here (cf. Bachrach & Katzir 2007).

(34)

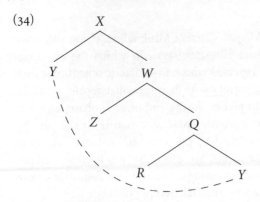

In (34), a schematized version of *wh*-movement, we would like to say that the higher occurrence of Y, standing for the *wh*-element, is pronounced while the lower occurrence is not. This is not possible by talking about Y alone. If Z is a phase head, it will trigger the Spell-Out of the set of terminals dominated by its sister, Q, including Y. Under a copy theory of movement we could mark the lower copy of Y as phonologically null (cf. Chomsky 2004a). Remerge makes this impossible. There is only one occurrence of Y in the structure, and if it is marked as phonologically null it will not be pronounced anywhere at all. The fact that multiple dominance complicates the notion of occurrence is not necessarily a serious problem, and proposals such as Frampton (2004) have offered ways to address the issue. Our only point here is that such proposals provide additions to the theory. The minimalist framework on its own does not offer a solution.

A second concern regarding cyclic Spell-Out is that it involves a counter-cyclic operation, at least as formulated by Chomsky (2001, 2004a). In (34), for example, the phase head Z merges Y as its specifier and spells out its sister Q. In order to avoid spelling out Y in its lower position, the order of operations must not be changed: Q can be spelled out only after the tree has been extended by remerging Y. As with the notion of occurrence, the counter-cyclic behavior of Spell-Out can be addressed in any of a variety of ways. All things being equal, however, it would be reassuring to have a system where the issue does not arise in the first place.

11.4.2.3 *Redefining Spell-Out Domains*   As a first step towards integrating Remerge and cyclic Spell-Out we propose the following definitions for complete dominance and for Spell-Out domains:[11]

(35) **Complete Dominance:** A node X completely dominates a node Y iff (a) X is the only mother of Y, or (b) X completely dominates every mother

---

[11] A different definition for complete dominance is offered by Wilder (1999).

of *Y*. The set of nodes completely dominated by *X* will be called the *Complete Dominance Domain* of *X*, written $CDD(X)$.

(36) **Spell-Out Domain (Revised):** The Spell-Out domain of a node *X* is $CDD(X)$.

(37) **Phase Node (replaces Phase Head):** A designated syntactic object that triggers Spell-Out of its Spell-Out domain.[12]

(38) **Spell-Out (Repeated from (33)):** A syntactic structure transferred to the interfaces is mapped onto an object that cannot be modified by further operations. In the case of the phonological interface, the resulting immutable object is a string.

The new definitions have the immediate result of making Spell-Out a cyclic operation. Going back to the schematized *wh*-movement example in (34), notice first that we now have *X* as a phase node instead of *Z* as a phase head. This is a minor modification. The significant change is that under the new definition, *Y* is not completely dominated by *X*: *X* is not the only mother of *Y*, since *Q* is also a mother of *Y*; furthermore, *X* does not dominate every mother of *Y*, since *X* does not dominate itself. Consequently, *Y* is not in $CDD(X)$, and when *X* is spelled out, *Y* will not be affected. More generally, our new definition exempts remerged specifiers, but not uniquely merged specifiers, from Spell-Out by their mothers.[13] Notice that as soon as we merge a new object as a sister of *X* in (34), *Y* becomes completely dominated by the new root:

(39)

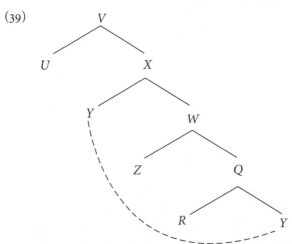

If *V* is a phase node, *Y* will now be subject to Spell-Out.

----

[12] For the purposes of this chapter we will assume that *v*P and CP are the only relevant phases.

[13] This raises several questions with respect to the interaction of Spell-Out and predicate-internal subjects. We will have to assume that subjects are first merged at a position that is higher than any *v*P/VP-internal phase node, though we will have nothing to say about what that position is.

11.4.2.4 *Successive Cyclic Movement*   Consider the following case of long-distance *wh*-movement:

(40) $[_{CP_2}$ What$_i$ did Mary$[_{vP_2}$ t_i say$[_{CP_1}$ t_i that John $[_{vP_1} t_i$ $[_{VP}$ ate $t_i?]]]]]$

What is initially merged as the object of the embedded verb *ate*. At this point it is completely dominated by the verb phrase, but since VP is not a phase, this has no Spell-Out effect. The first phase is the embedded vP_1, and *what* is remerged at its daughter, triggering Spell-Out. As described above, a remerged daughter is not completely dominated by its mother and is therefore not part of its Spell-Out domain. Consequently, *what* is not spelled out by vP_1. We will discuss the results of Spell-Out in more detail below. For our immediate purposes we only need the part of (38) that says that Spell-Out creates a string that cannot be altered later on. In the current case, the string will consist of *ate* alone. At the next few merges, *what* is again completely dominated, but since the next phase has not yet been reached, no Spell-Out takes place. The next phase is the embedded CP_1. Here again *what* is merged as a specifier, allowing it to escape Spell-Out, which now results in the string *that John ate*. Similar application of Remerge and Spell-Out happens in the matrix vP_2 and CP_2.

Notice that by our definitions *what* is not completely dominated at the root level. A potential concern at this point is that *what* will never be spelled out. A possible explanation is that the whole sentence is the daughter of a higher root node, which triggers one final Spell-Out. In that case, since *what* is now completely dominated, it will be spelled out. An alternative is to say that while not being completely dominated allows an element to escape Spell-Out, it does not force it to do so. We do not have data that would suggest which option is correct.[14]

We can also now block successive cyclic movement when an intermediate position is occupied. Consider the following ill-formed sentence:

(41)   * $[_{CP_2}$ What$_i$ did John $[_{vP_2} t_i$ know a man $[_{CP_1}$ who $[_{vP_1} t_i$ ate $t_i?]]]]$

As before, *what* is initially merged as the sister of *ate*, and escapes the first Spell-Out, at the embedded vP_1, by being remerged at its specifier. At the second phase, however, *who* is merged as the first specifier of CP_1, triggering Spell-Out. The phase node CP_1 completely dominates all the mothers of *what*, and so by our definitions it completely dominates *what*. This, in turn, means

---

[14] Similar considerations arise in the framework of Chomsky (2001, 2004*a*).

that *what* is part of the Spell-Out domain of CP₁. Spell-Out of CP₁ results in the string *who what ate*. Since strings are immutable (33), no subsequent operation will be able to extract *what* from its current position and cause it to appear in the position required for (41). Notice that we do not need any constraint on the number of possible specifiers in order to derive the blocking of *what* by *who*. All we require is the general restriction to binary branching, which makes it impossible for the two *wh*-words to be daughters of the same phase node. This ensures that the phase node that is the mother of *who* will completely dominate *what*.[15]

11.4.2.5 *Application to RNR*   Our derivation of long-distance *wh*-movement in the examples above involved successive cyclic movement. In a way, though, this was an accident. All that was needed for long-distance dislocation to work was that the *wh*-element remain only partially dominated during each of the intermediate phases. Successive Remerge into phase specifiers was one way to do that, but our analysis predicts that any other operation that prevents the *wh*-element from being completely dominated at Spell-Out would license the same kind of long-distance result. RNR allows us to test this prediction. Recall our multiple-dominance structure for RNR:

(42)

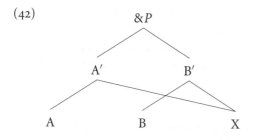

The first step in generating the structure in (42) is an application of Parallel Merge that combines *X* with *A* to form *A′* and with *B* to form *B′*. At this point, *X* is not completely dominated by anything in the structure. This means that even if *A′* or *B′* are phases, *X* will not be spelled out. The first occasion on which *X* becomes completely dominated is when *A′* and *B′* combine to form &*P*. If &*P* is not a phase, and if it has a specifier position, *X* can be remerged above both conjuncts:

---

[15] A question that arises at this point is how multiple *wh*-movement can be accounted for. We just saw that in our system at most one constituent can escape Spell-Out. This makes the prediction that if two (or more) *wh*-elements are to move outside of an embedded clause, they must first cluster together to form one constituent. Discussing the implications of this prediction for instances of long-distance multiple *wh*-movement lies outside the scope of this chapter.

(43)

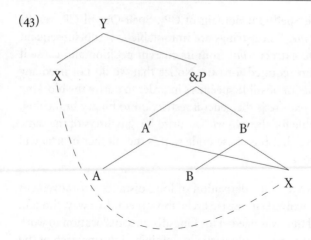

Crucially, Spell-Out inside the conjuncts cannot freeze X. We therefore expect islands below the conjunction to be transparent for extraction from RNR. As we have seen above, this is indeed the case:

(44) **Which book**$_i$ did [John meet the man who wrote ___], and [Mary meet the man who published ___] t_i?

Consider now the effect of islands above conjunction. X in (42) is completely dominated by $\&P$. At the next phase, X will be spelled out unless it is remerged as a daughter of that phase node. The same will apply for every subsequent phase. If X cannot be remerged to one of these phase nodes, it cannot be extracted further. Above conjunction, then, we expect island effects to reappear. Again, this prediction is confirmed:

(45) a.   **Which book**$_i$ did John say that he met [the man who wrote ___], and [the woman who published ___] t_i?

  b. * **Which book**$_i$ does John know a reporter who made famous [a man who published ___], and [a woman who published ___] t_i?

11.4.2.6 *Interim Summary*   We have seen that the combination of cyclic Spell-Out and Remerge, under their current formulations in the literature, gives rise to certain difficulties. Remerge allows multiple occurrences for a single object, requiring special care in the discussion of what gets pronounced where. Successive cyclic movement requires a counter-cyclic Spell-Out operation. We solved these problems by making cyclic Spell-Out sensitive to the notion of complete dominance we have defined.

By our new definition a multiply merged object is not completely dominated by any of its mothers, which makes remerged specifiers available for subsequent operations. This obviated the need for a counter-cyclic definition of Spell-Out. The task of specifying where an object is spelled out was relegated to the phonological interface: Strings can be concatenated but not internally changed, so once two objects are spelled out next to each other, they cannot be reordered or separated by future Spell-Out operations. The choice of occurrence is a by-product of this interface condition, the definition of multiple dominance, and the timing of Spell-Out. One further factor in determining where an object is pronounced is the linearization component, described in detail in the next section.

Finally, and most importantly, we saw how our definitions predict that multiply dominated elements will be available for Remerge even in the absence of movement-like operations. We noticed that this is exactly the pattern of interaction between RNR and *wh*-movement observed in Section 11.3. Missing at this point is the specification of ordering within any particular phase. This will require a more detailed discussion of the linearization of syntactic structures, to which we now turn.

11.4.3 *Linearization*

Linearizing two objects, A and B, with respect to each other is often implemented by requiring every element in A to be ordered in a certain way with respect to each element in B. The ordering of choice is usually strict precedence (Kayne 1994; Chomsky 2004a), written here as $<$:

(46)   *Strict Linearization*
     If A is linearized before B then $\forall a \in A.\forall b \in B.a < b$

Multiple dominance poses an immediate problem for this definition. If A and B share an element X, ordering A before B will result in X being ordered strictly before itself. This predicts, for example, that any instance of *wh*-movement will give rise to a linearization contradiction, as in (47). A similar problem arises with respect to RNR, as in (48).

(47)   a.   **What**$_i$ did John eat **What**$_i$
     b.   **What** $\not<$ **What**

(48)   a.   [John bought ___] and [Mary sold ___] **books about bats.**
     b.   **books about bats** $\not<$ **books about bats**

To resolve the linearization conflict in (47), standard solution is to state that when one position of a remerged element c-commands another position of the same element, the two positions are exempt from (46) with respect to each other. While this kind of solution does not solve the problem of multiple dominance of the Parallel Merge type, as in (48), it can be extended to such cases by requiring an additional movement (or Remerge) of the shared material to a position c-commanding both *A* and *B*. If only the highest occurrence is taken into account for linearization, as assumed by Nunes (2004) and Citko (2005), no contradiction arises. As we have seen, however, there are many reasons to reject a movement analysis for RNR.

A way to reconcile (46) with multiple dominance while maintaining an *in situ* approach to RNR has been developed by Wilder (1999), who proposes to exempt from the linearization of *A* any element not completely dominated by *A*.[16] We will not be able to discuss Wilder's proposal in any detail in this chapter. The proposal predicts correctly many of the properties of RNR; as noticed by Sabbagh (2007), however, it also makes the incorrect prediction that the RN can sometimes be non-rightmost within its conjunct.[17] In particular, the following is predicted to be grammatical:

(49)   * [A man who loves ___ sang a song], and [a woman who hates ___ read a book] **the new headmaster.**

The ungrammaticality of (49) suggests that excluding elements from linearization is incorrect, and that the well-formedness of the ordering of *A* and *B* depends on all the elements within them, including elements that are not completely dominated.

11.4.3.1 *Reflexive Linearization*   We believe that the incompatibility of multiple dominance and (46) is fundamental. Rather than trying to find a better method to exempt elements from linearization, either in the configuration of Internal Merge or in that of Parallel Merge, we propose to weaken the linearization principle itself. As we will see, the resulting system will capture both kinds of configurations, as well as their interaction. Informally speaking, we will replace the total ordering requirement in (46) with a condition on the edges of the linearized objects only, and we will avoid the ordering violation in (47) and (48) by replacing the irreflexive $<$ in (46) with its reflexive version $\leq$:

(50)   a.   **What**$_i$ did John eat **What**$_i$

        b.   **What** $\leq$ **What**

(51)   a.   [John bought ___] and [Mary sold ___] **books about bats.**

        b.   **books about bats** $\leq$ **books about bats**

---

[16] Wilder's definitions are different from ours, but the difference does not affect the current point.
[17] We will have more to say about the linear conditions in RNR shortly.

More formally, we separate linearization into two well-formedness conditions. The first condition concerns the well-formedness of linearization within each node. We represent the information about linearizing a node X by associating X with a list of nodes, $<x_1, \ldots, x_n>$, which we refer to as the *D-list* of X. The list contains all the terminal nodes that X dominates and nothing more. The possible D-lists of a node are determined compositionally by the D-lists of its daughters: If X is a terminal node, and its lexical content is x, the D-list of X is $<x>$; if X has daughters, the D-list of X is determined by a function that maps positions on the D-list of the daughter nodes of X onto positions in the D-list of X. Below we will see the details of how D-lists are constructed in several simple cases. Multiple occurrences of a single terminal node are allowed, but only for nodes that are not completely dominated by X, using the same notion of complete dominance as before (35). We define the condition as follows:

(52)   *Linearization Well-Formedness Condition*

   a.   The D-list for a node X has all the terminals dominated by X as members, and only them.

   b.   If $y \in CDD(X)$ then y appears on the D-list of X exactly once.[18]

While (52) allows multiple occurrences of elements that are not completely dominated, the availability of such multiple occurrences will be limited. The reason is that, as mentioned above, the D-lists for non-terminal nodes are the image of a function from the positions on the D-lists of the daughter nodes. This means that every occurrence of an element on the D-list of a mother has to have at least one corresponding position on some daughter D-list.

   The mapping from the D-lists of the daughters to the D-list of the mother is further constrained by the weakened linearization condition hinted at above. The first half of the condition (53a) involves the replacement of the universal condition with two existential ones, and the replacement of the strict $<$ with the reflexive $\leq$: It requires that the left edge of the left daughter reflexively precede the left edge of the right daughter, and that the right edge of the left daughter reflexively precede the right edge of the right daughter. The second half of the condition (53b) is more standard. It requires that the elements of the D-list of a daughter node stay in their original order when mapped onto the D-list of a mother node.[19]

---

[18]   We use (52b) to ensure that the D-list for X induces a linear ordering on $CDD(X)$.

[19]   Under its present formulation, (53) makes it difficult to get rid of multiple occurrences of material that is not completely dominated. Once a D-list is formed with two non-adjacent occurrences of the same element α, conservativity (53b) will prevent them from being mapped onto a D-list with only one occurrence of α. As soon as complete dominance is reached, such a D-list will be ruled out by (52b).

(53)   *Linearization Mapping Condition*
In ordering $A = <a_1, \ldots, a_m>$ to the left of $B = <b_1, \ldots, b_n>$, written
$A \bullet B$, the following must hold:

   a.   *Edge Alignment:* $a_1 \leq b_1$ and $a_m \leq b_n$

   b.   *Conservativity:* $a_1 \leq a_2 \leq \ldots \leq a_m$ and $b_1 \leq b_2 \leq \ldots \leq b_n$

Before discussing the predictions of these linearization conditions for multiple-dominance structures such as *wh*-movement and RNR, it will be helpful to observe their consequences for structures that do not involve multiple dominance. First, notice that linearization is unambiguous for atomic objects. If A consists of a single element a, and if B consists of a single element b, the only way to order A before B is by mapping them to an object where a precedes b:

(54)   Linearizing atomic objects: $< a > \bullet < b > \Rightarrow < a, b >$

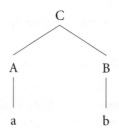

The ordering of a before b satisfies Edge Alignment: the left edge of A is a, and it is linearized to the left of b, the left edge of B; similarly, the right edge of A is a, and it is linearized to the left of b, the right edge of B. Ordering a to the right of b would have violated Edge Alignment. Conservativity is trivially satisfied in our example: A and B are atomic, and so nothing can change in their internal ordering. The two conditions of (52) are similarly satisfied: The D-list for each node contains exactly the terminals dominated by it—A linearizes a, B linearizes b, and C linearizes a and b—and every element that appears in a D-list appears there exactly once. Consequently, every D-list induces a linear order over its elements. Condition (52) would rule out a configuration where A and B above are mapped onto C with anything other than one occurrence of a and of b. For example, the D-list $< a, b, c >$ is excluded since it includes terminals not dominated by C, and the D-list $< a, a, b >$ is excluded since it has two occurrences of $a \in CDD(C)$.

This problem will get in our way in derivations such as (61) below, and we will then suggest a slight modification to (53) that will make such derivations possible.

If *A* and *B* are not atomic, more mappings are possible. Consider, for example, the following linearization configuration:

(55)   Linearizing complex objects:

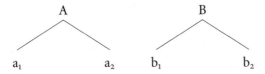

As in the case of atomic objects, concatenating the contents of *A* to the left of the contents of *B* is possible. The edges of the two daughters are aligned correctly, the internal ordering within each daughter is preserved, and all the relevant linearization relations are linear orderings:

(56)   √ Concatenation: $< a_1, a_2, b_1, b_2 >$

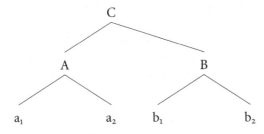

Next, notice that the linearization conditions rule out wrapping of the elements of one daughter around the elements of its sister. Such a configuration would violate Edge Alignment:

(57)   * Wrapping: $< a_1, b_1, b_2, a_2 >$

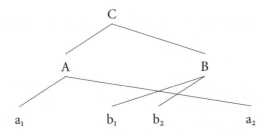

Finally, our conditions make possible the interleaving of the elements of *A* with those of *B* as long as the edges are aligned correctly:

(58)   √ Interleaving: $< a_1, b_1, a_2, b_2 >$

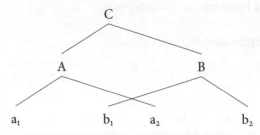

This last point might be seen as a cause for concern. After all, interleaving is not normally considered a possible outcome of combining two syntactic objects. Notice, however, that we use our linearization conditions in a system that includes a cyclic Spell-Out mechanism. Under normal conditions, by the time two complex objects are merged together, at least one of them has already undergone Spell-Out. Assume, for example, that A in (58) above has been spelled out before the merger of A with B. Recall that the output of Spell-Out is a string, in this case "a_1a_2," which is an immutable object. While interleaving in the syntax is licensed, the output of the next Spell-Out will contain the substring "$a_1b_1a_2b_2$." This result cannot be obtained without modifying the previous output, "a_1a_2," and the attempt to modify an immutable object will crash the derivation.[20]

11.4.3.2 *Linearizing Multiple-Dominance Structures*   We have seen how our linearization conditions (53) and (52) account for the possible linear orderings of disjoint objects. The motivation behind our change from $<$ to $\leq$, however, came from multiple-dominance structures, of both the Internal Merge and the Parallel Merge kinds. We are now in a position to test the predictions of the new definitions for these cases. We start by looking at *wh*-movement.

Simple *wh*-movement will have the following schematic form, where multiply dominated material is written within parentheses:

---

[20] In addition to categories such as *v*P and CP, which are treated here as designated Spell-Out nodes, one may want to consider various configurational notions of Spell-Out. Danny Fox (p.c.) suggests a condition that forces Spell-Out whenever multiple linearizations would otherwise arise. Alternatively, complex specifiers and adjuncts can be thought of as configurational Spell-Out domains. A proposal along different lines, suggested to us by Adam Albright (p.c.), is to embed the linearization within a competition framework, where interleaving is usually ruled out by markedness. We leave the investigation of these directions for future work.

(59) $< wh > \bullet < a, wh > \Rightarrow < (wh), a, (wh) >$

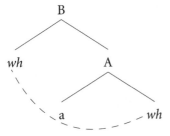

The D-list of B is $< wh, a, wh >$, which contains two occurrences of *wh*. We need to show that both of the linearization conditions, (52) and (53), are satisfied. The reason that *wh* can occur twice in the D-list for B without violating (52) is that *wh* is not completely dominated by B: It has been remerged as the daughter of B, which means that B is not the only mother of *wh* and that it does not completely dominate every mother of *wh*. Consequently, by definition (35), *wh* is not completely dominated by B. $CDD(B) = \{a\}$, and a has only one occurrence in the D-list, satisfying (52). As to (53), since we are linearizing $X =< wh >$ to the left of $Y =< a, wh >$, we need to check two things:

(60)   a. $\leq$ holds between the left edge of X and the left edge of Y, as well as between the right edge of X and the right edge of Y.

    b.   Conservativity holds.

$X =< wh >$ is atomic, which means that its two edges are identical. In this case, both are mapped onto the leftmost position in $< wh, a, wh >$, the D-list for B, and that position is to the left of where the edges of $Y =< a, wh >$ are mapped to. With respect to conservativity, since X is atomic we only need to check Y. By mapping $Y =< a, wh >$ onto the two rightmost positions of $< wh, a, wh >$, the D-list for B, we preserve the original ordering within Y. Notice that the appearance of *wh* in both positions in $< wh, a, wh >$ was crucial for (53): The leftmost position made possible the satisfaction of edge alignment with respect to the left edge of Y, and the rightmost position made possible the satisfaction of conservativity in Y. The appearance of *wh* in two positions, in turn, was made possible by the fact that it was not completely dominated by B: If it were completely dominated, (52) would be violated. Summing up, remerging an element in a c-commanding position allows reorganization of linear order by making the remerged element only partially dominated.

Consider now the next step in the derivation of long-distance *wh*-movement from (59). A new element, *c*, is merged to *B* in (59) to form *C*:

(61)

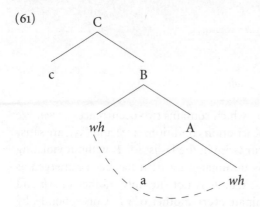

Since *C* completely dominates *wh*, the D-list < *c*, *wh*, *a*, *wh* >, in which *wh* occurs twice, is ruled out by (52b). As alluded to in *n.* 19 above, we will need to modify (53) in a way that would allow us to choose one occurrence of *wh* before it becomes completely dominated. The modification we propose is that the domain of the mapping in (53) can be somewhat smaller than all the positions on all the D-lists of the daughters. If some element α appears in more than one position on the same D-list, the mapping can ignore one or more of those positions, as long as at least one position of α is taken into account. Once we relax our definition in this way, two other D-lists become possible based on (53) and (52): < *c*, *wh*, *a* > and < *c*, *a*, *wh* >. In English, the former option is chosen.

Let us now turn to the linearization of multiple-dominance structures of the Parallel Merge kind. We start by looking at some empirical facts. RNR has been known to be subject to a strict constraint concerning the position of the RN. We model our characterization after Sabbagh (2007):

(62)   *Right-Edge Restriction (RER)*

    a.   The RN or a gap associated with it must be rightmost within each conjunct.

    b.   The RN cannot surface in a non-rightmost conjunct.

The RER covers judgements such as the following:

(63)   * John should [give ___ the book] and [congratulate ___] **that girl**

                                                   (Wilder 1999: 595 (34d))

(64) a. * [Joss will donate ___ to the library today ___], and [Maria will donate **several old novels** to the library tomorrow]

(Sabbagh 2007: 47 (87))

b. [Joss will donate ___ to the library today ___], and [Maria will donate ___ to the library tomorrow ___] **several old novels.**

In (64a), the RN *several old novels* appears before *to the library tomorrow*, which can only be interpreted inside the second conjunct. The RER is violated, and the result is ungrammatical. When *several old novels* is made rightmost within the second conjunct (64b), the result is grammatical.[21]

Let us now see how our linearization conditions capture the RER. We start with simple RNR, marking with parentheses any element on the D-list of X that is not in $CDD(X)$:

(65) $< a, (x) > \bullet < b, (x) > \Rightarrow < a, b, x >$

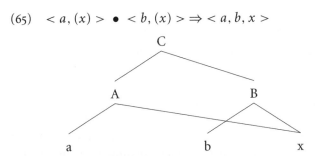

The correct linearization of the mother node, $< a, b, x >$ is the only one licensed by the linearization conditions. The left edge of A is a, and it is linearized to the left of b, the left edge of B. Similarly, the right edge of A is x, which is linearized to the (reflexive) left of x, the right edge of B. Notice that here, for the first time, reflexivity makes a difference. Conservativity is satisfied by the ordering $< a, b, x >$ since each of the internal orderings $< a, x >$ and $< b, x >$ is maintained. Conservativity would have ruled out the ordering $< a, x, b >$ since the original ordering of x to the right of b is not preserved. Finally, condition (52) rules out the potential ordering $< a, x, b, x >$, which includes two occurrences of $x \in CDD(C)$.[22]

Turning to more complex RNR configurations, we can see why RER violations are ungrammatical. The examples in (66) show an attempt to linearize $A =< a, x, a' >$ to the left of $B =< b, x >$:

---

[21] The RN is made rightmost through Heavy-NP Shift, an account of which falls outside the scope of the current chapter.

[22] Example (69) extends naturally to account for more complex cases, where each conjunct can contain more than one terminal before the RN. As long as the first conjunct is a Spell-Out domain, no interleaving will take place.

(66)   a.

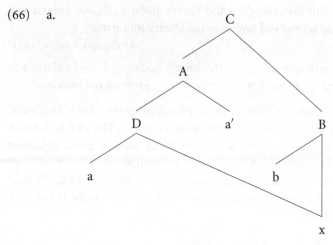

b. $< a, (x), a' > \bullet < b, (x) > \nRightarrow < a, x, a', b, x >$

c. $< a, (x), a' > \bullet < b, (x) > \nRightarrow < a, a', b, x >$

d. $< a, (x), a' > \bullet < b, (x) > \nRightarrow < a, x, a', b >$

By (52), x may only appear once in the result, as in the case of simple RNR, ruling out (66b). In the D-list for A, x occurs to the left of a'. Consequently, using Conservativity, the occurrence of x in the D-list for C must be to the left of a', ruling out (66c). At the same time, Edge Alignment requires that x be linearized to the right of a', ruling out (66d). No other ordering can rescue this structure, and so we correctly predict it to be bad.

The same reasoning does not apply to RER violations within the right conjunct:

(67) $< a, x > \bullet < b, x, b' > \nRightarrow < a, b, x, b' >$

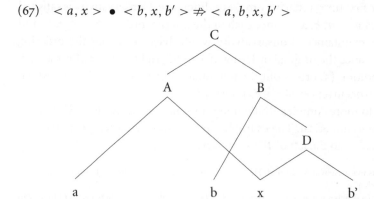

Edge Alignment is satisfied by (67): a is linearized before b, and x is linearized before b'. Similarly, Conservativity is satisfied, since no internal ordering is changed. Finally, all three D-lists, $< a, x >$, $< b, x, b' >$, and $< a, b, x, b' >$, are linear orderings. But in fact orderings like (67) are bad:

(68)   * [John congratulated ___] and [Mary gave **the winner** the prize].

Our explanation for the ungrammaticality of (68) is based on Spell-Out, and follows the explanation for the ungrammaticality of most interleaving configurations. Each conjunct within (68) is a clause, which under standard assumptions means it will undergo Spell-Out before conjunction takes place. At that point, the shared material is not completely dominated within either conjunct. Consequently, it is not spelled out: The left conjunct maps onto the string *John congratulated*, and the right conjunct maps onto *Mary gave the prize*. While the ordering of (68) according to the schema in (67) is licensed by the syntax, the next Spell-Out will attempt to modify the string of the right conjunct to insert *the winner* between *gave* and *the prize*. Since strings cannot be modified, the derivation crashes.[23]

The timing of the change between complete and partial dominance is an important difference between *wh*-movement and RNR. In *wh*-movement the remerged material is not completely dominated at the relevant point in the derivation, allowing reorganization of overt material. In RNR, the remerged material was not completely dominated within each conjunct, but it becomes completely dominated once the two conjuncts are merged together. Consequently, the shared material must satisfy (52) and appear only once:

(69) $< a, (x) > \bullet < b, (x) > \Rightarrow < a, b, x >$

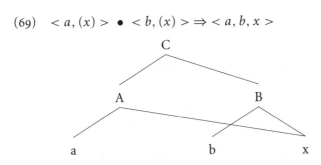

Since the shared material may have only one occurrence in the linearization of conjunction, Conservativity has a restrictive effect, ruling out reorderings:

---

[23] The fact that (67) crashed at Spell-Out and not because of linearization means that if we prevented the shared material from being spelled out in its conjunct-internal position, the structure could be rescued. We believe this to be the case and discuss it elsewhere.

(70) $< a, (x), a' > \bullet < b, (x) > \nRightarrow < a, a', b, x >$

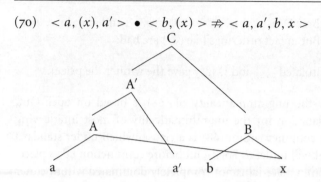

11.4.3.3 *Putting It All Together*   We conclude this section by showing the linearization steps involved in *wh*-movement from within RNR:

(71)   **Which book**ᵢ did [John meet the man who wrote ___], and [Mary meet the man who published ___] t_i?

We start at the point in the derivation where both conjuncts have been formed but before conjunction has taken place. The shared material *which book* is linearized at the right within each conjunct. It is not yet completely dominated at this point, hence the parentheses:

(72) TP_1 <John, meet, the man who wrote, (which book)> ,
       TP_2 <Mary, meet, the man who published, (which book)>

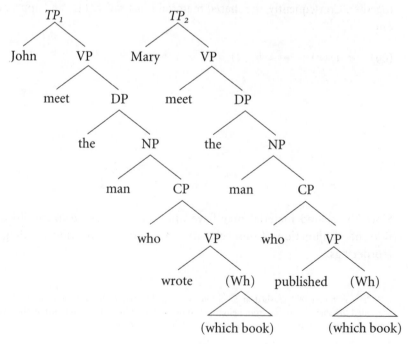

At the next step, the conjuncts are merged together to form TP_3 (or perhaps $\&P$ if conjunction projects a phrase; we will not try to settle this matter here, and we also leave out the terminal $\&$ in the current examples). The shared material is now completely dominated by TP_3 (or $\&P$). As discussed above, the D-list of TP_3 may only include one occurrence of *which book*. Conservativity requires that this instance be on the right:[24]

(73) $TP_1 \bullet TP_2 \Rightarrow$
       TP_3 <John, meet, the man who wrote, Mary, meet, the man who pub-
       lished, which book>

---

[24] Our claim has been that derivations such as the current one, where an element is extracted across conjunct-internal islands, must involve an RNR configuration. We argued, on the basis of cases like (17) above, that when an RER violation makes an RNR configuration impossible, extraction is ungrammatical. As pointed out to us independently by Klaus Abels and Danny Fox, our system currently does not predict this dependence on RNR. In the current derivation, for example, there is nothing to prevent the *wh*-element from being remerged on the left edge of each conjunct, as in standard ATB movement, resulting in the following D-lists: <(which book), John, meet, the man who wrote, (which book)> for TP_1, and <(which book), Mary, meet, the man who published, (which book)> for TP_2. This, in turn, will make it possible to combine the two conjuncts via a form of *Left*-Node Raising (LNR), regardless of the original position of the RN inside each conjunct. If LNR can allow us to extract across islands regardless of linearization, our system is in trouble. We acknowledge the problem, of course, but we think that there is an asymmetry between the RNR-based extraction and the LNR-based extraction that has the potential of explaining why only the former can be used to obviate islands. In RNR, the RN starts its way as being incompletely dominated inside each conjunct. When conjunction is formed, the RN becomes completely dominated. For *wh*-movement, the first time in which the RN must be remerged is after it has already been completely dominated by conjunction. By being remerged it changes its status once again. Each time the RN is remerged, then, results in a change of either dominance or complete dominance. In LNR, the RN also starts its way as being incompletely dominated, but then it must be remerged conjunct-internally, in a way that changes neither dominance relations nor complete dominance relations. If we require that every operation of Merge must change either dominance or complete dominance, shared material will no longer be allowed to remerge conjunct-internally. While restoring order to the domain of extraction across islands, such an economy condition seems to prohibit any form of ATB movement from non-edge positions. This, we suggest, can be solved once the relativization of complete dominance to workspaces is made more explicit. In RNR, each conjunct must be aware of the other conjunct for purposes of complete dominance. In our current derivation, for example, it is only by taking into account the use of the RN in TP_2 that TP_1 can exempt it from complete dominance and consequently from Spell-Out. Awareness of other workspaces (under currently ill-understood conditions) is what allows RNR to happen. But there is no reason to think that awareness of other workspaces is always required. If it is possible to choose not to see other workspaces, the RN will be considered completely dominated within each conjunct. This will mean that conjunct-internal Spell-Out will trap the RN inside the conjunct, but it will also mean that the economy condition on Merge, suggested above, will not block the RN from being remerged conjunct-internally. The RN will start its way as being completely dominated inside each conjunct. By being remerged in a conjunct-internal c-commanding position, the RN will become incompletely dominated inside that conjunct. This, we suggest, can be the explanation for simple ATB movement from non-edge positions. Exploring the implications of this condition in any detail is beyond the scope of the current chapter.

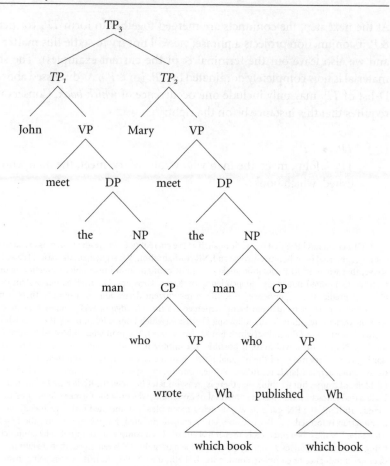

TP_3 is not a phase, and consequently *which book* is not yet spelled out. The next phase is the root CP, the result of remerging *which book* with TP_3. Spell-Out takes place, but since *which book* is not completely dominated by CP, it is not spelled out, and can feed subsequent operations:

(74)   *Wh* • TP_3 ⇒
        CP <(which book), John, meet, the man who wrote, Mary, meet, the man who published, (which book)>

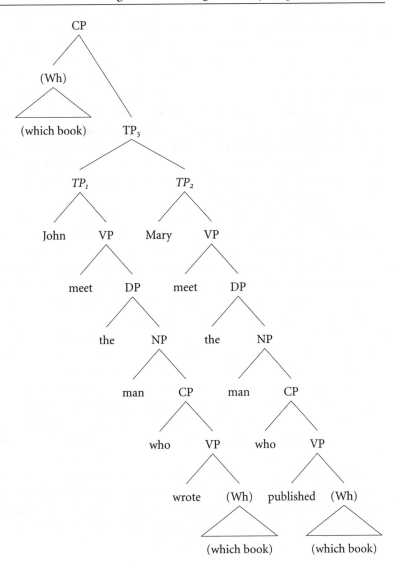

11.5 Conclusion

In this chapter we explored the consequences of reformulating movement as a special case of syntactic sharing, or Remerge, thus making it more similar to another case of sharing, namely RNR. Since in this framework there is no primitive movement operation, all known features of dislocation phenomena must follow from more general principles. In particular, the grammar cannot make reference to traces or copies, and locality cannot be defined via constraints on movement operations. In agreement with the general guidelines of the Minimalist Program, we turned to the interfaces, and in particular to the cyclic operation of Spell-Out of the syntactic structure, as the locus of explanation. We proposed that the major import of syntactic sharing is in altering the (complete) dominance relations within the syntactic object. (In)complete Dominance, in turn, plays an important role both in the definition of the Spell-Out domain of phases and in the well-formedness of the linearization list of each node in the structure.

The double role of (in)complete dominance gives rise to two independent effects which are usually difficult to distinguish in movement phenomena but which are dissociated in RNR. Incompletely dominated objects are not part of the Spell-Out of a phase. Consequently, these objects are not frozen and remain available for manipulation in consequent stages of the derivation. This freedom underlies cyclic *wh*-movement but is also found in RNR, where it explains the possibility of the RN surfacing separately from the material in all non-final conjuncts, giving rise to the appearance of rightward dislocation but without requiring a high attachment site for the RN. The same freedom also enables the RN to be available for further operations, such as *wh*-movement, regardless of any conjunct-internal Spell-Out. The other effect of incomplete dominance is in permitting the same object to appear twice in the D-list of a single node. This is the only source for reordering within the D-list, and it arises only in a restricted set of configurations, when an object is also dominated by its sister. In other words, reordering is possible only in a configuration that corresponds to movement to a c-commanding position. Only in such cases will the linearization list of the mother contain two incompletely dominated instances of the same object. This explains why only cases of Remerge at a c-commanding position allow for reordering, while other cases of syntactic sharing such as RNR do not.

12

The Ellipsis Movement Generalization and the Notion of Phase*

MASANORI NAKAMURA

12.1 Introduction

The notion of phase plays an integral part in the current version of the minimalist approach. It has been proposed that derivations proceed phase by phase, handing a specified portion of syntactic structure over to the phonological component as soon as a phase is fully constructed (Chomsky 2000, 2001, 2008; see also Fox & Pesetsky 2005 for relevant discussion).[1] The adoption of phase enables us to build a theory of grammar whereby the derivational system of human language attends only to a limited part of structure at one time, severely lessening the computational burden.

If it is correct to capture derivational cyclicity by the notion of phase or to view it as a result of syntax-phonology interactions, there is a good possibility that pre-minimalist theories have missed some generalizations regarding the impact of phonology on syntax. Building on previous works, this chapter presents one such generalization, dubbed the Ellipsis Movement Generalization (EMG): If a language allows ellipsis of a particular category (e.g. VP

* An earlier version of this contribution has been presented at the *InterPhases* conference (Nicosia, Cyprus, May 2006). My heartfelt thanks go to the organizer of the conference Kleanthes Grohmann, who did his very best to make the occasion extremely stimulating, rewarding, and enjoyable. For their valuable comments and suggestions, I would also like to thank Jason Merchant and an anonymous reviewer for this volume as well as the participants of the conference, especially Hee-Don Ahn, Masaaki Kamiya, Richard Kayne, Howard Lasnik, Máire Noonan, Jairo Nunes, Masayuki Oishi, and Takashi Toyoshima. As always, I alone am responsible for any remaining errors and oversights. This work was supported by a Senshu University Grant for Individual Research for the academic year 2006–7 (Project Title: *Ellipsis and Movement*), for which I am grateful.

[1] The operation Transfer is assumed to map a designated syntactic object not only to the phonological component but also to the semantic component (Chomsky 2001, 2008). Given the topic of this chapter, I focus primarily on the mapping to the former.

in English) in a certain structure, that category cannot undergo movement except when it is phonologically null. It is proposed that the generalization can be explained by a modified characterization of phase.

The basic layout of this chapter is as follows. In Section 12.2, I touch upon McCloskey's (2004) observation regarding the behavior of *v*P in Irish and his account of it. Specifically, he observes that Irish *v*P can undergo ellipsis and that it exhibits equivocal behavior with respect to movement: It cannot be moved if it has phonological content, but it can if it is a null operator. With McCloskey's observation as a background, in Section 12.3, I proceed to discussion of some pertinent data from English and Japanese. It is shown that VP and (finite) IP in English and a certain kind of CP in Japanese conform to the EMG. It is also shown that McCloskey's original analysis of *v*P in Irish does not extend to the English and Japanese cases. Section 12.4 presents a phase-based alternative analysis, which makes crucial use of Holmberg's (2001) analysis of ellipsis as non-pronunciation of material transferred to the phonological component. I argue that it offers a unified account of the EMG. Section 12.5 consists of a summary and implications of the analysis put forth here.

12.2 McCloskey's Observation: Irish

Irish finite clauses have the rigid word order of VSO, as in (1) (taken from McCloskey 2004).

(1) Sciob   an cat an t-eireaball den luch.
     snatched the cat the tail   from-the mouse
     'The cat cut the tail off the mouse.'

Under the widely accepted analysis of Irish clausal architecture (McCloskey 1991, 1996), verbs must raise out of VP to I and subjects stay where they are generated—in Spec of *v*P in current terms. The rough structure of (2) is as follows:

(2)

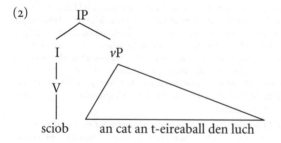

Observe the following examples of ellipsis, uttered in response to (1) (McCloskey 1991, 2004):[2]

(3) a. Ar   sciob?
         INTERR-PAST snatched
         'Did it?'

     b. Creidim gur   sciob.
         I-believe C-PAST snatched
         'I believe it did.'

In (3a) the confirmation question is formed by repeating the finite verb, with the interrogative particle attached to it. The rest of the structure, including the subject, has been deleted. In (3b) only the verb follows the complementizer *gur*. Then what has been elided in both cases must be *v*P. It cannot be IP, because the verb in I survives the ellipsis. It cannot be VP, either, because the *in-situ* subject is included in the elided domain.

McCloskey (2004) makes the interesting observation that although *v*P cannot be overtly moved, the same category can undergo movement if it is phonologically null.[3] Consider (4) (McCloskey 2002: 189).

(4) Teach beag a   cheannaigh muid.
     house little aL bought   we
     'It was a little house that we bought.'

(4) exemplifies clefting in Irish. There the noun phrase *teach beag* 'little house' has been extracted into Spec of CP, which results in the appearance of the morpheme *aL*, the morphosyntactic signature of *wh*-movement in Irish (see McCloskey 2002 among others). Turning now to *v*P, the following example of clefting shows that it cannot be extracted in the same way:

(5) * [$_{vP}$ An cat an t-eireaball den luch]   a   sciob t_{vP}.
         the cat the tail   from-the mouse aL snatched
         'It was the cat cutting the tail off the mouse that happened.'

In (5) the *v*P has undergone syntactic movement to the sentence-initial position. The movement is illegitimate, even though it has not crossed any island.

---

[2] The following abbreviations are used here:

ACC-accusative	C-complementizer	COND-conditional	COP-copula
DAT-dative	INTERR-interrogative	NEG-negative	NOM-nominative
Q-question particle	TOP-topic		

[3] A terminological note is in order. Throughout this chapter, a distinction is made between overt and covert movement in terms of the phonological content of moved categories, not in terms of the level at which movement takes place (i.e. pre-Spell-Out vs post-Spell-Out movement).

Based on Potts's (2002*a*, 2002*b*) work on *as*-parentheticals in English, McCloskey (2004) shows that Irish does have a null *v*P used in *mar*-parentheticals. Compare (6) with (7) (McCloskey 2002: 189–90, 2004).

(6)   a.   Céacu ceann a   dhíol tú?
          which one   aL sold you
          'Which one did you sell?'

   b.   an t-ainm a   hinnseadh dúinn a   bhí ar an áit
        the name aL was-told   to-us aL was on the place
        'the name that we were told was on the place'

(7)   Bhí lá galánta ann mar a   thuar   Proinnsíos a
      was day beautiful in-it as aL predicted Proinnsíos aL
      bheadh   *t*$_{v\mathrm{P}}$.
      be(COND)
      'It was a beautiful day, as Proinnsíos had predicted it would be.'

(6a) illustrates the Irish *wh*-interrogative. Notice the presence of the morpheme *aL* providing the indisputable evidence that syntactic movement has occurred. (6b) is an example of relativization. The two instances of *aL* indicate that the *wh*-movement (of an empty element) has taken place in a successive-cyclic fashion. (7) is an example of the Irish counterpart of the English parenthetical *as*-clause. The similarity between (6b) and (7) is obvious. As McCloskey (2004) notes, (7) clearly demonstrates two things. First, it shows that *mar*-parentheticals in Irish are derived by syntactic movement. Notice that the *mar*-clause in (7), just like the relative clause in (6b), contains two instances of *aL*, which proves the existence of successive-cyclic movement. Second, what has been extracted in (7) is the same constituent as is deleted in (3) and moved (without success) in (5), i.e. *v*P.[4] Since (7) involves the movement of a *v*P null operator, only the copular verb *bheadh*, directly inserted into I, appears in the embedded clause. The structure of the subordinate clause in (7) looks like the following:[5]

---

[4] Hence *v*P-ellipsis and *v*P-movement in Irish share an interpretative property in terms of missing subject, due to some semantic compatibility requirement (e.g. Merchant's 2001 notion of e-GIVENess); it must be coreferential with subject in an antecedent clause.

[5] To be precise, the movement in (8), subject to anti-locality (see Abels 2003*a* and also Grohmann 2003), must proceed via the edge of IP (it is suggested later that finite IP counts as a phase in Irish). This kind of complication is suppressed here and in English (26) below, where the movement must go through the edge of *v*P.

(8)   [_{PP} mar [_{CP} *Op* aL [_{IP} V [_{CP} *t′*_{*vP*} aL [_{IP} V *t*_{*vP*}]]]]]

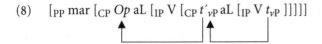

In (8) *mar* is taken to be a preposition selecting a CP, whose Spec hosts the null operator (see Potts 2002*b* for an analysis of its English equivalent *as*). The contrast between (5) and (7) highlights the above-mentioned observation made by McCloskey.

McCloskey (2004) suggests that the ill-formedness of (5), as opposed to the well-formedness of (7), is basically due to the presence of the stranded "copy" of V in the fronted constituent, acting like "a morphological orphan" (in McCloskey's terminology) to be merged with I (cf. Fiengo 1977). (7), on the other hand, is grammatical since the offending "copy" of V is absent (see McCloskey 2004 for details).

The next section shows that McCloskey's observation goes beyond Irish and is part of a more general phenomenon having to do with ellipsis and movement.

12.3 Towards a Generalization

Examining data from English and Japanese, this section argues for the following generalization:

(9)   *The Ellipsis Movement Generalization* (EMG)
        If a certain category can undergo ellipsis, it cannot undergo movement except when it is phonologically null.

(9) recognizes the direct connection between ellipsis and movement, which McCloskey (2004) does not mention.[6] Note that (9) correctly captures McCloskey's observation: In Irish *v*P can undergo ellipsis and cannot undergo movement except when it is a null operator. As we will see, McCloskey's approach to the contrast between (5) and (7) does not extend to the English and Japanese cases.

12.3.1 *English*

Consider the following English example (the elided constituent is indicated by strikethrough):

---

[6] The correlation should go in the opposite direction, too, i.e. if a certain category (such as *v*P in English) can be moved overtly, it cannot be elided. This applies to overt movement, but not to null operator movement.

(10)   John met Mary after Bill did [~~VP~~ ~~meet Mary~~].

(10) involves what has traditionally been called "VP-ellipsis" (see Lobeck 1995; Merchant 2001, 2008*b* among numerous others).

Given the clause structure assumed here (basically that of Chomsky 2000, 2001, 2008), there is a possibility, raised by Howard Lasnik, that what is elided in (10) is not VP but *v*P. Merchant (2008*b*) provides an insight in this regard, presenting an argument for VP ellipsis in examples like (10). His argument is based on the fact that the ellipsis of the relevant sort tolerates mismatches in voice between the elided constituent and its antecedent, as shown in (11) (taken from Kehler 2002):

(11)   a.   This problem was to have been looked into, but obviously nobody did [~~VP~~ ~~look into this problem~~].

      b.   Actually, I have implemented it (=a computer system) with a manager, but it doesn't have to be [~~VP~~ ~~implemented with a manager~~].

In (11a) the deleted constituent is in active voice, whereas its antecedent is in passive voice. In (11b), on the other hand, the ellipsis targets a verbal projection in passive voice, whose antecedent is in active voice. As Merchant (2008*b*) notes, the voice mismatches receive a natural account if we assume that what is elided is indeed VP rather than *v*P: The syntactic identity requirement on ellipsis implies that the elided structure in question must exclude *v*, which is assumed to determine the voice property of the clause.[7]

---

[7] Johnson (2004) claims that what is deleted in data like (10) is slightly larger than VP (the lower segment of *v*P excluding the thematic subject position or Asp(ect)P (see Travis 1991 among others)). One of his arguments is based on (i).

(i)   This can freeze. *Please do.

(i) shows that unaccusative/transitive alternations are not permissible under ellipsis. According to Johnson, a VP ellipsis analysis would leave the ill-formedness of the second sentence in (i) unaccounted for: What is elided would be [~~VP~~ ~~freeze this~~], which is assumed to have a legitimate antecedent in the first sentence and (i) would wrongly be expected to be fine. This account, of course, hinges on the correct analysis of argument structure alternations and I believe that there are real alternatives worth investigating. Even if Johnson's proposal turns out to be the right one, what is crucial for the purpose of this chapter is the thesis that the missing category in examples like (10) and that in "predicate *as*-parentheticals," to which we turn immediately, are of the same category (see *n.* 17 below). It is supported by the fact that the parentheticals behave in the same way as the ellipsis of the relevant kind with respect to transitivity alternations (as well as voice mismatches).

(ii)   *This can freeze, as I always do.

Let us continue to treat the ellipsis as targeting VP, with Johnson's suggestion in the back of our mind (see also *n.* 10).

Merchant (2008*b*) mentions that in contrast to VP ellipsis, pseudogapping (Jayaseelan 1990, Lasnik 1999*b*, among others) does not tolerate voice mismatches (but see his note 3), claiming that it is an

If the EMG is correct, VP in English cannot be overtly moved. In other words, the representation in (12a) should be impossible, whereas that in (12b) should be legitimate.

(12)   a.   * [$_{VP}$ eat the banana] Mary certainly did t_{VP}.

       b.   [$_{vP}$ t_{SUB} eat the banana] Mary certainly did t_{vP}.

Huang (1993) demonstrates that the fronted VP-like constituent in English contains the trace of subject, as in (12b), pointing to the impossibility of the representation in (12a). The contrast between (13) and (14) is familiar (Huang 1993; Abels 2003*a*).

(13)   John$_i$ wonders which pictures of himself$_{i/j}$ Bill$_j$ likes.

(14)   John$_i$ said that wash himself$_{*i/j}$ Bill$_j$ certainly would.

In (13) the *wh*-movement of *which pictures of himself* makes it possible for the anaphor to be bound by the matrix subject *John*. Without the movement, the only possible reading would be the one where *himself* is bound by the embedded subject *Bill*, as in *John wonders whether Bill likes pictures of himself*. In (14), on the other hand, the fronting of *wash himself* does not exhibit the same kind of effect: The only interpretation allowed is the one where the anaphor refers to *Bill*. The interpretative contrast can be explained if we assume that the fronted constituent in (14) is *v*P containing the subject trace, as in (15a).

(15)   a.   John said that [$_{vP}$ $t_{Bill}$$v$ [$_{VP}$ wash himself]] Bill certainly would t_{vP}.

       b.   * John said that [$_{VP}$ wash himself] Bill certainly would [$_{vP}$ t_{Bill} vt_{VP}].

Since the trace of *Bill* counts as the closest binder for *himself* in (15a), the matrix subject *John* has no chance to bind the anaphor. If the representation of (14) were (15b), the matrix subject, just like its counterpart in (13), would be able to qualify as a possible antecedent for the anaphor. The conclusion then is that what has been fronted in examples like (12) and (14) is *v*P, not VP.[8]

The EMG expects that VP in English, though immobile if it has phonological content, can undergo movement if it is null. This expectation is fulfilled

instance of *v*P-ellipsis. I will not consider pseudogapping here, mainly because its unique properties prevent us from testing the predictions that the present analysis makes about it, as far as I can see.

[8] Thus Johnson's (2001) hypothesis that VP ellipsis is licensed by VP topicalization (illustrated in (12a) and (15b)), followed by deletion, is untenable (see Johnson 2001 for other shortcomings).

One may appeal to the lexical integrity of *v* and V to explain why VP fronting is impossible (Heycock 1995; cf. Chomsky's (2008) treatment of the C-T/I relation and its extension to the *v*-V relation). This kind of attempt seems to fail, because, as we will see, VP can (and, in fact, must) move under certain circumstances (Potts 2002*b*) and because it does not cover the resistance to extraction of the complement of I in Irish ((5)) and FocP in Japanese ((28b) below). Note that (12b) and (15a) violate the Proper Binding Condition (Fiengo 1977), revealing its descriptive inadequacy.

by data on what Potts (2002b) calls "predicate *as*-parentheticals." Examples of relevant parentheticals are given below:

(16) a. He arrived on time, as I had said he would.

      b. I believe, as do all my friends, that war is now inevitable.

Notice that parentheticals of this sort pattern with VP ellipsis in that they tolerate voice mismatches between the missing constituent and its antecedent, as shown below:[9]

(17) a. This problem was looked into by Mary, just as everyone else did.

      b. I implemented it (=a computer system) with a manager, just as my boss had said it had to be.

(17a), like (11a), has a null category in an active clause and a passive antecedent, whereas (17b), like (11b), has a null category in a passive clause and an active antecedent. The similarity between (11) and (17) indicates that the inaudible constituents in the latter are of the same category as the one that undergoes deletion in the former, namely, VP.[10]

Potts (2002b) argues convincingly that *as*-clauses of the kind illustrated in (16) involve movement of null VP rather than VP ellipsis. He presents two main arguments.

First, there is a fundamental interpretative distinction to be made between the gap in predicate *as*-clauses and the VP-ellipsis site. Consider the example of ellipsis in (18) (Potts 2002b: 627; see also Kennedy & Merchant 2000).

(18) The fact that Sue read the map carefully probably means that she stayed on the trails. But we aren't sure whether Chuck did [$_{VP}$].

      a. [$_{VP}$] = stay on the trails

      b. [$_{VP}$] = read the map carefully

(18) is ambiguous. The elided VP can be interpreted either locally, as in the (a) interpretation, or non-locally, as in the (b) interpretation. (18) contrasts sharply with the following example involving an *as*-clause:

(19) The fact that Sue read the map carefully probably means that she stayed on the trails, as did Chuck.

---

[9] I wish to thank Jason Merchant (p.c.) for confirming the grammaticality of (17a,b).

[10] There is another empirical consideration that leads to the same conclusion. As we observed above (n. 4), true cases of *v*P ellipsis and null *v*P movement demand that the subject in the unpronounced constituent be coreferential with that in the antecedent clause. The fact that the subjects are different in the relevant English examples, such as (10) and (16b), demonstrates that they involve neither *v*P ellipsis nor null *v*P movement.

a. *as*-clause gap = stay on the trails

b. *as*-clause gap ≠ read the map carefully

Unlike (18), (19) permits only the local interpretation. This demonstrates that missing VP in VP ellipsis and its counterpart in *as*-parentheticals have different properties. Specifically, in (18) the ellipsis site can have two kinds of full-fledged VP structure with relevant lexical items corresponding to the two interpretations but gets deleted in PF (see Merchant 2001). In (19), on the other hand, a VP null operator is generated in the *as*-clause and undergoes movement (in the way depicted in (21) below). One general trait of a null operator is that it identifies itself with the closest possible antecedent. This accounts for the locality effect observed in (19).

Second, ellipsis is not subject to island constraints, whereas *as*-parentheticals are (see Ross 1967 for the initial observation). For instance, compare the following minimal pair:

(20) a.   Eddie fills his truck with leaded gas. They believed the report that he must [$_{VP}$].

b.   * Eddie fills his truck with leaded gas, just as they believed the report that he must.

(20a) is grammatical even though the elided VP is contained in the complex NP island headed by *the report*, indicating that the VP does not undergo movement. In contrast, (20b), where the elide VP is replaced with an *as*-clause gap, is ungrammatical, strongly suggesting that the gap is actually left by syntactic movement. In other words, (20b) violates the Complex NP Constraint.[11]

Potts maintains that the *as*-clause in (16b) is derived in the following manner:

(21)   [$_{PP}$ as [$_{CP}$ *Op* do [$_{IP}$ all my friends [$_{vP}$ t_{SUB} t_{VP}]]]]

A VP null operator (represented by *Op*) undergoes movement into the specifier of the CP selected by *as*, analyzed as a preposition.

Let us now turn to another celebrated case of ellipsis in English, i.e., what Ross (1969) calls sluicing. Merchant (2001) extensively argues that sluicing involves *wh*-movement in syntax, followed by IP deletion in the phonological component. Examples like (22) are typical.

[11] See Potts (2002b: 631–2) for examples in violation of other island constraints including the Adjunct Condition, the Subject Condition, and the *wh*-island Constraint.

(22)   Jack bought something, but I don't know [$_{CP}$ what [$_{IP}$ ~~Jack bought *t*~~]].

In the second conjunct of (22), the *wh*-phrase *what* moves to Spec of CP in the regular way, which is followed by the deletion of IP in PF.

The EMG predicts that IP of the kind illustrated in (22) cannot be overtly moved. Indeed, Abels (2003*a*) argues that that is the case, citing such examples as (23) and (24).[12]

(23)   a.   Frank saw a play that was long and boring yesterday.

b.   Frank saw a play yesterday [$_{CP}$ that was long and boring].

c.   * Frank saw a play that *t* yesterday [$_{IP}$ was long and boring].

(24)   a.   Mary told herself that John is a fool at least twice a day.

b.   [$_{CP}$ That John is a fool], Mary told herself *t* at least twice a day.

c.   * [$_{IP}$ John is a fool], Mary told herself that *t* at least twice a day.[13]

(23a) and (24a) are the baseline data. (23b-c) involve extraposition, whereas (24b-c) involve topicalization. If extraposition is a case of syntactic movement, as argued by Büring & Hartmann (1997) (see also Johnson 1985), ungrammatical (23c), as opposed to grammatical (23b), shows that (tensed) IP cannot undergo overt movement. The contrast between (24b) and (24c) in terms of topicalization points to the same conclusion.[14]

---

[12]   Abels (2003*a*) also cites examples of passivization like those in (i).

(i)   a.   Everybody believes fervently that John is a fool.

b.   [$_{CP}$ That John is a fool] is believed fervently by everybody.

c.   * [$_{IP}$ John is a fool] is believed (fervently that / that fervently) by everybody.

I exclude such examples from discussion, simply because the ungrammaticality of (ic) can be attributed to the EPP: It seems that in archetypical cases, only nominal categories, i.e. DP and CP can satisfy the EPP in English.

[13]   The acceptable bisentential reading with demonstrative *that* in (24c) is irrelevant here.

[14]   One may reasonably suggest that the ill-formedness of (23c) and (24c) is due to the *that-t* Filter (Chomsky & Lasnik 1977). Observe the following contrast (Browning 1996: 238):

(i)   a.   * I asked what Leslie said that *t* had made Robin give a book to Lee.

b.   I asked what Leslie said that in her opinion *t* had made Robin give a book to Lee.

(ia), containing the sequence *that t*, violates the *that-t* Filter. Examining data like (ib), Culicover (1993) claims that a filter-based account of the *that-t* effect is superior to an ECP-based account. In (ib) the adverbial phrase *in her opinion* intervenes between *that* and *t*, and that seems to ameliorate the violation detected in (ia). It is clear how the *that-t* Filter deals with the contrast in (i) (see Browning 1996 for an alternative minimalist account within the framework of Chomsky 1995).

If (23c) and (24c) were ruled out only by the *that-t* Filter, we would expect them to exhibit a mitigating "adverb effect" (Culicover 1993) similar to the one observed in (i). The expectation, however, is not fulfilled, as shown below:

(ii)   a.   Mary said that in her opinion John is a fool at least twice a day.

b.   * [$_{IP}$ John is a fool], Mary said that in her opinion *t* at least twice a day.

The EMG also predicts that tensed IP in English can undergo syntactic movement if it is phonologically empty. Unfortunately, it turns out that this prediction cannot be tested. In the present context, one might want to consider *as*-parentheticals of the following sort:

(25)   a.   I am, as I'm sure is all too obvious, very nervous.

       b.   We should resign right away, as I'm sure you'll agree.

Apparently, what is missing in (25) is "propositional." One might hope that (25a-b) represent a case involving an IP null operator. However, Potts (2002*a*, 2002*b*) argues persuasively that they involve a CP null operator instead.[15] Thus the relevant portion of (25b), for example, has the following representation:

(26)   [PP as [CP *Op* [IP I'm sure [CP *t′*CP[IP you'll agree *t*CP]]]]]

In (26) the CP null operator raises successive-cyclically from the complement position of the verb *agree* to the Spec of the CP selected by *as*.

The absence of IP null operators is understandable, given Potts's (2002*a*, 2002*b*) claim that *as*-parentheticals require operators denoting propositions, as in the case of CP and *v*P (Chomsky 2000, 2001, 2008) or properties, as in the case of VP (see Potts 2002*a*, 2002*b* for details). It appears that IP is simply incompatible with the semantics of *as*-parentheticals.

In brief, VP in English behaves in the way the EMG expects it to. In addition, the behavior of English finite IP is consistent with the EMG.

12.3.2 *Japanese*

Above, we examined three categories that can undergo ellipsis: VP (in English), *v*P (in Irish), and IP (in English). Let us now turn to ellipsis in Japanese, which is of interest because it targets yet another category, i.e. CP. (27) is an example of sluicing in Japanese (Takahashi 1994*b* among many others).

(27)   Taroo-ga   nanika-o   katta   ga, boku-wa [[FocP nani-o
       Taro-NOM something-ACC bought but I-TOP   what-ACC
       [CP ~~Taroo-ga *t* katta   no~~]   da] ka]   sira-nai.
            Taro-NOM bought C COP Q   know-NEG
       'Taro bought something, but I don't know what.'

In (ii), just as in (ib), the adverbial phrase *in her opinion* immediately follows the complementizer. Despite the lack of the offending *that-t* sequence, (iib) with the topicalization of IP is excluded, demonstrating the immobility of tensed IP.

[15] (25a) demonstrates that the null category in the example can satisfy the EPP. Thus it cannot be IP (see (ic) in *n*. 12).

Hiraiwa & Ishihara (2002) argue that in Japanese sluicing the focused *wh*-phrase moves to Spec of Focus Phrase (Rizzi 1997) headed by the copula *da* and the CP complement of the focus head undergoes deletion.

The EMG predicts that the CP headed by *no* in the focus construction cannot be moved. The prediction is borne out, as shown below:

(28) a. Boku-wa [[$_{\text{FocP}}$ [$_{\text{CP}}$ Taroo-ga uso-o   tuita no] da] to]
          I-TOP   Taro-NOM lie-ACC told C   COP C
          omotteita.
          thought
          'I thought that Taro told a lie.'

      b. * [$_{\text{CP}}$ Taroo-ga uso-o   tuita no] boku-wa [[$_{\text{FocP}}$ t_{CP} da]
            Taro-NOM lie-ACC told C   I-TOP   COP
          to] omotteita.
          C   thought
          lit. 'That Taro told a lie, I thought.'

(28a) illustrates the *in-situ* focus construction in Japanese, where nothing has moved into Spec of FocP and any element within the embedded IP can be focused if pronounced with heavy stress. The similarity between (27) and (28a) is straightforward (in fact, if ellipsis does not take place in (27), the *wh*-phrase *nani-o* 'what' can occupy its base-generated position). In (28b) the CP complement of the copula has undergone scrambling (see Saito 1985 among numerous others), and the sentence is ungrammatical.[16]

The EMG also predicts that the CP in question can move if it lacks phonological content. To test the prediction, let us consider the Japanese counterpart of the English *as*-parenthetical. First, observe the following contrast:

(29) a. Taroo-ga sinhannin dat-ta,   boku-ga t_{CP} omotteita
          Taro-NOM true culprit COP-PAST I-NOM   thought
          yooni.
          as
          'Taro was the true culprit, as I thought.'

---

[16] There is no general ban on extraction out of FocP, as shown in (i) (see also (30a)).

(i) Sono ie-o   boku-wa [[$_{\text{FocP}}$ [$_{\text{CP}}$ Taroo-ga   *t* katta   no] da] to] omotteita.
     that house-ACC I-TOP   Taro-NOM   bought C   COP C   thought
     'That house, I thought that Taro bought.'

   b. * Taroo-ga   sinhannin   dat-ta,   boku-ga t_{CP}
         Taro-NOM true-culprit COP-PAST I-NOM
         omotteita keizi-ni   atta yooni.
         thought   detective-DAT met as
         lit. 'Taro was the true culprit, as I met a detective who thought.'

(29a) exemplifies the *yooni*-parenthetical in Japanese. (29b) shows that the parenthetical involves syntactic movement and thus exhibits island effects. It is ruled out as a violation of the Complex NP Constraint because the gap is embedded in a relative clause. With this in mind, consider (30).

(30) a. Taroo-ga   uso-o   tuita no da, boku-ga t_{CP} da   to
        Taro-NOM lie-ACC told c   COP I-NOM   COP c
        omotteita yooni.
        thought   as
        'Taro told a lie, as I thought.'

   b. * Taroo-ga   uso-o   tuita no da, boku-ga t_{CP} da   to
        Taro-NOM lie-ACC told c   COP I-NOM   COP c
        omotteita keizi-ni   atta yooni.
        thought   detective-DAT met as
        lit. 'Taro told a lie, as I met a detective who thought.'

The crucial difference between (29) and (30) with respect to the parenthetical has to do with the presence of the copula or the focus head *da* (and the particle *to*) in the latter. In (29) the missing constituent is the CP complement of the verb *omotteita* 'thought.' In (30), on the other hand, what is missing is the CP complement of the focus head *da*, the same kind of constituent as the one elided in (27) and the one moved (unsuccessfully) in (28b). The grammaticality of (30a) demonstrates that the phonologically null CP can in fact undergo movement, as predicted by the EMG. (30b) shows that the null operator is indeed subject to the island constraints. The relevant structure of (30a) is assumed to be something like (31).

(31)   [$_{PP}$ [$_{CP}$ *Op* [$_{IP}$ boku-ga [[$_{FocP}$ t_{CP} da] to] omotteita] yooni]]

Drawing on Potts's (2002b) analysis, I tentatively take *yooni* as a species of postposition, selecting CP whose Spec requires a null operator to be present.

    In short, the EMG holds in the case of the CP complement of the FocP in Japanese.

12.3.3 *Summary*

The observations we have made so far are summarized in (32).

(32)

Elided Category	VP	vP	IP	CP
Language	English	Irish	English	Japanese
Overt Movement	*	*	*	*
Covert Movement	OK	OK	n/a	OK

As we saw above, they can be adequately captured by the EMG in (9). I conclude then that they do not represent separate phenomena and should receive a unified analysis.[17]

It is worth pointing out that McCloskey's (2004) account of the contrast between (5) and (7), making crucial use of V-to-I movement in Irish, is problematic at least in two respects.

First, it does not explain why the VP movement in (12a), the IP movement in (23c) and (24c), and the CP movement in (28b) are doomed. For instance, unlike Irish, English lacks overt verb movement and hence the fronted VP in (12a) does not contain any stranded "copy" of V. Similar remarks apply to the other cases: Neither the IP nor the CP in question seems to carry any "morphological orphan" in McCloskey's sense. It is commonly assumed that in English no I-to-C movement takes place in declarative clauses.[18] As for Japanese, there is no empirical motivation for positing C-to-Foc movement: Researchers such as Aoyagi (2006) have argued convincingly, contra Koizumi (1995), that the language lacks verb raising (or head raising in general).

Second and more generally, it offers no principled account of why there are correlations between ellipsis and movement described by the EMG: Under McCloskey's view, they are just a coincidence.[19]

---

[17] Richard Kayne asks how the present line of thinking is affected if a clause involves more structure than is assumed here (see, for example, Rizzi 1997 and subsequent works). No matter how articulated clausal architecture may turn out to be, the EMG is expected to hold. The challenge would always be to pin down exactly what syntactic category is targeted by ellipsis and movement.

[18] Pesetsky & Torrego (2001) present an interesting alternative view, where the complementizer *that* is analyzed as T/I moved to C. Even under this analysis, no "morphological orphan" should reside in T/I: *that* just doubles T/I and the latter is morphologically independent.

[19] McCloskey (2004) alludes to the possibility that what is extracted in predicate *as*-parentheticals is an actual contentful VP subject to the requirement that it delete in the operator position. If this were true, we would not be able to draw a distinction between the VP-ellipsis site and the gap in predicate *as*-parentheticals: Under the analysis to be presented below, movement of VP is possible in an *as*-clause, precisely because it is movement of a null operator inherently lacking phonological features. Therefore, this possibility is ruled out.

12.4 A Phase-Based Analysis

Given the problems of McCloskey's (2004) analysis, we need an alternative account. This section puts forth a unified account based on the notion of phase (Chomsky 2000, 2001, 2008).

As is well known, ellipsis is subject to a set of licensing and identification requirements (see Lobeck 1995, Merchant 2001 among others). Adopting the general framework of Chomsky (2000, 2001), Holmberg (2001) tries to shed a new light on the theory of ellipsis and presents an interesting proposal about the relationship between ellipsis and derivational cyclicity (see also Holmberg 1999*b* for a precursory idea). Specifically, he argues for the thesis that "an ellipsis is a phase that is spelled out as null" (Holmberg 2001:143, cf. Chomsky & Lasnik 1993; Merchant 2001).[20] Holmberg shows that his proposal, combined with a set of well-motivated auxiliary assumptions, accounts for the intricate behavior of the two kinds of yes/no replies (YNRs) in Finnish, simple YNRs without subject, as in (33a), and complex YNRs with subject, as in (33b).

(33) Onko Liisa kotona?
      is-Q Liisa at-home
      'Is Liisa home?'

  a. On.
      is
      'Yes, she is.'

  b. On se.
      is she
      'Yes, she is.'

According to Holmberg, simple YNRs like (33a) are derived by a species of IP ellipsis, whereas complex YNRs like (33b) are derived by a species of VP ellipsis (see Holmberg 2001 for details and complications).

Suppose, as Holmberg claims, that ellipsis is in fact governed by the theory of phase (as well as by the theory of licensing and identification). Suppose further that the operation Transfer (also called Spell-Out with an emphasis on the mapping to the phonological component), characterized in (34) (Nissenbaum 1998; Hiraiwa 2003; cf. Chomsky's 2000, 2001 Phase Impenetrability Condition), sends the complement of a designated phase head to the

---

[20] Following Chomsky (2001), Holmberg assumes the distinction between strong and weak phases: Only strong phases trigger Spell-Out of their previous phases. He also assumes that typical strong phases are CP and *v*P (though they can be weak in certain configurations), while weak phases include TP. As will be made clear, I depart from Holmberg in important points.

phonological component and that whether or not the transferred constituent receives a phonological interpretation is determined in the component ((34) is taken from Hiraiwa 2003).[21]

(34) *Transfer*
      In phase P with head H_p, Transfer applies to the complement domain of H_p as soon as the edge of P is extended.

Chomsky (2000, 2001, 2008) argues that phases are the "propositional" categories *v*P and CP. If this is correct, categories targeted by Transfer are VP and IP. When the transferred material (satisfying licensing and identification requirements) does not get pronounced, we end up with a case of ellipsis.[22] Notice that this line of thinking has an immediate, desirable result: It can capture the observed negative correlation, stated in the EMG, between ellipsis and movement: In a particular language, if a syntactic category can be elided, then that category cannot undergo overt movement (cf. Hiraiwa 2002).[23] For instance, VP cannot be overtly moved in English, because it gets transferred to the phonological component and becomes syntactically inert when its immediately dominating *v*P with subject is completed.

To account for the data reviewed above, however, (34) needs to be modified. In particular, it seems that edge extension is not a necessary condition for Transfer to apply.[24] Let us look at the Irish structure in (2) again. If Holmberg's (2001) proposal on the nature of ellipsis, endorsed here, is on the right track, one can use ellipsis as a diagnostic for phasehood. It must be then that IP in finite clauses qualifies as a phase in Irish and its complement domain *v*P is handed over to the phonological component when IP is completed. Notice that the edge of IP is not extended in (2). This means that (34) does not force the Spell-Out of *v*P in (2). Notice also that IP does not count as a phase within

---

[21] See Hiraiwa (2003) for empirical arguments that the adoption of (34) leads to the elimination of the Proper Binding Condition (Fiengo 1977).

[22] Holmberg (2001) tentatively adopts the copy theory of ellipsis (see Chung *et al.* 1995), but he admits that for his purposes, the choice between the copy theory and the deletion theory (see Chomsky & Lasnik 1993; Merchant 2001) is not crucial (Holmberg 2002: 143). It is worth pointing out that Holmberg's version of copy theory, in which a transferred constituent is replaced by a null category (formally Δ) in PF under ellipsis, is different from the standard copy theory, which posits empty categories in syntax. In light of Merchant's (2001) strong arguments, I advocate the deletion theory. As a matter of fact, this chapter provides indirect support for it. See below.

[23] We must somehow prevent the complement of a phase head from moving to the edge of the immediately dominating phase phrase (see Abels 2003*a*). Otherwise, the complement would be able to undergo movement, having escaped the Spell-Out domain. See below.

[24] Legate's (2003*b*) discussion of unaccusative and passive VPs as transferred domains may be relevant here.

Chomsky's (2000, 2001, 2008) framework. To accommodate the Irish facts, I propose (35) (cf. Svenonius 2004: sect. 4; Gallego 2006b).

(35)   *Transfer* (revised version)
Transfer applies to the complement domain of head H as soon as all of the uninterpretable features of H are eliminated.

(35) departs from Chomsky (2000, 2001) in adopting the hypothesis that any projection can in principle be a phase (cf. Chomsky 1986a).[25] If one regards edge extension as triggered by an uninterpretable feature (or an EPP feature), then (35) can subsume (34). According to (35), Irish vP in a finite clause gets transferred as soon as verb movement to I takes place to eliminate the interpretable feature of I. If transferred vP gets deleted in PF, the outcome is vP ellipsis of the kind illustrated in (3), which is superficially similar to IP ellipsis in Finnish in (33a).

The revised notion of Transfer is also needed to deal with the data related to IP in English and CP in Japanese. In (24) the embedded CP does not have a specifier, but its IP complement gets transferred to the phonological component and hence cannot be extracted, as in (24c). Similarly, in (28) the immobile CP headed by *no* is assumed to get spelled out, even though the edge of the FocP is not extended. The hypothesis about the proliferation of phases allows us to treat FocP in Japanese as a phase.

Given (35), the immobility of categories deletable under ellipsis (VP and IP in English, vP in Irish, and CP in Japanese) can be explained in terms of phase.

At this point, a remark is in order on one important caveat to the present phase-based analysis. It has to do with the kind of movement schematized in (36).

---

[25] An anonymous reviewer asks whether discounting the original motivation for postulating phase based on semantic independence (e.g. Chomsky 2000, 2001) is conceptually desirable. Gallego (2006a) proposes to analyze apparent cross-linguistic variation in terms of phase in a way that avoids the potential conceptual problem. Specifically, maintaining the universality of CP and vP phases, he argues that in Spanish, I inherits phase characteristics from v through v-to-I movement. His analysis nicely accounts for the phasehood of IP in Irish, a language with v-to-I movement. It is not clear, however, whether the analysis extends to the phasehood of FocP in Japanese, since there seems to be no C-to-Foc movement in the language. For this reason, I will stick to (35) (and (39) below), though Gallego's analysis and the present one yield the same results in many cases. They are similar in that they try to reduce parametric variation in terms of phase to morphological properties of heads (see also Gallego 2006b).

It is interesting to note that Chomsky (2008) states in passing "A stronger principle would be that phases are exactly the domains in which uninterpretable features are valued, as seems plausible." See Svenonius (2004) for an attempt to explore the possibility that categories other than CPs and vPs count as phases.

(36) H_pP

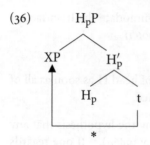

Suppose that H_p is a phase head. Suppose also that the complement of H_p, XP, moves to the edge of H_pP, as shown in (36). If such movement were possible, nothing would preclude further movement of XP. This is because by the time the complement gets transferred, it (or its copy) would have reached the "escape hatch" and hence should remain syntactically active. Therefore, it is crucial that the movement in question is prohibited.

Noting the impossibility of (36),[26] Abels (2003a) mentions possible ways to derive it from the theory of grammar. Any analysis would serve present purposes as long as it bans the movement in (36), but for the sake of concreteness, let us adopt an economy-based approach considered in Abels (2003a).[27] Assume following Chomsky (2001) that every step of movement must be motivated by feature checking. Assume further that mutual c-command suffices to establish checking relations (Epstein *et al.* 1998). Then all the relevant features on H_p will be checked against XP when H_p and XP are merged. This means in turn that no feature checking takes place as a result of the movement in (36). Since the movement is superfluous, it is forbidden.

So far, we have seen why the bad cases of extraction are ruled out. Let us now make sure that the good cases are indeed ruled in. Beginning with overt movement, take the *v*P-fronting in (12b) as a representative example. There are two questions to be addressed. First, why is it that *v*P in English, unlike *v*P in Irish, does not get spelled out even when IP is constructed above it? From the present perspective, it must be that the IP is not "complete" and thus does not force the Spell-Out of the *v*P. It has been noted for some languages that the property of I is somehow dependent on that of C. For instance, Chomsky (2008) suggests that I (T in his term) inherits features (such as an agreement feature) from C. Adapting this suggestion, suppose that English (tensed) I has uninterpretable features to be valued by C. Then it follows that *v*P remains

[26] Abels (2003a) states the relevant generalization as follows: No phrase can be both the complement and the specifier of the same head. It is worth pointing out that Grohmann's anti-locality framework does not categorically rule out (36) (Grohmann 2003: 194).

[27] Abels (2003a) also presents an account based on a graph-theoretic approach to phrase structure, which I omit here.

syntactically active in English because its sister head I bears uninterpretable features until C is merged to IP. Suppose further that Irish I has no such dependence on C, following Cottell's (1995) claim that C and I should both have an independent specification of Tense in Irish. If this is the case, then IP is "complete" in Irish, forcing the Spell-Out of *v*P.

The second question is: Why is it that the total elimination of uninterpretable features of I does not precede the *v*P movement? If it does, the *v*P in question would get spelled out and thus its movement would be impossible. Let us assume that the *v*P moves into Spec of CP and the movement is triggered by C. In other words, both operations are driven by the same "probe." Following Hiraiwa (2005), I regard such operations as simultaneous.[28] Then the *v*P-fronting is correctly expected to be possible, as in (12b).[29]

Let us turn our attention to covert movement. In light of the phase theory, which regards cyclicity as a result of syntax-phonology interactions in the course of derivations, a question arises as to whether phonological properties of syntactic categories have any impact on the way cyclicity operates. In particular, the question is: What happens if a category targeted by Transfer has no phonological features to be interpreted in the phonological component in the first place? It has been established above, in relation to English VP, Irish *v*P, and Japanese CP, that such a category remains active in syntax and therefore can undergo movement. Two ways to account for the fact come to mind immediately.

Under one account, we may choose to invoke a notion of economy. Specifically, there would simply be no point in sending a phonologically empty element to the phonological component. Exploring various issues related to the syntax-semantic interface, Fox (2000) argues for (37).

(37)   *Scope Economy*
        Scope-shifting operations (SSOs) cannot be semantically vacuous.

Fox (2000) shows that (36) correctly captures the interactions between ellipsis on the one hand, and QR (Quantifier Raising) and QL (Quantifier Lowering) on the other. A generalized version of (37) is (38) (cf. Chomsky 1995, ch. 4).

(38)   *Interface Economy*
        An operation is triggered only if it has an effect on output at the interface.

---

[28] Hiraiwa (2005) presents the following:

(i)   *The Principle of Simultaneity*
       Apply operations simultaneously in parallel at a probe level.

[29] Examples like (14), where *v*P-fronting has taken place within an embedded clause, would call for a CP-recursion analysis of the kind sought by Browning (1996).

If there exists an economy condition along the lines of (38), categories that are targeted by Transfer and can potentially undergo ellipsis should be able to undergo movement if it lacks phonological features.

However, this kind of global economy has come under scrutiny. It has often been suggested in the literature (notably, Collins 1997) that the minimalist derivational system should dispense with global economy conditions, because they allow for a considerable amount of look-ahead, which is undesirable from the viewpoint of minimal computation.[30] Illuminating as it may be, even Fox's (2000) analysis of scope-shift has been reinterpreted by Reinhart (2006), who argues that global computation based on reference sets (Chomsky 1995) is a last resort procedure available only at the interface and is not part of what Chomsky (2000, 2001, 2008) calls narrow syntax.

Then we should seek an alternative account that does not rely on the notion of global economy but takes advantage of local operations. The idea is simply that the operation Transfer itself is made sensitive to the presence of phonological features. (35) is now modified as in (39) (reminiscent of Chomsky's (1995: 297) discussion of the Minimal Link Condition as part of the definition of Attract), where "Φ-interpretable" means "interpretable in the phonological component."

(39)   *Transfer* (final version)

Transfer applies to the Φ-interpretable complement domain of head H as soon as all of the uninterpretable features of H are eliminated.

(39) correctly captures the observation that null operators (with intrinsic semantic features to be supplemented by those of their antecedents but without phonological features) are exempt from transfer even if they are complements of phase heads.

I have been concentrating on the phonological aspect of Transfer, but the operation is supposed to map a syntactic object not only to the phonological component but also to the semantic component, ideally at the same time (Chomsky 2008). In connection with this, an anonymous reviewer asks what would happen if the complement of a phase head is semantically null: Does it remain active in syntax just like a null operator?

I assume that there are no truly meaningless categories in natural language that appear as complements of a phase head (see for instance Kayne 2006 for discussion of English expletive *there*). At least in the cases considered here, this assumption is justified: VP, vP, IP, CP cannot be semantically empty. Then there is no need to take semantic (un)interpretability into consideration.

---

[30] See Toyoshima (forthcoming) for recent discussion of how much look-ahead is needed in the derivational process.

A seeming asymmetry between phonological and semantic properties in (39) stems from the presence of null operators and the absence of categories uninterpretable in the semantic component.

In a nutshell, the modified theory of phase, combined with Holmberg's (2001) characterization of ellipsis, derives the EMG properly.

12.5 Conclusion

To summarize, it has been argued, based on Holmberg's (2001) insight, that there are close relationships between ellipsis and movement. They are captured by what I call the Ellipsis Movement Generalization (EMG): If a certain category can undergo ellipsis, it cannot undergo movement except when it is phonologically null.[31] The EMG has been shown to be derivable from a version of phase theory (Chomsky 2000, 2001, 2008), whereby the total elimination of uninterpretable features on a head leads to the Spell-Out of the phonologically interpretable complement domain of that head.

To the extent that the present analysis is consistent and successful, it lends important empirical support to: (i) the basic framework of the Minimalist Program (Chomsky 2000, 2001, 2008), where cyclicity is regarded essentially as syntax-phonology interactions (see also Fox & Pesetsky 2005), and (ii) Holmberg's (2001) treatment of ellipsis as phase-related phenomena. Regarding the first point, I have been led to a significant departure from Chomsky's original system in that under the modified notion of Transfer, heads of any kind, not just C or *v*, can in principle define a phase. To put it differently, phases are parameterized across languages depending on morphosyntactic properties of functional categories (see Gallego 2006*a*, 2006*b* for relevant discussion). This modification has proved crucial in coming to grips with the Irish and Japanese data examined above.

In addition, the analysis advocated here provides interesting indirect evidence for the deletion theory of ellipsis (see Chomsky & Lasnik 1993, Merchant 2001 among others) and against the copy theory of ellipsis (see Chung *et al.* 1985 among others). Suppose, as the copy theory claims, that ellipsis involved generation of an empty constituent (such as an empty VP) and its content is recovered by copying an antecedent constituent at LF.[32] We would expect then that ellipsis and null operator movement should have the same property with respect to Spell-Out (*i.e.* they are not spelled out), because they both involve phonologically null constituents, though they differ in terms of movement properties. This much seems acceptable, but the problem is that we would

---

[31] See *n.* 6.   [32] See *n.* 22.

not expect a close connection between ellipsis and overt category movement: Transfer would be relevant only to the latter, but not to the former. In other words, under the copy theory, the EMG is merely a coincidence. On the other hand, the deletion theory, incorporating Holmberg's idea, correctly predicts the negative correlation between ellipsis and overt category movement: They are related to each other, precisely because they are both constrained by Transfer. This means that ellipsis sites do have full syntactic structure with lexical items containing phonological features.[33] In short, the deletion theory defended by Merchant (2001) is superior to the copy theory.

It remains to be seen whether the EMG holds in empirical domains other than those examined here, but that is a task for future research.

---

[33] It must be then that the hypothesis of Late Insertion advocated by Distributed Morphology (Halle & Marantz 1993), under which syntactic categories have no phonological content, is incorrect.

13

Island Repair, Non-Repair, and the Organization of the Grammar*

HOWARD LASNIK

13.1 Introduction

The phenomenon of island violation amelioration by ellipsis as in (1), first discovered by Ross (1969), has recently been the focus of much investigation, by Merchant (2001) and Lasnik (2001*b*), among many others.

(1) Irv and someone were dancing together, but I don't know who (*Irv and were dancing together). [Coordinate Structure Constraint]

On the face of it, this phenomenon is problematic for a strictly derivational theory. Since information about the violation would presumably be sent to the interface online, no later operation (deletion) should be able to repair it. One would expect persistence of violations, and, indeed, sometimes that is what we find, as in the case of P-stranding and possibly Superiority. For the surprising instances of amelioration, Lasnik (2001*a*) proposes a hybrid theory combining derivational and representational aspects. Fox & Pesetsky (2005) propose another sort of hybrid theory, which attempts to explain both island violations and their repair by ellipsis. At each phase, pairwise linear ordering statements are sent to PF. An island violation typically will result in some contradictory statements, so PF linearization will fail. Under their proposal that deletion of an element entails deletion of any ordering statement involving that element, repair by ellipsis follows. I will outline some further problems for cyclic Spell-Out and explore implications of possible solutions to those problems.

Another phenomenon I will be concerned with is the classic Subjacency vs ECP contrast, which shows up in two ways, as has been known since Huang

* I am grateful to Chizuru Nakao and to the participants of *InterPhases: A Conference on Interfaces in Current Syntactic Theory* at the University of Cyprus in May 2006 for helpful suggestions.

(1982). Island violations are usually worse with overt movement of adjuncts than with overt movement of arguments. Further, a *wh*-argument *in situ* inside an island is often fine, while an adjunct in comparable position is bad. Lasnik & Saito (1984) argued that this contrast is fundamentally one between overt locality constraints and covert ones. This is potentially supported by the fact that too long adjunct movement, unlike argument movement, is not repaired by ellipsis. Finally, Chung *et al.* (2006), further considering observations in Chung *et al.* (1995), propose that "Sprouting" (Sluicing where the *wh*-trace has no antecedent) involves LF movement (lowering, in particular), and that is why island effects are displayed. Once again, the architectural question arises: How can these patterns be made consistent with a single-cycle multiple Spell-Out type model?

13.2 Persistence of (Some) Syntactic Constraints under Ellipsis

It has been observed, most comprehensively by Merchant (2001), that in elliptical constructions, obedience to (at least certain) syntactic constraints persists. For example, Merchant massively documents conformity to the parametric prohibition of P-stranding. In languages that allow P-stranding (such as English), the survivor of Sluicing can be the bare object of a preposition; in languages that don't (such as Greek), it can't:

(2)   Anna was talking with someone, but I don't know who.

(3)   Who was Anna talking with.

(4)   I   Anna milise   me   kapjon,   alla dhe ksero   *(me) pjon.
      the Anna spoke with someone but not I.know   with who

(5)   * Pjon milise   me.
      who she.spoke with

As reported by Merchant, other languages that behave like English are Frisian, Swedish, Norwegian, Danish, and Icelandic. Languages like Greek that don't allow P-stranding are much more common. Merchant gives data from seventeen additional languages patterning with Greek, including German, Russian, Persian, Catalan, Hebrew, and Basque.

Another movement constraint that seems to be maintained under Sluicing is Superiority (though there are possibly interfering factors—see Grebenyova (2006) for discussion). Stjepanović (2003), developing ideas of Bošković (2002b), discusses several properties of *wh*-movement in Serbo-Croatian, a multiple *wh*-fronting language. One property is the apparent presence of

Superiority effects, as seen in the following example from Boeckx & Lasnik (2006).

(6)   Ivan i   Marko ne znaju ...
         Ivan and Marko neg know

  a.   ko   je šta   kupio.
        who is what   bought

  b. * šta   je ko   kupio.
        what is who bought
        'Ivan and Marko don't know who bought what.'

This effect is apparently preserved under Sluicing:

(7) A: (Somebody bought something, but)

     B: a. Ivan i   Marko ne znaju ko   šta.
             Ivan and Marko neg know who what

         b. *Ivan i   Marko ne znaju šta   ko.
             Ivan and Marko neg know what who
             'Ivan and Marko don't know who what.'

Merchant gives similar examples from Bulgarian, another multiple *wh*-fronting language.

(8) a.   Koj kogo e   vidjal?
          who whom AUX seen

     b. *Kogo koj e   vidjal?
          whom who AUX seen
          'Who saw whom?'

(9) a.   Njakoj e   vidjal njakogo, no ne znam koj kogo.
          someone AUX seen   someone but not I.know who whom

     b. *Njakoj e   vidjal njakogo, no ne znam kogo koj.
          someone AUX seen   someone but not I.know whom who

This is all exactly as one would expect under a single-cycle model of grammar (the multiple Spell-Out of Uriagereka (1999b) for example). Suppose that at the end of each cycle (or at each phase; the precise instantiation doesn't matter for now), the structure so far created is "shipped off" to the interfaces. In case there is some violation, external systems of mind then interpret the object as malformed.

  Merchant, developing an observation of Chung *et al.* (1995), presents data indicating that (some) island violations also persist under ellipsis, VP ellipsis this time:

(10)   * They want to hire someone who speaks a Balkan language, but I don't know which they do [vp ~~want to hire someone who speaks *t*~~].

Merchant (2001)

Again, this seems to be just what is expected in a single-cycle model.

13.3 Repair of Violations of Syntactic Constraints

13.3.1 *Phenomena*

Ross (1969) already noted a phenomenon that is problematic for such a model—island violation repair under Sluicing:

(11)   I believe that he bit someone, but they don't know who (I believe that he bit).

(12)   a.   * I believe the claim that he bit someone, but they don't know who I believe the claim that he bit.

> [Complex NP Constraint, noun complement]

   b.   (??) I believe the claim that he bit someone, but they don't know who.

(13)   a.   * Irv and someone were dancing together, but I don't know who Irv and were dancing together.   [Coordinate Structure Constraint]

   b.   (??) Irv and someone were dancing together, but I don't know who.

(14)   a.   * She kissed a man who bit one of my friends, but Tom doesn't realize which one of my friends she kissed a man who bit.

> [Complex NP Constraint, relative clause]

   b.   (??) She kissed a man who bit one of my friends, but Tom doesn't realize which one of my friends.

(15)   a.   * That he'll hire someone is possible, but I won't divulge who that he'll hire is possible.   [Sentential Subject Constraint]

   b.   (??) That he'll hire someone is possible, but I won't divulge who.

Based on this phenomenon, Ross explicitly argued against Markovian strictly monotonic cyclic derivation, given his powerful arguments earlier in that same paper for a movement and deletion analysis of sluicing. Ross notes that the phenomenon of island violation repair provides "evidence of the strongest sort that the theoretical power of [global] derivational constraints is needed in linguistic theory..." (p. 277):

If a node is moved out of its island, an ungrammatical sentence will result. If the island-forming node does not appear in surface structure, violations of lesser severity will (in general) ensue.   (Ross 1969: 277)

Wasow (1972) observed a related sort of problem (presented in somewhat different terms) for a one-cycle model, if ellipsis is instantiated by deletion. In this case, as in several others to be discussed, it seems that deletion is "too late" to have the effects it evidently does. Consider the familiar phenomenon of *do*-support under VP ellipsis:

(16) a. John will come if Bill comes.

 b. John will come if Bill does.

Wasow's point was that on the cycle of [Bill Infl come], Affix Hopping would apply. When VP deletion later operates, no stranded affix remains, so *do* would not be inserted. Wasow's conclusion was that ellipsis is not instantiated via deletion, but rather, by what would later be called LF copying. However, several of Ross's arguments, developed much more fully by Merchant, strongly implicate deletion.

The whole phenomenon of "repair by ellipsis," of which island violation repair is just one instance, raises a host of similar problems. In addition to island violation repair, there are circumstances where a normally obligatory instance of movement fails to take place, and ellipsis renders the resulting sentence acceptable, as discussed in Lasnik (1995a) and Lasnik (1999a). Here I assume the standard analysis of Sluicing as *wh*-movement followed by IP ellipsis (essentially Ross's account, taken up again by Saito and Murasugi (1990) and Merchant (2001)):

(17) Speaker A: Mary will see someone.

 Speaker B: I wonder [$_{CP}$ who [$_{IP}$ ~~Mary will see~~]].

As first argued by Rosen (1976), Sluicing is not limited to embedded questions. It can also occur in matrix *wh*-questions with all the same fundamental properties. (18) is a representative example.

(18) Speaker A: Mary will see someone.

 Speaker B: Who ~~Mary will see~~.

The relevant fact here is that the normally obligatory raising of Infl to C (in matrix interrogatives) does not apply:

(19) a. * Who Mary will see.

 b. Who will Mary see.

13.3.2 *Possible Analyses of These Phenomena*

13.3.2.1 *Islands*   As mentioned above, Ross had already argued that we need a strongly non-Markovian model to capture the facts. Chomsky (1972) on the other hand, rejects global derivational constraints, and suggests that * (# in Chomsky's presentation) is assigned to an island when it is crossed by a movement operation. An output condition forbidding * in surface structures accounts for the deviance of standard island violations. If a later operation (Sluicing in the example Chomsky discussed) deletes a category containing the *-marked item, the derivation is salvaged. (Chomsky's example, repeated here as (20), involves a complex NP with an infinitival complement to a noun, a very weak island even without Sluicing. But the logic of the account is clear enough.)

(20)   I don't know   CP

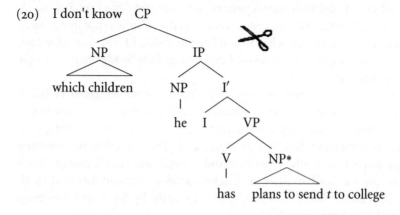

For Chomsky, the condition banning * applies at surface structure. The results are the same if, instead, it is a PF condition, as suggested by Lasnik (1995*b*, 2001*a*). This kind of analysis raises a host of problems. First, as Juan Uriagereka (p.c.) asks, if * is a symbol of the grammar that is subject to "collateral" deletion, why couldn't it be subject to primary deletion, thus resulting in the repair of islands even without ellipsis? Second, introduction of * into the structure seems to violate Inclusiveness, as pointed out by Kitahara (1999). Finally, as Lakoff (1972) observes, the account doesn't eliminate the globality in a deep sense. Rather, it encodes it.

13.3.2.2 *Failure to Move*   Assume, as is fairly standard, that matrix interrogative C contains the strong feature that triggers the overt raising of T, with the matching feature of Infl (presumably a tense feature) raising overtly to check it. Now, as proposed by Lasnik (1999*a*) roughly following Ochi (1999*a*), suppose that this leaves behind a phonologically defective Infl, which will cause a PF crash unless either pied-piping or deletion of a category containing that Infl (Sluicing) takes place. (21) illustrates the latter option.

(21)

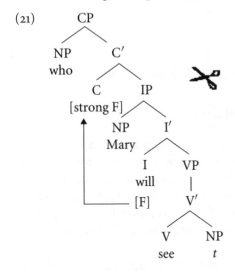

Wasow's problem writ large evidently arises again under these accounts. Deletion seems to be too late to rescue the violations.

At this point, it is worth considering whether an even more fundamental problem arises. If material is cyclically "shipped off" for interpretation at the interfaces, and deletion is late, then deletion is even too late to be deletion! Once material is already phonetically interpreted, how can it subsequently be rendered silent? The solution to this last problem will suggest a direction for the others. "Shipping the representation off" for interpretation cannot mean that it is actually interpreted at that point; just that it is made ready for interpretation with relevant properties presented. The ultimate interpretation it receives can be as silence.

For Wasow's specific problem, one compatible approach would be that suggested in Lasnik (1981) and Lasnik (1995c). Affix Hopping is merely low-level regrouping of an adjacent affix and verb. And *do*-Support merely reflects how Infl is phonologically realized when it has not been merged onto a verb.

13.4 Some New Approaches to Island Constraints and Repair by Deletion

Two recent approaches to islandhood and to successive cyclicity provide potential solutions to the repair problem without introducing * as a formative. They also refrain from actually fully interpreting all the material in a cyclic domain at the end of each cycle, hence avoiding the problems that that entailed. The first I will discuss is Multiple Spell Out (Uriagereka 1999*b*). Uriagereka was concerned to eliminate the stipulated induction step in Kayne's linearization algorithm:

(22) a. *Base*:
          If X asymmetrically c-commands Y, X precedes Y.

      b. *Induction*:
          If X is dominated by Z, and Z precedes Y, X precedes Y.

The induction step is needed for, e.g., complex specifiers, since terminals inside such a specifier don't c-command out of it, yet those terminals precede everything in the rest of the phrase. Uriagereka accepts the base step, and deduces the effects of the induction step as follows. Spell-Out "flattens" a complex specifier Z that dominates X and c-commands Y. This destroys internal boundaries, essentially turning C into a terminal. This allows it to linearize via (22a).

This deduces many islands—all specifiers, and, Uriagereka argues, adjuncts as well. Now suppose this flattening is optional. If it is not done, extraction will be possible, but linearization will ultimately fail (as the cycle demands that there will be no later opportunity to flatten). But it won't fail if the problematic material is rendered invisible to phonetics. Thus, repair of (at least these) islands by deletion.

Fox & Pesetsky (2005) present a way of forcing successive cyclic movement, hence, of deriving many islands (including some that are not encompassed by Uriagereka's approach). They propose that at each Spell-Out domain, linear ordering statements are added to an ever-growing Ordering Table. When movement does not proceed from each successive phase edge, contradictory ordering statements eventually appear in the Table. Phonetics would ultimately be incapable of responding to the resulting contradictory instructions. When deletion takes place, it can have a salvation effect by eliminating all statements involving deleted material, including the contradictory statements that can result from moving too far in one jump. Island violation repair is one such situation.

13.5 Apparent Failure of Island Violation Repair

As noted above, Merchant (2001), extending an observation of Chung *et al.* (1995), presents data indicating that (some) island violations persist under ellipsis, VP ellipsis (VPE) this time:

(23)   * They want to hire someone who speaks a Balkan language, but I don't know which they do [~~VP~~ ~~want to hire someone who speaks~~ *t*].

This is just what we would have expected under the strong single-cycle model, with all material shipped off for interpretation (including interpretation of deviance) at relevant cyclic points in the derivation. But we have now seen that that model seriously undergenerates. So what of the failure of VP deletion to repair island violations, as in (23)? Lasnik (2001*b*) points out that the generalization is actually much broader than Merchant indicated. Parallel "failure of repair" obtains even when there was no violation in the first place. That is, not only does VP deletion not repair a damaged structure, it seemingly creates its own damage. For example, extraction out of an embedded clause is typically fine and Sluicing is just as good, but VPE is bad:[1]

(24)   They said they heard about a Balkan language, but I don't know which Balkan language they said they heard about.

(25)   They said they heard about a Balkan language, but I don't know which Balkan language.

(26)   * They said they heard about a Balkan language, but I don't know which Balkan language they did.

Similarly for extraction out of an object NP:

(27)   They heard a lecture about a Balkan language, but I don't know which Balkan language they heard a lecture about.

(28)   They heard a lecture about a Balkan language, but I don't know which Balkan language.

(29)   * They heard a lecture about a Balkan language, but I don't know which Balkan language they did.

Fox & Lasnik (2003) propose an account of this asymmetry between Sluicing and VP ellipsis, based on a hybrid of the Chomsky (1972) theory of island marking and (a version of) the Chomsky (1986*a*) theory of islands. First, consider the nature of Sluicing:

---

[1]   The MaxElide principle of Merchant (2008*a*) is potentially relevant here. Compare (ia), where less was deleted than could have been (just the VP), with (ib) (where the whole IP is deleted).

(i)   Someone solved the problem.

    a.   ? Who did?

    b.   Who?

But this contrast seems far less than that seen between (26) and (25) and that between (29) and (28). Thus, something over and above MaxElide seems to be required.

(30) Fred said that Mary talked to a certain girl, but I don't know which girl
      <~~Fred said that Mary talked to~~ *t*>.

Suppose, following Chung *et al.* (1995), that the indefinite in the antecedent of
Sluicing must be bound by existential closure in a way that is parallel to the *wh*-
dependency in the sluiced clause. And suppose, contra Merchant (2001), that
formal parallelism is required for ellipsis. This is satisfied since the variables in
the antecedent and the elided clause are bound by parallel operators and from
parallel positions.

Now notice that in the structure shown, there are no intermediate traces in
the elided portion (in angle brackets), indicating that there were no intermediate landing sites in the movement. If there had been successive movement,
under plausible assumptions the relevant portions of the antecedent and the
ellipsis site would not be parallel, and this would prevent ellipsis. This seems
to be problematic under the assumption that successive cyclic movement is
required by considerations of locality. But as discussed earlier, considerations
of locality are nullified under deletion (island repair).

But why is there no such "repair" with VPE? VPE involves deletion of a
smaller constituent than the clause that is elided in sluicing (VP vs TP):

(31) which g(girl) [$_{TP}$ he T [$_{AspP}$ did <$_{VP}$ ~~say that I talked to g(girl)~~>]]

(32) *Fred said that Mary talked to a certain girl, but I don't know which girl
      he did.

The unacceptability of VPE follows if we assume that one of the remaining
maximal projections, say AspP or TP, is an "island" that must be circum-
vented by adjunction or repaired by deletion. This roughly follows the claim
of Chomsky (1986*a*) that all XPs are potential barriers. Since the island is
not deleted, the escape hatch is required, and a violation of parallelism is
unavoidable. Note that Fox & Lasnik simply assumed, for the sake of presentation, the Chomsky (1972) *-marking mechanism. As discussed above, this
has certain difficulties. Consider, then, the Fox & Pesetsky alternative. Under
that proposal, when there is extra long movement, at least some contradictory ordering statements will presumably remain in the Table of precedence
relations even after VPE (now assuming that all XPs are potentially relevant
points of Spell-Out). For Sluicing, since virtually everything is deleted, all
contradictory statements will be gone.

Since this account of the contrast between VPE and Sluicing relies crucially
on the fact that there is movement in the elided constituent but not in the
antecedent constituent, a prediction is that if the antecedent clause is replaced
with a clause that involves movement, both VPE and Sluicing would be possible. This prediction seems to be borne out:

(33) a. I know which book John said that Mary read, but YOU don't know which one.

   b. ? I know which book John said that Mary read, but YOU don't know which one he did.

(34) a. I know that John said that Mary read a certain book, but I don't know which one.

   b. *I know that John said that Mary read a certain book, but I don't know which one he did.

13.6 Non-PF Constraints

According to the theory outlined so far, if there are cases of true non-repair, they should involve constraints that do not have their roots in PF properties. It was suggested above that Superiority violations are not repaired. And, in fact, Merchant suggests that Superiority is a constraint on *derivations* rather than on output. The Minimal Link Condition of Chomsky (1995: 311) has this property, as does its forerunner, Shallowness of Oka (1993). Both of these are presumably instantiations of Relativized Minimality.[2] See Boeckx & Lasnik (2006) for some discussion.

Similarly, LF constraint violations should not be repairable by deletion. Long adjunct movement might be an instance of this. As pointed out by Huang (1982) and later discussed by Lasnik & Saito (1984), adjunct movement displays very strong island effects:

(35) ** How did [Mary meet [a student [who solved the problem *t*]]]?

These violations seem to persist under deletion:

(36) * Mary met a student who solved the problem (somehow), but I'm not sure exactly how [Mary met [a student [who solved the problem *t*]]]?

(37) * Which problem did Mary meet [a student [who solved *t*]]?

---

[2] This line of reasoning raises interesting questions about the *wh*-island constraint. This constraint is very often deduced from Relativized Minimality (RM), yet, as Chung *et al.* (1995) observe, violations are repaired under Sluicing:

(i) Sandy was trying to work out which students would be able to solve a certain problem, but she wouldn't tell us which one.

Is there any way that this could avoid falling under RM? Note that the RM treatment would appeal to Defective Intervention. Since *which students* has already moved to Spec of the embedded question it has thus checked its uninterpretable *wh*-feature, rendering it unavailable for further *wh*-movement. Yet under DI, it still would block access by the matrix C to *which one*. However DI has been called into question by, among others, Vukić (2003) and Chandra (2007). See Boeckx & Lasnik (2006) for discussion. It is important to note that the Fox & Pesetsky approach can easily handle *wh*-islands, and the fact that they are repaired by Sluicing.

(38)   Mary met a student who solved a problem, but I'm not sure exactly which problem ~~[Mary met [a student [who solved *t*]]]~~?

Further, as extensively discussed by Huang and by Lasnik & Saito, *wh*-adjuncts *in situ* show strong island effects. *Weisheme* inside an island in Chinese is extremely degraded, just as the trace of *why* is in English, strongly suggesting that the relevant constraint involves LF:

(39)   * Why do you believe [the claim [that [Lisi left *t*]]].

(40)   * Ni   xiangxin [[Lisi weisheme likai] de shuofa.   *Chinese*
         you believe   Lisi why   leave   claim

As discussed by Nakao (2007), if we follow Huang and Lasnik & Saito in treating this locality of adjunct movement as an LF effect, failure of repair follows, on the assumption that ellipsis is PF deletion.

Chung *et al.* (1995) and Chung *et al.* (2006) observe another instance of persistence of locality violations. They indicate that under Sprouting (Sluicing where there is no antecedent for the *wh*-trace) Sluicing seems not to repair violations:

(41)   * Sandy was trying to work out which students would speak but she refused to say who to/to who(m).

(42)   * Agnes wondered how John could eat, but it's not clear what.

(43)   * That Tom will win is likely, but it's not clear which race.

Chung *et al.* (2006) suggest a point in the derivation like (44), where deletion has taken place under identity, and where there is not yet a variable for *what* to bind.

(44)   Agnes wondered how John could eat, but it's not clear [what ~~[Agnes wondered how John could eat]~~].

Then LF lowering creates a copy of *what* that will be interpreted as the needed variable. As Chung *et al.* (2006) note, lowering ought to be completely symmetric with raising, so locality constraints ought to obtain. Since the movement operation is covert (unlike in standard Sluicing) PF deletion will have no saving effect. Interestingly, on the Lasnik and Saito account, the long adjunct movement situation discussed just above is actually parallel to the Chung *et al.* (2006) case, since Lasnik & Saito argue that adjuncts, unlike arguments, do not leave traces in overt syntax. Hence, covert lowering is crucially involved. In fact, the Lasnik and Saito account can now be simplified. They had argued that after lowering, there must be re-raising. But following Chung *et al.* (2006), instead we could say that the lowering already creates the required operator-variable chain.

13.7 Some Remaining Questions

13.7.1 *P-Stranding*

As noted earlier, P-stranding violations evidently cannot be repaired by ellipsis. This is mysterious, in fact paradoxical, if the P-stranding constraint is an "island constraint." Abels (2003*b*) shows that in one crucial respect, the P-stranding prohibition (in languages that exhibit it) does, indeed, diverge from standard island constraints: While the complement of the P cannot move, subextraction out of the PP is (sometimes) possible, as in these Russian examples:

(45) Ot čego sleduet otkaza'sja?
      of what follows give up-self
      'What should one give up?'

(46) * Čego sleduet otkaza'sja   ot?
      what follows give up-self of

(47) ? Na čto sleduet otkaza'sja   ot vsjačeskih   pretenzij?
      on what follows give up-self of whatsoever hopes
      'What should one rid oneself of any kind of hope for?'

(48) * Kakih argumentah protiv ehtoj točki zrenija ty   ešče ne
      which arguments   against this   point view   you yet not
      slyšal o?
      heard about

      'Which arguments against this point of view haven't you heard about?'

(49) ? Protiv kakov točki zrenija ty   ešče ne slyšal ob
      against which point view   you yet not heard about
      argumentah?
      arguments

      'Against which point of view haven't you heard about arguments?'

Standard island violations (at least most of them) do not show this pattern. Rather, extraction from deeper in the island is still bad:

(50) * That he'll hire someone is possible, but I won't divulge who that he'll
      hire is possible.   [Sentential Subject Constraint]

(51)   * That Mary thinks he'll hire someone is possible, but I won't divulge who that Mary thinks he'll hire is possible.

(52)   * She kissed a man who bit one of my friends, but Tom doesn't realize which one of my friends she kissed a man who bit.
                              [Complex NP Constraint, relative clause]

(53)   * She kissed a man who Bill said bit one of my friends, but Tom doesn't realize which one of my friends she kissed a man who Bill said bit.

Consider the possibility then that the P-stranding constraint is derivational, as in Merchant's account of persistence of Superiority under ellipsis. In the present instance a plausible candidate is the A-over-A. Chomsky (1973) proposed just this in anticipation of Postal's argument against successive cyclic *wh*-movement (Postal 1972). In English, preposition stranding is generally possible (54a). Sometimes pied-piping is as well, at least in fairly formal speech (54b). But once pied-piping takes place for the initial move, preposition stranding becomes impossible (54c).

(54)   a.   Who do you think (that) John talked to?

       b.   To whom do you think (that) John talked?

       c.   * Who do you think to (that) John talked?

To allow (54a) and (54b), Chomsky proposed that the *wh*-feature on *who(m)* can optionally extend to the PP *to whom* via "feature percolation." (54c) is still not possible, since the initial move of the PP means the feature has percolated, so the second step is disallowed by the A-over-A condition, presumably a constraint on derivations (and, not implausibly, an instance of Relativized Minimality).

One might further speculate then that the difference (or one of the differences) between languages that do and don't allow P-stranding in initial position is whether the *wh*-feature *can* or *must* percolate from DP to immediately dominating PP. In the latter type of language, even the first P-stranding step would violate the A-over-A. And if we continue to take that as a constraint on the operation of the transformation, P simply couldn't be stranded, so repair would never be a possibility.

13.7.2 *Unexpected Island Symmetry*

The next question might be the hardest of all. Following Uriagereka (1999*b*) and Fox & Pesetsky (2005), I have proposed that islands represent PF effects. But to the extent that the *LF* locality effects presented by Huang (1982), Lasnik & Saito (1984), and Chung *et al.* (2006) involve exactly the same islands, it is totally unclear why that should be so, or, indeed, why there should be LF locality effects at all. I will have to leave that question for future research.

13.8 Conclusion

One-cycle syntax with its concomitant cyclic Spell-Out has proven to be a very productive research idea. And, like so many productive ideas, it raises at least as many problems as it solves, as we have seen here, with respect to ellipsis phenomena and island constraints. Some of these problems have led to refinements of what, precisely, is meant by "Spell-Out," at least on the PF side. The remaining major problem—partial symmetry between "overt" and "covert" movement, alongside partial asymmetry—is more recalcitrant, possibly demanding a rethinking of the framework.

References

Abbott, Barbara. 1976. Right node raising as a test for constituenthood. *Linguistic Inquiry* 7: 639–42.

Abels, Klaus. 2003a. Phases, cyclicity, and stranding. Paper presented at the *IAP Workshop on EPP and Phases*. Massachusetts Institute of Technology, Cambridge (January 2003).

—— 2003b. *Successive-Cyclicity, Anti-Locality, and Adposition Stranding*. Ph.D. dissertation, University of Connecticut, Storrs.

Abney, Steven P. 1987. *The English Noun Phrase in Its Sentential Aspect*. Ph.D. dissertation, Massachusetts Institute of Technology, Cambridge.

—— 1991. Parsing by chunks. In Robert C. Berwick, Steven P. Abney & Carol Tenny (eds.), *Principle-Based Parsing*. Dordrecht: Kluwer.

Ackema, Peter & Ad Neeleman. 2002. Effects of short-term storage in processing rightward movement. In Sieb Nooteboom, Fred Weerman & Frank Wijnen (eds.), *Storage and Computation in the Language Faculty*. Dordrecht: Kluwer.

—————— 2004. *Beyond Morphology*. Oxford: Oxford University Press.

—————— & Weerman, Fred. 1993. Deriving functional projections. *Proceedings of the Twenty-Third Annual Meeting of the North-East Linguistic Society (NELS 23)*, vol. 1: 17–31.

Adger, David. 2003. *Core Syntax: A Minimalist Approach*. Oxford: Oxford University Press.

—— 2007. Stress and phasal syntax. *Linguistic Analysis* 33: 238–66.

Alexiadou, Artemis. 1997. *Adverb Placement: A Case Study in Antisymmetric Syntax*. Amsterdam: John Benjamins.

—— 1999. On the properties of some Greek word order patterns. In Artemis Alexiadou, Geoffrey Horrocks & Melita Stavrou (eds.), *Studies in Greek Syntax*. Dordrecht: Kluwer.

—— & Elena Anagnostopoulou. 1998. Parametrizing AGR: Word-order, V-movement and EPP checking. *Natural Language & Linguistic Theory* 16: 491–539.

Anagnostopoulou, Elena. 1994. *Clitic Dependencies in Modern Greek*. Ph.D. dissertation, Universität Salzburg.

Aoshima, Sachiko, Colin Phillips & Amy Weinberg. 2004. Processing filler-gap dependencies in a head-final language. *Journal of Memory & Language* 51: 23–54.

Aoun, Joseph & Elabbas Benmamoun. 1998. Minimality, reconstruction, and PF movement. *Linguistic Inquiry* 29: 569–97.

Aoyagi, Hiroshi. 2006. *Nihongo no Zyosi to Kinoo Hanchuu* (Particles and Functional categories in Japanese). Tokyo: Hitsuzi Shoboo.

Arregi, Karlos. 2002. *Focus on Basque Movements*. Ph.D. dissertation, Massachusetts Institute of Technology, Cambridge.

——2003. Nuclear stress and syntactic structure. Paper presented at the *1st North American Syntax Conference*, Concordia University, Montreal (May 2003).

Arvaniti, Amalia & Mary Baltazani. 2000. Greek ToBI: A system for the annotation of Greek speech corpora. *Proceedings of the Second International Conference on Language Resources and Evaluation (LREC 2000)*, vol. 2: 555–62.

Bachrach, Asaf & Roni Katzir. 2007. Spelling out QR. *Proceedings of Sinn und Bedeutung 11 (SuB 11)*: 63–75. [http://mutis.upf.es/glif/pub/sub11/individual/bach_katz.pdf]

Baker, Mark. 1996. *The Polysynthesis Parameter*. New York: Oxford University Press.

——2001. *The Atoms of Language: The Mind's Hidden Rules of Grammar*. New York: Basic Books.

——2008. The macroparameter in a microparametric world. In Biberauer (ed.).

Baltazani, Mary. 2002. *Quantifier Scope and the Role of Intonation in Greek*. Ph.D. dissertation, University of California, Los Angeles.

——& Sun-Ah Jun. 1999. Focus and topic intonation in Greek. *Proceedings of the XIVth International Congress of Phonetic Sciences*, vol. 2: 1305–8.

Baltin, Mark & Chris Collins (eds.). 2001. *The Handbook of Contemporary Syntactic Theory*. Malden, MA: Blackwell.

Bayer, Josef. 1996. *Directionality and Logical Form*. Dordrecht: Kluwer.

——1999. Final complementizers in hybrid languages. *Journal of Linguistics* 35: 233–71.

——2001. Two grammars in one: Sentential complements and complementizers in Bengali and other South-Asian languages. In Virginia Motapanyane (ed.), *Comparative Studies in Romanian Syntax*. Oxford: Elsevier.

——Tanja Schmid & Markus Bader. 2005. Clause union and clausal position. In Marcel den Dikken & Christina Tortora (eds.), *The Function of Function Words and Functional Categories*. Amsterdam: John Benjamins.

Belletti, Adriana. 2004a. Aspects of the low IP area. In Rizzi (ed.).

——(ed.). 2004b. *Structures and Beyond—The Cartography of Syntactic Structures*, vol. 3. New York: Oxford University Press.

Bianchi, Valentina. 2002. Headed relative clauses in generative syntax—Part II. *Glot International* 6: 1–13.

Biberauer, Theresa (ed.). 2008. *The Limits of Syntactic Variation*. Amsterdam: John Benjamins.

Bickmore, Lee. 1990. Branching nodes and prosodic categories: Evidence from Kinyambo. In Inkelas & Zec (eds).

Biskup, Petr. 2006a. Scrambling in Czech: Syntax, semantics and information structure. *Proceedings of the 21st North West Linguistics Conference—University of British Columbia Occasional Papers of Linguistics* 1: 1–15.

Biskup, Petr. 2006b. Adjunction, condition C, and the background adjunct coreference principle. *Proceedings of the 25th West Coast Conference on Formal Linguistics (WCCFL 25)*: 96–104.

——— Forthcoming. Adjunction. In Eva Lehečková & Jan Táborský (eds.), *Struktura, variety, funkce: Festschrift for Oldřich Uličný*. Prague: Slavica Pragensia.

Bittner, Maria & Kenneth Hale. 1996. The structural determination of case and agreement. *Linguistic Inquiry* 27: 1–68.

Bobaljik, Jonathan David. 1995. *Morphosyntax: The Syntax of Verbal Inflection*. Ph.D. dissertation, Massachusetts Institute of Technology, Cambridge.

——— 2002. A-chains at the PF-interface: Copies and "covert" movement. *Natural Language & Linguistic Theory* 20: 197–267.

——— & Susi Wurmbrand. 2003. Relativized phases. Ms., McGill University, Montreal & University of Connecticut, Storrs. [Revised version published as Bobaljik & Wurmbrand (2005).]

——— ——— 1999. Modals, raising and A-reconstruction. Paper presented at Leiden Universiteit (October 1999) & Universität Salzburg (December 1999).

——— ——— 2005. The domain of agreement. *Natural Language & Linguistic Theory* 23: 809–65.

Boeckx, Cedric. 2001. Scope reconstruction and A-movement. *Natural Language & Linguistic Theory* 19: 503–48. [Reprinted in Boeckx, Cedric. 2008. *Aspects of the Syntax of Agreement*. London: Routledge.]

——— 2003. *Islands and Chains: Resumption as Stranding*. Amsterdam: John Benjamins.

——— 2006. *Linguistic Minimalism: Origins, Concepts, Methods, and Aims*. New York: Oxford University Press.

——— 2008a. *Understanding Minimalist Syntax: Lessons from Locality in Long-Distance Dependencies*. Malden, MA: Blackwell.

——— 2008b. *Bare Syntax*. New York: Oxford University Press.

——— & Kleanthes K Grohmann. 2007. Putting Phases in Perspective. *Syntax* 10: 204–22.

——— & Howard Lasnik. 2006. Intervention and repair. *Linguistic Inquiry* 37: 143–54.

Boersma, Paul & David Weenink. 2006. Praat: Doing phonetics by computer (version 4.4.31). Speech analysis software, Universiteit van Amsterdam. [http://www.praat.org]

Booij, Geert E. 1985. Coordination reduction in complex words: A case for prosodic phonology. In Harry van der Hulst & Norval Smith (eds.), *Advances in Nonlinear Phonology*. Dordrecht: Foris.

——— & Jaap van Marle (eds.). 1999. *The Yearbook of Morphology 1998*. Dordrecht: Kluwer.

Borer, Hagit. 1984. *Parametric Syntax: Case Studies in Semitic and Romance Languages*. Dordrecht: Foris.

Bošković, Željko. 2001. *On the Nature of the Syntax-Phonology Interface*. Oxford: Elsevier.

—— 2002a. Expletives don't move. *Proceedings of the Thirty-Second Annual Meeting of the North-East Linguistic Society (NELS 32)*, vol. 1: 21–40.

—— 2002b. On multiple *wh*-fronting. *Linguistic Inquiry* 33: 351–83.

—— 2002c. A-movement and the EPP. *Syntax* 5: 167–218.

—— 2005. Left branch extraction, structure of NP, and scrambling. In Joachim Sabel & Mamoru Saito (eds.), *The Free Word Order Phenomenon: Its Syntactic Sources and Diversity*. Berlin: Mouton de Gruyter.

—— & Howard Lasnik. 1999. How strict is cycle? *Linguistic Inquiry* 30: 691–703.

—————— 2003. On the distribution of null complementizers. *Linguistic Inquiry* 34: 527–46.

Bouchard, Denis. 2002. *Adjectives, Numbers and Interfaces: Why Languages Vary*. Oxford: Elsevier.

Bresnan, Joan. 1971. Sentence stress and syntactic transformations. *Language* 47: 257–81.

—— 1972. Stress and syntax: A reply. *Language* 48: 326–42.

Brody, Michael. 1995. *Lexico-Logical Form: A Radically Minimalist Theory*. Cambridge, MA: MIT Press.

—— 2000. Mirror theory: Syntactic representation in perfect syntax. *Linguistic Inquiry* 31: 29–57.

Brosziewski, Ulf. 1994. *Extraposition im Deutschen*. M.A. thesis, Universität zu Köln.

Browning, Marguerite A. 1996. CP recursion and *that*-t effects. *Linguistic Inquiry* 27: 237–55.

Bruening, Benjamin. 2001. *Syntax at the Edge: Cross-Clausal Phenomena and the Syntax of Passamaquoddy*. Ph.D. dissertation, Massachusetts Institute of Technology, Cambridge.

Büring, Daniel. 1997. *On the Meaning of Topic and Focus: The 59th Street Bridge Accent*. London: Routledge.

—— & Katharina Hartmann. 1997. Doing the right thing. *The Linguistic Review* 14: 1–42.

Butler, Jonny. 2003. A minimalist treatment of modality. *Lingua* 113: 967–96.

Carnie, Andrew. 1995. *Non-Verbal Predication and Head Movement*. Ph.D. dissertation, Massachusetts Institute of Technology, Cambridge.

—— 2000. On the definitions of X^0 and XP. *Syntax* 3: 59–106.

—— 2008. Consonant mutations as evidence for a *v*P phase. Ms., University of Arizona, Tucson.

Carrier, Jill & Janet Randall. 1992. The argument structure and syntactic structure of resultatives. *Linguistic Inquiry* 23: 173–234.

Cecchetto, Carlo. 2004. Explaining the locality conditions of QR: Consequences for the theory of phases. *Natural Language Semantics* 12: 345–97.

—— & Gennaro Chierchia. 1999. Reconstruction in dislocation constructions and the syntax/semantics interface. *Proceedings of the 17th West Coast Conference on Formal Linguistics (WCCFL 17)*: 132–46.

Chametzky, Robert. 2000. *Phrase Structure*. Malden, MA: Blackwell.

—— 2003. Phrase structure. In Randall Hendrick (ed.), *Minimalist Syntax*. Malden, MA: Blackwell.

Chandra, Pritha. 2007. *(Dis)agree: Movement and agreement reconsidered*. Ph.D. dissertation, University of Maryland, College Park.

Chen, Matthew. 1987. The syntax of Xiamen tone sandhi. In Colin Ewen & John Anderson (eds.), *Phonology Yearbook 4*. Cambridge: Cambridge University Press.

Cheney, Dorothy L. & Robert M. Seyfarth. 1997. Why animals don't have language. *The Tanner Lectures on Human Values*, delivered at the University of Cambridge (March 1997). [http://www.tannerlectures.utah.edu/lectures/documents/Cheney98.pdf]

Cheng, Lisa L.-S. 2000. Moving just the feature. In Uli Lutz, Gereon Müller & Arnim von Stechow (eds.), Wh-*Scope Marking*. Amsterdam: John Benjamins.

Chierchia, Gennaro. 1995. *Dynamics of Meaning: Anaphora, Presupposition, and the Theory of Grammar*. Chicago: University of Chicago Press.

Chomsky, Noam. 1955. *The Logical Structure of Linguistic Theory*. Mimeograph, Harvard University, Cambridge, MA. [Revised version published as Chomsky (1975).]

—— 1965. *Aspects of the Theory of Syntax*. Cambridge, MA: MIT Press.

—— 1972. Some empirical issues in the theory of transformational grammar. In Stanley Peters (ed.), *Goals of Linguistic Theory*. Englewood Cliffs, NJ: Prentice-Hall.

—— 1973. Conditions on transformations. In Stephen R. Anderson & Paul Kiparsky (eds.), *A Festschrift for Morris Halle*. New York: Holt, Reinhart & Winston.

—— 1975. *The Logical Structure of Linguistic Theory*. New York: Plenum Press.

—— 1981. *Lectures on Government and Binding: The Pisa Lectures*. Dordrecht: Foris. [Subsequent editions published by Berlin: Mouton de Gruyter.]

—— 1986a. *Barriers*. Cambridge, MA: MIT Press.

—— 1986b. *Knowledge of Language: Its Nature, Origin and Use*. New York: Praeger.

—— 1993. A minimalist program for linguistic theory. In Hale & Keyser (eds.). [Reprinted in Chomsky (1995).]

—— 1994. Bare phrase structure. In Gert Webelhuth (ed.), *Government and Binding Theory and the Minimalist Program*. Malden, MA: Blackwell.

—— 1995. *The Minimalist Program*. Cambridge, MA: MIT Press.

—— 2000. Minimalist inquiries: The framework. In Martin *et al.* (eds.).

—— 2001. Derivation by phase. In Kenstowicz (ed.).

—— 2004a. Beyond explanatory adequacy. In Belletti (ed.).

—— 2004b. *The Generative Enterprise Revisited: Discussions with Riny Huybregts, Henk van Riemsdijk, Naoki Fukui, and Mihoko Zushi*. Berlin: Mouton de Gruyter.

—— 2005. Three factors in language design. *Linguistic Inquiry* 36: 1–22.

—— 2006. Turing's thesis. Keynote address, presented at *InterPhases: A Conference on Interfaces in Current Syntactic Theory*, Castelliotissa Hall, Nicosia (May 2006).

—— 2007a. Approaching UG from below. In Sauerland & Gärtner (eds.).

—— 2007b. Of minds and language. *Biolinguistics* 1: 9–27.

—— 2008. On phases. In Robert Freidin, Carlos P. Otero & Maria Luisa Zubizarreta (eds.), *Foundational Issues in Linguistic Theory: Essays in Honor of Jean-Roger Vergnaud*. Cambridge, MA: MIT Press.

—— & Morris Halle. 1968. *The Sound Pattern of English*. New York: Harper and Row.

—— & Howard Lasnik. 1977. Filters and control. *Linguistic Inquiry* 8: 425–504.

—— —— 1993. The theory of principles and parameters. In Joachim Jacobs, Arnim von Stechow, Wolfgang Sternefeld & Theo Vennemann (eds.), *Syntax: Ein internationales Handbuch zeitgenössischer Forschung / An International Handbook of Contemporary Research*, vol. 1. Berlin: Mouton de Gruyter.

Chung, Inkie. 2007. *Ecology at PF: A Study of Korean Phonology and Morphology in a Derivational Approach*. Ph.D. dissertation, University of Connecticut, Storrs.

Chung, Sandra, William A. Ladusaw & James McCloskey. 1995. Sluicing and logical form. *Natural Language Semantics* 3: 239–82.

—— —— —— 2006. Sluicing revisited. Paper presented at the *Linguistic Society of America (LSA) 2006 Annual Meeting—Symposium on Ellipsis*, Hyatt Regency Hotel/Albuquerque Convention Center, Albuquerque, NM (January 2006).

Cinque, Guglielmo. 1993. A null theory of phrase and compound stress. *Linguistic Inquiry* 24: 239–97.

—— 1999. *Adverbs and Functional Heads: A Cross-Linguistic Perspective*. New York: Oxford University Press.

—— (ed.). 2002. *Functional Structure in DP and IP—The Cartography of Syntactic Structures*, vol. 1. New York: Oxford University Press.

—— 2004a. Issues in adverbial syntax. *Lingua* 114: 683–710.

—— 2004b. "Restructuring" and functional structure. In Belletti (ed.).

Citko, Barbara. 2005. On the nature of merge: External merge, internal merge, and parallel merge. *Linguistic Inquiry* 36: 475–96.

Collins, Chris. 1997. *Local Economy*. Cambridge, MA: MIT Press.

—— 2002. Eliminating labels. In Epstein & Seely (eds.).

Cottell, Siobhan. 1995. The representation of tense in Modern Irish. *Geneva Generative Papers* 3.2: 105–24.

van Craenenbroeck, Jeroen & Marcel den Dikken. 2006. Ellipsis and EPP repair. *Linguistic Inquiry* 37: 653–64.

Culicover, Peter W. 1993. The adverb effect: Evidence against ECP accounts of the *that*-t effect. *Proceedings of the Twenty-Third Annual Meeting of the North-East Linguistic Society (NELS 23)*, vol. 1: 97–111.

D'Imperio, Mariapaola, Gorka Elordieta, Sónia Frota, Pilar Prieto & MarinaVigário. 2005. Intonational phrasing in Romance: The role of syntactic and prosodic structure. In Sónia Frota, Marina Vigário & Maria João Freitas (eds.), *Prosodies: With Special Reference to the Iberian Languages*. Berlin: Mouton de Gruyter.

Davidson, Donald. 1967. The logical form of action sentences. In Nicholas Rescher (ed.), *The Logic of Decision and Action*. Pittsburgh, PA: University of Pittsburgh Press.

Diesing, Molly. 1992. *Indefinites*. Cambridge, MA: MIT Press.

Dobashi, Yoshihito. 2003. *Phonological Phrasing and Syntactic Derivation.* Ph.D. dissertation, Cornell University, Ithaca, NY.

Donati, Caterina & Marina Nespor. 2003. From focus to syntax. *Lingua* 113: 1119–42.

Drubig, Hans Bernhard. 2003. Towards a typology of focus and focus constructions. *Linguistics* 41: 1–50.

Dryer, Matthew. 1980. The positional tendencies of sentential noun phrases in Universal Grammar. *The Canadian Journal of Linguistics* 25.2: 123–95.

Elordieta, Gorka. 2007. Segmental phonology and syntactic structure. In Ramchand & Reiss (eds.).

—— Sónia Frota, Pilar Prieto & Marina Vigário. 2003. Effects of constituent length and syntactic branching on intonational phrasing in Ibero-Romance. *Proceedings of the XVth International Congress of Phonetic Sciences*: 487–90.

—— —— & Marina Vigário. 2005. Subjects, objects and intonational phrasing in Spanish and Portuguese. *Studia Linguistica* 59: 110–43.

Embick, David. 2007. Linearization and local dislocations: Derivational mechanics and interactions. *Linguistic Analysis* 33: 303–36.

—— & Rolf Noyer. 2001. Movement operations after syntax. *Linguistic Inquiry* 32: 555–95.

Enç, Mürvet. 2004. Functional categories in Turkish. *Proceedings of the 1st Workshop on Altaic Formal Linguistics (WAFL 1)—MIT Working Papers in Linguistics* 46: 208–26.

Endo, Yoshio. 2006. *A Study of the Cartography of Japanese Syntactic Structures.* Ph.D. dissertation, Université de Genève.

—— 2007. *Locality and Information Structure: A Cartographic Approach to Japanese.* Amsterdam: John Benjamins.

Engdahl, Elisabet. 1986. *Constituent Questions: The Syntax and Semantics of Questions with Special Reference to Swedish.* Dordrecht: Reidel.

—— 2001. The role of syntactic features in the analysis of dialogue. In Rohrer *et al.* (eds.).

Epstein, Samuel David. 1999. Un-principled syntax: The derivation of syntactic relations. In Epstein & Hornstein (eds.).

—— Erich M. Groat, Ruriko Kawashima & Hisatsugu Kitahara. 1998. *A Derivational Approach to Syntactic Relations.* New York: Oxford University Press.

—— & Norbert Hornstein (eds.) 1999. *Working Minimalism.* Cambridge, MA: MIT Press.

—— & T. Daniel Seely. 2002a. Rule applications as cycles in a level-free syntax. In Epstein & Seely (eds.).

—— —— (eds.). 2002b. *Derivation and Explanation in the Minimalist Program.* Malden, MA: Blackwell.

—— —— 2006. *Derivations in Minimalism.* Cambridge: Cambridge University Press.

Ernst, Thomas. 2002. *The Syntax of Adjuncts.* Cambridge: Cambridge University Press.

Erteschik-Shir, Nomi. 1997. *The Dynamics of Focus Structure.* Cambridge: Cambridge University Press.

Fanselow, Gisbert. 1989. Coherent infinitives in German. In Christa Bhatt, Elisabeth Löbel & Claudia Schmidt (eds.), *Syntactic Phrase Structure Phenomena*. Amsterdam: John Benjamins.

—— & Damir Ćavar. 2002. Distributed deletion. In Artemis Alexiadou (ed.), *Theoretical Approaches to Universals*. Amsterdam: John Benjamins.

Felser, Claudia. 2004. *Wh*-copying, phases, and successive cyclicity. *Lingua* 114: 543–74.

Féry, Caroline. 2007. The prosody of topicalization. In Kerstin Schwabe & Susanne Winkler (eds.), *On Information Structure, Meaning and Form*. Amsterdam: John Benjamins.

—— & Katharina Hartmann. 2005. The focus and prosodic structure of German right node raising and gapping. *The Linguistic Review* 22: 69–116.

—— & Stavros Skopeteas. In progress. The prosodification of Greek adjuncts. Ms., Universität Potsdam.

Fiengo, Robert. 1977. On trace theory. *Linguistic Inquiry* 8: 35–61.

Fitch, W. Tecumseh & Marc D. Hauser. 2004. Computational constraints on syntactic processing in nonhuman primates. *Science* 303: 377–80.

Fitzpatrick, Justin & Erich M. Groat. 2005. The timing of syntactic operations: Phases, c-command, remerger, and Lebeaux effects. Handout from a paper presented at the *ECO5 Syntax Conference*, Harvard University, Cambridge, MA (March 2005). [http://web.mit.edu/jfitzpat/www/FitzpatrickGroat-ECo5.pdf]

Fodor, Jerry A. & Zenon W. Pylyshyn. 1988. Connectionism and cognitive architecture: A critical analysis. *Cognition* 28: 3–71.

Fox, Danny. 1999. Reconstruction, binding theory, and the interpretation of chains. *Linguistic Inquiry* 30: 157–96.

—— 2000. *Economy and Semantic Interpretation*. Cambridge, MA: MIT Press.

—— & Howard Lasnik. 2003. Successive cyclic movement and island repair: The difference between sluicing and VP ellipsis. *Linguistic Inquiry* 34: 143–54.

—— & David Pesetsky. 2005. Cyclic linearization of syntactic structure. *Theoretical Linguistics* 31: 1–45.

Frampton, John. 2004. Copies, traces, occurrences, and all that: Evidence from Bulgarian multiple *wh*-movement. Ms., Northeastern University, Boston, MA. [http://www.math.neu.edu/ling/pdffiles/CopiesTraces.pdf]

—— & Sam Gutmann. 2002. Crash-proof syntax. In Epstein & Seely (eds.).

Franks, Steven. 1995. *Parameters of Slavic Morphosyntax*. New York: Oxford University Press.

Frazier, Lyn. 1978. *On Comprehending Sentences: Syntactic Parsing Strategies*. Ph.D. dissertation, University of Connecticut, Storrs.

Frege, Gottlob. 1892. Sinn und Bedeutung. *Zeitschrift für Philosophie und philosophische Kritik* 100: 25–50.

Fukui, Naoki. 1995a. *Theory of Projection in Syntax*. Tokyo: Kurosio.

—— 1995b. The principles-and-parameters approach: A comparative syntax of English and Japanese. In Masayoshi Shibatani & Theodora Bynon (eds.), *Approaches to Language Typology*. London: Clarendon Press.

Fukui, Naoki (ed.). 2000. *Shintakusu to Imi: Harada Shin-ichi Gengogaku Ronbun Senshu* (Syntax and Meaning: Shin-ichi Harada's Collected Works in Linguistics). Tokyo: Taishukan.

—— 2005. Embed. Invited lecture presented at the *Third International Conference on Formal Linguistics*, Hunan University, Changsha (September 2005).

—— & Yuji Takano. 1998. Symmetry in syntax: Merge and demerge. *Journal of East Asian Linguistics* 7: 27–86.

Fuß, Eric. 2005. *The Rise of Agreement: A Formal Approach to the Syntax and Grammaticalization of Verbal Inflection*. Amsterdam: John Benjamins.

—— 2007. Cyclic spell-out and the domain of post-syntactic operations: Evidence from complementizer agreement. *Linguistic Analysis* 33: 267–302.

Gallego, Ángel J. 2006a. Phase sliding. Poster presented at *InterPhases: A Conference on Interfaces in Current Syntactic Theory*, Castelliotissa Hall, Nicosia (May 2006).

—— 2006b. Phase effects in Iberian Romance. *Selected Proceedings of the 9th Hispanic Linguistics Symposium*: 43–55.

—— 2007. *Phase Theory and Parametric Variation*. Ph.D. dissertation, Universitat Autònoma de Barcelona.

Gärtner, Hans-Martin & Markus Steinbach. 1994. Economy, verb second, and the SVO/SOV distinction. *Working Papers in Scandinavian Syntax* 53: 1–59.

Gee, James Paul & François Grosjean. 1983. Performance structures. *Cognitive Psychology* 15: 411–58.

Gentner, Timothy Q., Kimberly M. Fenn, Daniel Margoliash & Howard C. Nusbaum 2006. Recursive syntactic pattern learning by songbirds. *Nature* 440: 1204–7.

Georgiafentis, Michalis. 2004. *Focus and Word Order Variation in Greek*. Ph.D. dissertation, University of Reading.

Ghini, Mirco. 1993. Ø-formation in Italian: A new proposal. *Toronto Working Papers in Linguistics* 12: 41–78.

Giannakidou, Anastasia. 2000. Negative … concord? *Natural Language & Linguistic Theory* 18: 457–523.

Gibson, Edward. 1991. *A Computational Theory of Human Language Processing: Memory Limitations and Processing Breakdown*. Ph.D. thesis, Carnegie Mellon University, Pittsburgh, PA.

Giorgi, Alessandra & Fabio Pianesi. 1997. *Tense and Aspect: From Semantics to Morphosyntax*. New York: Oxford University Press.

Golden, Marija. 2003. Clitic placement and clitic climbing in Slovenian. *Sprachtypologie und Universalienforschung* 56: 208–33.

Grebenyova, Lydia. 2006. Sluicing puzzles in Russian. In Hana Filip, Steven Franks, James E. Lavine & Mila Tasseva-Kurktchieva (eds.), *Formal Approaches to Slavic Linguistics 14 (The Princeton Meeting, 2005)*. Ann Arbor, MI: Michigan Slavic Publications.

Green, Antony D. 2007. *Phonology Limited*. Potsdam: Universitätsverlag Potsdam.

Grewendorf, Günther. 1988. *Aspekte der deutschen Syntax*. Tübingen: Narr.

Grimshaw, Jane. 1990. *Argument Structure*. Cambridge, MA: MIT Press.

——2000. Locality and extended projection. In Peter Coopmans, Martin Everaert & Jane Grimshaw (eds.), *Lexical Specification and Insertion*. Amsterdam: John Benjamins.

Groat, Erich M. & John O'Neil. 1996. Spell-out at the LF interface. In Werner Abraham, Samuel David Epstein, Höskuldur Thráinsson, & C. Jan-Wouter Zwart (eds.), *Minimal Ideas*. Amsterdam: John Benjamins.

Grohmann, Kleanthes K. 2000. *Prolific Peripheries: A Radical View from the Left*. Ph.D. dissertation, University of Maryland, College Park.

——2003. *Prolific Domains: On the Anti-Locality of Movement Dependencies*. Amsterdam: John Benjamins.

——2007a. Deriving dynamic interfaces. *Linguistic Analysis* 33: 3–19.

——2007b. Transfer vs. spell-out and the road to PF. *Linguistic Analysis* 33: 176–94.

——2007c. Spelling out dynamic interfaces. *Linguistic Analysis* 33: 197–208.

——Forthcoming. Anti-locality. In Cedric Boeckx (ed.), *The Oxford Handbook of Linguistic Minimalism*. Oxford: Oxford University Press.

Grosu, Alex & Sandra A. Thompson. 1977. Constraints on the distribution of NP clauses. *Language* 53: 104–51.

Guimarães, Maximiliano. 1998. *Repensando a interface sintaxe-fonologia a partir do axioma de correspondência linear*. M.A. thesis, Universidade Estadual de Campinas.

Haegeman, Liliane. 1995. *The Syntax of Negation*. Cambridge: Cambridge University Press.

——& Raffaella Zanuttini. 1991. Negative heads and the NEG-criterion. *The Linguistic Review* 8: 233–51.

————1996. Negative concord in West Flemish. In Adriana Belletti & Luigi Rizzi (eds.), *Parameters and Functional Heads: Essays in Comparative Syntax*. New York: Oxford University Press.

Haider, Hubert. 1993. *Deutsche Syntax—Generativ*. Tübingen: Narr.

——1995. Downright down to the right. In Lutz & Pafel (eds.).

——1997. Extraposition. In Dorothee Beerman, David LeBlanc & Henk van Riemsdijk (eds.), *Rightward Movement*. Amsterdam: John Benjamins.

——2000. OV is more basic than VO. In Svenonius (ed.).

——2001. Heads and selection. In Norbert Corver & Henk van Riemsdijk (eds.), *Semi-Lexical Categories: The Function of Content Words and the Content of Function Words*. Berlin: Mouton de Gruyter.

——2003. V-clustering and clause union—Causes and effects. In Pieter A. M. Seuren & Gerard Kempen (eds.), *Verb Clusters in Dutch and German*. Amsterdam: John Benjamins.

——2005. How to turn Germanic into Icelandic—And derive the OV-VO contrasts. *Journal of Comparative Germanic Linguistics* 8: 1–53.

Hale, Kenneth & Samuel Jay Keyser. 1993a. On argument structure and the lexical expression of syntactic relations. In Hale & Keyser (eds.).

————(eds.). 1993b. *The View from Building 20: Essays in Linguistics in Honor of Sylvain Bromberger*. Cambridge, MA: MIT Press.

Halle, Morris & Alec Marantz. 1993. Distributed morphology and the pieces of inflection. In Hale & Keyser (eds.).

Harada, Shin-ichi. 1976. Arguments that Japanese *to*-complements are noun phrase complements. *Attempts in Linguistics and Literature* 3: 33–7. [Reprinted in Fukui (2000).]

Harley, Heidi. 1995. *Subjects, Events and Licensing*. Ph.D. dissertation, Massachusetts Institute of Technology, Cambridge.

—— 2003. Possession and the double object construction. In Pierre Pica with Johan Rooryck (eds.), *Linguistic Variation Yearbook 2 (2002)*. Amsterdam: John Benjamins.

Harlow, Steve. 1989. The syntax of Welsh soft mutation. *Natural Language & Linguistic Theory* 7: 289–316.

Hartmann, Katharina. 2000. *Right Node Raising and Gapping: Interface Conditions on Prosodic Deletion*. Amsterdam: John Benjamins.

Hauser, Marc D., Noam Chomsky & W. Tecumseh Fitch. 2002. The faculty of language: What is it, who has it, and how did it evolve? *Science* 298: 1569–79.

Hawkins, John A. 1990. A parsing theory of word order universals. *Linguistic Inquiry* 21: 223–61.

—— 1994. *Performance Theory of Order and Constituency*. Cambridge: Cambridge University Press.

—— 2004. *Efficiency and Complexity in Grammars*. Oxford: Oxford University Press.

Hayes, Bruce. 1989. The prosodic hierarchy in meter. In Paul Kiparsky & Gilbert Youmans (eds.), *Rhythm and Meter—Phonetics and Phonology*, vol. 1. Orlando, FL: Academic Press.

Heim, Irene & Angelika Kratzer. 1998. *Semantics in Generative Grammar*. Malden, MA: Blackwell.

Hendriks, Herman. 1993. *Studied Flexibility*. Ph.D. dissertation, Universiteit van Amsterdam.

Heycock, Caroline. 1995. Asymmetries in reconstruction. *Linguistic Inquiry* 26: 547–70.

Hinzen, Wolfram. 2003. Truth's fabric. *Mind and Language* 18: 194–219.

—— 2006. *Mind Design and Minimal Syntax*. Oxford: Oxford University Press.

—— 2007. *An Essay on Names and Truth*. Oxford: Oxford University Press.

—— & Juan Uriagereka. 2006. On the metaphysics of linguistics. *Erkenntnis* 65: 71–96.

Hiraiwa, Ken. 2003. Movement and derivation: Eliminating the PBC. *Proceedings of the 26th Penn Linguistics Colloquium (PLC 26)—UPenn Working Papers in Linguistics* 9.1: 89–103.

—— 2005. *Dimensions of Symmetry in Syntax: Agreement and Clausal Architecture*. Ph.D. dissertation, Massachusetts Institute of Technology, Cambridge.

—— & Shinichiro Ishihara. 2002. Missing links: Cleft, sluicing, and "no da" construction in Japanese. *MIT Working Papers in Linguistics* 43: 35–54.

Hirose, Yuki. 1999. *Resolving Reanalysis Ambiguity in Japanese Relative Clauses*. Ph.D. dissertation, City University New York.

—— 2003. Recycling prosodic boundaries. *Journal of Psycholinguistic Research* 32: 167–95.

Höhle, Tilman N. 1986. Der Begriff "Mittelfeld": Anmerkungen über die Theorie der topologischen Felder. In Walter Weiss, Herbert Ernst Wiegand & Marga Reis (eds.), *Textlinguistik contra Stilistik*. Tübingen: Narr.

Holmberg, Anders. 1999a. Remarks on Holmberg's Generalization. *Studia Linguistica* 53: 1–39.

—— 1999b. Yes and no in Finnish: Ellipsis and cyclic spell-out. *MIT Working Papers in Linguistics* 33: 83–110.

—— 2001. The syntax of yes and no in Finnish. *Studia Linguistica* 55: 141–75.

Hopper, Paul J. & Elisabeth C. Traugott. 1993. *Grammaticalization*. Cambridge: Cambridge University Press.

Hornstein, Norbert. 1998. Movement and chains. *Syntax* 1: 99–127.

—— 2001. *Move! A Minimalist Theory of Construal*. Malden, MA: Blackwell.

—— 2005. What do labels do? Some thoughts on the endocentric roots of recursion and movement. Ms., University of Maryland, College Park.

—— Forthcoming. *A Theory of Syntax*. Cambridge: Cambridge University Press.

—— Jairo Nunes & Kleanthes K. Grohmann. 2005. *Understanding Minimalism*. Cambridge: Cambridge University Press.

—— & Juan Uriagereka. 2002. Reprojections. In Epstein & Seely (eds.).

Horrocks, Geoffrey. 1994. Subjects and configurationality: Modern Greek clause structure. *Journal of Linguistics* 30: 81–109.

Huang, C.-T. James. 1982. *Logical Relations in Chinese and the Theory of Grammar*. Ph.D. dissertation, Massachusetts Institute of Technology, Cambridge.

—— 1993. Reconstruction and structure of VP. *Linguistic Inquiry* 24: 103–38.

Iatridou, Sabine. 1990. The past, the possible and the evident. *Linguistic Inquiry* 21: 123–9.

—— 1991. *Topics in Conditionals*. Ph.D. dissertation, Massachusetts Institute of Technology, Cambridge.

Inaba, Jiro. 2007. *Die Syntax der Satzkomplementierung: Zur Struktur des Nachfeldes im Deutschen*. Berlin: Akademie Verlag.

Inkelas, Sharon. 1989. *Prosodic Constituency in the Lexicon*. Ph.D. dissertation, Stanford University, CA.

Inkelas, Sharon & Draga Zec (eds.). 1990. *The Phonology-Syntax Connection*. Chicago: University of Chicago Press.

Ishihara, Shiniriro. 2000. Stress, focus, and scrambling in Japanese. *MIT Working Papers in Linguistics* 39: 142–75.

—— 2003. *Intonation and Interface Conditions*. Ph.D. dissertation, Massachusetts Institute of Technology, Cambridge.

—— 2004a. Focus intonation inside another: A multiple spell-out account. Handout from a paper presented at the *27th GLOW (Generative Linguistics of the Old World) Colloquium 2004*, Aristotle University of Thessaloniki (April 2004). [http://www.sfb632.uni-potsdam.de/homes/s_i/talks/7glow04_a.pdf]

—— 2004b. Prosody by phase: Evidence from focus intonation-*wh*-scope correspondence in Japanese. *Working Papers of SFB 632—Interdisciplinary Studies on Information Structure* 1: 77–119.

Itô, Junko & Armin Mester. 1992. Weak layering and word binarity. *Linguistics Research Center Report LRC–92–09*, University of California, Santa Cruz. [Revised version published in Takeru Honma, Masao Okazaki, Toshiyuki Tabata & Shin-ichi Tanaka (eds.), *A New Century of Phonology and Phonological Theory: A Festschrift for Professor Shosuke Haraguchi on the Occasion of His Sixtieth Birthday*. Tokyo: Kaitakusha, 2003.]

—— 1995. Hierarchical alignment and binarity. Paper presented at the *Trilateral Phonology Weekend (TREND)*, University of California, Santa Cruz (April 1995) and the *18th GLOW (Generative Linguistics of the Old World) Colloquium 1995: Phonology Workshop*, Universitetet i Tromsø (May 1995).

Jackendoff, Ray. 1969. *Some Rules of Semantic Interpretation in English*. Ph.D. dissertation, Massachusetts Institute of Technology, Cambridge.

—— 1996. *The Architecture of the Language Faculty*. Cambridge, MA: MIT Press.

Janssen, Theo M. V. 1983. *Foundations and Applications of Montague Grammar*. Amsterdam: Mathematisch Centrum.

Jayaseelan, K. A. 1990. Incomplete VP deletion and gapping. *Linguistic Analysis* 20: 64–81.

Johnson, Kyle. 1985. *A Case for Movement*. Ph.D. dissertation, Massachusetts Institute of Technology, Cambridge.

—— 2001. What VP ellipsis can do, what it can't, but not why. In Baltin & Collins (eds.).

—— 2003. Towards an etiology of adjunct islands. *Proceedings of the 19th Scandinavian Conference in Linguistics (SCL 19)—Nordlyd* 31: 187–215.

—— 2004. How to be quiet. Paper presented at the *Fortieth Regional Meeting of the Chicago Linguistic Society (CLS 40)*, University of Chicago (April 2004).

Jones, Morris & Alan R. Thomas. 1977. *The Welsh Language: Studies in Its Syntax and Semantics*. Cardiff: University of Wales Press.

Jun, Sun-Ah. 2003. The effect of phrase length and speech rate on prosodic phrasing. *Proceedings of the XVth International Congress of Phonetic Sciences*, vol. 1: 483–6.

Junghanns, Uwe. 2002. Klitische Elemente im Tschechischen: Eine kritische Bestandsaufnahme. In Thomas Daiber (ed.), *Linguistische Beiträge zur Slavistik IX*. Munich: Sagner.

Kahnemuyipour, Arsalan. 2004. *The Syntax of Sentential Stress*. Ph.D. dissertation, University of Toronto.

—— 2005. On the nature of the syntax-phonology interface: The case of sentential stress. Paper presented at the *Mediterranean Syntax Meeting Workshop on Interfaces*, University of the Aegean, Rhodes (June 2005).

Kaisse, Ellen M. 1985. *Connected Speech: The Interaction of Syntax and Phonology*. New York: Academic Press.

Kayne, Richard S. 1994. *The Antisymmetry of Syntax*. Cambridge, MA: MIT Press.

—— 2000. *Parameters and Universals*. New York: Oxford University Press.

—— 2002. Pronouns and their antecedents. In Epstein & Seely (2002*b*).

—— 2006. Notes on full interpretation. Invited lecture presented at *InterPhases: A Conference on Interfaces in Current Syntactic Theory*, Castelliotissa Hall, Nicosia (May 2006).

Kehler, Andrew. 2002. *Coherence, Reference and the Theory of Grammar*. Stanford, CA: CSLI Publications.

Kempson, Ruth, Wilfried Meyer-Viol & Dov Gabbay. 2001. *Dynamic Syntax: The Flow of Language Understanding*. Oxford: Blackwell.

Kennedy, Christopher & Jason Merchant. 2000. Attributive comparative deletion. *Natural Language & Linguistic Theory* 18: 89–146.

Kenstowicz, Michael (ed.). 2001. *Ken Hale: A Life in Language*. Cambridge, MA: MIT Press.

—— & Charles Kisseberth. 1979. *Generative Phonology*. New York: Academic Press.

Kimball, John P. 1973. Seven principles of surface structure parsing in natural language. *Cognition* 2: 15–47.

Kiss, Tibor. 1995. *Infinitive Komplementation*. Tübingen: Niemeyer.

Kitagawa, Yoshihisa. 2005. Prosody, syntax and pragmatics of *wh*-questions in Japanese. *English Linguistics* 22: 302–46.

Kitahara, Hisatsugu. 1997. *Elementary Operations and Optimal Derivations*. Cambridge, MA: MIT Press.

—— 1999. Eliminating * as a feature (of traces). In Epstein & Hornstein (eds.).

Ko, Heejeong. 2005. *Syntactic Edges and Linearization*. Ph.D. dissertation, Massachusetts Institute of Technology, Cambridge.

—— 2007. Asymmetries in scrambling and cyclic linearization. *Linguistic Inquiry* 38: 49–83.

Koeneman, Olaf. 2000. *The Flexible Nature of Verb Movement*. Utrecht: LOT Publications.

Koizumi, Masatoshi. 1995. *Phrase Structure in Minimalist Syntax*. Ph.D. dissertation, Massachusetts Institute of Technology, Cambridge.

—— 2000. String vacuous overt verb raising. *Journal of East Asian Linguistics* 9: 227–85.

Koopman, Hilde. 1984. *The Syntax of Verbs: From Verb Movement Rules in the Kru Languages to Universal Grammar*. Dordrecht: Foris.

Kotzoglou, George. 2005. Wh-*Extraction and Locality in Greek*. Ph.D. dissertation, University of Reading.

Kratzer, Angelika. 1981. The notional category of modality. In Hans-Jürgen Eikmeyer & Hannes Rieser (eds.), *Words, Worlds, and Contexts*. Berlin: Walter de Gruyter.

—— 1991. Modality. In Arnim von Stechow & Dieter Wunderlich (eds.), *Semantik / Semantics: Ein internationales Handbuch zeitgenössischer Forschung / An International Handbook of Contemporary Research*. Berlin: Walter de Gruyter.

—— & Elisabeth O. Selkirk. 2005. Focuses, phases and phrase stress. Paper presented at the *Mediterranean Syntax Meeting Workshop on Interfaces*, University of the Aegean, Rhodes (June 2005).

Kratzer, Angelika & Elisabeth O. Selkirk. 2007. Phase theory and prosodic spellout: The case of verbs. *The Linguistic Review* 24: 93–135.

Krejnovich, Eruhim A. 1937. *Fonetika Nivxkogo Jazyka* (Phonetics of the Nivkh [Gilyak] Language). Leningrad: Uchpedgiz.

Krifka, Manfred. 1992. A compositional semantics for multiple focus construction. In Joachim Jacobs (ed.), *Informationsstruktur und Grammatik*. Opladen: Westdeutscher Verlag.

Kuno, Susumo. 1974. The position of relative clauses and conjunctions. *Linguistic Inquiry* 5: 117–36.

Ladd, D. Robert. 1986. Intonational phrasing: The case for recursive prosodic structure. *Phonology* 3: 311–40.

Ladusaw, William A. 1992. Expressing negation. *Proceedings of the Second Conference on Semantics and Linguistic Theory (SALT II)*: 237–59.

Laka, Itziar. 1990. *Negation in Syntax: On the Nature of Functional Categories and Projections*. Ph.D. dissertation, Massachusetts Institute of Technology, Cambridge.

Lakoff, George. 1972. The arbitrary basis of transformational grammar. *Language* 48: 76–87.

Larson, Richard K. 1985. Quantifying into NP. Ms., Massachusetts Institute of Technology, Cambridge. [To be published in Larson, Richard K. Forthcoming. *Interface Studies*. London: Routledge.]

—— 1988. On the double object construction. *Linguistic Inquiry* 19: 335–91.

—— 1990. Double objects revisited: Reply to Jackendoff. *Linguistic Inquiry* 21: 589–632.

—— 1991. The projection of DP and DegP. Ms., State University of New York, Stony Brook. [Published in Larson, Richard K. Forthcoming. *Essays on Shell Structure*. London: Routledge.]

—— 2004. Sentence-final adverbs and "scope". *Proceedings of the Thirty-Fourth Annual Meeting of the North-East Linguistic Society (NELS 34)*, vol. 1: 23–43.

Lasnik, Howard. 1981. Restricting the theory of transformations: A case study. In Norbert Hornstein & David Lightfoot (eds.), *Explanation in Linguistics: The Logical Problem of Language Acquisition*. London: Longmans. [Reprinted in Lasnik (1990).]

—— 1990. *Essays on Restrictiveness and Learnability*. Dordrecht: Kluwer.

—— 1995a. A note on pseudogapping. *Papers on Minimalist Syntax—MIT Working Papers in Linguistics* 27: 143–63. [Reprinted in Lasnik (1999).]

—— 1995b. Notes on ellipsis. Lecture series given at the Forschungsschwerpunkt Allgemeine Sprachwissenschaft, Berlin (June 1995).

—— 1995c. Verbal morphology: *Syntactic Structures* meets the minimalist program. In Hector Campos & Paula Kempchinsky (eds.), *Evolution and Revolution in Linguistic Theory: Essays in Honor of Carlos Otero*. Washington, DC: Georgetown University Press. [Reprinted in Lasnik (1999).]

—— 1998. Some reconstruction riddles. University of Pennsylvania *Working Papers in Linguistics* 5.1: 83–98.

—— 1999a. On feature strength: Three minimalist approaches to overt movement. *Linguistic Inquiry* 30: 197–217. [Reprinted in Lasnik (2003).]

—— 1999b. *Minimalist Analysis*. Malden, MA: Blackwell.

—— 2001*a*. Derivation and representation in modern transformational syntax. In Baltin & Collins (eds.).

—— 2001*b*. When can you save a structure by destroying it? *Proceedings of the Thirty-First Annual Meeting of the North-East Linguistic Society (NELS 31)*, vol. 2: 301–20.

—— 2002. The minimalist program in syntax. *Trends in Cognitive Sciences* 6: 432–7.

—— 2003. *Minimalist Investigations in Linguistic Theory*. London: Routledge.

—— & Mamoru Saito. 1984. On the nature of proper government. *Linguistic Inquiry* 15: 235–89. [Reprinted in Lasnik (1990).]

—— & Juan Uriagereka with Cedric Boeckx. 2005. *A Course in Minimalist Syntax: Foundations and Prospects*. Malden, MA: Blackwell.

Lebeaux, David. 1988. *Language Acquisition and the Form of the Grammar*. Ph.D. dissertation, University of Massachusetts, Amherst.

Lechner, Winfried. 2006. Linearization and locality. Lecture notes, Universität Stuttgart. [http://vivaldi.sfs.nphil.uni-tuebingen.de/%7Ennsleo1/HS2006.htm]

—— 2007. Interpretive effects of head movement. *LingBuzz* 000178. [http://ling.auf. net/lingBuzz/000178]

Lee-Schoenfeld, Vera. 2005. *Beyond Coherence: The Syntax of Opacity in German*. Ph.D. dissertation, University of California, Santa Cruz.

Legate, Julie Anne. 2003*a*. Identifying phases. Paper presented at the *IAP Workshop on EPP and Phases*, Massachusetts Institute of Technology, Cambridge (January 2003). [Published version appeared as Legate, Julie Anne. 2004. Phases and cyclic agreement. *Proceedings of the MIT Workshop on Phases—MIT Working Papers in Linguistics* 47: 147–56.]

—— 2003*b*. Some interface properties of the phase. *Linguistic Inquiry* 34: 506–16.

Lehmann, Christian. 1982. Nominalisierung—Typisierung von Propositionen. In Hansjakob Seiler & Christian Lehmann (eds.), *Apprehension: Das sprachliche Erfassen von Gegenständen—Teil I: Bereich und Ordnung der Phänomene*. Tübingen: Narr.

Lenertová, Denisa. 2008. On the syntax of left peripheral adverbial clauses in Czech. In Luka Szucsich, Gerhild Zybatow, Uwe Junghanns & Roland Meyer (eds.), *Recent Issues in Formal Slavic Linguistics*. Frankfurt am Main: Peter Lang.

Lightfoot, David. 1999. *The Development of Language: Acquisition, Change and Evolution*. Malden, MA: Blackwell.

Lobeck, Ann. 1995. *Ellipsis: Functional Heads, Licensing, and Identification*. Oxford: Oxford University Press.

Longobardi, Giuseppe, Chiara Gianollo & Cristina Guardiano. 2008. Three fundamental issues in parametric linguistics. In Biberauer (ed.).

Lutz, Uli & Jürgen Pafel (eds.). 1995. *On Extraction and Extraposition in German*. Amsterdam: John Benjamins.

McCarthy, J. John. 1986. OCP effects: Gemination and antigemination. *Linguistic Inquiry* 17: 207–63.

—— & Alan Prince. 1993. Generalized alignment. In Booij & van Marle (eds.).

McCawley, James D. 1968. *The Phonological Component of a Grammar of Japanese*. Hague: Mouton de Gruyter.

McCawley, James D. 1982. Parentheticals and discontinuous constituent structure. *Linguistic Inquiry* 13: 91–106.

—— 1988. *The Syntactic Phenomena of English*. Chicago: University of Chicago Press.

McCloskey, James. 1991. Clause structure, ellipsis and proper government in Irish. *Lingua* 85: 259–302.

—— 1996. Subjects and subject positions in Irish. In Robert Borsley & Ian Roberts (eds.), *The Syntax of the Celtic Languages: A Comparative Perspective*. Cambridge: Cambridge University Press.

—— 2001. The morphosyntax of *wh*-extraction in Irish. *Journal of Linguistics* 37: 67–100.

—— 2002. Resumption, successive cyclicity, and the locality of operators. In Epstein & Seely (eds.).

—— 2004. Three puzzles about head-movement. Paper presented at the *Workshop on Morphosyntax*, Universidad Nacional del Comahue, Buenos Aires (July 2004).

McDaniel, Dana. 1989. Partial and multiple *wh*-movement. *Natural Language & Linguistic Theory* 7: 565–604.

McGonigle, Brendan & Margaret Chalmers. 2006. Ordering and executive functioning as a window on the evolution and development of cognitive systems. *International Journal of Comparative Psychology* 19: 241–67.

—————— & Anthony Dickenson. 2003. Concurrent disjoint and reciprocal classification by *Cebus Apella* in seriation tasks: Evidence for hierarchical organization. *Animal Cognition* 6: 185–97.

Mahootian, Shahrzad. 1997. *Persian*. London: Routledge.

Martin, Roger. 1996. *A Minimalist Theory of PRO*. Ph.D. dissertation, University of Connecticut, Storrs.

—— David Michaels & Juan Uriagereka (eds.). 2000. *Step by Step: Essays on Minimalist Syntax in Honor of Howard Lasnik*. Cambridge, MA: MIT Press.

—— & Juan Uriagereka. 2000. Some possible foundations of the minimalist program. In Martin *et al.* (eds.).

Marušič, Franc Lanko. 2005. *On Non-Simultaneous Phases*. Ph.D. dissertation, Stony Brook University, NY.

—— 2007. On the lack of a (PF) phase in non-finite complementation. *Proceedings of ConSOLE XIV*: 203–25.

—— 2008. CP under control. In Luka Szucsich, Gerhild Zybatow, Uwe Junghanns & Roland Meyer (eds.), *Recent Issues in Formal Slavic Linguistics*. Frankfurt am Main: Peter Lang.

—— Tatjana Marvin & Rok Žaucer. 2002. Secondary predication in control sentences. *Snippets* 6: 10–11.

—————— 2003. Depictive secondary predication in Slovenian. In Wayles Browne, Ji-Yung Kim, Barbara H. Partee & Robert A. Rothstein (eds.), *Formal Approaches to Slavic Linguistics 11 (The Amherst Meeting, 2002)*. Ann Arbor, MI: Michigan Slavic Publications.

—— & Rok Žaucer. 2005. On phonologically null verbs: GO and beyond. *Proceedings of ConSOLE XIII*: 231–48.

————2006. On the intensional FEEL-LIKE construction in Slovenian. *Natural Language & Linguistic Theory* 24: 1093–59.

Matushansky, Ora. 2003. DPs and phase theory. Handout from the TSSS-Lecture given at Utrecht Institute of Linguistics-OTS (January 2003).

——2004. Going through a phase. *Perspectives on Phases—MIT Working Papers in Linguistics* 49: 157–81.

May, Robert. 1985. *Logical Form: Its Structure and Derivation*. Cambridge, MA: MIT Press.

Meinunger, André. 2000. *Syntactic Aspects of Topic and Comment*. Amsterdam: John Benjamins.

Megerdoomian, Karine. 2003. Asymmetries in form and meaning: Surface realization and the interface conditions. Paper presented at *Approaching Asymmetry at the Interfaces*, Université de Québec à Montréal (October 2003).

Merchant, Jason. 2001. *The Syntax of Silence: Sluicing, Islands, and the Theory of Ellipsis*. New York: Oxford University Press.

——2006. Why no(t). *Style* 20: 20–3.

——2008*a*. An asymmetry in voice mismatches in VP-ellipsis and pseudogapping. *Linguistic Inquiry* 39: 169–79.

——2008*b*. Variable island repair under ellipsis. In Kyle Johnson (ed.), *Topics in Ellipsis*. Cambridge: Cambridge University Press.

Mihara, Ken-ichi. 1994. *Nihongo no Togo-kozo* (The Syntactic Structures of Japanese). Tokyo: Shohakusha.

Mluvnice češtiny 3. Skladba (Grammar of Czech 3. Syntax). 1987. Prague: Academia.

Moro, Andrea. 2000. *Dynamic Antisymmetry*. Cambridge, MA: MIT Press.

——2004. Linear compression as a trigger for movement. In Henk van Riemsdijk & Anne Breitbarth (eds.), *Triggers*. Berlin: Mouton de Gruyter.

Morrill, Glyn. 2002. Islands, coordination and parasitic gaps. In V. Michele Abrusci & Claudio Casadio (eds.), *New Perspectives in Logic and Formal Linguistics*. Roma: Bulzoni Editore.

Müller, Gereon. 1995*a*. Anti-Rekonstruktion. Ms., Universität Tübingen.

——1995*b*. On extraposition & successive cyclicity. In Lutz & Pafel (eds.).

——2007. Towards a relativized concept of cyclic linearization. In Sauerland & Gärtner (eds.).

Munakata, Takashi. 2006. Japanese topic-constructions in the minimalist view of the syntax-semantics interface. In Cedric Boeckx (ed.), *Minimalist Essays*. Amsterdam: John Benjamins.

——2007. *Throwing In & Kicking Out. Proceedings of the 2nd Workshop on Altaic Formal Linguistics (WAFL 2)—MIT Working Papers in Linguistics* 54: 259–73.

——Forthcoming. Intermediate agree: Complementizer as a bridge. *Proceedings of the 3rd Workshop on Altaic Formal Linguistics (WAFL 3)—MIT Working Papers in Linguistics*.

Nakao, Chizuru. 2007. Copy free movement, swiping and the ECP. Ms., University of Maryland, College Park.

Nakau, Minoru. 1973. *Sentential Complementation in Japanese*. Tokyo: Kaitakusha.

Neeleman, Ad & Hans van der Koot. 2006. On syntactic and phonological representations. *Lingua* 116: 1524–52.

—— & Kriszta Szendrői. 2004. Superman sentences. *Linguistic Inquiry* 35: 149–59.

Nespor, Marina & Irene Vogel. 1986. *Prosodic Phonology*. Dordrecht: Foris.

Newell, Heather & Tobias Scheer. 2007. Procedural first. Paper presented at the *38th Poznan Linguistic Meeting (PLM 2007)*, Gniezno (September 2007).

Newmeyer, Frederick J. 2004. Against a parameter-setting approach to language variation. In Pica with Rooryck & van Craenenbroeck (eds.).

—— 2005. *Possible and Probable Languages: A Generative Perspective on Linguistic Typology*. New York: Oxford University Press.

—— 2006. Newmeyer's rejoinder to Roberts and Holmberg on parameters. *LingBuzz* 000248. [http://ling.auf.net/lingBuzz/000248]

Nilsen, Øystein. 2003. *Eliminating Positions*. Utrecht: LOT Publications.

Nissenbaum, Jonathan W. 1998. Derived predicates and the interpretation of parasitic gaps. *The Interpretive Tract—MIT Working Papers in Linguistics* 25: 247–95.

—— 2000. *Investigation of Covert Phrase Movement*. Ph.D. dissertation, Massachusetts Institute of Technology, Cambridge.

Nunes, Jairo. 1995. *The Copy Theory of Movement and Linearization of Chains in the Minimalist Program*. Ph.D. dissertation, University of Maryland, College Park.

—— 1999. Linearization of chains and phonetic realization of chain links. In Epstein & Hornstein (eds.).

—— 2004. *Linearization of Chains and Sideward Movement*. Cambridge, MA: MIT Press.

—— & Juan Uriagereka. 2000. Cyclicity and extraction domains. *Syntax* 3: 20–43.

O'Grady, William. 2005. *Syntactic Carpentry*. Mahwah, NJ: Laurence Erlbaum.

Ochi, Masao. 1999*a*. Some consequences of Attract F. *Lingua* 109: 81–107.

—— 1999*b*. Multiple spell-out and PF adjacency. *Proceedings of the Twenty-Ninth Annual Meeting of the North-East Linguistic Society (NELS 29)*, vol. 1: 293–306.

Oehrle, Richard T. 1990. Categorial frameworks, coordination, and extraction. *Proceedings of the 9th West Coast Conference on Formal Linguistics (WCCFL 9)*: 411–25.

Ogihara, Toshiyuki. 2006. Tense, adverbials and quantification. In Raffaella Zanuttini, Hector Campos, Elena Herburger & Paul Portner (eds.), *Negation, Tense and Clausal Architecture: Cross-Linguistic Investigations*. Georgetown, DC: Georgetown University Press.

Öhl, Peter. 2003. *Economical Computation of Structural Descriptions in Natural Language*. Ph.D. dissertation, Universität Stuttgart.

Oka, Toshifusa. 1993. Shallowness. *Papers on Case and Agreement II—MIT Working Papers in Linguistics* 19: 255–320.

Parsons, Terence. 1990. *Events in the Semantics of English: A Study in Subatomic Semantics*. Cambridge, MA: MIT Press.

Partee, Barbara H. 1984. Compositionality. In Fred Landman & Frank Veltman (eds.), *Varieties of Formal Semantics*. Dordrecht: Foris.

—— 1992. Topic, focus, and quantification. *Proceedings of the First Conference on Semantics and Linguistic Theory (SALT I)*: 159–87.

—— 2004. Bound variables and other anaphors. In Barbara H. Partee, *Compositionality in Formal Semantics: Selected Papers by Barbara H. Partee*. Malden, MA: Blackwell.

Pesetsky, David. 1995. *Zero Syntax: Experiencers and Cascades*. Cambridge, MA: MIT Press.

—— 1998. Some optimality principles of sentence pronunciation. In Pilar Barbosa, Danny Fox, Paul Hagstrom, Martha McGinnis & David Pesetsky (eds.), *Is the Best Good Enough? Optimality and Competition in Syntax*. Cambridge, MA: MIT Press and MIT Working Papers in Linguistics.

—— & Esther Torrego. 2001. T-to-C movement: Causes and consequences. In Kenstowicz (ed.).

—— —— 2006. Probes, goals and syntactic categories. *Proceedings of the 7th Annual Tokyo Conference on Psycholinguistics*: 25–60.

—— —— 2007. The syntax of valuation and the interpretability of features. In Simin Karimi, Vida Samiian & Wendy K. Wilkins (eds.), *Phrasal and Clausal Architecture: Syntactic Derivation and Interpretation*. Amsterdam: John Benjamins.

Philippaki-Warburton, Irene. 1987. The theory of empty categories and the *pro*-drop parameter in Modern Greek. *Journal of Linguistics* 23: 289–318.

—— 1989. Subject in English and Greek. *Proceedings of the 3rd Symposium on the Description and/or Comparison of English and Greek*: 11–32.

—— & Vassilios Spyropoulos. 1999. On the boundaries of inflection and syntax. In Booij & van Marle (eds.).

—— Spyridoula Varlokosta, Michalis Georgiafentis & George Kotzoglou. 2004. Moving from theta-positions: Pronominal clitic doubling in Greek. *Lingua* 114: 963–89.

—— & Jannis Veloudis. 1984. I ypotaktiki stis sympliromatikes protasis (The subjunctive in complement clauses). *Studies in Greek Linguistics* 5: 87–104.

Phillips, Colin. 1996. *Order and Structure*. Ph.D. dissertation, Massachusetts Institute of Technology, Cambridge.

—— 1999. Categories and constituents in the neuroscience of language. Lecture given at Keio University, Tokyo (July 1999).

—— 2003. Linear order and constituency. *Linguistic Inquiry* 34: 37–90.

—— 2005. How is grammar so fast? Lecture given at Sophia University, Tokyo (August 2005).

Piattelli-Palmarini, Massimo & Juan Uriagereka. 2004. The immune syntax: The evolution of the language virus. In Lyle Jenkins (ed.), *Variation and Universals in Biolinguistics*. Oxford: Elsevier.

Pica, Pierre with Johan Rooryck & Jeroen van Craenenbroeck (eds.). 2004. *Linguistic Variation Yearbook 4 (2004)*. Amsterdam: John Benjamins.

Pietroski, Paul. 2002. Function and concatenation. In Gerhard Preyer & Georg Peters (eds.), *Logical Form*. Oxford: Oxford University Press.

—— & Juan Uriagereka. 2002. Dimensions of natural language. In Uriagereka (2002c).

Poeppel, David & David Embick. 2005. Defining the Relation between Linguistics and Neuroscience. In Anne Cutler (ed.), *Twenty-First Century Psycholinguistics: Four Cornerstones*. Mahwah, NJ: Lawrence Erlbaum. [Reprinted in Anna Maria Di Sciullo (ed.). Forthcoming. *Biolinguistics*. Cambridge, MA: MIT Press.]

Pollock, Jean-Yves. 1989. Verb movement, universal grammar, and the structure of IP. *Linguistic Inquiry* 20: 365–424.

Portner, Paul & Katsuhiko Yabushita. 2002. Specific indefinites and the information structure theory of topics. *Journal of Semantics* 18: 271–97.

Postal, Paul M. 1972. On some rules that are not successive cyclic. *Linguistic Inquiry* 3: 211–22.

—— 1974. *On Raising: One Rule of English Grammar and Its Theoretical Implications*. Cambridge, MA: MIT Press.

Potts, Christopher. 2002a. The lexical semantics of parenthetical-*as* and appositive-*which*. *Syntax* 5: 55–88.

—— 2002b. The syntax and semantics of *as*-parentheticals. *Natural Language & Linguistic Theory* 20: 623–89.

—— 2002c. No vacuous quantification constraints in syntax. *Proceedings of the Thirty-Second Annual Meeting of the North-East Linguistic Society (NELS 32)*, vol. 2: 451–70.

Povinelli, Daniel J. 2004. We don't need a microscope to explore the chimpanzee's mind. *Mind and Language* 19: 1–28.

Prieto, Pilar. 1997. Prosodic manifestation of syntactic structure in Catalan. In Fernando Martínez-Gil & Alfonso Morales-Front (eds.), *Issues in the Phonology of the Major Iberian Languages*. Washington, DC: Georgetown University Press.

—— 2005. Syntactic and eurhythmic constraints on phrasing decisions in Catalan. *Studia Linguistica* 59: 194–222.

Prince, Alan & Paul Smolensky. 1993. Optimality theory: Constraint interaction in generative grammar. Report no. RuCCS-TR-2, Rutgers University Center for Cognitive Science, New Brunswick, NJ. [Published as Prince, Alan & Paul Smolensky. 2004. *Optimality Theory: Constraint Interaction in Generative Grammar*. Malden, MA: Blackwell.]

Pustejovsky, James. 1995. *The Generative Lexicon*. Cambridge, MA: MIT Press.

Radford, Andrew. 1997. *Syntactic Theory and the Structure of English: A Minimalist Approach*. Cambridge: Cambridge University Press.

—— 2004. *Minimalist Syntax: Exploring the Structure of English*. Cambridge: Cambridge University Press.

Ramchand, Gillian Catriona. 2008. *Verb Meaning and the Lexicon: A First Phase Syntax*. Cambridge: Cambridge University Press.

—— & Charles Reiss (eds.). 2007. *The Oxford Handbook of Linguistic Interfaces*. Oxford: Oxford University Press.

Reinhart, Tanya. 2000. Strategies of anaphora resolution. In Hans Bennis, Martin Everaert & Eric Reuland (eds.), *Interface Strategies*. Amsterdam: Royal Netherlands Academy of Arts and Sciences.

—— 2006. *Interface Strategies: Optimal and Costly Computations*. Cambridge, MA: MIT Press.

—— Forthcoming. Processing or pragmatics?—Explaining the coreference delay. In Edward Gibson & Neal Pearlmutter (eds.), *The Processing and Acquisition of Reference*. Cambridge, MA: MIT Press.

Reuland, Eric. 2001. Primitives of binding. *Linguistic Inquiry* 32: 439–92.

Revithiadou, Anthi. 2004a. Prosodic cues in p-phrasing: The case of Greek declaratives. *Studies in Greek Linguistics* 24: 580–91.

—— 2004b. Phonological vs. interface grammars of p-phrasing in Greek. Ms., University of the Aegean, Rhodes.

—— 2005. Prosodic phrasing and focus in Greek declaratives. *Proceedings of the 6th International Conference of Greek Linguistics (ICGL 6)*, vol. 1: 64–74.

—— & Vassilios Spyropoulos. 2003. Trapped within a phrase: Effects of syntactic derivation on p-phrasing. *Proceedings of IP2003—Prosodic Interfaces*: 167–72.

—— —— 2005. The multiple spell-out hypothesis and the phonological component: Evidence from Greek. *Proceedings of the Thirty-Fifth Annual Meeting of the North-East Linguistic Society (NELS 35)*, vol. 2: 523–37.

Richards, Marc. 2004. *Object Shift and Scrambling in North and West Germanic: A Case Study in Symmetrical Syntax*. Ph.D. dissertation, University of Cambridge.

—— 2007. On feature inheritance: An argument from the phase impenetrability condition. *Linguistic Inquiry* 38: 563–72.

Richards, Norvin. 2002a. A distinctness condition on linearization. *Proceedings of the 20th West Coast Conference on Formal Linguistics (WCCFL 20)*: 470–83.

—— 2002b. Movement in a top-down derivation. In Epstein & Seely (eds.).

van Riemsdijk, Henk. 1978. *A Case Study in Syntactic Markedness: The Binding Nature of Prepositional Phrases*. Lisse: Peter de Ridder.

—— & Edwin Williams. 1981. NP-structure. *The Linguistic Review* 1: 171–217.

—— —— 1986. *Introduction to the Theory of Grammar*. Cambridge, MA: MIT Press.

Rizzi, Luigi. 1986. Null objects in Italian and the theory of *pro*. *Linguistic Inquiry* 17: 501–57.

—— 1990. *Relativized Minimality*. Cambridge, MA: MIT Press.

—— 1997. The fine structure of the left periphery. In Liliane Haegeman (ed.), *Elements of Grammar: Handbook in Generative Syntax*. Dordrecht: Kluwer.

—— 2001. Relativized minimality effects. In Baltin & Collins (eds.).

—— (ed.). 2004. *The Structure of CP and IP—The Cartography of Syntactic Structures*, vol. 2. New York: Oxford University Press.

Roberts, Ian. 1997. The syntax of direct object mutation in Welsh. *The Canadian Journal of Linguistics* 42: 141–68.

—— 2005. *Principles and Parameters in a VSO Language: A Case Study in Welsh*. New York: Oxford University Press.

Roberts, Ian & Anders Holmberg. 2005. On the role of parameters in universal grammar: A reply to Newmeyer. In Hans Broekhuis, Norbert Corver, Riny Huybregts, Ursula Kleinhenz & Jan Koster (eds.), *Organizing Grammar: Linguistic Studies in Honor of Henk van Riemsdijk*. Berlin: Mouton de Gruyter.

—— & Anna Roussou. 2002. The extended projection principle as a condition on the tense dependency. In Svenonius (ed.).

Rochemont, Michael S. & Peter W. Culicover. 1990. *English Focus Constructions and the Theory of Grammar*. Cambridge: Cambridge University Press.

Rohrer, Christian, Antje Roßdeutscher & Hans Kamp (eds.). 2001. *Linguistic Form and Its Computation*. Stanford, CA: CSLI Publications.

Rosen, Carol. 1976. Guess what about. *Proceedings of the Sixth Annual Meeting of the North-East Linguistic Society (NELS 6)*: 205–11.

Rosengren, Inger. 1992. Zum Problem der kohärenten Verben im Deutschen. In Peter Suchsland (ed.), *Biologische und soziale Grundlagen der Sprachfähigkeit*. Tübingen: Niemeyer.

Ross, John R. 1967. *Constraints on Variables in Syntax*. Ph.D. dissertation, Massachusetts Institute of Technology, Cambridge. [Revised version published as Ross, John R. 1986. *Infinite Syntax!* Norwood, NJ: Ablex.]

—— 1969. Guess who? *Papers from the Fifth Regional Meeting of the Chicago Linguistic Society (CLS 5)*: 252–86.

Roussou, Anna. 2000. On the left periphery: Modal particles and complementizers. *Journal of Greek Linguistics* 1: 65–94.

Rubin, Edward J. 2003. Determining pair-merge. *Linguistic Inquiry* 34: 660–8.

Ryalls, Jack H. 1996. *A Basic Introduction to Speech Perception: Speech Science Series*. San Diego, CA: Singular.

Sabbagh, Joseph. 2007. Ordering and linearizing rightward movement. *Natural Language & Linguistic Theory* 25: 349–401.

Safir, Ken. 1999. Vehicle change and reconstruction in A-bar chains. *Linguistic Inquiry* 30: 587–620.

Saito, Mamoru. 1985. *Some Asymmetries in Japanese and Their Theoretical Implications*. Ph.D. dissertation, Massachusetts Institute of Technology, Cambridge.

—— 2003a. A derivational approach to the interpretation of scrambling chains. *Lingua* 113: 481–518.

—— 2003b. On the role of selection in the application of merge. *Proceedings of the Thirty-Third Annual Meeting of the North-East Linguistic Society (NELS 33)*: 323–45.

—— & Keiko Murasugi. 1990. N'-deletion in Japanese. *University of Connecticut Working Papers in Linguistics* 3: 87–107.

Sandalo, Filomena & Hubert Truckenbrodt. 2001. Some notes on phonological phrasing in Brazilian Portuguese. *Phonological Questions (and Their Corresponding Answers)—MIT Working Papers in Linguistics* 42: 81–105.

Sato, Yosuke. 2006a. Nuclear stress, phase theory and the syntax-prosody interface. Ms., University of Arizona, Tucson.

—— 2006*b*. Multiple spell-out, cliticization and the syntax-prosody mapping. Ms., University of Arizona, Tucson.

Sauerland, Uli. 2003. Intermediate adjunction with A-movement. *Linguistic Inquiry* 34: 308–14.

—— 2005. DP is not a scope island. *Linguistic Inquiry* 36: 303–14.

—— & Paul Elbourne. 2002. Total reconstruction, PF movement, and derivational order. *Linguistics Inquiry* 33: 283–319.

—— & Hans-Martin Gärtner (eds.). 2007. *Interfaces + Recursion = Language? Chomsky's Minimalism and the View from Syntax-Semantics*. Berlin: Mouton de Gruyter.

Schneider, David A. 1999. *Parsing and Incrementality*. Ph.D. dissertation, University of Delaware, Newark.

Scott, Gary-John. 2002. Stacked adjectival modification and the structure of nominal phrases. In Cinque (ed.).

Selkirk, Elisabeth O. 1972. *The Phrasal Phonology of English and French*. Ph.D. dissertation, Massachusetts Institute of Technology, Cambridge.

—— 1974. French liaison and the X′ notation. *Linguistic Inquiry* 5: 573–90.

—— 1978. *On Prosodic Structure and Its Relation to Syntactic Structure*. Bloomington, IN: Indiana University Linguistics Club.

—— 1980. Prosodic domains in phonology: Sanskrit revisited. In Mark Aronoff & Mary-Louise Kean (eds.), *Juncture*. Saratoga, CA: Anma Libri.

—— 1981. On prosodic structure and its relation to syntactic structure. In Thorstein Fretheim (ed.), *Nordic Prosody II*. Trondheim: TAPIR.

—— 1984. *Phonology and Syntax: The Relation between Sound and Structure*. Cambridge, MA: MIT Press.

—— 1986. On derived domains in sentence phonology. *Phonology Yearbook* 3: 371–405.

—— 1995. The prosodic structure of function words. *Papers in Optimality Theory— University of Massachusetts Occasional Papers in Linguistics* 18: 439–69.

—— 2000. The interaction of constraints on prosodic phrasing. In Gösta Bruce & Merle Horne (eds.), *Prosody: Theory and Experiment—Studies Presented to Gösta Bruce*. Dordrecht: Kluwer.

—— 2006*a*. Contrastive focus, givenness and phrase stress. Ms., University of Massachusetts, Amherst.

—— 2006*b*. Strong minimalist spellout of prosodic phrases. Paper presented at the *Tokyo Circle of Phonologists*, University of Tokyo (March 2006) and the *29th GLOW (Generative Linguistics of the Old World) Colloquium 2006: Prosodic Phrasing Workshop*, Universitat Autònoma de Barcelona (April 2006).

—— & Tong Shen. 1990. Prosodic domains in Shanghai Chinese. In Inkelas & Zec (eds.).

—— & Koichi Tateishi. 1991. Syntax and downstep in Japanese. In Carol Georgopoulos & Roberta Ishihara (eds.), *Interdisciplinary Approaches to Language Essays in Honor of S.-Y. Kuroda*. Dordrecht: Kluwer.

Seyfarth, Robert M., Dorothy L. Cheney & Thore J. Bergman. 2005. Primate social cognition and the origins of language. *Trends in Cognitive Science* 9: 264–6.

Sgall, Petr, Eva Hajičová & Eva Buráňová. 1980. *Aktuální členění větné v češtině*. Prague: Academia.

Shibatani, Masayoshi. 1978. *Nihongo no Bunseki: Seisei-bunpo no Hoho* (Analyses of Japanese: A Generative Method). Tokyo: Taishukan.

Shiobara, Kayono. 2001. The weight effect as a PF-interface phenomenon. *Linguistic Research—University of Tokyo Working Papers of English Linguistics* 18: 61–96.

—— 2004. *Linearization: A Derivational Approach to the Syntax-Prosody Interface*. Ph.D. dissertation, University of British Columbia, Vancouver.

—— 2007. Why are grammars the way they are: A functional formalist view (Review article of *Efficiency and Complexity in Grammars*, by John A. Hawkins.) *English Linguistics* 24: 599–626.

—— Forthcoming. Prosodic phases and left-to-right structure-building. *The Canadian Journal of Linguistics (Special Issue on Interfaces)*.

Sigurðsson, Halldór Árman. 1991. Icelandic case-marked PRO and the licensing of lexical arguments. *Natural Language & Linguistic Theory* 9: 327–63.

—— 2004. Meaningful silence, meaningless sounds. In Pica with Rooryck & van Craenenbroeck (eds.).

—— Forthcoming. Remarks on features. In Kleanthes K. Grohmann (ed.), *Explorations of Phase Theory: Features and Arguments*. Berlin: Mouton de Gruyter.

Simpson, Andrew & Zoe Wu. 2002. IP-raising, tone sandhi and the creation of S-final particles: Evidence for cyclic spell-out. *Journal of East Asian Linguistics* 11: 67–99.

Singh, Udaya. 1980. *Bole*: An unresolved problem in Bengali syntax. *Indian Linguistics* 41: 188–95.

Speas, Margaret J. 1990. *Phrase Structure in Natural Language*. Dordrecht: Kluwer Academic Publishers.

—— 2004. Evidentiality, logophoricity and the syntactic representation of pragmatic features. *Lingua* 114: 255–76.

Sportiche, Dominique. 1988. A theory of floating quantifiers and its corollaries for constituent structure. *Linguistic Inquiry* 19: 425–49.

—— 1997. Reconstruction & constituent structure. Handout from a lecture given at the Massachusetts Institute of Technology, Cambridge (October 1997). [http://www.linguistics.ucla.edu/people/sportich/papers/mittalk97.pdf]

—— 2005. Division of labor between merge and move: Strict locality of selection and apparent reconstruction paradoxes. *LingBuzz* 000163. [http://ling.auf.net/lingBuzz/000163]

Spyropoulos, Vassilios. 1999. *Agreement Relations in Greek*. Ph.D. dissertation, University of Reading.

—— 2001. I nomimopoiisi tou ipokimenou stin Elliniki: Ptosi, symphonia ke polisynthesy (The licensing of subject in Greek: case, agreement and polysynthesis). *Proceedings of the 4th International Conference on Greek Linguistics (ICGL 4)*: 209–16.

—— 2003. The syntactic status of head-movement: Evidence from Greek. Paper presented at the *26th GLOW (Generative Linguistics of the Old World) Colloquium 2003*, Lunds Universitet (April 2003).

—— & Irene Philippaki-Warburton. 2002. Subject and EPP in Greek: The discontinuous subject hypothesis. *Journal of Greek Linguistics* 2: 149–86.

—— & Anthi Revithiadou. 2007. Subject chains in Greek and PF processing. Paper presented at the *Workshop on Greek Syntax and Semantics*, Massachusetts Institute of Technology, Cambridge (May 2007).

Starke, Michal. 2001. *Move Dissolves into Merge: A Theory of Locality*. Ph.D. dissertation, Université de Genève.

—— 2004. On the inexistence of specifiers and the nature of heads. In Belletti (ed.).

von Stechow, Arnim. 2002. Temporal prepositional phrases with quantifiers: Some additions to Pratt and Francez (2001). *Linguistics & Philosophy* 25: 755–800.

—— 2005. LF in einem Phasenmodell: Bemerkungen anhand von Fischers Bindungstheorie. Handout from a paper presented at the *31. Tagung zur generativen Grammatik des Südens (GGS 31)*, Universität Tübingen (May 2005). [http://www2.sfs.uni-tuebingen.de/~arnim10/Handouts/LF-Phasen.doc.pdf]

Steedman, Mark. 1987. Combinatory grammars and parasitic gaps. *Natural Language & Linguistic Theory* 5: 403–39.

Stepanov, Arthur. 2000. The timing of adjunction. *Proceedings of the Thirtieth Annual Meeting of the North-East Linguistic Society (NELS 30)*, vol. 2: 597–611.

—— 2001. Late adjunction and minimalist phrase structure. *Syntax* 4: 94–125.

Sternefeld, Wolfgang. 2001. Semantic vs. syntactic reconstruction. In Rohrer *et al.* (eds.).

Stjepanović, Sandra. 2003. Multiple *wh*-fronting in Serbo-Croatian matrix questions and the matrix sluicing construction. In Cedric Boeckx & Kleanthes K. Grohmann (eds.), *Multiple* Wh-*Fronting*. Amsterdam: John Benjamins.

Stowell, Tim. 1981. *Origins of Phrase Structure*. Ph.D. dissertation, Massachusetts Institute of Technology, Cambridge.

Stroik, Thomas. 1990. Adverbs as V-sisters. *Linguistic Inquiry* 21: 654–61.

Stump, Gregory. 1988. Non-local spirantization in Breton. *Journal of Linguistics* 24: 457–81.

Suzuki, Satoko. 2000. *De dicto* complementation in Japanese. In Kaoru Horie (ed.), *Complementation*. Amsterdam: John Benjamins.

Svenonius, Peter (ed.). 2000. *The Derivation of VO and OV*. Amsterdam: John Benjamins.

—— 2002a. Subject positions and the placement of adverbials. In Svenonius (ed.).

—— (ed.). 2002b. *Subjects, Expletives, and the EPP*. New York: Oxford University Press.

—— 2004. On the edge. In David Adger, Cécile de Cat & George Tsoulas (eds.), *Peripheries: Syntactic Edges and Their Effects*. Dordrecht: Kluwer.

Svenonius, Peter. 2007. Interpreting uninterpretable features. *Linguistic Analysis* 33: 375–413.

de Swart, Henriëtte & Ivan Sag. 2002. Negation and negative concord in Romance. *Linguistics & Philosophy* 25: 373–417.

Swingle, Kari. 1995. On the prosody and syntax of right node raising. Ms., University of California, Santa Cruz.

Szabó, Zoltán G. 2000. Compositionality as supervenience. *Linguistics & Philosophy* 23: 475–505.

Takahashi, Daiko. 1994a. *Minimality of Movement*. Ph.D. dissertation, University of Connecticut, Storrs.

—— 1994b. Sluicing in Japanese. *Journal of East Asian Linguistics* 3: 265–300.

Takezawa, Koichi & John Whitman. 1998. *Kaku to Gojun to Togo-kozo* (Case, Word Order, and the Syntactic Structure). Tokyo: Kenkyusha.

Tallerman, Maggie. 1990. VSO word order and consonant mutation in Welsh. *Linguistics* 28: 389–416.

—— 1993. Case-assignment and the order of functional projections in Welsh. In Anna Siewierska (ed.), *Eurotyp Working Papers*. Strasbourg: ESF Programme in Language Typology.

—— 2006. The syntax of Welsh "direct object mutation" revisited. *Lingua* 116: 1750–76.

—— 2007. Did our ancestors speak a holistic protolanguage? *Lingua* 117: 579–604.

Tenny, Carol & James Pustejovsky. 2000. A history of events in linguistic theory. In Carol Tenny & James Pustejovsky (eds.), *Events as Grammatical Objects: The Converging Perspectives of Lexical Semantics and Syntax*. Stanford, CA: CSLI Publications.

Terada, Hiroshi. 2002. On θ-checking. *English Linguistics* 19: 1–28.

Terrace, Herbert S. 2005. Metacognition and the evolution of language. In Herbert S. Terrace & Janet Metcalfe (eds.), *The Missing Link in Cognition*. Oxford: Oxford University Press.

Tokizaki, Hisao. 2006. *Linearizing Structure with Silence: A Minimalist Theory of Syntax-Phonology Interface*. Ph.D. dissertation, University of Tsukuba.

Toyoshima, Takashi. Forthcoming. Dynamic economy of derivation. In Kleanthes K. Grohmann (ed.), *Explorations of Phase Theory: Interpretation at the Interfaces*. Berlin: Mouton de Gruyter.

Travis, Lisa deMena. 1984. *Parameters and Effects of Word Order Variation*. Ph.D. dissertation, Massachusetts Institute of Technology, Cambridge.

—— 1991. Derived objects, inner aspect and the structure of VP. Paper presented at the *Twenty-Second Annual Meeting of the North-East Linguistic Society (NELS 22)*, University of Delaware, Newark (October 1991).

Truckenbrodt, Hubert. 1995. *Phonological Phrases: Their Relation to Syntax, Focus, and Prominence*. Ph.D. dissertation, Massachusetts Institute of Technology, Cambridge.

—— 1999. On the relation between syntactic phrases and phonological phrases. *Linguistic Inquiry* 30: 219–55.

—— 2006. On the semantic motivation of syntactic verb movement to C in German. *Theoretical Linguistics* 32: 257–306.

Tsimpli, Ianthi-Maria. 1990. The clause structure and word-order in Modern Greek. *UCL Working Papers in Linguistics* 2: 226–55.

Uned Iaith Genedlaethol Cymru (U.I.G.C.). 1976. *Gramadeg Cymraeg Cyfoes.* Y Bontfaen: D. Brown a'i Feibion.

Uriagereka, Juan. 1998. *Rhyme and Reason: An Introduction to Minimalist Syntax.* Cambridge, MA: MIT Press.

—— 1999a. In defense of deep-structure, Ms., University of Maryland, College Park. [Published in Uriagereka (2008a).]

—— 1999b. Multiple spell-out. In Epstein & Hornstein (eds.).

—— 2002a. Introduction. In Uriagereka (2002c).

—— 2002b. Warps: Some thoughts on categorizations. In Uriagereka (2002c).

—— 2002c. *Derivations: Exploring the Dynamics of Syntax.* London: Routledge.

—— 2008a. *Syntactic Anchors: On Semantic Structuring,* Cambridge: Cambridge University Press.

—— 2008b. *Spell-Out Extensions.* Book ms., University of Maryland, College Park.

—— & Ángel J. Gallego. 2006. (Multiple) agree as local (binding and) obviation. Handout from a paper presented at *Going Romance XX*, Vrije Universiteit Amsterdam (December 2006). [http://seneca.uab.es/ggt/membres/professors/gallego/pdf/Uriagereka_Gallego_Binding(ho).pdf]

—— & Roger Martin. 1999. Lectures on Dynamic Syntax. Ms., University of Maryland, College Park & Kanda University of International Studies.

Vangsnes, Øystein A. 2002. Icelandic expletive constructions and the distribution of subject types. In Svenonius (ed.).

Vukič, Saša. 2003. *On Features and the MLC.* Ph.D. dissertation, University of Connecticut, Storrs.

Wasow, Thomas. 1972. *Anaphoric Relations in English.* Ph.D. dissertation, Massachusetts Institute of Technology, Cambridge. [Revised version published as Wasow, Thomas. 1979. *Anaphora in Generative Grammar.* Ghent: E. Story-Scientia.]

Webelhuth, Gert. 1992. *Principles and Parameters of Syntactic Saturation.* New York: Oxford University Press.

Weerman, Fred & Ad Neeleman. 1997. *Flexible Syntax.* Dordrecht: Kluwer.

Weinberg, Amy. 1988. *Locality Principles in Syntax and in Parsing.* Ph.D. dissertation, Massachusetts Institute of Technology, Cambridge.

—— 1999. A minimalist theory of human sentence processing. In Epstein & Hornstein (eds.).

Wenck, Günther. 1974. *Systematische Syntax des Japanischen—Band III: Syntaktische Produktion oberhalb des einfachen Satzes.* Wiesbaden: Franz Steiner.

Wexler, Kenneth & Peter W. Culicover. 1980. *Formal Principles of Language Acquisition.* Cambridge, MA: MIT Press.

Wiklund, Anna-Lena. 2005. *Syntax of Tenselessness: On Copying Constructions in Swedish.* Ph.D. Dissertation, Lunds Universitet.

Wilder, Chris. 1997. Some properties of ellipsis in coordination. In Artemis Alexiadou & Tracy Alan Hall (eds.), *Studies on Universal Grammar and Typological Variation*. Amsterdam: John Benjamins.

——1999. Right-node raising and the LCA. *Proceedings of the 18th West Coast Conference on Formal Linguistics (WCCFL 18)*: 586–98.

Williams, Edwin. 2003. *Representation Theory*. Cambridge, MA: MIT Press.

Willis, David. 2000. On the distribution of resumptive pronouns and *wh*-trace in Welsh. *Journal of Linguistics* 36: 531–73.

Windfuhr, Gernot. 1987. Persian. In Bernard Comrie (ed.), *The World's Major Languages*. Oxford: Oxford University Press.

Witkoś, Jacek. 2003. *Movement and Reconstruction: Questions and Principle C Effects in English and Polish*. Frankfurt am Main: Peter Lang.

Wolf, Matthew. 2007. For an autosegmental theory of mutation. *Papers in Optimality Theory III—University of Massachusetts Occasional Papers in Linguistics* 32: 315–404.

Wöllstein-Leisten, Angelika. 2001. *Die Syntax der dritten Konstruktion*. Tübingen: Stauffenburg.

Wu, Zoe. 2004. *Grammaticalization and Language Change in Chinese: A Formal View*. London: Routledge.

Wurmbrand, Susanne 2001. *Infinitives: Restructuring and Clause Structure*. Berlin: Mouton de Gruyter.

——2007. Infinitives are tenseless. *Proceedings of the 30th Penn Linguistics Colloquium (PLC 30)—UPenn Working Papers in Linguistics* 13.1: 407–20.

Zanuttini, Raffaella. 1997. *Negation and Clausal Structure: A Comparative Study of Romance Languages*. New York: Oxford University Press.

Zec, Draga & Sharon Inkelas. 1990. Prosodically constrained syntax. In Inkelas & Zec (eds.).

Zeijlstra, Hedde. 2004. *Sentential Negation and Negative Concord*. Utrecht: LOT Publications.

——2006. The ban on true negative imperatives. *Empirical Issues in Formal Syntax and Semantics* 6: 405–26.

——2007. Modal concord is syntactic agreement. *LingBuzz* 000494. [http://ling.auf. net/lingBuzz/000178, to appear as "Modal concord" in *Proceedings of the Seventeenth Conference on Semantics and Linguistic Theory (SALT XVII)*.]

——2008. On the syntactic flexibility of formal features. In Biberauer (ed.).

——Forthcoming. Dislocation triggers uninterpretability. *Linguistic Analysis* 35.

Zubizarreta, Maria Luisa. 1998. *Prosody, Focus and Word Order*. Cambridge, MA: MIT Press.

Zwart, C. Jan-Wouter. 1997. *Morphosyntax of Verb Movement: A Minimalist Approach to the Syntax of Dutch*. Dordrecht: Kluwer.

Author Index

Language Index

Subject Index

OXFORD STUDIES IN THEORETICAL LINGUISTICS

PUBLISHED